AFRICAN WOMEN AND FEMINISM

AFRICAN WOMEN AND FEMINISM: REFLECTING ON THE POLITICS OF SISTERHOOD

EDITED BY
OYÈRÓNKÉ OYEWÙMÍ

AFRICA WORLD PRESS

TRENTON | LONDON | CAPE TOWN | NAIROBI | ADDIS ABABA | ASMARA | IBADAN | NEW DELHI

AFRICA WORLD PRESS
541 West Ingham Avenue | Suite B
Trenton, New Jersey 08638

First Printing 2003

Book design: 'Damola Ifaturoti
Cover design: Roger Dormann
Cover photograph: Nyokabi Muthama

Library of Congress Cataloging-in-Publication Data

African women and feminism : reflecting on the politics of sisterhood / edited by Oyeronke Oyewumi.
    p. cm.
  Includes bibliographical references and index.
  ISBN 0-86543-627-4--(hc) -- ISBN 0-86543-628-2 (pbk.)
  1. Women--Africa--Social conditions. 2. Feminism. 3. Feminist theory. I. Oyewumi, Oyeronke.

HQ1787 .A372 2000
305.42'096--dc21

                                                          00-027033

Contents:

"SISTERHOOD"

white sister told me
all women are one
united in de face
of chau'vism.
(pa'don my engilis)

I smiled

pa...paa
pa..tri..archy is the cross
women carry, she charged
we must unite
to fight it
with all our might.

I laughed ...

racked by spasm
my head jerked back
and crazily wobbled
from side to side.
pampered sister
titillates herself
to frenzy
with quixotic tales
of male 'xploitation.

I ...

"dumb" black woman
laughed mirthlessly on
flicking away tears
of pain from eyes.

I looked up
from my chore
on the kitchen floor
where, new found sister
had ordered me to be
on knees

to scrub the floor clean
for the pittance she paid:
on knees
to scrub the floor clean
for sisterarchy.

Nkiru Nzegwu

28/7/90

1.
INTRODUCTION:
Feminism, Sisterhood, and *Other* Foreign Relations

Oyèrónké Oyewùmí

Currently, feminism as an ideology if not as a social movement, is subject to many qualifications. Thus scholars differentiate between white feminism, black feminism, Western feminism, Third world Feminism, and African feminism. These distinctions reflect the contestations that have become very much a part of the history and worldwide development of feminist ideas. This book focuses on the contentious relationship between feminism and African women. As its title indicates, African women and feminism are at odds because despite the adjectives used to qualify feminism, it is Western feminism that inevitably dominates even when it is not explicitly the subject under consideration. This feminism usually travels without any qualifications but with a lot of baggage.

The volume engages with Western feminism as it has been articulated in Europe and America and subsequently carried forward in an imperial march across the globe. A distinction must be made between the noun *feminism* and the adjective *feminist*. The term *feminism* usually refers to a historically recent Europe and American social movements founded to struggle for female equality. *Feminism* by this designation has become a global political project. But the adjective *feminist* has a broader reach in that it need not be confined by history; in fact it describes a range of behavior indicating female agency and self-determination. In many traditional African societies, a certain measure of self-determination was a value, and practiced as a matter of course and as a way of life for all adults, male and female. In the 1980s, Filomina Steady called attention to this African value when she wrote about Africa as the original home of feminist principles (Steady 1981). In this sense, then, African feminism is a tautology.

However, this very tradition of African self-determination—personal, cultural, and political—has been truncated by a series of successive global historical processes most notably the Atlantic Slave Trade and European colonization. Over the past five centuries, these developments have made Africa politically, economically, and culturally dependent on Western Europe and North America. As a result, Africa has become the recipient of ideas and goods of dubious and often harmful value. In order to transform the many types of degradation and dependency that Africans face today, we must be cognizant of this complex history and its enduring effects as well as the multiple forms of oppression from which African peoples continue to suffer.

Feminism is primarily concerned with the liberation of women. Given the aforementioned historical occurrences and the fact that in many African societies the category *woman* cannot be isolated raises the question of the relevance and value of Western feminism. In much of Africa, "womanhood" does not constitute a social role, identity, position, or location. This is because each individual occupies a multiplicity of overlapping and intersecting positions, with various relationships to privilege and disadvantage. In addition, local situations are themselves in a state of flux, given the disproportionate influence of external agents in African life. It would be counterproductive in the African setting to single out gender, which thus far has been elaborated only as a biologistic category—a body-based identity—as the primary source and focus of political agitation. As Oyeronke Oyewumi noted in her book *The Invention of Women: Making an African Sense of Western Gender Discourses*, despite the many feminist claims that gender is a socially constructed category, in reality "in Western conceptualization, gender [the purported social category] cannot exist without sex [the biological category] since the body sits squarely at the base of both categories" (1987:8). Thus in the West, the distinction between gender and sex cannot be sustained. In many African societies however, there are many social categories that do not rest on the bodily distinctions of gender. A good example is the "female husband" of Igbo culture (Amadiume 1987).

Yet, we cannot discount the growing presence of gender consciousness and the ongoing establishment of male superiority which has been unleashed by Africa's encounter with Europe and the Arab world, and by the current gendered practices of institutions such as the World Bank, the United Nations, and various governmental and non-governmental organizations that promote the tenets of Western feminism in the rest of the world. In its various guises and disguises, feminism continues to be the most avid manufacturer of gender consciousness and gender categories, inevitably at the expense of local categories such as ethnicity, seniority, race, and generation that may be more locally salient.

The feminism that we engage extensively in this book, then, is Western feminism, a feminism that is entangled with the history and practice of European and North American imperialism and the worldwide European colonization of Africa, Asia, and the Americas. Since the fifteenth century, European nations have been engaged in imperialistic ventures that laid the foundation of globalization. Thus global feminism forms a part of Europology— an elaboration of what is a distinctly European phenomenon into a human universal—which is then imposed on all cultures. Gender as essentialized ontology is one of these pseudo-universals deriving from Western culture that is being exported worldwide. Thus feminism's role in the projection of Western culture and cultural forms in the contemporary period must not be underestimated.

This volume therefore is also about imperialism—defined as a set of hierarchical relationships between and among nations, peoples, cultures, and regions. The project addresses imperialism as a metascript of domination and oppression, revealing itself variously in the realms of culture, nationality, race, ethnicity, gender, and class. Imperialism is also manifested in interpersonal relationships. It incorporates, produces, and is constituted by multiple axes of social relations, including race and gender. This anthology fundamentally implicates cultural imperialism. Central to this introduction, which was written as a companion piece to the book, is the following question: What are the implications for Africans of uncritically adopting Western social categories, concerns, and interpretations of reality as their own? The erasure of history and the discounting of cultural norms and institutions are the issues at stake here.

Using the discourse of sisterhood—a mantra which assumes the common victimhood of all women—we examine the effects of unthinkingly adopting Western language and cultural terms of discourse. Notwithstanding the equality and homogenization of positions of women worldwide that the concept of sisterhood is meant to convey, the reality is that women are linked together in a variety of unequal relationships an idea eloquently expressed in the preceding poem by Nkiru Nzegwu (see p. vii). Nzegwu reminds us that it is a myth that sisters are ever equal because the sisterhood is, in fact, always a "sisterarchy."

Sisters in the Global Hood

Sisterhood has emerged as the dominant model for feminist intercommunity relations. A term of political solidarity, "sisterhood" bespeaks women's activism. The meaning it carries for the white feminist who initiated its use in yet another wave of American feminism is one of shared oppression, solidarity, common victimization, community of interests and political activism. Whether it refers to interracial, international, transglobal, or cross-cultural relations, the ideal promoted is couched in the rhetoric of kinship and family bonds. Nevertheless, many feminists have criticized this use of the term. African American feminists have, for example, pointed out what they consider the hypocrisy and the dishonesty of white feminists in advocating an unconditional love and solidarity amongst all women, even as they exercised their race and class privileges on the backs of non-white women. Given this insightful critique of sisterhood as a model for inter-racial relations, one is surprised that the term still has currency in certain feminist circles. Unlike the word "feminism," which has engendered new concepts such as womanism for example, "sisterhood" has not generated alternative terms of political solidarity. African American feminists, in particular, have pointed out the limitations of the term "sisterhood," attempting to reformulate it to carry the weight of experiences beyond those of white women. Audre Lorde (1984) writes about the "sister outsider," an oxymoron which suggests that the problem is not really the notion of sisterhood but the way it has been used in the women's movement. Another black feminist, bell hooks (1995), writes about "false sisterhood," indicating that the term's early meanings were not realized in the lives of contemporary feminists. She writes:

> Sisterhood became yet another shield against reality, another support system. Their [white feminists'] version of Sisterhood was informed by racist and classist assumptions about white womanhood, that the white "lady" (that is to say the bourgeois woman) should be protected from all that might upset or discomfort her and shielded from negative realities that might lead to confrontation. (hooks 1995:296)

Sisterhood amongst women of a racially and culturally diverse group, hooks concluded, is possible, but only with a great deal of unrelenting work against all sorts of divisions, most importantly, race. Thus, for hooks, the problem with the concept of sisterhood is that it takes political solidarity for granted rather than as a goal to be worked at and achieved.

From its inception a recurrent criticism of white feminism, as manifested also in the hooks quote above, is that white feminists have considered their experience of womanhood in their culture as the prototypic female experience and have used it to define feminism. I contend that the articulation of sisterhood as a framework for cross-boundary feminist relations is very much tied to the use of white women's experiences as the basis for feminist engagements. If the danger of "white solipsism" that is the tendency "to think, imagine and speak as if whiteness described the world" (Rich 1979:299) is taken seriously, then the concept of sisterhood itself, given that it originated with white women, needs to be interrogated.

At issue here are the politics of culture, the cultural meaning of sisterhood, and the need to examine the viability of such a relationship given diverse cultural experiences. We must question the very foundation of sisterhood, both as a concept and as a desirable relationship. Undoubtedly a cultural understanding is expressed in the choice of "sisterhood" over other terms to describe relations between white and black women. Race was the first border it had to cross before sisterhood went global. One must ask: What is sisterhood and how did it become an ideology through which interracial, cross-cultural, and transnational relations are to be negotiated? Is the term transcultural?

The reason for the selection of sisterhood over other terms of solidarity—such as friend, comrade, or compatriot—is not obvious. Even if we grant that sisterhood had a head start over comrade and friend in that it is a kinship term, suggesting family ties, unconditional love and loyalty, but what about a term deriving from motherhood or its variant. I say this because there are two immediately apparent models of female solidarity deriving from the family: one based on motherhood and the other stemming from the bond between sisters. Western readers will be quick to respond that motherhood introduces a generation gap, which itself signals inequality, the very thing that feminism was founded to wipe out. This reaction, of course, is very much tied to the social context of motherhood in contemporary Western cultures, where it is a solitary experience, a social role that is perceived to be occupied by one person at a time within the nuclear family. To an African reader (or even a Chicana), the model of motherhood is absolutely natural, because if anything binds women together in collective experience, it is childbearing and the mothering of children, and consequently the nurturing of community. Because of the tradition of multiple mothers African "sisterly" relations are more likely to be found in co-mothering. Mothers were present in all generations within and without the household and the family, and motherhood in a sense is a great leveler of women in that the experience is considered to be an equalizer.

Beyond the dichotomous cultural geography implicit in a comparison of African and Western cultures, however, the tradition of multiple and nonexclusive mothering is also present within African American and Chicano cultures in the United States and in a number of Afro-Caribbean societies. Patricia Hill Collins (1990) writes about the tradition of Other Mothers in African American social practice. Sociologist Denise Segura points out that the term *comadre*–co-mother–is an expression of sisterhood amongst Chicanas. In a paper on Chicana/o family structure, Segura and Jennifer Pierce draw attention to multiple mothering figures as a feature of family life as mother and aunts "work together both to make meals and to nurture the family and each other" (Segura and Pierce 1993:62). In a number of the Caribbean Islands, including Trinidad, St. Lucia, and Haiti, the term *macomere* is used to express friendship amongst women. This term essentially encapsulates a particular kind of relationship amongst women that is founded on trust and an expectation of mutual support– material and otherwise– particularly with regard to the raising of children, which is the most important and lifelong charge of women. In St. Lucia, a close friend is a *macoum.*

According to the prefatory note of the premier issue of Macomeré (The Journal of Caribbean Women Writers and Scholars), Macomeré is a term

> widely used by women in the Caribbean to mean 'my best friend and close confidante,' 'my bridesmaid or another female member of a wedding party of which I was bridesmaid,' 'the godmother of the child to whom I am also godmother,' 'the woman who, by virtue of the depth of her friendship, has rights and privileges over my child and whom I see as a surrogate mother.'

Against this background, we must ask again: Why was "sisterhood" chosen as the basis of feminist alliances? Why not "co-mother"? The point is that there is nothing inherent in the concept of sisterhood to describe interracial, cross-cultural, or any social relationships. The privileging of the ideology of sisterhood over an ideology of shared nurturing embodied in the institution of motherhood, for example, must be sought within the specific culture and history of Euro-Americans. My goal in this essay is to examine the cultural basis of sisterhood as a kinship term, as a metonym for family, an ideology of solidarity, and a political model used as a bridge across communities. Simply put, since sisterhood is a kinship term that emerges from the logic of the nuclear family, which is a specifically Euro-American family form, one must ask why Africans and other peoples whose family systems may have a different logic and hence articulate and privilege a different set of kinship and non-kin relations should adopt the term.

Sisterhood, just like the term feminism, need to be re-examined in the light of the fact that though its origins are very much tied to a specific culture, its intended application is ultimately transglobal. What meaning does it carry as it crosses boundaries, if indeed it ever does cross boundaries? Should it carry the same meaning? Can it carry the same meaning, given that its conceptualization is informed by specific cultural assumptions and histories? What exactly are the implications of the cross-cultural use of sisterhood, given that the meaning shifts depending on a host of factors. It is also pertinent to question whether the desired relationship apparent in the use of sister-hood initiated by white women is matched by the desire of other women to relate to them and others in that way.

Sisterhood: A Legacy of the White American Nuclear Family

The privilege of naming the model for a cross-border would-be relationship among women regardless of race, color, culture, and geography fell to white, American, middle-class women. Their very first invitation was extended to African American women. What kind of sorority were black women being invited to join? What was it in the family experience of white American women that privileged sisterhood over other terms of political solidarity? Feminist philosopher Maria Lugones questions why white American feminists would go inside the patriarchal nuclear family institution to select a model for female solidarity. Lugones considers this odd behavior and questions whether any-thing can really be salvaged from this oppressive institution. Lugones goes on to suggest that perhaps the model of sisterhood that white American femi-nists were proposing did not derive from their family situation but instead was borrowed from elsewhere (Lugones 1995:136).

I would however argue that there is nothing odd in the white feminist usage of sisterhood as a model for female solidarity. In fact, one of the places where the model of sisterhood makes sense is within the social organi-zation of the white American nuclear family and the ideologies that flowed from it. Gender distinctions are fundamental to the institutions of Western culture on which the white American family is based, and the family as an institution is at the cutting edge of gender attribution and manufacture. With the development in the United States of a distinct form of the nuclear family in the nineeenth century, gender became even more important as the line of fracture in the family, given that the family became smaller and more isolated and that the generational difference that was the hallmark of the European-type stem family did not transfer to the U.S. Thus, gender was the fundamen-tal organizing principle of the nuclear family, and gender distinctions were the basic source of hierarchy and oppression within it. By the same token, gender sameness is perceived to be the primary source of identification and solidar-ity in this family type. Thus daughters identified as females with their mother and sisters (Chodorow 1978).

In fact, the mother-daughter relationship is key to understanding the motivations of white women in the early part of second-wave feminism. These feminists viewed the nuclear family in its most patriarchal dimension, focusing on the way in which it had juvenilized their mothers and stripped them of autonomy. Writing about the mother-daughter relationship and its impact on feminist activism for white women, Jill Lewis (Joseph and Lewis

1986) noted the sources of feminist negative attitudes towards motherhood:

> The fear of becoming our mothers, our refusal to emulate them, … is a fear of
> the specific conditions of motherhood and womanhood, which necessitate
> our oppression. It is a rejection of the nonviable patriarchal separation of
> nurturance and autonomy, caring and achievement, loving and power. The
> fear stems from our knowledge that, through our relationship with our moth-
> ers, we are cyclically part of those conditions, … (Joseph and Lewis 1986:139-
> 140)

In the nuclear family, the gender identification of children with their mothers underscores the fact that the mother is first and foremost (even to children) the patriarch's wife. The gender-based division of power in the nuclear family permanently cast the mother in the powerless role of a victim. It is not surprising then that motherhood never ranked high in the kin relationship or role to which middle-class white American feminists aspired. They could, on the other hand, identify with their sisters, who not only grew up under the terrifying shadow of the patriarchal father but also shared the same difficult gender-identification with the powerless mother and the need to distance themselves from her. Sisterly relations emerged out of their family heritage as the only viable model: the mother-daughter relationship was hierarchical, but sisters were equal. Sisterhood, which developed to signal the gender exclusivity necessary for white women to escape male control, also symbolized common victimhood and shared oppression, which made for equal relations and solidarity.   Here in lies the historical and cultural roots of sisterhood.

The African American Connection
Any engagement with feminist interracial, cross-cultural relationships must start with the United States where black-white relations constituted the testing ground of 'difference' which proved to be a dress rehearsal for the global sisterhood. As I mentioned earlier, some of the most astute interpreters of the African American feminist experience do not jettison sisterhood, they only seek to make it more honest by reformulating it. The refusal to subvert the concept of sisterhood may be due to the fact that African American feminists recognize themselves in its usage. The kin terms "sister" and "brother" are central to the black experience in the United States. An enduring legacy of plantation slavery, these are political terms that immediately establish solidarity and a sense of connection and community among black people. Pat Alake Rozelle points out:

> The slave experience is the beginning of 'sister' and 'brother.' When a people

> are bastardized, raped, and fragmented from their families, they have to create family. Then it is a political act to call those who are not your blood, but who are your people 'brother' and 'sister' (Rozelle 1995:139).

Rozelle suggests that white feminism appropriated the term "sisterhood" from the black experience following the participation of many white women in the Civil Rights struggle. It is well documented that the second-wave feminist movement derived from and developed within the black Civil Rights movement. Rozelle argues that white women who had participated in the movement, having had such a positive encounter in this community of resistance, naturally tried to borrow the language of the black experience of which "sister" was a part. She points out that because of their racism, however, they were unable to replicate the meaning and function which the term had in the black community (Rozelle 1995:141).

A close examination of the ways in which these kinship models are used in the black community and among white feminists reveal a gulf in what they symbolize and the meaning attached to them in these two settings. This difference in usage suggest that interpretation must proceed from differing cultural and historical experiences. The use of kinship terms in African American communities differs markedly from their use by white feminists. For one thing, African Americans make use of *both* kinship terms "brother" *and* "sister"–always the pair. On the other hand, "sisterhood," a collective noun, is the predominant term used to express kinship in white feminism. Sisterhood is a metaphor, denoting a collectivity, and it operates at a more abstract and generalized level than the terms "sister" and "brother" amongst black Americans, which are most often used on a personalized, one-to-one basis.

More fundamentally, "sisterhood" or gender-specific kinship terms in feminism are deployed to signal an exclusive female community. For African Americans, despite the fact that these terms are gender specific, both "brother" and "sister" transcend gender solidarity and are used to signal racial communion. In the black community, "sister" does not imply a desire for a female exclusive community (of interests), which is precisely what is at its base in white feminism. It is not surprising, then, that use of the collective noun "sisterhood" is rare in the African American experience. Even when "sisters" in contrast to "brother" are singled out in the black community for special recognition, it is an acknowledgment of the gender-specific burden that black women have borne historically, way beyond the other forms of oppression that they share with black men. The sense of community that the use of kinship terms was designed to convey represented one of the strategies black Americans employed in their efforts to resist white supremacy and its debilitating effects on the psyche and the community during the period of enslavement and beyond.

Africa and Diaspora: A (Dis)Connection

The notion of gender inclusiveness that is present in African American usage of "sister" and "brother"–terms which superficially suggest gender-specific bonds and interests need to be further analyzed. Although the African American usage of brother/sister appears to be linguistically almost identical to their use by feminists, the meaning and function of these kinship terms seem to derive more from an African notion of family and kin relations. In African social organization, household and family are not identical or co-terminous; therefore there are always primary family members who live elsewhere. Without denying the importance of slavery in the African American experience, it would appear that the gender-inclusive use of the pair brother/sister may have derived from West African cultures from which many black Americans originated. The languages that many of the enslaved West Africans brought to the Americas did not contain linguistic equivalents of the kin terms "brother" and "sister" because many African languages do not express gender-specificity in sibling designation. Though one is unable to establish the exact moment at which the enslaved Africans started to address each other in these terms in the Americas, it is clear that such usage evolved with the experience of slavery and acculturation. The consciousness of racial affinity as the basis of solidarity must have developed as soon as enslaved Africans were all put in the same boat and in company of the white slavers. At that moment, race became the signifier of kinship. The consciousness of gender distinctions in social experience must have been reinforced also by the slavers' practice of putting male and female slaves in different parts of the ship. Language subsequently emerged to acknowledge the gender-specificity of the experience of slavery but never the exclusive interest of one gender, separate from those of the whole group.

Nevertheless, it is significant that for many of the enslaved Africans, gender was not coded linguistically in their original languages. Indeed the kinship categories "brother" and "sister" do not exist in Yoruba, Igbo, Efik, Wolof, Songhoi, Benin, Manding and Fulani to name some of the West African languages and nationalities from which many black Americans originated. In a book documenting the African heritage of the Georgia islands (United States), we catch a glimpse of how a black American grandson of an enslaved African woman navigates the English language without much attention to the gender-specific nature of pronouns. Ben Sullivan, one of the oldest men living on the island in the 1940s, said the following to the researchers about his African roots: "Muh granmothuh Hettie, duh mothuh uh muh Bella, *he* come from Africa too an *he* huzbun come frum Africa" [my emphasis] (Savannah Unit Georgia Writers' Project 1940: 181). His speech, reminiscent of a number of West African pidgins, uses the English masculine pronoun to refer to both genders as if it were equivalent to the non-gendered subject pronouns of many African languages. It also brings to mind the experience of Mary Kingsley, the nineteenth-century English explorer who was repeatedly referred to as "sir" by West Africans as she traveled through the region. This reference to Kingsley was an indication not that she had been turned into an honorary male, but of the gender-free nature of many African languages, and indeed a lack of gendered notions of power and hierarchy in African cultures generally. The way in which the concepts of brother and sister emerged in the African American experience recalls an African understanding, whereas the gender predilection in the English language itself imposed a restriction. In any discussion of sisterhood for Africans, the question of language is even more central than usual.

Mothernity: An African Communitarian Ideology and Ideal

With regard to Africa, the most important question under consideration turns on the issue of cultural imperialism. On what basis are feminist concepts, developed from Western social categories, transferable or exportable to other cultures that display a different social organization and cultural logic, and what are the implications? A careful history and deconstruction of the concept of sisterhood grounds it in the patriarchal Euro-American nuclear family, with all its well-documented negative effects on females. What relevance or interest does such a deeply gendered social organization, whose social categories and cultural logics are different, hold for Africa? Despite the great impact of Christianity, the institutionalization of a European-derived colonial legal system,and the ongoing practices of modern global institutions, the nuclear family remains a mirage on the African continent.

More significant is the fact that many West African languages do not contain gender specific kinship terms,as I pointed out earlier. In a sense then, sister indeed is a foreign relation. The comparable category in sentiment in many West African cultures to the concept of "sister" in Western culture—that is, sister as sibling who has a common interest because of shared experience and social location and whose love and loyalty are supposed to be unconditional— is a category that literally translates as "my mother's child/ren". In Yoruba it is *omoya*. The following is a sample of the term in some West African languages: *Nwanne* (Igbo), *Omwiyemwen* (Benin), *Doo mi ndey* (Wolof), *N ba den* (Bamana), *Gna'izo* (Songhoi-Hombori), *Eyen-eka* (Efik), *Badenya* (Manding), *Biddo yaya'm* (Fulani).

The term *omoya* and sister give us clues as to which categories are considered primary in the different cultural contexts in which they developed. I have elucidated the Western cultural context of "sister" as one in which gender is a fundamental and therefore a primary category. Hence, it was imperative for family members to be categorized as male or female, boy or girl, because this is necessary for determining their place and function within the family. Because of the matrifocality of many African family systems, the mother is the pivot around which familial relationships are delineated and organized. The category of *omoya* transcends gender; sometimes it is used to refer to an individual, but what it encapsulates is the collectivity. It functions to locate the individual within a socially recognized grouping and underscores the significance of mother-child ties in delineating and anchoring a child's place in the family. These relationships are primary and privileged, and it is understood that they should be protected above others. *Omoya* is the primary category in the sense that it is the first and fundamental source of identification for the child in the household. To put it crudely, in the traditional Yoruba household, the first thing you need to know is not whether you are a boy or a girl but who are your *omoya*–siblings with whom you share the same mother. Symbolically, *omoya* emblematizes unconditional love, togetherness, unity, solidarity, and loyalty.

Within the household and family, treatment of any one individual and behavior toward that person is *always* filtered through the knowledge of who is the person's mother and *omoya*. Because of the social importance of the *omoya* category, an only child is disadvantaged within the household, not simply due to being outnumbered by some other group but because there is a social role elaborated for siblings. There are certain things that cannot be done, experienced, or enjoyed throughout the life course except by *omoya*, individually with each other, and collectively as an interest group. Furthermore, the *omoya* category extends beyond the patrilineage (household) in that the category includes cousins related to one on the mother's side. Matrilateral cousins as *omoya* are considered as close as siblings, but closer than half-brothers and half-sisters with whom one shares the same father and who often live in the same residence. Thus, the most important shared experience that *omoya* recalls and builds on is the fact that the group of siblings shared the womb of the mother. They are what has been called uterine/womb siblings. The experience of the mother's womb is not gendered–it carries both male and female babies; therefore the social grouping of *omoya* does not anticipate any gender commonality amongst its members, and the elaboration of their emotional closeness does not rest on it. Sisterhood, in contrast, is defined solely by gender commonality and the anticipated similarity in social experience as a result of having what Western culture designates as the inferior body-type–the female one.

What emerges from such African household and family organization is the importance of motherhood, the fact that mother-derived ties are the most culturally significant, and that mothers have agency and power. Fundamentally, motherhood is not usually constructed in relation to or in opposition to fatherhood; it is conceived in its own right. Mothers are perceived as especially powerful–literally and mystically, in regard to the well being of the child. They are therefore the pivot around which family life is structured and the child's life rotates.

In this family system, unlike in the nuclear family, motherhood is the most important source and model of solidarity, and being a mother is perceived as an attractive and desirable goal to achieve. The privileging of motherhood in the African family organization contrasts with the ambivalence about motherhood in feminism, and the deliberate elevation there of sisterhood as the only positive female relationship model. As I pointed out in my earlier discussion, the very definition of sisterhood rests on an assumption of gender as an essential category in society and the need for female solidarity in the face of this body-based oppression. Given these fundamental differences between the social organization of family and kinship in Africa, in contrast to kinship in the Euro-American nuclear family, why then should Africans adopt sisterhood as a model for solidarity, or for anything else for that matter? Significantly, what cultural norms are being injected into African forms? And, for what purpose and to what effect?

In many African societies, there is no sisterhood without motherhood. The most profound sisterly relations are to be found in co-mothering, which is the essence of community building. Co-mothering as a communal ideal and social practice is not reducible to biological motherhood; it transcends it. The fact that the children of one's *omoya* are regarded as one's children demonstrates this ideal. Furthermore, in the consanguinally-based African family, the reality is that children experience many mothers. Notwithstanding the voluminous "co-wife" literature that Western anthropologists have used to define African marriage, "co-mother" is the preferred idiom in many African cultures for expressing the relationship amongst women married into the same family. In Yoruba culture, for example, all women who have married into the family–even when they are married to different brothers–relate to each other as if they have one and the same husband, since marriage is a collective act contracted not between two individuals but two clans. A younger wife refers to a senior one as *Iyale*, literally mother of the house.

1 Sisterhood: Bridge or Barricade

Before any discussion of African models of solidarity, the question of how African female associations have been interpreted by some black feminists in the West requires some attention. A number of African American scholars have misrepresented a range of institutions and social practices in West African societies as evidence of culturally sanctioned and institutionalized forms of lesbianism. That I am compelled to address this question is an indication of the extent to which Africa remains for many in the Western world a tabula rasa upon which anything can be written. That African articulations do not count—even amongst some black feminists, whose politics is centered on their consanguinal ties to Africa—speaks volumes about the complexity of cultural imperialism and its various practitioners.

It is perhaps not surprising that the search for Africa continues to structure questions of black identity in the United States. This quest for Africa, often articulated as a theme of "paradise lost," is an idea whose resonance partially rests on the infinite plasticity and malleability of Africa in the black American imagination. "What is Africa to me?" the poet Countee Cullen asks. For some African Americans, Africa really has no reality or meaning independent of what it means to them individually and as members of particular sub-groupings. All too often, the only way that Africa participates in this discourse about black identity is in its remaking in the image of whichever political grouping it is called upon to serve within this Diaspora community.

Lately, black feminists have arisen as one constituency that Africa must serve both positively and negatively. Their discourse about black feminist identity oscillates between what I would characterize as notions of "paradise recognized" and "paradise demonized"—concepts which are not mutually exclusive. A clear example of the latter is detailed in my paper (in this volume) "Alice in Motherland: Reading Alice Walker on Africa and screening the Color Black" in which I interrogate Alice Walker's representation of Africa as the ultimate fountainhead of misogyny.

What I am concerned about here, however, is the representation of Africa by black lesbian feminists as a paradise in which lesbianism is not only accepted, but is institutionalized in women's everyday relationships. Audre Lorde (1983) to my knowledge was the first to claim that the "woman-to-woman marriages" found in some African societies are actually lesbian unions, a claim which she then uses to underwrite her own identity as a black lesbian. Lorde makes cryptic allusions to the *ahonsi* (popularly represented in the Western imagination as Amazons), a military regiment of female soldiers in the Dahomean army in the nineteenth century, as an example of traditional African lesbian sisterhood (Lorde 1983). With all due respect to Lorde's pioneering and insightful writings on feminism, race, and difference, her representation of these African institutions is utterly without foundation. It should be made clear that the issue here is not whether homosexuality exists in Africa or not. For me, that debate (if ever there was one) is moot since homosexuality is part of the human condition. The important issue at hand is not homosexuality but the culture of misrepresentation that pervades the depiction of

African peoples, institutions and forms especially by people living in the Northern hemisphere. This culture of misrepresentation is built on the devaluation of African experiences and leads to the silencing of African voices in the articulation of their own realities.

Both the organization of "woman marriage" and the "*ahonsi*" who are "wives of the king" in Dahomean society, demonstrate the broad and complex meaning of marriage as a social (not necessarily sexual) institution in African societies. The role of "wife" encapsulates the relationship of women who enter a particular lineage through marriage, in contrast to their husbands—defined as men, women, and children (both boys and girls)—who are members of the lineage by birth. The definition of marriage does not depend on there being a sexual relationship between two people. Rather, it is often a social, non-sexual relationship, indicating the place of an individual in the family. Thus, in yet another configuration a woman marries a woman in order for the "female husband" to be able to have children that she can claim customarily as heirs. The "female wife" is a wife to the female husband in that she (the husband) has jural rights to her and the children produced within the marriage despite the fact that they do not engage in sexual intercourse. A male recruited by the husband (female) impregnates the wife. Similarly, the *ahonsi* are called wives of the king of Dahomey despite the fact that the king does not necessarily engage in sexual relationships with them.

In a host of African societies, marriage is predicated on a contractual agreement, cemented by the giving of bridewealth by the family of the husband to the family of the wife. What these two examples speak to is not same-sex marriage, but that the category of "wife" in patrilineal African societies is a catch-all for relationships between those who are blood relations (male and female) on the one hand, and those women who come into the family through marriage on the other. Wives are women who are recruited into the family through affinal and other non-blood relationships. Consequently, in many West African societies, including Yoruba and Igbo, women married into the family are not just the wives of males, they are also wives of females. The point is that "woman-to-woman" marriage is not the only instance of a socially recognized marriage form that does not involve sexual relations. Thus, in a West African context where these practices still obtain, there is no indication that they are associated with homosexuality in theory or in fact.

What is also remarkable is that many of the African social practices that are at issue here are not outmoded, but are living traditions that have been well documented by Africans; therefore, writers who distort them cannot take refuge in the assumption that their meanings are lost in time. Consider the following example, articulated by Nigerian, Harvard-educated anthropologist Felicia Ekejiuba about her family's experience of woman marriage in Igboland in the contemporary period: "My maternal aunt, for instance, emerged from a 'failed,' childless marriage to re-establish her 'hearth-hold.' ... She later became a 'female husband' ... by 'marrying' her own wife who increased the 'hearthold' by producing four more children for her" (Ekejiuba 1995:48). Unfortunately, the issue is not the reality of African social institutions and cultural practices but the various agendas of "blackness," and "womanism" that Africa is called upon to serve in the United States and other parts of the African Diaspora. Such concerns cannot define African institutions; they must be articulated on their own terms.

Beyond Lorde's original use of Africa to account for her own homosexuality, in a more recent paper on Afro-Surinamese working class women, anthropologist Gloria Wekker discusses the institution of "mati work"–a social practice which she claims involves lesbian relationships. Wekker speculates that *mati* work is an elaboration of Surinamese West African heritage and that "although the origin of the *mati* work is often associated with the departure of men to do migrant labor ... from my perspective, there is no good reason to suppose that *mati* work was not already present in West Africa ..." (Wekker 1997:338). Wekker, like Lorde before her, does not provide any evidence for this assertion other than the work of two founding fathers of African anthropology Melville Herskovitts and E. E. Evans-Pritchard. Both scholars conducted research in the forties and sixties, when the discipline of anthropology, as part of the colonial enterprise was imbricated in exoticizing Africa, an orientation that proved useful in justifying European exploitation and dominance. Wekker ignores the more recent scholarship of African anthropologists like Ifi Amadiume, who has written on woman-to-woman marriage and other family forms in Igbo society of southeastern Nigeria. Amadiume's research shows that woman-to-woman marriage is not about same-sex sexual relations, but that it is based on social relations of family formation and maintenance (Amadiume 1981). The issue is no longer whether there is documentation of these institutions from African perspectives, instead, it is a question of whose claims are preferred—those of Western anthropologists over African scholars many of who have personal knowledge of these institutions. The cryptic phrase "there is no reason to suppose," in Wekker's account quoted above, is vintage Evans-Pritchard, who, in his paper on what he claims to be Azande homosexuality, writes that "there is no reason to suppose it was introduced by the Arabs" (Evans-Pritchard 1971:1429).

African Models of Solidarity

Organizing–associating to attain a purpose–is the process by which traditional Africans wove the very fabric of their societies. Because of the strong sense of community and the fact that individual experience could best be realized in a group, formal organizations became a way of life. Besides kinship organizations, age grades, occupational guilds, and religious, social, and political organizations are all features of African community life. In Yorubaland as one case, associations were called *egbe*, which also means peer group. Members of a convivial *egbe* referred to each other as *oore*–friend. In fact, in Yoruba society, no one, male or female, can go through life without *oore*, as a formalized category. During celebrations, especially those associated with rites of passage or other major life events, one relies on one's *oore* for support. Sociologist N. A. Fadipe, elaborating the function of one's *egbe*, wrote:

> In case of death in the family of any member, he or she was helped by the rest of the *Egbe*. They helped her perform tasks that needed to be done as well as to make the occasion grand with dancing, singing and feasting.... During the period of courtship, a young man had the support and co-operation of members of his *Egbe* in whatever labour services were required by custom to be rendered to the parents-in-law (Fadipe 1970:258).

For a female upon marriage, it is members of her *egbe*, childhood friends who join her in chanting the *ekun iyawo* (bridal chants when it was still customary to do so) and who accompany her to the house of the groom. Subsequently, new friends are also made, and much of female friendship centers around experiences of shared mothering and continuous mutual support from friends who are at a similar stage in the life cycle. Friendship based on socially defined mutual interest is the model for non-kin relations. Although mature friendship often is expressed in the idiom of kinship, the important point is that it is never the starting point. African American anthropologist Niara Sudarkasa's experience in Aawe, a Yoruba town in which she conducted research in the early 1960s, is telling:

> To most people in Awe [Aawe] I was known only in the role of researcher.... A relatively small group of women, ranging in age from about twenty five to forty, became my friends. We used the term "Ore" [*oore*] (literally, "friend") as one would use a personal name... This was the group of women with whom I often exchanged visits and presents, for whom I did special favors ... with whom I gossiped, to whom I went for advice... (Sudarkasa 1996:205-206)

Maria Lugones, in her discussion of why friendship and not sisterhood should be the model for feminist intergroup relations, writes: "Unlike 'sisters,' which presupposes the institution of the family and takes as model a particular relation... friendship is not an institutional relationship.... There are no rules specifying the duties and rights of friends" (Lugones 1995:141-142). Such a statement cannot bear scrutiny even in American society especially post Lewinsky/Linda Tripp saga! Lugones' observation does not hold for many African societies. To continue with our case study, in Yoruba society, friendship is institutionalized and has specific rights and obligations. For elucidation, let us revisit Sudarkasa's experience in Aawe as an indication of prevailing expectations held about friendship. She writes that it was to her group of *oore* to:

> whom I reported most of my movements, and whenever I was away from the town, it was from them that people made inquiries about my whereabouts. *Ore* [*Oore*] were the only ones in town who regularly called me aside to give me advice on personal matters…. If I wanted straightforward information on anything going on in the town, I went to … my special friend. Whenever anything happened about which they thought I had not heard, they would send someone to inform me (Sudarkasa 1996:206).

Another example of institutionalized friendship in an African setting is the Chinjira, a non-kin relationship between women in Southern Malawi. It is a special friendship that involves social, ritual, and economic obligations, and this relationship is especially called forth at times of crisis in a woman's life. At such times, the *anjira* (friend) is obligated to provide emotional, material, and ritual support—whatever the occasion demands (Vaughan 1983:275-283).

Equally important as friendship groups and convivial everyday clubs are associations formed to attain a specific purpose. Traditionally, these would include trading guilds, which established prices of goods and commodity standards. During the colonial period, a number of anti-colonial movements constituted by women emerged in Southern Nigeria. The three most important resistance movement took place in Aba, Lagos, and Abeokuta; in these three cities, women organized to fight many oppressive colonial policies focusing on unjust taxation, price controls, and the colonial imposition of dictatorial male chiefs. Although these organizations have been labeled women's organizations, it is clear that they were constituted by women but not by women *qua* women. In Lagos and Abeokuta, the basis of these groups did not stem from some notion of womanhood or gender consciousness but rather from the fact that these Yoruba women were traders: occupational commonality, not gender, was the primary basis of solidarity.

Even in the case of the Women's War of the southeast, which stemmed from the Igbo and Ibibio traditional dual-sex political system, it was not the inherent consciousness of gender as identity that informed the forming of organizations but rather the fact of the social positioning of women as wives who are strangers in a particular village. According to Kamene Okonjo, because Igbo marriage was "exogamous and patrilocal" (Okonjo 1976:51), almost all adult women in a village would be wives and therefore the *inyemedi* is actually an organization of wives, not of women in general. As a corollary, the *umuada* (daughters of the lineage) had a separate organization, and their status was superior to that of the wives. It is important to emphasize that each adult woman played both roles of wife and daughter, albeit in different villages. None of these political organizations could be represented as a sisterhood in the contemporary feminist sense of a solidarity organization based on gender. In fact, in many African societies, any notions of a universal female sisterhood will immediately run up against the differing and often opposed interests of women as daughters and women as wives in the lineage and in the society at large. Gender is not viewed as a source of political identity, and where it may appear to play a role, such politics are related to social location, recognizing that identities are situational and that they emanate from multiple social positionings. Motherhood is another basis for political action in many African societies. However, the understanding of the institution in Africa transcends narrow gender considerations.

In African societies, the question of organizing to attain a political goal speaks to the issue of forming political alliances, and not sisterhood, since group identity is constituted socially and is not based on any qualities of shared anatomy popularly called gender. Consequently, it would be impractical and counterproductive to approach community building and the struggle for a just society as projects constituted on the basis of an exclusive sisterhood of the body. Coalition politics seems to be the practical, age-old system of furthering group interest only, of course, if a group has identified a common interest. Women do not constitute such a group unambiguously or continuously. In the oft-repeated, eloquent words of Bernice Reagon, a "coalition is not home" (Reagon 1983:359). So if a coalition is not home, why are we looking for sisters within it.

The Order of Things: An Overview

A number of the essays in the volume focus on the role of imperialism in the constitution of knowledge about Africa. Oyeronke Oyewumi sets the tone of the book in "White Women's Burden: The African Woman in Western Feminist Discourse" as she calls attention to the implications for Africa of the dominance of Western travelers/scholars in the production of knowledge. She shows that certain images of Africa have emerged over the four centuries of Africanist discourse, images which from time to time are refurbished and re-presented. The latest make-over has been achieved in recent studies by Western feminists portraying African women solely as abject victims. These victims stand in stark contrast to the feminists' own liberated selves who are positioned, in their view, to take on a world-wide messianic role. Oyewumi insists that African Studies is composed mainly of Euro/American travel tales; the inflections in the corpus reflect not African interests and realities, but the identity, concerns, and predilections of the "safari" scholars.

In his paper "Feminism and Africa: Some Reflections on the Poverty of Theory," Olufemi Taiwo takes up the theme of misrepresentation. He draws attention to the cost of this culture of misrepresentation to Africans who must spend time and energy struggling against it (as we are doing in this volume), at the expense of building knowledge on the specificities of the human condition in Africa and having genuine dialogues with other world civilizations. Taiwo goes on to elucidate the various forms of what he terms the "poverty of theory in feminism," drawing out its role in marginalizing Africa and stereotyping African women. Despite the fact that both Oyewumi's and Taiwo's papers were written more than a decade and half ago, we chose to include them in the volume because the issues they raise are unfortunately still very current in studies on Africa and African women. Our position is validated by the result of Mojubaolu Okome's examination of the more recent literature. In "What Women? Whose Development? A Critical Analysis of Reformist Feminist Evangelism on African Women" Okome interrogates the discourse and practice of international development pertaining to Africa and African women. She challenges the imperial practice of what she terms "feminist evangelism" and calls into question the believability of the fictional "African women" of its creation. Okome argues that sisterhood notwithstanding, the depiction of African women as objects and victims in this scholarship is inevitable given the hegemony of Western women in the representation of African women. Okome then goes on to question the very meaning and purpose of scholarship if it bears no relation to reality, even as she points to the fact that such research unavoidably functions as a tool of domination.

In "O Africa: Gender Imperialism in Academia," Nkiru Nzegwu gives us a detailed and richly textured analysis of the functioning of imperialism in the academic system. A review of an art catalogue by an obscure graduate student provides an entrance into the invisible, subtle politics of racial and sexual difference, and to the "silencing" strategies utilized to erase the Other and to re-inscribe privilege. Written in multiple shifting voices, the essay examines the social, psychic, and political effects of "whiteness" in academia and the varied forms of gender imperialism that arise from that base. Nzegwu's lucid definition of "whiteness" mirrors the way in which some of the other contributors (Oyewumi, Okome) deploy the term "Western": "Whiteness refers to a euroethnic world view, ... it comprises a shifting assortment of attitudes and beliefs.... It is a supremacist belief system embodying its own logic, whose ultimate aim is to uphold the power, the world-view, and the privileges of white people." It becomes clear that although the concept of "whiteness" or "Western" may have originated with euroethnic peoples, such concepts are no longer limited to them. Western cultural dominance is undoubtedly reinscribed when the starting point of feminist inter-community relations is framed in terms of sisterhood, a concept which privileges Euro/American experiences and summons "Other" women to accede to its terms of unconditional love among the members of this would-be global sorority.

In "Alice in Motherland: Reading Alice Walker and Screening the Color Black" Oyewumi argues that Walker's journey back to Africa, though presented as a loving return to the motherland, actually follows an imperial path. In analyzing Walker's representation of Africa, Oyewumi makes visible her debt to nineteenth-century European racist discourse on African primitiveness. Using the same time-tested imperial strategies of Othering, pathologizing, homogenizing, exceptionalizing, and colorizing African cultures, the picture of African womanhood that Walker paints takes its place among other imperial fictions of our time. Even as Walker invokes a doubly privileged consanguinal relationship of a common race and gender with African women, what she brings to this age-old discourse of African primitivism is no more than a masked reworking of those stereotypical claims under the rubric of "progressive" politics such as feminism.

In a similar vein, Nontsasa Nako takes up Alice Walker's self-representation, her portrayal of Africa, and the representation of African women as Other in *Possessing the Secret of Joy*. Nako's reading is a delightful literary evaluation of Walker's two mutually exclusive positions: of "being possessed of the Other's voice" and simultaneously locating herself as the vessel by which the Other gains voice. She shows us that despite Walker's apparently polyphonic textual approach and seemingly democratic narrative strategy, the Western worldview is the yardstick with which everything is measured. From the vantage point of South Africa from which Nako is writing, a place where the two categories African and black coexist and have currency at the level of the every day, her interrogation of these categories remind us of the complexity and fluidity of social identities.

Legal scholar L. Amede Obiora, in "The Little Foxes that Spoil the Vine: Revisiting the Feminist Critique of Female Circumcision," states that feminist sisterhood should be no excuse for marginalizing African women's own efforts at self-determination. Engaging the discourse of female circumcision, she examines the practical and policy implications of Western intervention in the struggle to eradicate the practice. Obiora cautions against an ill-conceived, externally imposed campaign which will not only risk illegitimacy and effectiveness, but which also erect walls instead of bridges in the attempt to build cross-continental understanding.

Likewise, Chikwenye Ogunyemi explores the discourse on female circumcision as she addresses issues of sisterhood, patriarchy, privilege, and exclusion in the construction of knowledge. She deploys ectomy as a trope and a lens for interpreting both the fictional writings of "Africa's daughters" and what she sees as their ostracism in both local and global centers of power. Applying the Western notion of excision as exclusion, Ogunyemi shows that imperialism is the supreme form of ectomy.. Her juxtaposition of the fictional writings of African and African American women as daughters of Africa illumines a host of questions, particularly regarding motherhood as a social institution and the symbolic motherhood that Africa represents to all her daughters, wherever they are located.

Ogunyemi in bringing together Africans and African American women as daughters of Africa prefigures Abena Busia's insistence that the tragic history of slavery and dispersal notwithstanding, these two groups of women remain sisters. In "In Search of Chains Without Iron: On Sisterhood, History, and the Politics of Location," Busia brings "home" in a forceful way the tortured personal and political history of sisterhood among white Americans, black Americans, and Africans. Using a series of personal stories, she explores the meaning of her identity as an African as she moves from one location to the other and the presumptions that each group makes borne of particular understandings of history. We start the volume with a poem on the real meaning of sisterhood in an unequal world; we end with Busia's poem forcefully reclaiming motherhood as the source of agency from which new relationships must be forged and new histories made.

All the contributors to the volume are Africans. All but one is a woman. This fact underscores the point made variously in all the papers about the necessity for self-representation as a first step in constituting knowledge about any specific social grouping. Here, we have taken this step as individuals and as a group; our hope is that we as Africans can define ourselves, our interests, and our concerns on our own terms, and can put behind us once and for all a culture of misrepresentation and marginalization which absorbs so much of our creative energy. We will continue to define ourselves and our concerns on our own terms.

WORKS CITED:

Amadiume, Ifi. *Male Daughters, Female Husbands: Gender and Sex in an African Society*. London: Zed Press, 1987.

Appiah, Anthony. "In My Father's House." *Hypatia* 11.12 (1996): 175.

Chodorow, Nancy. *The Reproduction of Mothering: Psychoanalysis and the Sociology of*

Gender. Berkeley: University of California Press, 1978.

Collins, Patricia Hill. *Black Feminist Thought: Knowledge, Consciousness, and the Politics of Empowerment*. Boston: Unwin Hyman, 1990.

Ekejiuba, Felicia I. "Down to Fundamentals: Women-centered Hearth-holds in Rural West Africa." *Women Weilding the Hoe*. Ed. Deborah Fahy-Bryceson. Oxford: Oxford University Press, 1995.

Evans-Pritchard, E. E. "Sexual Inversion among the Azande." *American Anthropologist* 72 (1970): 1428-1433.

Fadipe, N. A. *The Sociology of the Yoruba*. Ibadan, Nigeria: Ibadan University Press, 1970.

Herskovits, Melville J. "A Note On 'Woman Marriage' in Dahomey." *Africa* 10 (1937): 335-41.

hooks, bell. "Sisterhood: Political Solidarity between Women." *Feminism and Community*. Ed. Penny A.Weiss and Marilyn Friedman. Philadelphia: Temple University Press, 1995.

Joseph, Gloria I. and Jill Lewis. *Common Differences: Conflicts in Black and White Feminist Perspectives*. Boston, MA: South End Press, 1986.

Lorde, Audre. *Sister outsider: Essays and Speeches*. New York: Crossing Press, 1984.

__________. *Zami, a new spelling of my name*. New York: Crossing Press, 1983.

Lugones, Maria C. "Sisterhood and Friendship as Feminist Models." *Feminism and Community*. Ed. Penny A.Weiss and Marilyn Friedman. Philadelphia: Temple University Press, 1995.

Mikell, Gwendolyn. ed., *African Feminism: The Politics of Survival in Sub-Saharan Africa*. Philadelphia: University of Pennsylvania Press, 1997.

Nzegwu, Nkiru. "Questions of Identity and Inheritance: A Critical Review of Kwame Anthony Appiah's *In My Father's House*." *Hypatia* 11.1 (1996): 175-202.

Okonjo, Kamene. "The Dual-Sex Political System in Operation: Igbo Women and Community Politics in Midwestern Nigeria." *Women in Africa: Studies in Social and Economic Change*. Ed. Nancy J. Hafkin and Edna G. Bay. Stanford: Stanford University Press, 1976.

Oyewumi, Oyeronke. *The Invention of Women: Making an African Sense of Western Gender Discourses*. Minneapolis: University of Minnesota Press, 1997.

Reagon, Bernice Johnson. "Coalition Politics: Turning the Century." *Home Girls: A Black Feminist Anthology*. 1st ed. Ed. Barbara Smith. New York: Kitchen Table– Women of Color Press, 1983.

Rich, Adrienne. *On Lies, Secrets, and Silence*. New York: Norton, 1979.

Rosezelle, Pat Alake. "Sisterhood and Friendship as Feminist Models." *Feminism and Community*. Ed. Penny A.Weiss and Marilyn Friedman. Philadelphia: Temple University Press, 1995.

Savannah Unit Georgia Writers' Project. *Drums and Shadows: Survival Studies among the Georgia Coastal Negroes*. Athens, Georgia: The University of Georgia Press, 1940.

Segura, Denise A. and Jennifer L. Pierce. "Chicana/o Family Structure and Gender Personality: Chodorow, Familism, and Psychoanalytic Sociology Revisited." *Signs* 19.1 (Autumn 1993): 62-91.

Steady, Filomina Chioma. "The Black Woman Cross-Culturally: an Overview" in *The*

Black Woman Cross-Culturally. Cambridge, Mass. : Schenkman Pub. Co., 1981.
Sudarkasa, Niara. "Female Employment and Family Organization in West Africa." *The Black Women Cross-Culturally*. Ed. Filomina Chioma Steady. Cambridge: Schenkman Publishing Company, Inc., 1981.
Vaughan, Megan. "Which Family?: Problems in the Reconstruction of the History of the Family as an Economic and Cultural Unit," *Journal of African History* 24 (1983): 275-283.
Wekker, Gloria. "One Finger Does Not Drink Okra Soup: Afro-Surinamese Women and Critical Analysis." *Feminist Genealogies, Colonial egacies, Democratic Futures*. Ed. M. Jacqui Alexander and Chandra Talpade Mohanty. New York: Routled

2.
THE WHITE WOMAN'S BURDEN[1]:
African Women in Western[2] Feminist Discourse

Oyèrónké Oyewùmí

By persistent reiteration, a manner of speaking can become the substance of what is said.
-The Africa That Never Was, (Hammond and Jablow 1970:14)

Travelers with closed minds can tell us little except about themselves.
-"An Image of Africa" Chinua Achebe (Achebe 1978:12)

There is no question that in order to investigate the construction of gender in any contemporary African society, the role and impact of the West must be examined, not only because most African societies came under European rule by the end of the nineteenth century, but also because of the continued dominance of the West in the production of knowledge. In African studies, historically and currently, the creation, constitution, and production of knowledge remains the privilege of the West. In the last three decades, feminism has played a significant role in perpetuating certain myths about Africa. However, unlike the previous four centuries of Africanist scholarship, which focused on men, contemporary feminist discourse centers on African women.

From the outset, it should be made clear that feminism is one of the most important approaches to the interpretation of Western society that has been developed in recent times. It is invaluable to a total comprehension of Euro-American societies; and as such it expands our understanding of colonization and other processes unleashed by the West on Africa. Feminism without doubt elucidates the European world view and the socio-political organizations and processes that flow from it. Nevertheless, with regard to Africa, feminist scholarship in the main has not provided any serious departures from the "Othering" of Africa which has characterized Western writings on Africa. Therefore, my concern in this paper is not with feminism in its land of origins *per se*, but with feminism as it engages Africa and its peoples.

Predating feminist scholarship is the centuries-old Africanist discourse which has been well documented by a number of researchers, including Winthrop Jordan (1968), Hammond and Jablow (1970), Philip Curtin (1974), and Christopher Miller (1985). The consensus among these scholars is that Western writings on Africa have been racist and ethnocentric, projecting Africans, among other things, as savage, subhuman, primitive, and hyper-sexed. I contend that such images are re-presented in feminist discourse on Africa today. Thus, parallels can be drawn between the images of Africa in traditional Africanist discourse and those in the more recent feminist writings. In fact, there is a marked continuity of themes, images, and declared motivations of the scholars participating in these two phases of Africanist discourse. I am suggesting that despite the professed epistemologically "radical" shift that feminism represented in Western thought, with regard to the representation of Africans, such a radical shift is not apparent. Feminism is essentially a continuation of the traditional Africanist scholarship.

The historical context within which Africanist discourse was produced was a period of unprecedented European expansion and domination of non-European peoples. In Africa, it was the period during which the Atlantic slave trade flourished, imperialism thrived, and the framework for eventual colonial domination was put in place. Not surprisingly, the tone, content, and form of this literature were imperialistic and racist, designed to justify and rationalize European plunder and domination. Africans were projected as inferior to prove their need for the "guiding hand" of Europeans. Remarkably, Africans, were uniformly framed by European writers regardless of their station. As Jablow and Hammond noted:

> what is more significant is that this [racist] idiom should have dominated so many other writers on Africa. Traders, settlers, prospectors, and tourists tended to be equally imperialist in sentiment. It is as if the nineteenth century never ended for them. (Hammond and Jablow 1978:117-118)

Western feminists, as "heiresses" to this tradition, are no exception. It appears as though the nineteenth century is an especially long one, its prejudices endured into the opening year of the twenty-first century.

The concern in this paper is to explicate a certain mode of appropriation and codification of knowledge. I shall examine the images of African women depicted in Western feminist discourse and analyze the implications of the fact that the scholarship is dominated by white women, many of whom have not managed to avoid the racism and ethnocentrism that have characterized Western writings on Africa generally. The intention is not to undertake a discussion of the so-called status of women in Africa. Rather, I pursue the question of how Western writings affect the subjects under consideration. More precisely, the aim is to show how the way in which African women are constituted, conceptualized, and theorized in Western scholarship creates its own reality. Literally, the image not only makes the woman; the image becomes the woman. It is the discursive domination of the West that I call into question. In her discussion of how anthropology as a study of the Other conjures up its object, Min-ha writes:

> What we "look for" is unfortunately what we shall find. The anthropologist, as we already know does not *find* things; s/he *makes* them. And makes them up. The structure is therefore not something given entirely external to the person who structures, but a projection of that person's ways of handling realities (Min-ha 1989:141).

These comments also describe the way in which feminist scholarship has created its very own African woman.

Universalizing Women's Defeat

The "world historic defeat" of women theorized by Engels did not take place on any grand battlefield, but happened at the stroke of the pen with the declaration of the universal subordination of women in the early 1970's by groups of feminist scholars. The introductory chapter of Michele Rosaldo and Louise Lamphere's *Women, Culture and Society*, a collection widely regarded as seminal in women studies, exemplifies how the defeat of women was engineered. Patriarchy was created largely through a process of flitting from one society to the other, all over the globe, without reference to region, nation, race, cultural boundaries, or even history. Ignoring local specificities, Rosaldo and Lamphere declared that "sexual asymmetry is presently a universal fact of human social life" (1974:3). In spite of the fact that the editors of this collection argued that the anthropological literature has ignored women and thus "tells us relatively little about women," and despite the claim that they suffered from "lack of both materials and theories" (Ibid:vi), they were still able to reach their grand conclusion about the state of the world's women of all time. But they were only able to achieve this feat by recreating all women in the image of the Western woman, who found herself in a male-dominated society. Lack of cross-cultural data did not seem to constitute a problem for these scholars. Karen Sacks identified two lines of argument through which this universe of women's inequality is created:

> The first manifests in defining or conceptualizing equality in a slippery way, whatever women lack is the crucial marker. The second utilizes ad hoc reasoning to explain the conditions that underlie men and women's social positions: if the data do not fit the theory, an unusual circumstance has overridden biology… Thus… women in some necessarily unformulated way, are always subordinate to men. It is a theory that cannot be disproved by contradictory data. (Sacks 1979:94)

The ethnocentric idea that the white woman (or man) is the norm—measure of all things—is ethnocentric, and has dominated Western scholarly writings in at least the last two centuries. Consequently, cross-cultural women's studies have largely focused on finding patriarchy, and deciding what strategy Western feminists can use to liberate women of Africa, Latin America, and Asia from its shackles. There have been few genuine scholarly attempts to uncover and analyze the role and importance of gender differences in other societies and cultures. Scholars have simply assumed that if gender is salient in the West, it must be salient in all societies across time and space.

The feminist movement of the early 1970's in Europe and North America provided the historical context in which feminist discourse was produced and proliferated. In fact, the discipline of Women's Studies, has been characterized as the academic arm of the feminist movement. (Farnham 1987:1) This combination of scholarship and political activism meant that feminist scholars were not just content to identify and describe gender inequality; they also sought to eradicate it wherever it reared its ugly head. Hence, feminist theories are simultaneously a description of gender asymmetry and a prescription for eliminating it. Discussing their own research, Alison Jaggar and Paula Rothenberg noted that they, like other feminists, were "motivated by our deep belief, as feminists, that changes were urgently required in the position of women.... It came from our recognition as activists, that not only our political activity be guided by theory but our theory must be evaluated by its success in practice" (Jaggar and Rothenberg 1978:xii).

However, political activism and academic theorizing are often a long-distance "affair" carried out as anthropological studies and "Women in Development" projects in African, Asian, and Latin-American societies. Feminism, like imperialism, discovered its social mission, which was global in scope, and like the white man's burden of the nineteenth century, the white woman's burden of the twentieth century was born. The burden, from these feminists' vantage point, entailed rescuing the exploited, helpless, brutalized, and downtrodden African woman from the savagery of the African male and from a primitive culture symbolized by barbaric customs.

In their passionate zeal, it was inconceivable to some white women that there might be any society in the world in which women fare better than they do in the West. In their perception, the West represented the height of civilization. This was in keeping with traditional European ideas about the evolutionary stages of human progress, which posited that the position of women in any society was closely tied with the position of the society in the evolutionary hierarchy. Curtin cites Millar, who in 1777 created a four-stage schema on the place of women as a means for determining the position of a society: the more "liberated" the women, the more civilized the society (Curtin 1964:64). Because European women were said to enjoy very high status, their society was deemed the most civilized. Predictably, according to this formulation, African women were at the very bottom.

Given this way of thinking in the West about Africa, it is not surprising that feminist studies conducted on African women usually confirmed their "sorry" state. The premises of such studies represented their conclusions; as a result, no new "discoveries" were possible. Moreover, the fact that Western women were the researchers studying other women was seen as proof in itself that they were better off in their own situation, this was evidenced by their new-found position as creators of knowledge. This "positional superiority," to borrow Edward Said's term, put them in a powerful position *vis-à-vis* Africans, Asians, and Latin Americans, male and female. Western feminists did not explain their privileged status, however, in terms of their race and the internationalization of a Western-originated capitalist system; they took for granted that it was a result of how far they had progressed as women in their own society. What white women did not realize was that if they were motivated by women's subordination in their own society to study "Other" women, it was their economic and racial dominance in the global system that made it possible. After all, they were in an equally privileged position *vis-à-vis* African men. Their positional superiority is reinforced by their capacity to create knowledge about Africa and Africans. Edward Said, commenting on the relationship between power and knowledge, observed that:

> ...the object of such knowledge is inherently vulnerable to scrutiny.... To have such knowledge of such a thing is to dominate it, to have authority over it" (Said 1978:32)

and hence to recreate it in an image that fits one's fantasy, I might add.

Scholarly "Reflections" or Mirror on the Wall

For Western feminism, Africa represented the place *par excellence* for the realization of both the academic project of theorizing gender and the social mission of liberating women. According to Basil Davidson, historically, in Africanist discourse, "Africa was represented as some kind of human reserve where the nature and condition of Ancient Man could be studied in all its simplicity and savage innocence: a reserve, moreover, in which the Negroes occupied the lowest place in the hierarchy of achievement" (Davidson 1964:37). In this case, the achievement or lack of it on the part of Africans (read, African men) was that they oppressed "their" women. This view of a time-less, eventless, and changeless Africa, so well summarized by Davidson, is evident in feminist writings. In an ethnography of the !Kung, a people in Southern Africa, Shostak writes:

> Their culture, unlike ours, was not being continuously disrupted by social and political factions.... Although the !Kung were experiencing cultural change, it was still quite recent and subtle and had thus far left their traditional value system mostly intact. A study revealing what !Kung women's lives were like today might reflect what their lives had been for generations, possibly even for thousands of years. (Shostak 1983:6)

Shostak makes this assumption of !Kung stasis, in spite of the fact that the !Kung had been the basis of a Harvard University anthropological project for years, which must have been quite an event for the !Kung (if not for the anthropologists). The idea that the West could learn about itself and hence that feminists could find themselves in Africa was not a new one. Ranging from the explorers who used their (mis)adventures in Africa to test their manhood, through the Christian missionaries proselytizing for the sake of their own salvation, to the feminists in search of themselves, Africa repre-sented a mirror to the Westerners in which they perceived themselves. Rosaldo and Lamphere, summarizing the questions that reflect their concerns about women cross-culturally, concluded, "ultimately, of course, all of these ques-tions revolve around a need to re-examine the ways in which *we* think about *ourselves* "[my emphasis]. (Rosaldo and Lamphere 1974:v) And Shostak ex-plains the reason for her interest in !Kung women: "The Women's Movement had just begun to gain momentum, urging re-examination of the roles West-ern women had traditionally assumed. I hoped the field trip might help *me* to clarify some of the issues the Movement had raised" (Shostak 1983:5). At a certain level, cross-cultural research was primarily a narcissistic undertaking.

The notion of a static, unchanging Africa is clearly ahistorical. One of the major critiques leveled by feminist anthropologists against their discipline is its ahistorical approach (Leacock 1981:33-81), depicted by the tendency to treat the present circumstances of the so-called traditional cultures as if they were identical to past circumstances. Accordingly, Duley and Edwards understand the problem inherent in this kind of thinking:

> We cannot assume, as many have done, that the present set of relationships
> between men and women are necessarily those of the past, and efforts to
> analyze the origins of gender stratification may be seriously flawed by failing to
> recognize this fact. (Duley and Edwards 1986:29)

Yet, in the declaration of a universal subordination of women and in the search for origins of male dominance, many Western feminists make no reference to history—the history of slavery, imperialism, colonization, and racial domination of non-Western peoples, and the emergence of Western hegemony world-wide. In Gayatri Spivak's words, they deny the "worlding" of the Third World—which is a denial of the impact of the West on the rest of the world. According to Spivak, "the information retrieval approach to non-Western peoples suggests that despite centuries of imperialism and colonial exploitation non-Westerners still have a rich, intact, cultural heritage waiting to be recovered, interpreted, and curricularized for the benefit of the West" (1985:262). It is the curricularization of African women in feminist literature that I call into question.

"Customizing" Women's Oppression

Inherent in the notion of cultural stasis is the idea of a primitive Africa where humans have remained in their original state, a state of nature, for ages. Indeed, the characterization of Africa as the dark continent is undergirded by this notion. Alta Jablow and Dorothy Hammond posit that two contradictory images of Africans flow from this characterization—the Noble Savage and the Bestial Savage (1970:20). But in relation to "his" women, the African male could not be portrayed as anything but a bestial savage. In this regard, polygamy was singled out and represented as a special evil, symbolizing the degradation of African women and hence the low state of Africans. Likewise, polygamy has been a focus of attention for feminist scholars. Perhaps the two questions that are most asked by Westerners of African women are the ones Shostak asked !Kung women—"how it felt to share a husband with another woman?" (18) and "did spouses love one another?" (5). No doubt, foreigners are often obsessed with perceived curiosities they encounter in other cultures. However, the problem is that in feminist discourse, these questions are rhetorical not because they demand no answers, but because they have pre-ordained answers, such as, monogamy is the only "normal" (read "civilized," "true") form of marriage, and polygamy and love are mutually exclusive. For many Western feminists, polygamy is barbaric, it degrades and oppresses women, and it is alien to the civilized (read "Western") societies from which they come. No attention is paid to the feelings and perspectives of those who experience it as the only form of marriage, and no examination is made of its implications for social organization. For example, though many feminists promote women's employment outside the home, they fail to acknowledge that women in some African societies are able to earn income by engaging in non-home-based work because of the division of labor among women that polygamy makes possible. Child-care, for instance, can be shared among women, allowing them to pursue different occupations without being handicapped by children's needs. Despite decades of feminist scholarship on Africa, interpretations of polygamy and bride price remain ethnocentric if not racist, reinforcing the beast-of-burden image as a manifestation of African "tradition."

Violence plays an important role in the painting of negative pictures of Africa. It has been powerful in the depiction of Africa as the "dark continent" and it is no less important in the representation of the woman in the "heart of darkness." According to Brantlinger, negative images are created by the constant association of Africa with evil, disease, and brutality. He notes that in nineteenth-century European writing, from abolitionist propaganda to travel tales, violence is depicted in excruciating detail to feed the European imagination. Signs of such "X-rated" concern are apparent in feminist writing. For example, Shostak's choice of Nisa as the !Kung woman to be studied, was determined in part by the woman's alleged story about having committed infanticide. Another case in point is Western women's obsession with and sensationalization of female circumcision—a practice found in some communities of Africa. Their preoccupation with this practice was made obvious during the conference of the United Nations Decade for Women, held in Copenhagen in 1980. The insistence on the part of Western women to label what African women call female circumcision "mutilation" was the fist visible sign of deep divisions between them and many of their African counterparts. Although many of the African delegates voiced their interest in seeing an end to the practice, "they stressed that the abolition of these practices is not a priority for them—sufficient food and clean water having a far greater importance."[3] For Western feminists, the position taken by African women was unacceptable and, like the proverbial mourners who wail at the funeral more than the bereaved, they continue to focus on female circumcision as the number-one problem of African women. This presumption on the part of Western women to define the meaning and goals of the lives of "Other" women did not bode well for the sisterhood that was being advocated at these international conferences. The conflict was bound to come to a head, as it did in subsequent international meetings.

A number of other African institutions that Westerners view as barbaric include arranged marriages, levirate, and child betrothal. These practices are misrepresented as misogynistic and are not placed in their cultural and social contexts that would allow Westerners to discern their meaning from the perspective of African societies. Solange Falade, commenting on arranged marriages, condemns the self-righteous attitude of Euro/Americans and informs us that in Senegalese society:

> It is indeed parents who choose the marriage partner. I do not think it is necessary to regard this as nothing but a heartless trick, or something done for egoistic reasons, on the part of the parents. It is not a question merely of a union between two individuals, but of a union between two families. (Falade 1963:220)

In fact, the time seems ripe for many feminists to critically analyze the alternative of arranged marriages—the so-called personal choice or "love" marriages—that are prevalent in the West today, and indeed in Africa where women as individuals are said to choose their own mates. As the popular books with telling titles like *Smart Women, Foolish Choices,* and *Men Who Hate Women and the Women Who Love Them,* suggest that personally choosing a marriage partner does not necessarily guarantee personal safety, self-fulfillment, or eternal bliss in marriage. The institutional and social context of marriage is paramount in assessing the welfare of both men and women.

The Creation of Patriarchy or "Feminist" Male-Centeredness

The strategy in Western feminist discourse of singling out women without corresponding attention to men is used to create an impression that African societies are male-dominated and anti-women. For example, Nancy Folbre, establishing patriarchy among the Shona of Zimbabwe, points out that "a woman's consent to marriage was not required and many young girls were promised at an early age in return for a portion of the bride wealth payment" (Folbre 1988:64). What she failed to mention is that marriage was arranged for both boys and girls. Bride wealth is portrayed as "buying a wife," yet no attention is paid to bride service, whereby men may have to provide services to their in-laws for the duration of their lives. The lack of attention to men in much of feminist writing on Africa has produced gross distortions and misrepresentations in the understanding of gender relations. Christine Oppong noticed this unfortunate development and acting to avoid it in a book she edited writes: "In putting together this volume, we have sought to avoid a currently pervasive neo-sexist trap: the study of women, by women, for women! We have sought rather to assemble male and female accounts and observations of female and male relationships" (Oppong 1983:xv-xvi).

Moreover, the creation of patriarchy through denial of female power and agency is pervasive in the feminist literature. An outgrowth of this practice is the image of a weak and helpless African woman who needs to be saved from barbaric customs and a brutal, all-powerful, misogynistic group of men. Jean Henn, in the process of instituting a continent-wide patriarchal mode of production in Africa, dismisses roles symbolizing female importance and power: "Such roles for women can be variously interpreted as the means by which the patriarchal class co-opted particularly capable and potentially rebellious women" (Henn 1988:47). In one quick stroke of the pen, Henn co-opts the counter-evidence, and we are back to the image of the weak, helpless, and subjugated African woman. This discursive practice demonstrates very clearly how "research" can constitute its own subject.

Perhaps one is not surprised at the racist and ethnocentric perspectives displayed in some feminist scholarship on Africa, given that it is part of a larger Africanist discourse that has consistently inferiorized Africans. However, one is taken aback at the androcentricity of feminist discourse, mainly because male bias has been the cornerstone of the feminist critique of traditional Western writing and thought. The androcentrism of four hundred years of Africanist discourse is glaring because of the absence of women as objects of study. In feminist scholarship, women are presented, but like African men, are presented as objects. Men are absent, but their presence is maintained as a *male*volent, all-powerful, omnipresent force labeled "patriarchy," directing everything women do. To that extent, such analyses are male-biased. Women are presented, but silenced. Their experience is not validated, thus perpetuating the marginalization of females. In this light then, although a body of knowledge has been produced on African women, much of the new research is no less male-biased than traditional Western scholarship. As a matter of fact, even neutral concepts like "elders" and "in-laws" are masculinized. One wonders whether African women ever aged or had any relationship with the spouses and families of their children.

As a consequence of this androcentrism, much power is attributed to African men, even in situations where they are victims themselves. A good example is Folbre's paper on gender relations in colonial Zimbabwe, where she alleges a patriarchal alliance between African men and white colonial masters, to the detriment of African women. But she fails to explain why such an "unholy alliance" between white men and African men (in which they were assumed to be "partners") kept white women in a state of permanent leisure and African men as their domestic servants. Other scholars have noted the pervasive denial of race as an important category in Western feminist analyses (Davis 1982; hooks 1982; Amadiume 1987).

The stereotyping of Africans in Western writings as a servile, childlike people who need to be rescued and protected by one Western group or another is an enduring practice. Throughout the different phases of the encounter between Africa and the West, the image has been used to justify European domination both on the continent and in its Diaspora. In the process of constituting African women as objects of discourse, some feminists focus on the most downtrodden groups among women, leaving the impression that African women are all the same—equally oppressed, equally wretched, and equally in need of deliverance. In creating this homogeneous, downtrodden mass, differences and distinctions of age, class, rank, kinship affiliation, marital status, and seniority are ignored as if they do not exist. Amadiume points out that the "picture of Black women as universally deprived only reinforces racism" (Amadiume 1987:5).

In fact, racism is demonstrated in the debate about the impact of colonization on African women; there is a tendency to identify all positive social change as externally derived and all Western practices as good. Anthropologist Jane Guyer, whose work is relatively more sensitive to issues of cross-cultural representation, also displays this tendency. Reiterating the positive impact of European domination on Beti women of Cameroon, she offers this lamentation, which a native male informant is said to have made to an earlier anthropologist:

> Why did whites make us clothe our wives? I used to have twenty wives. When they went naked, it was enough that I growl here in my *abaa* (men's house) for them to stop talking in their twenty kitchens. When they had dresses and wrappers, I grumbled here in vain, and they continued to chat as if nothing was going on. (Guyer 1984:6).

Guyer fails to contextualize and interrogate these assertions. Left uninterpreted, their implications are clear enough: African women have a lot for which to thank the West, not the least of which is their newfangled assertiveness (and, of course, their clothes). The agency of African women is again denied; the social mission of feminist imperialism will be thwarted if they are portrayed as self-determining. The need for white women to engage in a rescue operation is certainly made more urgent by this picture of naked and victimized African women.

The Beast of Burden
In contrast with the image of the weak African woman is one of immense physical strength. Despite the fact that many Western feminists in their own societies glorify women's physical strength as a sign of equality with men, in their writings on Africa the concept of strength is used negatively to construct

a beast-of-burden image for the African woman. Clearly, white women as the bearers of the beast of burden have a more difficult task than their nineteenth-century male counterparts. In Boserup's (1970) "female farming systems" and the "prostitution for survival" stereotype, the African woman is pictured as a mule and a drudge. Few studies of African women fail to make this point, mostly by highlighting what women do and omitting what men do, or by concentrating on what African men do not do—tasks that have been defined as a man's job based on the European experience. This belabored image of the overworked African woman complements the image of African men as lazy and indolent in traditional Africanist discourse. Curtin notes that in constructing what Europeans called the African character in the nineteenth century, laziness and indolence topped the list (1964:223). Of course, in this male-as-norm discourse, "African" meant the African male unless otherwise stated. It logically follows that if men were so lazy, "their women," who were perceived as slaves by Europeans, were doing all the work. Furthermore, in the mind of many Westerners, male and female, African women's gainful employment suggest indolence on the part of the African male. Therefore, the fact of women's very active and visible engagements met with negative interpretations about African societies as a whole.

Summarizing the image of African women in the popular literature of the nineteenth century, Jablow and Hammond conclude that "the assumption that she the African woman is nothing but a drudge, completely subjugated if not actually enslaved, is reinforced by superficial knowledge of the bride-price and polygamy" (Jablow and Hammond 1970:150). Interestingly, the continent of Africa itself has been depicted by various writers as a woman emphasizing her fecundity, helplessness, sexuality and over-burdenedness. Reade, a popular nineteenth century English writer, exhorts readers to "look at the map of Africa. Does it not resemble a woman with a huge burden on the back?" (Ibid:72) In this image, the savage environment and its helpless and hapless victim are united as one.

Womanhood as Prostitution

One of the recurrent images of African womanhood in feminist writings is that of prostitute. In what Amina Mama appropriately called a "groin-centered" analysis, Cutrufelli states that "either overtly or covertly, *prostitution* is still the main if not the *only source of work* [my emphasis] for African women" (Cutrufelli 1983:33). Concluding a discussion of the informal sector and women, Parpart and Stichter write: "It is difficult to imagine the informal sector in Africa being eliminated in the foreseeable future; local *food distribution* and *sexual services* in particular, the *two areas of women's greatest specialization* [my emphasis mine] (Parpart and Stichter 1988:20). Likewise, in an essay on women and social change on the Zambian copper belt, Parpart asserts: "Playing on their scarcity, women soon learned to bargain with male partners; *changing partners became an accepted way to improve one's living standards* [my emphasis]" (Ibid:115). Similarly, MacGaffey states: "Women in Kinshasa earned money in two primary ways: through *petty trade* and through *prostitution* [my emphasis]" (MacGaffey 1988:164). In contrast, there have been very few studies of prostitution as a distinct occupational category in African societies. In the literature, the impression created is that African women, apart from being peasants, traders, wives, clerks, child-care workers or, whatever, are also always prostitutes.

This image of the prostitute cannot be separated from the association of Africans with strong sexual desire, which reaches back into centuries of European fantasy. Polygamy was interpreted as a sign of innate lust and sexual indiscipline on the part of the African man, and was regarded as proof of his primitivism. In the European mind, civilization is based on the repression of instincts (sexual and otherwise), but primitivism was associated with unbridled sexuality. The labeling of African women as primitive, and therefore more sexually intensive, was antithetical to the portrayal of the European woman as sexually passive. In an informative essay on female sexuality in nineteenth century Europe, Sander Gilman argues that the perception of the black merged with the perception of the prostitute: "The primitive is black, and the qualities of blackness, or at least of the black female, are those of the prostitute" (Gilman 1985:248). It is remarkable that European prostitutes during this period were visually portrayed with steapopygia, as if they were black. Steapopygia was perceived as the physical manifestation of black women's hypersexuality; thus they were defined as prostitutes. The image was pervasive then and it remains persistent; being part of a particular reality written by both white men and white women.

Conceiving Women or Barren Ideas

The ethnocentrism of some Western feminists ranged from the idea that there is a universal woman who is white (like them), to the imposition of Western concepts and values to interpret the experiences of "Other" women. Based on their own limited experience, they had declared women's subordination a universal fact and had reached a conclusion about how to eradicate it. According to Amadiume:

> this kind of global presupposition is itself ethnocentric. Furthermore, the domestic/public dichotomy which led them to the conclusion that maternal and domestic roles were responsible for the supposed universal subordination of women was a feature of their particular class and culture. (Amadiume

1987:4)

The public/private concept has been uncritically applied to Africa despite the fact that various researchers have noted that in Africa, the gender division of labor does not organize itself according to any public/private divide. As a matter of fact, the reduction of gender relations to the economics of women's lack of access to land, labor, men, and jobs is a function of both the application of public/private concept and the economic monism of the West. The public/private conceptualization lacks any clear definition; it is shifted around at will, chasing women about and defining the women's sphere, wherever it is deemed to exist, as private. In contrast, men's location is always defined as public. Thus, the preoccupation in the literature is to get women out of their private sphere and into the public sphere of men as a means of abolishing their subordination. A new vocabulary has developed around this concept in the "Women in Development" literature, integrating women into development is code for moving them out of subsistence production (private world) into the cash cropping (public world) of men. Other ways of maintaining the public/private dichotomy in different terms such as modern/traditional or formal/informal, both of which connote male/female space, respectively. Based on this usage of the public/private concept, it is not farfetched to suggest that a female head of state of any country is operating in the private sphere of women, since by definition it is the presence of women which defines the sphere (a very radical interpretation of the "kitchen cabinet").

Another over-used concept in the "Women in Development" literature, handed down directly from the Euro-American experience, is female-headed households. Female-headed households in the West are perceived as abnormal and male-deprived, and as a result beset with a host of problems. The concept presupposes that households are normally organized around one male authority figure directing all other members of the household. In many societies in Africa, this is not the case; authority is more dispersed in consanguinallly-based, multi-generationally based households in which the spheres of control for a variety of individuals, fathers and mothers, siblings and wives are delineated. In addition, the fact that women hold positions of authority within the household does not necessarily suggest male absence or the pathologies associated with female-headed households in the West. It is against this background that Felicia Ekejiuba's concept of "hearthhold," (Ekejiuba 1984) put forward to describe African families which are organized around a mother and her children in polygamous households is especially appropriate. It is necessary to examine concepts critically, taking into account the African experience, because all concepts come with baggage, some of it alien to the cultures to which we apply them. Other concepts, such as marriage, family, wife, and husband, all bear the taint of "Westocentricity"[4] in their usage; therefore, they should always be defined when applied.

Within the context of this ethnocentric world view, the Western family organization in the contemporary period is perceived as egalitarian, and this is the outcome that is advocated for Africans. Sharon Stitcher, in a study of middle-class families in Kenya, poses her major concern thus:

> The underlying comparative question is whether more egalitarian and more "joint" relations are coming into being in the domestic domain, such as are said to exist in contemporary European and American middle-class families…. Changes in gender relations in the family can be seen as part of the broader question of whether a transition to the western "bourgeoisie" family is taking place in urban Africa. (Stitcher 1988:178)

Apart from the fact that the observation that the Western middle-class family as egalitarian is debatable, the assumption that joint conjugal relations are necessarily egalitarian is unproven, even in the West. The imposition of Western concepts and values on African material has not gone unnoticed by other African writers. Wole Soyinka, for example, commenting on this unfortunate practice, writes:

> We Black Africans have been blandly invited to submit ourselves to a second epoch of colonization—this time by universal humanoid abstraction defined and conducted by individuals whose theories and prescriptions are derived from their history, their social neuroses, and their value systems. (Soyinka 1972:x)

The feminist project definitely fits into Soyinka's definition of a second epoch of colonization.

These images of Africa in Western writing are made possible by the projection of a powerful myth of Africa as a homogeneous, unitary state of primitivism. The characterization of a vast continent of diverse nations and peoples as if it were one village can be termed the "villagization of Africa." The "Othering" of this homogenized collectivity is done in binary opposition to the West. Because Africa has been projected as that which the West is not, it becomes absolutely necessary to impose an appropriate identity on the homogenized mass. To be sure, there are commonalities among Africa's cultures, nations, states, and peoples; however, sources of diversity are so many that scholars should be cautious, if not wary, of making overly generalized statements. With regard to gender relations and family structure, even apparent common practices like polygamy and bride wealth transfers have varied meanings in different historical epochs and cultural contexts. Yet, overly generalized statements about these social practices abound.

A Question of Power

The hegemony of the West and the monopoly of scholarship on Africa by white men traditionally, and more recently by white women, is largely responsible for the persistence of these images and misrepresentations. In a sense, feminist discourse, as the better half of Africanist discourse, has completed the picture of Africa started hundreds of years ago. It is remarkable that, through four centuries of "progress," "enlightenment," scientific discoveries, and space exploration, with technological advancements in information gathering and dissemination, the images of Africa (by the West and for the West) have hardly changed. Information generated through research coded as knowledge is a major tool of domination. In this day of policy studies, the impact of scholarly assumptions and practices is immediately felt by the subjects of research. "Women in Development" studies and their consequent implementation as policy by international organizations and governments are cases in point. Barbara Rogers conducted an informative study on how Western gender assumptions embedded in development policies have negatively affected African women (Rogers 1980).

With regard to women, most feminists postulate gender as a social construct in opposition to the biological constructionists who define women as inferior by nature. Paradoxically, the universality attributed to gender asymmetry by Western feminists suggests a biological rather than a cultural basis, given that human biology is universal, but cultures speak in myriad voices. In fact, the categorization of women as a homogeneous group, always constituted as powerless and victimized, does not reflect the fact that gender relations are social relations and therefore historically grounded and culturally bound.

I have argued that women are not just women; factors of race, class, regional origins, age, and kinship ties are central to the understanding of inter-gender and intra-gender relations, locally and globally. It has been demonstrated that the biological similarity of all women cannot be taken for granted as the basis of solidarity (sisterhood) in the face of a multitude of differences that emerge contextually and situationally. At the level of scholarship, in particular, white women occupy a position of power, and this has serious implications for their relationship with women from other societies. According to Saddeka Arebi (1986: 17), "in a discourse of other cultures, questions of who speaks, what is and what is not discussed, how it is discussed, what questions may be asked, who defines the reality, and what is true or false take on new significance." Such questions have been central in this study. However, these questions have not received much attention in Western feminist discourse, in spite of the fact that scholars from different parts of the world continue to call attention to them, challenging the positions and presuppositions of Western women (Mohanty 1984; Amadiume 1987; Ong 1988; Minh-ha 1989). It remains to be seen whether the increasing presence of scholars from Africa, Asia, and Latin America will result in more accurate and contextualized portrayals of people from different cultures and societies.

NOTES

1. This paper was originally presented at the conference *In Search of New Paradigms in African Development* (ISENPAD) held in Nairobi, Kenya in June 1988. I was drawn to Rudyard Kipling's poem on the white man's burden the source of an apt phrase for describing the way in which Western feminist scholars went about their business in Africa, Asia, and Latin America. Of course to make it more appropriate, I gendered it. A version of this paper is the first chapter of my dissertation (*Mothers Not Women: Making an African Sense of Western Gender Discourses*, submitted in the Dept. of Sociology UC Berkeley, 1993). Though the paper is a fourteen years old, the issues it examines are still current.

2. The discourse in origins is Euro-American; therefore, it is overly determined by their interests and concerns. It should be made clear, however, that Eurocentric views of the world are no longer limited to European peoples. Because this paper focuses on the inception of the discourse, its concern is to examine the implications of the fact that feminist scholarship on Africa was created and continues to be dominated by Euro-American women.

3. Minority Rights Group *Report, #47:* 10. The point that is being made here by the African delegates is that with regard to priorities, putting the question of eradicating female circumcision over basic needs like food and water amounts to rearranging the deck chairs on the Titanic. More importantly, they are asserting their rights to self-definition.

4. In the light of the dominance of North America, I felt the need for a word that would not just specify Europe but incorporate other centers of Western culture.

WORKS CITED

Achebe, Chinua. "An Image of Africa." *Research in African Literatures 9* (1978): 2, 12.

Amadiume, Ifi. *Male Daughters, Female Husbands: Gender and Sex in an African Society.* London: Zed Press, 1987.

Arebi, Saddeka. "Field Statement on the Anthropological Study of Gender." Department of Anthropology, University of California at Berkeley, 1986. Unpublished.

Boserup, Ester. *Women's Role in Economic Development*. St. Allen's Press, Inc., 1970.

Brantlinger, Patrick. "Victorians and Africans: The Genealogy of the Myth of the Dark Continent." *"Race," Writing and Difference*. Henry Louis Gates, Jr. Chicago, London: University of Chicago Press, 1985.

Curtin, Phillip. *The Image of Africa: British Ideas and Action, 1780-1850*. University of Wisconsin Press, 1964.

Cutrufelli, Maria Rosa. *Women of Africa: Roots of Oppression*. London: Zed Press, 1983.

Davidson, Basil. *The African Past: Chronicles from Antiquity to Modern Times*. New York: The Universal Library, Grosset & Dunlap, 1964.

Duley, Margo and Mary Edward. *The Cross-cultural Study of Women*. New York: The Feminist Press at the City University of New York, 1986.

Ekejiuba, Felicia. "Contemporary Households and Major Socio-economic Transitions in Eastern Nigeria." Paper presented at the Workshop on Conceptualizing the Household: Issues of Theory, Method and Application. Cambridge, MA, 1984.

Engels, Frederick. *The Origin of the Family, Private Property and the State*. Moscow: Foreign Languages Publishing House, 1891.

Falade, Solange. "Women of Dakar and the Surrounding Urban Area." *Women of Tropical Africa*. Berkeley and Los Angeles: University of California Press, 1963.

Farnham, Christie, ed. *The Impact of Feminist Research on the Academy*. Bloomington and Indianapolis: Indiana University Press, 1987.

Folbre, Nancy. "Patriarchal Formation in Zimbabwe." *Patriarchy and Class: African Women at Home and in the Work Force*. Ed. Sharon Stitchter and Jane Parpat. Boulder and London: Westview Press, 1988.

Foucault, Michel. *The History of Sexuality*, Vol. 2. New York: Vintage Books, 1980.

Gilman, Sander. "White Bodies, Black Bodies: Toward a Iconography of Female Sexuality in Late 19th Century Art, Medicine and Literature." *"Race," Writing and Difference*. Henry Louis Gates, Jr. Chicago, London: University of Chicago Press, 1985.

Guyer, Jane. *Family and Farm in Southern Cameroon*. Boston University, African Studies Center, 1984.

Hammond, Dorothy and Alta Jablow. *The Africa that Never Was: Four Centuries of British Writing About Africa*. New York: Twayne Publishers, Inc, 1970.

Henn, Jeanne. (1988). "The Material Basis of Sexism: A Mode of Production Analysis." *Patriarchy and Class: African Women at Home and in the Work Force*. Ed. S. Stitchter and Jane Parpart. Boulder and London: Westview Press, 1988.

Jaggar, Alison and Paula Rothenberg. *Feminist Frameworks*. McGraw-Hill, 1978.

MacGaffey, Janet. "Evading Male Control: Women in the Second Economy in Zaire." *Patriarchy and Class: African Women at Home and in the Work Force*. Ed. S. Stitchter and Jane Parpart. Boulder and London: Westview Press, 1988.

Mama, Amina. "African Women Fight Back," *West Africa* (December, 1984): 10.

Miller, Christopher. "Theories of Africans: The Question of Literary Anthropology." *Race, Writing and Difference*. Chicago, London: University of Chicago Press, 1986.

______. *Blank Darkness: Africanist Discourse in French*. Chicago and London: University of Chicago Press, 1985.

Minh-ha, Trinh. *Woman, Native Other: Writing Post Coloniality and Feminism*. Bloomington and Indianapolis: Indiana University Press, 1989.

Minority Rights Group. "Female Circumcision, Excision and Infibulations: The Facts and Proposal for Change." *Report No. 47*, published by Minority Rights Group, London.

Mohanty, Chandra. "Under Western Eyes: Feminist Scholarship and Colonial Discourses." *Boundary 2* (Spring/Fall, 1984).

Ong, Aihwa. "Feminism and the Critique of Colonial Discourse," *Inscriptions* 3-4 (1988).

Oppong, Christine, ed. *Male and Female in West Africa*. London: George Allen & Unwin, 1983.

Parpart, Jane. "Sexuality and Power in the Zambian Copperbelt." *Patriarchy and Class: African Women at Home and in the Work Force*. Ed. S. Stitchter and Jane Parpart. Boulder and London: Westview Press, 1988.

Rogers, Barbara. (1980). *The Domestication of Women Discrimination in Developing Societies* (Reprint). London: Tavistock Publications, Ltd., and Methuen, Inc. (1983).

Rosaldo, Michelle and Louise Lamphere. *Women, Culture and Society*. Stanford University Press, 1974.

Sacks, Karen. *Sister and Wives: The Past and Future of Sexual Equality*. Urbana, London, Chicago: University of Illinois Press, 1979.

Said, Edward. *Orientalism*. New York: Vintage Books, 1978.

Shostak, Marjorie. *Nisa: The Life and Words of a !Kung Woman*. New York: Vintage Books, 1983.

Soyinka, Wole. *The Man Died: Prison Notes*. New York: Penguin Books, 1972.

Spivak, Gayatri. "Three Women's Texts and a Critique of Imperialism." *"Race," Writing and Difference*. Henry Louis Gates, Jr. Chicago, London: University of Chicago Press, 1985.

Stitchter, Sharon. "The Middle Class Family: Changes in Gender Relations." *Patriarchy and Class: African Women at Home and in the Work Force*. Ed. S. Stitchter and Jane Parpart. Boulder and London: Westview Press, 1988.

Stitchter, Sharon and Jane Parpart, eds. *Patriarchy and Class: African Women in the Home and in the Work Force*. Boulder and London: Westview Press, 1988.

3.
FEMINISM AND AFRICA:
Reflections on the Poverty of Theory

Olufemi Taiwo

African scholars in the humanities and social sciences labor under a burden imposed by the misrepresentation, falsehoods, and half-truths which characterizes much of Euro-American scholarship on Africa. African historians spent the 1950s and 60s trying to refute the racist contention, ridiculous as it must sound to contemporary ears, that Africans had no history before the arrival of Europeans. It is no accident, therefore, that a nationalist problematic still dominates much of African historiography. Much of the substantive academic philosophizing from Africa is of recent origin. During most of the 1970s, valuable time was needlessly expended on the question of whether or not African philosophy even exists. Many African scholars sojourning in Europe and North America, either as graduate students or teachers, have encountered what amounts to a culture of misrepresentation and have spent time and energy assailing it.

Every time African scholars are forced into these sterile but needed efforts to assert that we *are* or we *think*, the urgent tasks of identifying and explicating *what* we are or *what* we think remain undone or only partly done, and the possibility of a genuine dialogue with other world civilizations is aborted. The world, especially the Western world, and we ourselves, are the worse for it. We must decry this unfortunate situation and lament the fact that an end is nowhere in sight. But we must not despair. We must continue, in spite of all odds, to struggle against the misrepresentation of our situation in Western (that is European and North American) media, scholarship, politics, history, and other areas.

This paper is a response to a manifestation of this culture of misrepresentation in the area of women's studies. It would not have been necessary had I not noticed that the culture of misrepresentation is alive and well, even if largely unacknowledged, in feminist writings about Africa.[1] In what follows, I shall cite evidence to buttress my claim and indict those who perpetuate this culture. But first, a clarification.

Anyone who is familiar with women's studies must think that there is a paradoxical ring to the title of this paper. The paradox lies in the fact that whereas feminism is suffused with theory, in its application to Africa and in feminist writings on or about African women, one finds a profound poverty of theory. Before I explain the nature of the poverty, it is necessary to explain what I mean by theory.

We never apprehend reality directly or *immediately*. The categories with which we analyze, organize, and synthesize phenomena as interconnected and internally coherent wholes are theories. In this paper, however, I am using theory as applied to whole, synthetic, identified, and individuated phenomena–i.e., the business of establishing patterns of determination in diverse phenomena. This is what natural scientists do with nature and what social scientists do with social phenomena. To relate this conception to the issue of feminism and Africa, I will use "theory" to refer to the conceptual tools with which we identify patterns of determination in social phenomena regarding women and their place in society–that is, I will find out the whats, hows, and whys of the situation of women, in our case, in Africa; the causes, courses, and consequences of regularities discernible in the social phenomena concerning women. By so doing, I hope to facilitate an understanding of the realities of African women, a fundamental precondition for the more arduous task of changing for the better those realities that require transformation.

It may be urged against my title that theories of the sort I have described abound in feminism. So why talk of the poverty of theory? Let us explain the notion of poverty. Poverty can refer to two things, among others: an absence and a deficiency. An absence must be taken in its literal sense: an emptiness, a void. The poverty of theory where it refers to absence can mean the utter lack of theory. But poverty may also refer to an insufficiency: not the lack of the thing (theory), but its presence in insufficient quantities or the presence in it of too few building blocks, for example, data. Insufficiency may itself be of two kinds: it may be used to refer to inadequacy or to incorrectness–either way, we mean it is not good enough. And it may be used to refer to irrelevance–that is the theory proposed is not suited to the reality it purports to explain. In other words, there is a lack of fit, a disjuncture, between theory and reality. As will presently become clear, feminism, the kind that I treat here, suffers from a poverty of theory in the various forms just adumbrated.

I should point out that my focus in this paper is in those variants of feminism that claim to be interested in the liberation of women worldwide. For in most of the feminist writings that dominate the discourse in the United States and Canada, the same provincialism is prevalent that afflicts the thoughts of their male counterparts. In fact, one can say that poverty-as-absence is the dominant feature of American feminist writings that affirm, wittingly or unwittingly, an identity between American women's experience and the experience of women *simpliciter*.[2] Those who concern themselves with Africa usually fall within the socialist-feminist or the Marxist-feminist categories.[3] The differences between them matter less, given the aim of this paper. My primary concern is with theory; politics, although relevant, is secondary.

The distinction between feminists and Marxist-feminists turns on the level of emergency which either of them gives to the women's struggle in relation to the class struggle against capitalism. For Marxist-feminists, feminist issues are not placed on the level of primary emergency. The oppression of women is seen as only one form of oppression, one which is an integral part of capitalism. For them, while there is need to struggle against women's oppression, national oppression, racial oppression, and so on, such a struggle should not be allowed to obfuscate the ultimate goal of overthrowing the basis of all oppression in the present epoch–capitalism. For feminists, however, feminist issues are primary. In fact, radical feminists see "feminist issues not only as *women's* first priority, but as central to any larger revolutionary analysis" (Firestone 1970:37). Socialist feminists try, on the other hand, to combine what they see as the best insights of radical feminism and Marxism. In this view, it is not the case that Marxian class analysis is incorrect but that it is inadequate for the purposes of women's liberation. Gender analysis must combine with class analysis. Gender struggle and class struggle are both of primary and equal importance. In dealing with women's oppression, we are not dealing with one system (capitalism) of which the oppression of women is a feature. We have two systems (capitalism and patriarchy), the first of which oppresses everyone through class rule and the second of which alone can explain the oppression of women *qua* women. This is what has come to be known as the Dual Systems Theory.[4]

What I have tried to do in the last few paragraphs is to render, in a capsule, the distinction between the two groups of feminists I am considering in this paper. I have chosen to focus on these two categories because they are the loudest in their verbal and written professions of commitment to the cause of women's liberation in Africa, Asia, and Latin America. Others are simply unaware of Africa or can't be bothered about it. It is among the former that the diverse manifestations of the poverty of theory are most to be found. As we would say in Yoruba, *O n pami, o lo n gbami* (You are killing me but you insist that you are saving me): in succumbing, wittingly or unwittingly, to the danger of the poverty of theory, these authors are actually demeaning the peoples of Africa, women as well as men, in the name of representing them. How does the poverty of theory express itself?

According to socialist feminists, whereas Marxism can explain the exploitation of women as workers, capitalists, and so on, it cannot explain the exploitation of women as women. For it is not capitalism which is responsible for the oppression of women; rather it is *patriarchy*. According to Heidi Hartmann, patriarchy is defined "as a set of social relations between men, which have a material base, and which, though hierarchical, establish or create interdependence and solidarity among men that enable them to dominate women" (Hartman 1981:14). Patriarchy is seen as constituting a separate and autonomous totality of relations independent of the economic relations of production rooted in capitalism. Even though patriarchy is hierarchical and, implicitly, some men are dominated by other men, both male dominator and male dominated are united in their common objective of dominating women. In order to support the independence of patriarchal relations of the determining influence of the capitalist mode of production, defenders of socialist feminism assert that patriarchy has a material base which lies "most fundamentally in men's control over women's labour power" (Hartman 1981:14). Through patriarchy, men exclude women from access to the essential productive resources in society and channel their sexuality in the direction of producing and rearing children. When a theory that apprehends reality with only two categories–"men" and "women"–confronts Africa, the result is a litany of confusion and nonexplanations.

The theory is not equipped to deal with the complexity of the African, nor with any other situation. Talk about Africa's bewildering diversity is one of the real legends of all time. It is quite diverse in its demographic constitution, the cultural practices contained within it, its history, and so on. One assumes that this forbidding diversity will, at the least, have a sobering effect on any researcher interested in truth to approach his or her subject with considerable respect. In other words, any researcher working on Africa will be less prone to generalizations, to asserting uniformities in advance of more adequate knowledge and information about the peoples and cultures of the continent. This is an important point. Most aspects of African life and thought remain unresearched or underresearched. The reasons for this go beyond the scope of this paper. One consequence is that for most areas of life and thought, even the most diligent scholar must lament the paucity of relevant and useful data. But a disinclination to generalize on the basis of limited evidence and respect for the diversity of African phenomena are a rare in feminist theory as applied to Africa. This is one aspect of the poverty of theory that I speak of in this paper. I give some illustrations, beginning with the sexual division of labor.

Almost every human society can be said to have had some variant or other of the sexual division of labor. It is perhaps the first division of labor known to history. The sexual division of labor may or may not be based on superordination and subordination. Either way, one must never discount the exigencies of coordination that are forever present in even the most primitive divisions of labor. Many African societies have had variants of the sexual division of labor. I grant that some may have been structures of domination and others purely technical. This would have to be established for each society at given periods in its development. Any judgment on the peculiar character of a given division of labor, however, can only come at the conclusion of an analysis; it cannot be a presupposition of one.[5] And it is not an exaggeration to suggest that we know very little of the history of diverse social formations on the African continent in both remote antiquity and the period just before the irruption of European colonialism and capitalism.[6] Hence one must draw conclusions with ample caution and hesitation. But caution is exactly what feminists find extremely difficult to exercise.

For some of them, *a priori*, the sexual division of labor is *prima facie* oppressive. The reason for this manner of proceeding is easy to locate. Recall that the two concepts in their theory are "men" and "women." Given that all societies hitherto have been patriarchal societies, it stands to reason, *ex definitione*, that they all have been oppressive of women. When you add to this situation the fact that women's contributions have historically not always been fully acknowledged and have often gone unacknowledged, one begins to understand the reception that greeted Ester Boserup's book, *Woman's Role in Economic Development*. (Boserup 1970) As Lourdes Beneria and Gita Sen have pointed out in their reexamination of the contributions of Boserup to women's studies:

> When Boserup's work was published in 1970, it represented a comprehensive and pioneering effort to provide an overview of women's role in the development process. In the literature on development the specific role of women had been largely ignored, particularly the question of how development affects women's subordinate position in most societies (Beneria and Sen 1981:279).

Boserup contended that women's role as food cultivators around the world has usually remained unacknowledged, the reason being that the "subsistence activities usually omitted in the statistics of production and income are largely women's work" (Boserup 1970:163.) Boserup's work and her record of the predominantly female labor in agriculture that goes largely unreported has become cant on the lips of feminists. If any "facts" were needed to buttress their point about patriarchy, Boserup supplied them.[7] Since then we have been treated to homilies and polemics on the evils of patriarchy in Africa.

Every new paper or chapter on women in Africa opens with a recitation of how women do sixty to eighty percent of agricultural work in Africa. Ruby R. Leavitt asserts:

> In view of the important role of women throughout Southeast Asia in producing essential staple foods, it is surprising to find a statement by so distinguished an anthropologist as Margaret Mead to the effect that men everywhere are the primary food producers…. At any rate there is no question that in Africa virtually all rural women do farm work "and the agricultural force is predominantly female". In Africa, especially south of the Sahara, where shifting cultivation is practiced, men usually fell the trees to clear the land, but women remove and burn the trees, sow and plant in the ashes, weed the crops, and harvest and store them (Leavitt 1971:287).

In a paper on women and development in Northern Zambia, we find the following:

> It is important to stress that my definition of the basic unit of production as a woman plus her dependent children is limited to cultivation. In other spheres the unit often differs; in the case of hunting and fishing, for instance, men constitute the basic unit of production. But if, at least for cultivation, women and their children constitute the basic unit, where do men fit in? Are men simply to be tacked on in some spiteful feminist parody of the male bias of so much anthropological and sociological writing? No. The key point is that *men gain access to the products of cultivation primarily through their relationships to women* (Emphasis added) (Crehan 1983:59).

It is curious that the writer of the passage just quoted does indeed believe that she is different from the anthropological writers she implicitly criticizes. After all, for her and for them, in this and other areas as well, the men reap where they do not sow. They appropriate women 's produce just by virtue of being male. Kate Crehan cites the ideological constraints on women to give to the men the products of their agricultural labor. Ultimately, these and other feminist writers about Africa insist that women are the mainstays of African agriculture.

Reading all these assertions about women and agriculture in Africa, one often wonders what the men do while the women are busy breaking their backs on the fields. I will let some of these writers speak for themselves, beginning with Barbara Deckard:

In Africa, for example, the women used the hoe to conduct almost all of the agricultural production, while the men limited themselves mostly to hunting and warfare. The advent of European colonialism ended the intertribal war activities of the men. Since the African men then appeared idle to the Europeans, they used every means to force them into farming. The Europeans believed that agriculture is by nature a male job. Therefore, they never perceived that almost all African agriculture was done by women (Deckard 1975:239).

Leavitt writes:

> Before European colonization the chief occupations of the African male were warfare, hunting, and felling trees. When Europeans abolished intertribal warfare, the men seemed to be idle most of the time, and the Europeans stigmatized them as lazy…. To the Europeans, 'cultivation is naturally a job for men', and African 'men could become far better farmers than women, if only they would abandon their customary "laziness" (quoting Boserup) (Leavitt 1971:287).

Of course both writers draw their evidence from Boserup, using almost exact wording. But neither of these women is convincing. In the first place, due to intellectual indolence and imperialist arrogance, they keep referring to "Africa." One gets the impression that Africa is as homogeneous as the inhabitants of a beehive. No sociologist would regard Paris or Toronto as a homogeneous entity, and Toronto has only slightly over two million people. But Africa is "Africa" and it is said that Africans all look the same. References to Africa as if the continent were a homogeneous village are clearly nonsense. Perhaps it needs to be said again and again that long before the ancestors of these feminist descendants of Count de Gobineau even knew of the existence of the African continent, this continent had generated cultures of varying degrees of material and ideological development. Whereas some might have looked like what is described by the feminist writers cited above, clearly not all did.

In the first place, it is problematic to say that African men did not engage in agriculture until they were forced to do so by Europeans. For a continent that is regarded as the birthplace of agriculture, it would be strange indeed if men did not take part in it until the nineteenth century. Secondly, only a culpable penchant for homogenization would lead one to put a continent of Africa's diversity and complexity into a monocultural or simple cultural frame.[8] Thirdly, there is evidence that men *did* practice agriculture. Consider the following:

> Although there was no actual prohibition of women from hoeing and plant-

ing in kitchen gardens inside the towns, the Yoruba, as a whole, did not make use of the labour of women on their farms in these capacities. Women were only expected to harvest crops…. The more important part of women's work on the farm, however, consists of changing the form of the various crops harvested so as to bring them a stage or two nearer the point of ultimate consumption (Fadipe 1970:147-8).

Reading Boserup and the others, one who is not familiar with African history is likely to get the impression that all that African men did before European colonialism was kill game (hunting) and kill one another (intertribal warfare) and that European colonialism in fact saved the continent of Africa from itself. This is profound ignorance masquerading as scholarship, and it is even more offensive because the scholars concerned show no hint of embarrassment.[9] Their imperialistic arrogance, however, is undercut by the poverty of their theory.

Given the fact that these scholars have not bothered to study reality and allow it to guide and discipline their theoretical flights of fancy, it is no wonder that they do not even begin to pose the relevant questions; much less are they competent to give the right answers. The problem lies in the theory that sees men and women in antagonistic relationships in which the women always are the victims. Such a theory is apt to ignore the profound cleavages—class, ethnic, national, and so forth—among African men and women *qua* men and women in fighting imperialist and neocolonial domination of various African countries. As Achola Pala reminds us:

> The position of women in contemporary Africa is to be considered at every level of analysis as an outcome of structural and conceptual mechanisms by which African societies have continued to respond to and resist the global processes of economic exploitation and cultural domination. I am suggesting that the problems facing African women today, irrespective of their national and social class affiliations, are inextricably bound up in the wider struggle by African people to free themselves from poverty and ideological domination in both intra- and international spheres (Pala 1977:9).

Bolanle Awe observes:

> Many of our assumptions about the universality of female interest and objectives are questionable. Apart from the distinctions of class, occupation, environment, etc., the position of women differs nationally and, even more significantly, from Third World to developed countries. The problems of women, therefore, have to be examined within many contexts and with an awareness of differences (Awe 1977:314).

It is exactly these differences and specificities that feminism willfully blocks out of its theoretical mindset. To confront these differences is to unearth the ugly fact that women never experience their oppression in the same ways; the wife of a wealthy peasant, for instance, may not be "a typical rural African woman," and the possibilities of accumulation may vary from place to place and from class to class. These differences have generated serious divergences among African women concerning their understanding of their situation. That was why, for example, a few African countries sent two delegations each to the Beijing Conference and why, in Nigeria, two of the umbrella women's organizations, the National Council of Women's Societies and Women in Nigeria, are ideologically opposed to each other.

The poverty of theory has another significant dimension. One of the central aims of feminists is the reclamation of the power of naming and language for women. One cannot overstress this political goal. Language has usually been the prime tool with which oppressors have defined those whom they oppress and the vehicle through which the oppressed interiorize the images of themselves fabricated by their oppressors. It is ironic, therefore, that feminists could be charged with appropriating the power of naming from some other women. I suggest that feminists do indeed deny the power of naming to African women and that one of the goals of women's movements in Africa is, and for some time to come will be, to reclaim language and the power of naming from feminist pretenders to theory.

In the extant international political economy, Western feminists stand in a relation to the women and men of Africa in exactly the same manner as their male counterparts do. There is no doubt that at the worst of times, feminism is an aspect of the imperialism of culture. In exactly the same way as Christian missionaries defined our foreparents as pagans before forcing them to become children of God, feminists desire to demonize African men in the name of saving African women. This is easy for them to do. Feminists, by virtue of belonging to the dominant capitalist economies which oppress the rest of us, have all the resources–capital, journals, conferences, and so on– that make it possible for them to stake various portions of the continent and secure their deeds of conveyance over our realities merely by publishing one or two papers from one or two brief visits to Africa in the worst traditions of safari scholarship. They define our realities as backward and underdeveloped. Given what I said earlier about *a prior-ism* in the analysis of the sexual division of labor and the *prima facie* oppression of women, sometimes they do not even set foot in Africa before they feel qualified to pontificate on how oppressed African women are, even when most of them could not identify an oppressed African woman when they saw one. But they can make unwarranted knowledge claims with little fear of being caught. After all, we are not in a position to vet their scholarship as they are to vet ours, and most members of their audience hardly know better.[10] Ignorance multiplies, and the perpetrators get tenure on the basis of libels, half-truths, and untruths. Indeed, the political economy of "universal sisterhood" looks more like the makings of a new gold rush–the difference in this case being that the prospectors do not have to leave the coziness of their Boston, Santa Cruz, and London offices to be showered with the yellow dust of academic respectability.

Talking about Western ethnocentrism and perceptions of the harem, Leila Ahmed writes:

> What compels one is not only that Americans by and large know nothing at all about the Islamic world, which is indeed the case, ...: it is, rather, that Americans 'know', and know without even having to think about it, that the Islamic peoples–Arabs, Iranians, whatever they call themselves–are backward, uncivilized peoples totally incapable of rational conduct.... Just as Americans 'know', that Arabs are backward, they know also with the same flawless certainty that Muslim women are terribly oppressed and degraded. And they know this not because they know that women everywhere in the world are oppressed, but because they believe that, specifically, Islam monstrously oppresses women (Ahmed 1982:521-2).

Ahmed's paper was published in 1982. It is a mark of how much truth is contained in the paper that a paper published in *Signs* two years later by Barbara K. Larson included the following:

> The traditional role of an Arab woman has generally been one of subservience and subordination to men, with some variation in degree according to her class, way of life, and, more recently, degree of westernization.... For most women, the formal strictures of Islam and/or the prevailing codes of honour and shame reinforce patterns of subordination (Larson 1984:421).

That there is not a single reference to Ahmed's article in Larson's paper indicates the degree to which Western feminists listen to their (in this case, Arab) counterparts. Ahmed's article was published in *Feminist Studies*. Clearly Barbara K. Larson was not reading *Feminist Studies*. Nor did it occur to any of *Signs*'s referees to require Larson to show familiarity with Ahmed's work before accepting her piece for publication. No Arab or African scholar qualifies as required or even recommended reading.

I would like to give another illustration. Simi Afonja published a paper in *Signs* in 1981 in which she presented a nuanced discussion of the sexual division of labor in Yoruba country (Afonja 1981:299-313). There she struggled with the complexity of Yoruba life and tried valiantly to point out the dynamism of material processes in that life. In 1988, Jeanne Koopman Henn, a supposed authority on African women, wrote a paper titled "The Material Basis of Sexism: A Mode of Production Analysis," (Henn 1988:27-59) in which Afonja's paper does not rate even a listing in the references. But she had the presence of mind to cite a paper, about which I shall have more to say presently, by Kate Crehan that came out in 1984, and included as well several irrelevant but pseudo-sophisticated citations of works by Paul Lovejoy, the editor of the series in which the book is included, by Ernesto Laclau, Heidi Hartmann, and Wally Seccombe, and finally a book by Barry Hindess and Paul Hirst, whose thesis the authors themselves had repudiated by 1988. Meanwhile, Simi Afonja, in spite of her extensive publication in industrial sociology, was not invited to contribute. In fact, the only contribution from the continent came from South Africa and this at a time when apartheid was still in force! Again, *O n pami, o lo n gbamii*. Apparently, neither the editor of the series, nor the editors of the anthology, nor those from whom Henn solicited reactions to her draft, nor the reviewers for the press, not one of them had either read Afonja in *Signs* or, if they had, thought enough of it to ask that Henn engage its arguments. I am suggesting that the Western feminist arrogance of which Leila Ahmed complained is especially serious in the case of Africa. Pala has protested the misrepresentation of African women's realities by these latter-day civilizers in feminist garb:

> Like the educational systems inherited from the colonial days, the research industry has continued to use the African environment as a testing ground for ideas and hypotheses the locus of which is to be found in Paris, London, New York, or Amsterdam. For this reason, the primary orientation to development problems tends to be created on the basis of what happens to be politically and/or intellectually significant in the metropoles. At one time, it may be family planning; at another, environment; at yet another, human rights and women's social conditions.... I have visited villages where, at a time when the village women are asking for better health facilities and lower infant-mortality rates, they are presented with questionnaires on family planning. In some instances, when women would like to have piped water in the village, they may be at the same time faced with a researcher interested in investigating power and powerlessness in the household. In yet another situation, when women are asking for access to agricultural credit, a researcher on the scene may be conducting a study on female circumcision (Pala 1977:10).

In a review of a book by an Italian Marxist feminist sociologist written in the worst traditions of colonial anthropology, Amina Mama avers:

> Cutrufelli [the author] mirrors African women's realities about as well as a handful of shattered glass, providing us with a fine example of the contradictions implicit in international feminism, universal sisterhood and other such loose concepts pervasive on the current international academic scene. We have recently been subjected to a barrage of books on 'African women', the majority of which have been researched and written by non-African women. The danger of such work is that of our intensified objectification, to use Fanon's term. By this he meant the process by which our reality is constructed by others (oppressors in the colonial and neocolonial contexts), to serve their psychological and political needs, and then projected on to us and internalised. In a context where our own interpretations and accounts are as yet largely unpublished, others become the experts on us, and this monopoly on knowledge about us must be seen as imperialistic. While some of this knowledge may be well researched, much of it is partial and particular, and does not serve our interests as a group, or our psychological and intellectual development. All that imperial feminism has meant here, is that it is European (and North American) women's preoccupations rather than those of men which have come into vogue (Mama 1984:253).

In the cases referred to by Pala we have poverty as irrelevance of theory, and for Mama, both an absence of theory and a malicious appropriation of African women's realities. It is a new form of imperialism.

If I am correct that feminist writings suffer from the poverty of theory in some of the ways I have described, it is right to reflect a bit on the consequences of this poverty. One consequence is that one invariably finds that many feminists use anthropological paradigms and concepts— concepts that they have not bothered to interrogate; concepts that are products of a racist, ethnocentric way of looking at Africans and their realities. Many of the papers read more like anthropological travelogues than serious attempts at analysis. What we find are cases of selective vision, which is manifested in two ways.

In the first place, there is an overweening, one is tempted to say unseemly, concentration on rural Africa. This is usually justified by the apologia that the rural areas are where most Africans live. This is quite consistent with the popular conception that the greater percentage of African labor is to be found in agriculture. Even if the numbers bear out this claim—it is becoming increasingly difficult to support in light of current developments in the continent—one is right to suspect that there is more to this concern than merely following the research subjects to where they live. To begin with, being involved with agriculture does not necessitate being rural. At least such associations are not made in the American or Canadian cases. Were we to use the absence of what are generally regarded as urban trappings to define rural areas, then few places in Africa would escape the "rural" designation. But such an outcome is counterintuitive. For anyone who knows, say, Western Nigeria, also knows that it is more urban than Utah, Wyoming, Idaho, the Dakotas, Arkansas, or Mississippi, to mention just a few areas of the United States.

So why the fixation on rural Africa? I suggest that it is because the appellation fits the *a priori* conception of Africa as backward and its people as still mired in stages of evolution that so-called developed societies have superseded. In light of this, "rural Africans" who speak in "strange 'tribal' tongues" and have "quaint beliefs and funny cuisines" must be more "authentic" than the English-speaking, ale-swilling, Hume-quoting, Shakespeare-loving bourgeois sybarite of the African city. The problem is that it is only by deliberately *ignoring*–viewing selectively–the corruption of many areas by what are usually associated with urban populations that we can justifiably call those areas rural. It is not unlikely that the "rural woman" who is such a staple of feminist safari scholarship probably finished elementary school or at least had a few years of schooling, spends part of the year selling in the city and may also sell sorts of nonrural goods in the so-called rural area. Finally, such scholarship ignores the complexity of the so-called rural areas, some of which are seats of local government complete with state institutions, schools, hospitals, and, lately, banks, postal agencies, and so on. In presenting such unidimensional pictures of most of rural Africa, our feminists make simple what is complex and, in doing so, miseducate their audience.

The other manifestation of selective vision is generated by the feminists' theoretical parsimony. Theories are regulative principles which encourage us to seek explanations for social phenomena in one direction while turning us away from some others. Since there is little that a theoretical paradigm that can only accommodate men and women can tell the analyst, the pressure to fill the pages is satisfied by the usual colonial anthropological tactic of emphasizing the exotic at the expense of genuine study. In fact I want to suggest that much feminist writing about Africa is in quest of *exotica*. I give some illustrations.

Kate Crehan, in her paper, "Women and Development in North Western Zambia: From Producer to Housewife," (Crehan 1983)[11] could not resist the temptation to tell us that the Kaonde still view Europeans–any one–as know-it-alls. At the risk of boring the reader, I will quote her at length. There is sexual division of labor in Mukunashi, where she did her study. But there is some blurring of the lines in the possession of certain skills.

The only partial exception concerns the skills of certain individuals, both male and female, in divination and healing, though these too are matters of which most people have a fair degree of basic knowledge. This was brought home to me when I arrived in Mukunashi. As soon as my presence became known, people began coming to me, often walking many miles, to ask for western drugs and general medical aid. Since I have no medical training and had only a tiny supply of medicines, it seemed irresponsible to set myself up as some kind of dispensary. So at the risk of seeming callous, I tried to make it clear that I was not a doctor and could not offer treatment. Although people learnt that I was not a source of drugs, gradually I realised that my careful explanations about not being a doctor and not having any kind of medical skills were totally meaningless to the villagers. From their point of view I was a European and, therefore, obviously knew all about Western medicine, just as they all knew the essentials of Kaonde medicine. Throughout my stay, particularly after beer drinks when the alcohol had eroded some of the layers of customary politeness, I was periodically accosted by unsteady figures demanding that I exercise my European curative skills, my protestations of medical ignorance being greeted with knowing smiles (Crehan 1983:54).

I have read this article, which was published in the *Review of African Political Economy*,[12] several times, and I have not been able to discern the point of the story just quoted. If the inhabitants of Mukunashi had approached Crehan because she is a woman, there would be nothing worth recounting–after all, every male and female is expected to have some healing and divination skills. An alternative explanation might be that they had always had European health personnel. If this is the case, then there is nothing unusual in the association made by the residents of Mukunashi between being European and being a medical practitioner. Crehan's point seems to be that she was approached as a European *qua* European. If this is correct, how does this story differ from the stereotypical stories in which natives ascribe to the European some magical powers? If that is the significance of the story, it is not much different from old-time colonial anthropology. And Crehan poses as a feminist and her paper is published in a radical journal. Incidentally, the essay would not have lacked anything had this passage been omitted. But the lure of exotica was too great–more potent in this case because it was obviously unconscious. And it is even more significant that this titillating interlude escaped the leftist editors of the *Review of African Political Economy*.

Another aspect of this quest for exotica is the choice of subjects for study. African urban centers are hardly studied. The ways in which the ethos of capitalism and individualism have embroidered, challenged, distorted, and reordered the reality of Africans, rural and urban alike, are rarely highlighted in the studies. This is not surprising. Talk of African equivalents of capitalist institutions is unlikely to arouse curiosity and, in any case, such talk will have to rely on male political scientists, anthropologists, and other scholars. Hence the overarching effort to strip various phenomena of their historicity. The result is that many Africans who read some of the offerings barely recognize their realities in them. For instance, Simi Afonja argues:

> What is missing in studies of Yoruba women's economic activities, therefore, is an explanation of how trade is integrated with other areas of production and reproduction in an economy characterized by a low level of specialization. Also missing is an analysis of the social relations generated by this integrated economic structure and of the ways in which these relations have been altered by the transformation to commercial and industrial capitalism (Afonja 1981:300).

Meanwhile, a theory that is very limited in its applicability is likely to be a poor theory. Thus theorists are pressed to make their theories as general and as widely applicable as possible. Feminist theorists are no different, except that they start out with very few categories and this inexorably leads them to blind generalizations that are easily falsifiable. In fact, one might say that the fallacy of insufficient evidence has taken up residence in feminist theory and is doing quite well.

> *While the countries of the Third World vary tremendously in culture and social structure and, thus, in the position that women hold, they resemble one another in that they all are less economically developed than the countries that were discussed earlier (i.e., capitalist and socialist countries of Europe and North America).* They remain very poor, rural, agricultural, with high rates of disease and illiteracy—in other words, they resemble countries in Western Europe in 1750 (Emphasis added) (Deckard 1975:239).

Similarly, Kate Crehan could not resist the urge to include the following in her introductory remarks:

> The research was carried out between 1979 and 1981 during which time I lived for 18 months in one small Kaonde community in North Western Zambia. The main research method used was participant observation. *Although the paper is in one sense specific and particular, the underlying processes described are similar to those found in many rural areas of sub-Saharan Africa* (Emphasis Added) (Crehan 1983:52).

In an article on the Kaguru we have the following:

The purpose of this study is to examine women's perceptions of how family relationships, land-holding customs, household power structures and other social and familial realities may stimulate or stymie the educational opportunities and household, agricultural and income-earning work of rural Kaguru women. Obtaining information from women themselves is essential for the formulation of policies and programs that are relevant to the needs of rural African women…. *While the situation of women in other societies may be different, many of the issues addressed by Kaguru women are relevant for other rural African societies* (Emphasis added) (Meeker and Meekers 1997:36).

The preceding quotes, especially the emphasized portions, typify the tendency to baseless generalization that we have identified. They follow the same pattern: What you disclaim in one half of the sentence you proclaim in the other. All such locutions must raise our suspicion. Why is it necessary to generalize from Kaonde or Kaguru women to African women at large? What is it about Kaguru or Kaonde women that magically transforms them into typical African women unless we already assumed the coherence of the phrase or have decided that all African women are the same? It is problematic enough, once one sets out with some respect for the complexity of one's subject matter, to speak of Kaguru women. How much more so will it be to speak of Tanzanian, not to talk of East African, or African women? This penchant for generalization must be traced to a fundamental lack of respect for the complexity of African life.

We find the most ridiculous example of the urge to generalize in the following cycle culled from the pages of the *Review of African Political Economy*:

A WOMAN'S WORK IS NEVER DONE

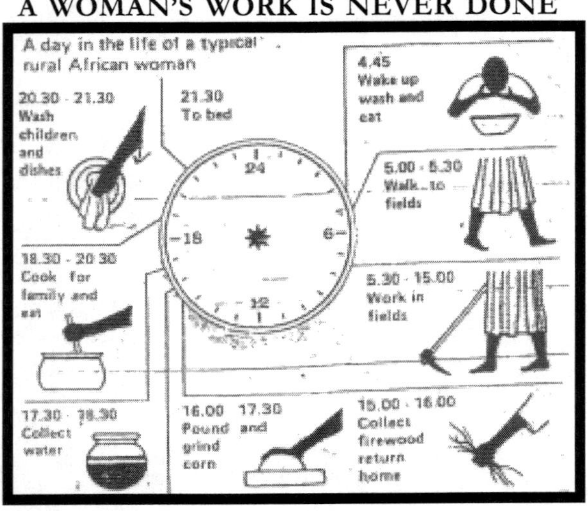

Do the women typified in the cycle have friends? Do they ever exchange visits? Do they ever sit down with kith and kin to discuss family affairs or engage in other activities that take up part of the day of most families? Do they go to church? To the mosque? The fact is that women who lead normal lives are not fit and proper subjects to sate the thirst for exotica. A normal life for women in Yorubaland would depend on whether or not they live in rural areas or in urban centers, whether they are lower, lower middle, upper middle, or upper classes, and so on.[13]

Closely related to this quick resort to generalizations are the obscure concepts that are often substituted for hard and serious theoretical exertion. Most readers of this paper will be familiar with phrases like "traditional Africa," "traditional African values," "'traditional African woman," "precolonial Africa," and so forth, which are in widespread use but are theoretically vacuous. Granted, Africans are partly to blame for the creation of this escape hatch from theoretical responsibility. African scholars started using these phrases to counter the previous descriptions of Africa as "savage" or "primitive." They themselves never really asked whether their substitutes are theoretically fecund. They are not. These substitutes are bogus concepts. For example, who is a "typical rural African woman"? In Nigeria, for instance, especially in those areas where Christianity and commerce have deep and long-standing roots, even the most rural of villages would not uphold the stereotype illustrated in "A Woman's Work is Never Done." This stereotype was inaccurate from the moment of the cartoon's publication in 1983, which predated the present cycle of economic crisis, when many rural households especially in Southern Nigeria were increasingly using kerosene stoves.

What really is traditional Africa? Is it Africa before the advent of Europeans? Or the one before the coming of colonialism? Is it Africa at the beginning of time or Africa of the fifteenth century? Who is a traditional African woman? Must she be totally innocent of formal education to qualify? Is she Muslim or Christian? Is she the same person in the urbanized culture of the Hausa and the Yoruba as in the village-based communities of Igboland? Of course it is a lot easier to invoke vacuous concepts like "traditional Africa" and the like than to work seriously to study Africa in its richest detail and with an awareness of the complexity of its social formations. Social formations are very complex phenomena, and they often have articulated within them several modes of production. Certainly, there usually is a dominant mode to which the rest are subordinate. It is this complexity that notions like "traditional Africa" tend to obscure. A very good example of the way in which these vacuous notions can vitiate analysis is Simi Afonja's paper, already cited. In this paper, we find references like "the African subsistence mode of production," "Yoruba production modes," "traditional economic formations," without serious attempts to clarify what precisely each of these notions entails. She is, however, still better than many others because she, at least, tries to point out variations in the content and context of women's experiences. She insists that:

> In order to explain the relationship between the cause and the effect of female subordination, therefore, one must analyze the continuity between historical and contemporary patterns of the sexual division of labour in production and reproduction. This is imperative in African studies, because the labels 'traditional' and 'modern', 'colonial', and 'precolonial', draw arbitrary lines through the historical process of change and, as Audrey Smock and Alice Schlegel suggest, encourage the analyst to transpose the phenomena of the present onto the past (Afonja 1981:300).

What emerges from the discussion so far is the need for feminists to take Africa seriously and to stop handling discussions about the continent as if they are talking about a borough in London. Taking Africa seriously means listening well to what African women themselves have to say. Feminists must restore to African women the power of naming and recognize the legitimacy and expertise of African women's voices. Serious efforts must be made to abandon the arrogant pretense to theory and its corollary assumption that African women have or know no theory. As Leacock recognizes, "it behooves Western feminists to listen to such women and learn from them, rather than prejudging or delimiting the many forms that struggle for women's liberation can take" (Leacock 1981:491). Taking Africa seriously means abandoning safari scholarship and the attitude that assumes knowledge where there is glaring and culpable ignorance. It will also mean that research will be adapted to the real need to promote knowledge rather than individual careers. Taking Africa seriously means confronting the specificities of women's oppression in various parts of Africa. Whether or not we will have a theory that can generalize across these diverse specificities will be the conclusion of our research: it cannot be the beginning. We should heed Pala's caution below:

> In considering the issue of the impact on women of colonial and/or neocolonial socioeconomic processes, it is well to bear in mind that, although such processes have enslaved women in the reserves and exploited their labour while withdrawing men to work in wage-earning jobs, in reality wages alone cannot constitute an argument that men have benefited from those systems of oppression. In fact peoples who are dominated by a repressive regime, whether they are men or women, share a similar subordinate structural position vis-a-vis the dominant culture. What we must look for, then, is not how

> African women lost their development opportunity during colonial or con-
> temporary neocolonial periods (since our men have also suffered the same
> loss) but, rather, the differential impact of such socioeconomic conditions on
> men and women. (Pala 1977:11)

Perhaps I have painted too negative a picture of the field. I do not wish to suggest that the prospects are bleak or that all feminists are as insensitive as some of those I have cited. Far from it. My optimism is buoyed by the fact that there are feminists who have begun to address some of the issues raised here. In addition to those I have cited, there is the special issue of *FRONTIERS*, Volume 8, Number 2 (1983), devoted to the issue of Feminism and the Non-Western World and the quite refreshing introduction to the edition by Barbara Alpern Engel. Some other contributions would surely include the Reflections on the Conference on Women and Development held in 1976 at Wellesley College.[14] What I have tried to do in this essay is to focus on some aspects of feminist writings about Africa that I believe portray a poverty of theory. If I have sensitized a few readers to the need for a little respect and caution, my job will have been done.

NOTES:

1. Some atonements have been made. But I have yet to see a vigorous criticism of some of the worst examples, on which I will focus here. It will not do to object to what follows by pointing out the various books and anthologies that have tried not only to portray Africa in a good light but have striven to present it in its complexity. That such instances are few and far between corroborates my thesis. More importantly, my hope in sharing what follows is to identify the many pitfalls that one often encounters in women's studies concerning Africa and call on scholars to work scrupulously in the future to avoid and correct them.
2. Take any text you care to choose. It always surprises me that the women who edit many feminist texts do not apprehend either the irony of passing off American women's experience <u>as</u> women's experience or the kinship between these feminists and their male colleagues who do exactly the same thing to them and to the rest of us.
3. I have omitted the uninformed references to the African experience to be found in Mary Daly, *Gyn\ecology: The Metaethics of Radical Feminism* (Boston: Beacon Press, 1978).
4. See Iris Young, "Beyond the Unhappy Marriage: A Critique of the Dual Systems Theory," in Lydia Sargent, ed., *Women and Revolution* (Boston: South End Press, 1981), pp. 43-69.
5. Some African women scholars have started doing the kind of regional investigations that are *conditio sine qua non* for any meaningful continental generalizations. See

the works by Nkiru Nzegwu, Oyeronke Oyewumi, Nakanyike Musisi, and others.

6. Here I have in mind regional studies of those far off periods and a proper periodization of them rather than suspect generalizations that are obvious instances of the fallacy of insufficient evidence.

7. They reject Boserup's more cautious approach and insistence on the significant differences in women's work across countries and regions. See Beneria and Sen, "Accumulation, Reproduction and Women's Role in Economic Development.," p. 280.

8. There are ready indices to identify this penchant in locutions like "Women in Other Cultures," which is about *all* women other than those of the Euro-American White variety; "The Precarious Socio-Economic Position of Women in Rural Africa: The Case of the Kaguru of Tanzania." The Kaguru are not even the majority in Tanzania. Not only that, they live in a very small part of the country. How one makes the leap from "Kaguru" to "Africa" remains both unexplained and unexplainable. In addition, by objectifying "The Kaguru," there is no room to apprehend the many ways in which different Kaguru live.

9. I have yet to see an internal feminist critique of these views. Quite the contrary, whereas Asians have in part been able to fight off this intellectual imperialism, Africa has yet to get the respect it deserves in this area.

10. This is an important point. I have often been tempted to collect the sometimes scandalous comments that referees write on our submitted and rejected manuscripts. Just take a look at the editorial boards of the "leading" journals and try to explain what qualifies some of their members to judge scholarship about Africa.

11. The same one cited by Henn.

12. *Review of African Political Economy* is a journal that prides itself, and not without good reasons, as a leading radical platform for alternative scholarship about Africa.

13. For a rich description which captures in fascinating detail the complexity of life in Yorubaland as far back as the eighteenth century, see Fadipe, *The Sociology of the Yoruba*. On division of labour and occupational specialization in Yorubaland, see T. M. Ilesanmi, *Olootu, Ise*.

14. The Wellesley Editorial Committee, ed., *Women and National Development*, pp. 313-329. See also Zenebeworke Tadesse, "Women and Technology in Peripheral Countries: An Overview," in Pamela M. D'Onofrio-Flores and Sheila M. Pfafflin, eds., *Scientific-Technological Change and the Role of Women in Development* (Boulder, Colorado: Westview Press, 1982), pp. 77-111; Stephanie Urdang, "The Last Transition? Women and Development in Mozambique," and Deborah Gaitskell, et al., "Class, Race and Gender: Domestic Workers in South Africa," both reprinted in *Review of African Political Economy*, No. 27/28 (1983); Gay W. Seidman, "Women in Zimbabwe: Post-Independence Struggles," *Feminist Studies* (10) 3 (Fall 1984).

WORKS CITED:

Afonja, Simi. "Changing Modes of Production and the Sexual Division of Labor Among the Yoruba". *Signs* 7, no. 2 (1981). Pp. 299-313.

Ahmed, Leila. "Western Ethnocentrism and Perceptions of the Harem," *Feminist Studies* 8, no. 3 (Fall 1982). Pp. 521-522.

Awe, Bolanle. in The Wellesley Editorial Committee, ed., *Women and National Development: The Complexities of Change*, Chicago: University of Chicago Press, 1977.

Beneria, Lourdes. and Gita Sen, "Accumulation, Reproduction and Women's Role in Economic Development: Boserup Revisited," *Signs* 7, no. 2, (1981), p. 279.

Boserup, Ester. *Woman's Role in Economic Development*, London: Allen & Unwin, 1970.

Crehan, Kate. "Women and Development in North Western Zambia: From Producer to Housewife," *Review of African Political Economy* 27/28 (1983), p. 59.

Daly, Mary. *Gyn\ecology: The Metaethics of Radical Feminism*, Boston: Beacon Press, 1978.

Deckard, Barbara. *The Women's Movement*, New York: Harper & Row, 1975.

Fadipe, N.A. *The Sociology of the Yoruba*, Idaban: Ibadan University Press, 1970.

Firestone, Shulamith. *The Dialectic of Sex*, New York: William Morrow & Co., 1970.

Gaitskell, Deborah. et al., "Class, Race and Gender: Domestic Workers in South Africa," *Review of African Political Economy*, No. 27/28 (1983).

Hartmann, Heidi. "The Unhappy Marriage of Marxism and Feminism: Towards a More Progressive Union," in Lydia Sargent ed. *Women and Revolution: A Discussion of the Unhappy Marriage of Marxism and Feminism*. Boston: South End Press, 1981.

Larson, Barbara K. "The Status of Women in a Tunisian Village: Limits to Autonomy, Influence, and Power". *Signs* 9, no. 3 (1984): p. 421.

Leacock, Eleanor. "History, Development and the Division of Labour by Sex: Implications for Organization," *Signs* 7, no. 2 (1981), p. 491.

Leavitt, Ruby R. "Woman in Other Cultures," in Vivian Gornick & Barbara Moran, eds., *Woman in Sexist Society*, New York: Basic Books, 1971.   p.287.

Mama, Amina. "African Women Fight Back" *West Africa*, 10 December, 1984, p. 253.

Meeker, Jeffrey and Dominique Meekers, "The Precarious Socio-Economic Position of Women in Rural Africa: The Case of Kaguru of Tanzania," *African Studies Review* 40, no. 1 (April 1997): p. 36.

Pala, Achola. in The Wellesley Editorial Committee, ed., *Women and Na-tional Development: The Complexities of Change*. Chicag: University of Chicago Press, 1977. p. 9.

Seidman, Gay W. "Women in Zimbabwe: Post-Independence Struggles," *Feminist Studies* No. 10, 3 (Fall 1984).

Stichter, Sharon and Jane L. Parpart, eds., *Patriarchy and Class: African Women in the Home and the Workforce*, London: Westview Press, 1988.

Tadesse, Zenebeworke. "Women and Technology in Peripheral Countries: An Overview," in Pamela M. D'Onofrio-Flores and Sheila M. Pfafflin, eds., *Scientific-Technological Change and the Role of Women in Development* Boulder:

Westview Press, 1982. pp. 77-111.

Urdang, Stephanie. "The Last Transition? Women and Development in Mozambique," *Review of African Political Economy*, No. 27/28 (1983).

Young, Iris. "Beyond the Unhappy Marriage: A Critique of the Dual Systems Theory," in Lydia Sargent, ed., *Women and Revolution*, Boston: South End Press, 1981. pp. 43-69.

4.
WHAT WOMEN, WHOSE DEVELOPMENT?
A Critical Analysis of Reformist Feminist Evangelism on African Women

Mojúbàolú Olúfúnké Okome

Reformist Western Feminist Evangelism

Western feminist discourse on African women is characterized by what I will call reformist feminist evangelism. As such, it replicates, the missionary evangelism exhibited by the seventeenth-, eighteenth- and nineteenth-century colonialists, missionaries, anthropologists, and sundry adventurers when they explored, brutally "pacified," Christianized, and colonized Africa. It was these Europeans who invented the notion of Africa as the dark continent and the African as the exotic antithesis of the enlightened, progressive Westerner. This invention continues to permeate religious and secular thought alike and remains pervasive in contemporary Western thought. (Mudimbe 1988:1-23) Mainstream feminist writings tend to portray African women as confused, powerless, and unable to determine for themselves both the changes needed in their lives and the means to construct these changes. Thus, Western feminists, acting like superiors who hand down valuable knowledge, define the relevant issues for African women, how these issues ought to be promoted and pursued, and what the end result should be.

There are striking parallels between the activities of contemporary feminists and the colonialist missionaries in Africa. Both groups actively prospect for converts through widespread proselytization that rejects all other sources of knowledge, casting them illegitimate and inferior. Western trends are idealized as both modern and desirable. Indeed, they are presented as the only pool from which viable solutions to human problems should be drawn. In the past, feminist literature drew out polygamy as a symbol of male domination. Today, female circumcision is the focus, the argument being that men imposed circumcision on women to prevent them from enjoying sex, to keep them celibate, to own them as just so much property. In this work, I reject the usage of the term that has come to be dominant in discussions concerning African women's genitalia: "Female Genital Mutilation" [FGM]. Instead, I use the term, "female genital surgeries." The usage of the term FGM is rejected because of its overt assumption that African societies which practice these procedures deliberately set out to disfigure their women. Indeed, the practice of female genital surgeries has been identified by Western feminists as the ultimate signifier of African male dominance and women's powerlessness. In response, several groups have emerged within the boundaries of the African continent and in the West that assert their commitment to the eradication of FGM. The term FGM is problematic not only because it emerges from an assumption that the intent of societies in which these procedures are practiced is to control women by wreaking violence on them, but also these societies are presumed to desire to butcher, mangle, deform, assault, and batter their women en masse, an assumption that has not been conclusively proven.

The term female genital surgeries is also preferable because, if the intent is to eliminate these practices, serious scholars must move away from sensationalism and headline-grabbing and endeavor to make thoughtful enquiries into why they persist.

Doing so would facilitate the engineering of appropriate, relevant, and lasting solutions. In this regard, Esther Hicks' study of infibulation in Islamic Northeastern Africa exemplifies a sensible, even-handed scholarly approach. This work recognizes that for some societies, the practice is the norm, and subjects the reasons why it is normative to serious scholarly inquiry. According to Hicks, female genital surgeries are but one of the ties that bind the community, one of the mechanisms through which the communities have chosen to define roles and identities (Hicks 1993). To the extent that this is true, it is essential to undertake clear-headed gender analyses that clearly explicate the nature and form of patriarchy and other forms of hierarchical relationships in these societies. When such an analysis is done, it is possible to identify and understand structural institutions within communities more concretely. The kinds of power and agency that women have within such societies is seen more clearly, and the choices that women make on how to treat their bodies are revealed, albeit within the constraints of institutions that exist in their societies. It is this power and agency that must be deployed in culturally specific ways to assert new understandings of identity and their deployment in social relations. Thus, women's power and agency can be turned toward the end of transforming their condition in society.

Reformist feminist evangelism reveals the hallmarks of the traditional evangelist mission which, for V.Y. Mudimbe, is characterized by a "holier than thou" attitude, proselytization, ethnocentrism, and imperialism (Mudimbe 1988:64-83; Serequeberhan 1991). In the main, these attitudes and practices are made possible by three factors: Western hegemony in scholarly discourse; the character of the international system; and the colonial origin of African states, which defines the nature and form of the contemporary African state. The production of knowledge has been internationalized to such an extent that at conferences, in courses, and in scholarly debates on women, one observes a remarkable degree of convergence.

Frantz Fanon's *The Wretched of the Earth* explores the nature and impact of colonialism's evangelistic project:

> The colonial world is a Manichean world. It is not enough for the settler to delimit physically, with the help of the army and the police force, the place of the native. As if to show the totalitarian character of colonial exploitation, the settler paints the native as a sort of quintessence of evil. Native society is not simply described as a society lacking in values. It is not enough for the colonist to affirm that those values have disappeared from, or still better, never existed in, the colonial world. The native is declared insensible to ethics; he represents not only the absence of values, but also the negation of values. He is, let us dare to admit, the enemy of values, and in this sense, he is the absolute evil. He is the corrosive element, destroying all that comes near him. He is the deforming element, disfiguring all that has to do with beauty or morality; he is the depository of maleficent powers, the unconscious and irretrievable instrument of blind forces. All values, in fact, are irrevocably poisoned and diseased as soon as they are allowed in contact with the colonized race. The customs of the colonized people, their traditions, their myths—above all, their myths—are the very sign of that poverty of spirit and their constitutional depravity. That is why we must put the DDT which destroys parasites, the bearers of disease, on the same level as the Christian religion which wages war on embryonic heresies and instincts, and on evil yet unborn. The Church in the colonies is the white people's Church, the foreigner's Church. She does not call the native to God's ways but to the ways of the white man, of the master, of the oppressor. And as we know, in this matter, many are called, but few chosen. (Fanon 1963:40-41)

Western feminism has elements of Fanon's colonialist-native relationship, and missionary-native proselytization. When it directs its gaze at African societies, it justifies its intrusive intervention as "helping" African women "to help" themselves. Instead, what occurs suggests what is described by Rousseau as "forcing (them) to be free." Thus, a broad brush is used to paint African societies. If they treat their women in the inhuman ways that they do, they must be depraved, sub-human, cruel beyond belief. Any society that performs genital surgeries is performing *"mutilation."* It should be reviled, brought to task, berated, shamed into converting. The force of international and domestic laws must be brought to bear in order to reflect "the principles of *civilized* societies" and bring Africans into the mainstream of the modern or postmodern contemporary world. They must be made to adopt *civilized* norms of behavior. A campaign must thus be mobilized to raise consciousness on the problem, the solutions, and the processes needed to generate change. This campaign must, of course, be drawn from Western experience, values, and ethics. *Everyone knows* that these are the ideals to which all human beings must aspire.

What this kind of thinking and action does is to totally cancel out any opportunities of dialogue between the "primitive African mutilators" and "progressive" Western feminist evangelists. There is, of course, only one right perspective, and *everyone* is presumed to know what that is. My critique of Western feminist evangelists is by no means an advocacy of the perpetuation of female genital surgeries. I am also not proposing that Western feminists are always wrong and Africans always right. I am questioning the mindset that presumes that Africans cannot apprehend reality independently of Western intervention, that they always need help, and that their "voiceless" women can only be given voice by the "progressive, sympathetic" Western feminist. This kind of stance is extremely patronizing. In essence, it denies the humanity of the African. It establishes a rigid hierarchy of knowledge, where Western thought remains superior *ad infinitum*. African societies are, I argue, able to identify their problems and to prioritize their goals. If women in Africa are not jumping *en masse* on the bandwagon of the anti- "genital mutilation" militia, there ought to be a re-thinking of why this is so. Presuming that African women are acting out of false consciousness or ignorance or that they are being irredeemably oppressed by male patriarchy is absurd.

It is curious that there have been debates within Africa on the question of female genital surgeries, but that here in the West, it is assumed that, without Western feminist intervention, nothing has been or will be done. It is amazing that people have presented spurious figures on the number of "mutilated" African women, and no one questions the accuracy of the statistics. *The Hoskens Report*, which is published by Fran Hoskens, one of the foremost campaigners in the anti-FGM militia, is a case in point. This report presents information which claims that the overwhelming majority of African women have been subjected to some kind of genital surgery. The report is much quoted, without being subjected to critical scrutiny. It is astounding that even within one ethnic group, the Yorùbá, some sub-groups practice female genital surgeries and others do not. Those who do not practice these procedures engage those who do in arguments, discussion, and debates on the whys and wherefores. Here in the West, however, it seems as though there is widespread African female complacency, which only *civilized, humanitarian* intervention can shake up, for mobilization to occur. Nigeria has an untold number of national groups, thus, the situation regarding the generalizability of any social phenomenon is extremely complex. Making sense of the African reality must stop being the domain of "kamikaze" scholarship that dives in quickly for a brief period, observes the natives in one small pocket "doing their thing" and draws broad conclusions which grossly exaggerate one's findings.

One very good example where "kamikaze" scholarship was displayed to the core is Hanny Lightfoot-Klein's travelogue, *A Woman's Odyssey into Africa: Tracks Across a Life*. Lightfoot-Klein traveled to parts of Sudan, Egypt, and Kenya, but wrote a travelogue in which she generalizes on the African experience. It cannot be overstressed that Africa, is a huge, diverse continent where generalizations are very hard to make, because there are often as many examples of exceptions to rules as there are of phenomena that confirm general rules. Lightfoot-Klein speaks of "The Barbaric Practice" which is practiced on the "Dark Continent," which persists despite British colonial intervention, the earlier intervention of the Prophet Mohammed, and the postcolonial government's legal intervention. For Lightfoot-Klein, "the barbaric practice" continues because:

> Custom in Africa is stronger than domination, stronger than law, stronger even than religion. Over the years, customary practices have been incorporated into religion, and ultimately have come to be believed by their practitioners to be demanded by their adopted gods, whoever they may be. Throughout the centuries, slavers, marauders and bandits have roamed the Dark Continent. Only the protection of a male-defended family compound offered any kind of security from these predators to unarmed women and their children. Would it be any wonder in circumstances such as this for a woman ... willingly to submit to the sacrifice of her sexual organs as a proof of her subservient respectability? And would it be any wonder that she would then subject her daughters to the same procedure to safeguard their virginity and enable them to offer living proof of their full deservingness? But that is all within the realm of speculation. It does not really matter with whom the Barbaric Practice actually began. What matters is that female sexual mutilation is to this very day ubiquitous in the greater part of Sub Saharan Africa and Central Africa (Lightfoot-Klein 1989:47).

How does Lightfoot-Klein know all this? According to her, from trekking through three countries in Africa. Lightfoot-Klein also goes on to say:

> The number of affected women has been variously estimated to be 30 mil-
> lion, 80 million, and over 100 million, and the relative accuracy of these figures
> is sometimes hotly debated. This always strikes me as pointless as arguments
> about the precise accuracy of statistics on the numbers of human beings
> destroyed in the Holocaust. A precise statistical accounting is not really the
> crucial issue. All that we need to know in either instance is that we are talking
> about the destruction or torture of many millions of human beings (Ibid:49).

Lightfoot-Klein is absolutely right in one respect, and dead wrong in another. If this were not presented as a scholarly study, "the result of three-year long treks through Sudan, Kenya and Egypt," of interviews of "over 400 people in all walks of life in regard to psychological, sociological, historical, sexologi-cal, medical, religious and legal aspects of female circumcision," then, one could be persuaded as to the fact that statistics are irrelevant. However, if statistics are so relevant and necessary in the West, so should they be in Africa. This is the work of a person who presents herself as a scholar and who should be mindful of accuracy and the dangers of overgeneralization.

Lightfoot-Klein's book is absolutely astounding. However, her penultimate chapter, which is titled "Karen Blixen Never Returned to Africa," goes over the top. It is an account of the moment of Lightfoot-Klein's transportation to a higher plane, a higher level of consciousness, after seeing the film version of Blixen's "Out of Africa." It is disturbing that this most racist, patronizing depiction of Africans is glorified so passionately. The African for Blixen, as for Lightfoot-Klein, is a child, who must be led by the hand in order to be able to recognize what's good for her. Ngugi wa Thiong'o in *Moving the Centre* (1993) gives a concise, trenchant critique of the kind of work that is pro-duced by Blixen. For Ngugi, Blixen's work is grounded in racist ideology which presumes that the African is a perpetual child, an irresponsible, some-times charming and innocent child who must be led by the hand and guided into developing good work habits, truth-telling, responsible social behavior. The African is presented as the quintessence of savagery, the human being in the proverbial state of nature. For Blixen, the duty of the enlightened Euro-pean is to help these poor Africans to help themselves. Thus, in one fell swoop, the colonization, brutalization, and extreme exploitation of the African is justified. These gross injustices are also characterized as being necessary for the African's own good. I classify Lightfoot-Klein's work as one of the most blatant examples of Western colonialism and feminist evangelism in Africa.

Alice Walker in *Warrior Marks* (1996) and *Possessing the Secret of Joy* (1992) does something very similar. Straddling the academy and the realm of pure fiction, she presents the accounts of fictional and real live Africans whom she interviewed in order to throw her weight behind the mission to eradicate of the African man's inhumanity to his woman. "FGM" for her is so dangerous as to cause mental illness. For Walker, if you lose your clitoris, you lose your mind. While I think it is unneccessary for people's private parts to be tampered with in any way, yet I fail to see why female genital surgeries are more important an issue than maternal mortality or death from diseases like malaria, small pox, typhoid, or yellow fever. I see it as no more important than the fact that women remain marginalized economically and politically. Alice Walker also indicts African women even more than the men. They are presented as deceptive, capricious, and clueless. The older ones are presented as preying on younger generations in order to enhance their power, and to shore up the structures of male patriarchy. Indeed, solutions to African degradation must be fashioned, but not by the Lightfoot-Kleins, Walkers, and other Western feminist evangelists. African women, some of whom belong with the Western feminist evangelist camp, need to take their societies seriously as subjects of study. They need to decolonize their minds and consider ways in which their societies were able to solve problems in the past, and to direct their efforts at finding solutions for problems that they identify as important. They ought to lead whatever movement exists, to delineate the priorities and strategies, and to stop seeking "aid" from those for whom the African continent remains "dark" and its people "barbaric."

Western feminists often attempt to fit Africa and Africans forcibly into theories and models that cannot be reasonably applied to Westerners themselves. The focus of such study thus far has been on the inability of the continent and its peoples to achieve progress and advancement in a manner that replicates the historical experience of the West. The Western feminist desire to "reform" and "uplift" the African woman is couched in seemingly innocuous phrases such as "sisterhood is global." Sisterhood appears to be global, however, only to the extent that Western feminists can dictate the acceptable standards by sharing their "good news of great joy" with women in other parts of the world. The first part of the news is that women are oppressed by male domination and patriarchy. The second part is that their Western big sisters will help to set these "powerless" and "voiceless" women free. The third part of the news concerns gender. Clearly, for the concept to be meaningful, it must be socially constructed, but only the West's construction is acceptable as valid. Western feminists, as it were, present themselves as humanitarians who are helping their African sisters by bringing gender discourses to a higher level. The prevailing attitude seems to be that Western feminists have either solved these elementary problems that are thrown up by gender relations at an earlier historical period or that, like doctors in the itinerant medicine shows of old, they have what the Yorùbás refer to as *oògùn gbogboònse,* the cure-all elixir, the bag of tricks, from which they pull out remedies that can serve to cure all gender-related maladies that are suffered by their disadvantaged sisters in Africa.

The literature on *Women and Development* manifests all the worst traits of Western feminist evangelism. It grossly over-generalizes the condition of women in African societies who are described as oppressed, downtrodden, and immiserated. African women are treated as an undifferentiated mass of humanity. Neither class nor status is taken into consideration. Even where there are attempts to grapple with the implications of class and status, African women are viewed as objects of history rather than as active agents. The result is the conceptualization of feminine gender in Africa as a disability across the board. When this scholarly depiction is juxtaposed with the situation of living and breathing women in Africa, its one-dimensional nature is revealed, and the question "What women?" becomes relevant.

One of the more recent examples of the negative scholarly depiction of African women, particularly by those who consider themselves to be the "friends" of the African women, is that of Catherine Coquery-Vidrovitch, a respected French historian of Africa, who has now turned her hand, as many have done recently, to Women's Studies. For Coquery-Vidrovitch, African women are impeded from developing a sense of the self because they remain the quintessential "beasts of burden": "They are so overburdened with tasks of all kinds that they hardly have time to bemoan their fate or even to wonder about it. Their image of themselves remains cloudy" (Coquery-Vidrovitch 1997:1). For this reason, Coquery-Vidrovitch directs her attention "primarily to understand why African women have lacked the leisure and often even the right to observe themselves" (Ibid). This work is presented as a serious scholarly effort which not only furnishes women's history, but "highlights a perspective: the history of the whys and wherefores of society from women's viewpoints" (Ibid:2). Coquery-Vidrovitch, however, falls short of fulfilling this self-imposed "noble" task. In the first place, she attributes only to women, or only to men, some of the roles that are generalizable to both. For example, she makes the mistake of locating the role of oral historian as the exclusive preserve of men among the Sahelian peoples of West Africa and of women among the Yorùbá of Nigeria (Ibid:2). In each of these cases, she is wrong. There are indeed male *griots* in Sahelian societies, but female griottes also abound. There are Yorùbá female specialists in *oríkì.*, as there are men. Even when trying to acknowledge the contributions of women in society, an effort at empirical accuracy is imperative. This is a minor point of criticism. The most damning critique of Coquery-Vidrovitch's work is that she continues the negativities that she so vociferously critiques. Her accounts of women's oppression are ethnocentric to the extreme. A few examples will suffice.

Directly following from her assumption that African women are over-burdened, Coquery-Vidrovitch uses the characterization "Beasts of Burden" as a subtitle in her first chapter, giving the case of the Tswana as an example (Ibid:13-14). She also has for her second chapter the title "Slave Women" and the sub-title "Was Every Woman a Slave?" (Ibid:26-27). In these sections of her work, as well as in many other respects, Coquery-Vidrovitch presents a beleaguered African woman who is unable to help herself, with the exception of the few elite women (Ibid:34-44), the "free women" or prostitutes (Ibid:117-135), and drug traffickers, who in her thinking, exhibit a great deal of entrepreneurship, chutzpa, and drive. Consider, for example, the following statement: "Currently, Yorùbá women's adventurous spirit has led some of them to exercise their talents in overseas trade. In 1991, in Britain, of 267 women arrested for drug trafficking, 81 were Nigerian" (Ibid:100). Taken at face value, this statement not only implies that women who go into drug trafficking are doing so out of some higher-order motivation, and the element of panache is emphasized, without considering that the personal histories of these women, as told by themselves, reveals that they are driven into being *mules* in the drug trade by poverty, deprivation, and desperation. Many of them give as the reason why they became couriers their inability to fend for their children otherwise. They usually leave their children home alone, under the supervision of magnanimous neighbors, because they expect to be back within a brief period of time. Many speak of having lost spouses, or having been separated from their spouse, and thus having no other recourse. Many of them, rather than being smart entrepreneurs, have the lowest possible return from their efforts in the drug-trafficking hierarchy, while facing an overwhelming proportion of the risk. My analysis is the result of face-to face interviews with approximately 100 drug traffickers, men and women, as a freelance interpreter-translator for the US Department of Justice from 1989 to 1996. These women are called mules because they are, in essence, used almost as "pack animals" by higher-ups in the drug-trafficking networks that employ their services for a fee. They often have no idea who exactly owns the drugs that are packed in either balloons, or condoms, which they swallow. Were these drugs to burst open in their intestines, they would face instant paralysis or certain death. They are often not told to whom exactly they are to deliver the drugs. They are assured that the individual will recognize them or meet them in a designated place, often a cheap hotel room. They are given sums as low as $500.00 as deposits, and promised $1500 on their successful return to Nigeria after delivering the drugs. In what sense are these entrepreneurs? Indeed, what this example suggests is an analysis of the very personal toll of Africa's incorporation into a capitalist international system continues to take.

Of course, there are entrepreneurs in the drug trade, and some of them are women, but often they are not the ones who end up in jail. If they get arrested, they do not depend, as the *mules* do, on court-appointed attorneys, some of whom have been known to fall asleep in court. They hire skilled, highly-paid, articulate defenders who dazzle all in court with their erudition and expertise. Juxtaposing the evidence of my research with the assertions in Coquery-Vidrovitch's work, one can see that scholars are wont to say almost anything about Africa and its people and get away with it. This practice, I argue, did not start yesterday. It has deep roots in Western scholarly and academic tradition. (Davidson 1992; Fanon 1963; Rodney 1981; Mudimbe 1988; Boahen 1987).

A second troubling point is that for a scholar of her stature, Coquery-Vidrovitch's work reveals a great deal of ignorance and limitations of using gender as the main analytic category in understanding the political economy of drug trafficking. Are we to assume that all Nigerian drug traffickers are Yorùbá or that they are all women? Does her statement enable one to make a determination on these questions one way or the other? I assert that the book is replete with similar careless assertions and lack of rigor.

Reformist feminist evangelism emerges from the ideological, political, and economic hegemony which privileges all things Western. The assumption is that Westerners, whether feminist or otherwise, are better able to apprehend and interpret reality than Africans. Some of the clearest evidence of Western feminist evangelism in contemporary scholarship is found in the discourse on female circumcision, in which Africans are thought of as always benefiting from the contact with the West. Like the encounter between Africa and the European invaders from the seventeenth to nineteenth centuries, this contact is perceived as a way for Africans "to evolve from their frozen state to the dynamism of Western civilization." (Mudimbe 1988: 67, 76) Western feminist discourse on female circumcision continues the colonial tradition of the enlightened Westerner attempting to reform the "backward" populations of Africa (Sanderson 1981:1-12; Koso-Thomas 1987:1-14; Hoskens 1979).[1] Thus, the crucial question in the debate on circumcision is conceptualized by mainstream feminist theorists as involving right versus wrong and civilization versus barbarity, continuing the colonialist effort to interpret indigenous African culture and, thereby, dominate it. Yet this effort at understanding another is seriously limited by an absolute abhorrence of the otherness of the subject and a striving for sameness through the imposition of a conception of human civilization which is exclusively Western.

Many feminist arguments on female circumcision automatically assume that women subject themselves to this procedure only at the insistence of males. This assumption ignores the likelihood that, for some women, female genital surgeries are a choice regarding the manner in which they want to treat their bodies. For others, it is just one of the manifestations of socially accepted norms. These actions are no different from the predominant assumptions within the dominant culture in the U.S. that when boys are birthed, they are circumcised, an assumption that is so normalized that when a woman gives birth to a boy in the hospital, she is immediately asked whether she wants him circumcised. When the woman responds positively to the hospital's inquiry, how informed is she about the implications of her choice? How knowledgeable is she about what she has chosen, and why? The point is that choices are made in societies on the basis of the assumption that individuals do not have to "re-invent the wheel" concerning problems that have been resolved and normalized. It is precisely because social norms differ in specific times and places that what constitutes solid, well-considered, and sensible choice is eternally contestable.

Comparative analyses of various African societies on why some choose female genital surgeries and others reject it are thus necessary. Opponents and supporters of female genital surgeries in Africa must also engage in debate that incorporates the critiques of the opponents and rationale of the supporters. If the goal is eradication, appropriate strategies must be jointly devised. These strategies will work best if a new hegemonic consensus emerges within communities and societies which practice these procedures; where people delve into social constructions of identity such that powerful alternatives are constructed. To date, this has not been done. Scholars and activists of Western and African derivation have engaged in top-down attempts and very sterile debates on practices which remain little understood. A second possibility is that practices which are of limited utility to a society are bound to wither away. The task for abolitionist activists and scholars, then, is to find productive ways of speeding the process along. *How* this is done is as important as *what* is being done. In contrast to African social practices, Western mutilations, which take the form of elective cosmetic surgery, are touted as a sign of women's liberation. In fact, these practices seem sane only when viewed against the background of their culture and society. Although it is highly unpopular to say so, the same can be said of social practices in Africa. Acknowledging that Africans exercise choices such as these, however, is frowned upon and condemned through what Elmer Eric Schattschneider refers to as the "mobilization of bias" (Schattschneider 1975). Applied to scholarly discourse on female genital surgeries, this is a process where the more powerful determine, prior to public debate, what the relevant issues are and to keep issues which they determine to be unsuitable out.

This paper, then, considers questions that will illuminate the mobilization of bias in feminist theorizing on female genital surgeries: Who has the capacity and knowledge to speak on the issue? Is objective analysis on this subject possible? Are the questions that are being asked relevant? How can the subject best be studied? (Mudimbe 1988:64) Answering these questions is facilitated by applying Mudimbe's critique of missionary discourse on Africans to feminist scholarship on African women. Intellectually, African women are considered either "pure children or incipient human beings in need of tutoring" due to their failure to meet Western standards, a replication of colonial standards of judgment (Mudimbe 1988:68). Hence, the overwhelming majority of writings and discourse on African women fail to acknowledge the reality informed by the multidimensional nature of African women in terms of both their experiences and the articulation of their goals. Women's objectives and policy preferences from pre-colonial times to the present and their struggle to shape their own destinies are ignored in favor of a sensationalized presentation of the abuses to which they are subjected.

Finally, if it is possible, as Joyce Gelb did, in a comparative study of feminism and politics, to "demonstrate how differences in British, American and Swedish feminism relate to systemic and cultural differences"(Gelb 1989:1), it is inevitable that the forms and the expressions taken by women's struggles in each African society will differ from the other and that these struggles will not replicate the experience of Western women. Too many feminist scholars and activists have refused to acknowledge this basic fact and have continued to churn out studies that present African women as nothing but a compendium of problems.

The thrust of my argument is that African women, like any other group, are able to articulate their needs, evaluate the alternative courses of action, and mobilize for collective action where necessary. Sometimes they have even successfully changed the course of history.[2] If the objectives and policy preferences of women are not studied as part of a dialectical historical process, feminist scholarship will forever be damned with the curse of unidimensionality and all avenues to the production of new knowledge will be blocked. The complexity which exists in real-life situations, an essential component of any human situation or condition, will go unrecognized.

The term "Western feminists" in this paper is not used geographically, to apply only to feminists in or of the West. Rather, it describes a mindset that has come to be shared worldwide due to the hegemony of the West in scholarship and in the production of knowledge. In this sense, some African scholars are also Western feminists in their consciousness, approaches, and recommendations.[3] For example, there is very little difference between mainstream Western feminist thought and that found in the Economic Commission for Africa's 1981 study by Belkis Wolde Giorgis, for whom "Patriarchal family structures assign women a subordinate role in the household and community. Women's subordinate role is maintained by cultural practices designed to control women's reproductive capacity. One such practice is female circumcision" (Giorgis 1981:1). Giorgis essentially claims the victimization of African women by society thus: "Left out of the new structures or remaining marginal to them, women are victims of traditional practices that are often harmful to their well-being and that of their children" (Ibid). Like many feminist analysts, Giorgis contends that African women are treated no differently from children and, moreover, that children in African societies are not nurtured but subjected to abusive treatment due to the wrong-headed maintenance of harmful, outdated tradition. In this view, women as well as children are jural minors and African societies have neither the capacity nor capability to offer them the equal protection of the laws or conventions. She loses sight of the central point of gender analysis, which is that gender is socially constructed. Of course there is considerable inequality between men and women, this is incontrovertible. To argue, however, that all men stand in a position of privilege *vis-à-vis* women is absurd. Clarity is important. What women are we referring to? Women are not an undifferentiated mass. Quite apart from class cleavages, there are degrees of hierarchy that are manifested in socially specific ways between individuals, men and women alike. To illustrate this point, in Yorùbá society, a younger woman is *not* equal to an older one. A wife is *not* equal to the daughters of the house or family into which she marries. Younger wives are *not* equal to older wives. A poor man is *not* equal to a wealthy woman, and neither is a poor woman. A woman who is a chief has more power than a woman or man who is not. These are important relational principles which affect the conceptualization of power in society and the capacity to exercise power. Understanding them facilitates the explanation of why people make choices and how to structure incentives such that the process of change is accelerated. It is also crucial to recognize that African societies differ markedly depending on the issue area. Comparative analysis of these several societies is more fruitful than globalization of an African reality which exists only within scholarly imagination.

An additional flaw in Giorgis' work is the use of the entire continent of Africa as a single unit of analysis, leading to the gross conflation of many dissimilar situations. In spite of these flaws, however, she offers some valuable insights, first on the issue of the causal factors responsible for the definition of Africa's socio-economic structures, and second on the analysis of the struggle between Western women and their "desire to perform a civilizing mission and African women's desire to define their own ways and means of struggling against oppressive structures and building alternatives" (Ibid:2-3).

These insights get lost, however, in an analysis which replicates the same problems that Giorgis identifies so accurately.

To reiterate, reformist feminist evangelism is regressive as well as sterile. Countless studies are churned out on helpless and hapless African women that do not always reflect social, political, and economic reality. The issue of female circumcision is over-sensationalized due to the need of some to play a messianic role. If scholarship is to be meaningful, it is only as a quest for knowledge, a portrayal of reality that is as accurate as possible. If African women cannot recognize themselves in our portrayals of them, we will have failed as scholars. According to Mudimbe:

> Anthropologists, sociologists, and theologians from foreign Churches have been studying us for many years.... We have become a fertile field for the kind of research that will enable a person to write an 'interesting' thesis and obtain an academic degree. It is therefore not surprising that we do not recognize ourselves in their writings (Mudimbe 1988:5).

This time-honored tradition continues today, making it impossible for one to recognize anything remotely approaching reality in the scholarly, journalistic, and popular depictions of African women in the overwhelming majority of Western works, feminist or otherwise.

Colonialism and the African State

In the introduction to their edited volume on women and class in Africa, Claire Robertson and Iris Berger contend that "Colonialism not only exacerbated inequality, but ultimately turned over mechanisms for extracting wealth to new African [male] ruling classes" (Robertson and Berger 1986:6). However, Robertson and Berger state that the essays they collected hesitate to blame:

> African women's deprivation solely on colonialism and capitalism and support the Western feminist argument that the household as well as the international economy is a prime locus of women's oppression. Household here must be more broadly defined to include household relations of production, which may be manifested in productive work done outside the home, thus blurring the public-private distinction (Ibid:12).

This statement reveals curious reasoning on two counts. First, and most troubling, Robertson and Berger assume that the household mode of production is separable from the capitalist system within which it operates and also that the household mode of production as it exists today represents pre-colonial African socioeconomic systems held constant over time. Both assumptions are problematic, as indicated in Bonnie Kettel's study in the same volume.

It is instructive to consider Kettel's chapter in the Robertson and Berger volume. Kettel begins her chapter by stating her essay "is about cows and women" (Kettel 1986:47). The insight revealed in Kettel's analysis into the nature of social relations among the Tugen of Kenya is limited by a sensational introductory statement that clearly categorizes women as being no more important than cattle, cattle and women being just so much male property (Ibid:47). This is amazing, especially given the focus of Kettel's analysis as stated below:

> I suggest that research on gender relations among the East African cattle-keepers has been biased, not by insensitive male chauvinism, but by a "received view" on the significance of property in social life, by the assumption that differential rights in property are inevitably associated with differential rights in society. This interpretation ... results from our attempt to understand social relations based on gender from the vantage point of developed capitalism, and thus with an ethnocentric set of assumptions of power in society and in the household. It has caused us to read the present into the past and to assume that the male dominance which is characteristic of so much of present day life in this context is an enduring feature of social reality that has somehow survived untouched by the impact of colonial rule (Ibid:48).

Kettel understands the erroneous Western feminist tendency to assume that observed forms of social relations in contemporary Africa exist exactly as they did in pre-colonial times. However, she is equally wrong when she puts women and cattle in one and the same category. To casually throw around depictions which reinforce the reduction of women to men's property is to accept that women have absolutely no agency. If indeed they do not, why? Have they always lacked agency? How and when did they lose their agency? These are relevant, appropriate, and legitimate questions that must be addressed. It is important to be clear about what is and is not characteristic of pre-colonial gender relations. The scholarship that exists to date has not answered these questions conclusively, thus, gender analysis in Africa cannot claim to have answered the essential question of the social construction of the concept. What we have so far are modest beginnings, and this ought to be acknowledged.

In Africa, the political arm of Western hegemony was established during the "pacification" and the subsequent colonization process, when the European state form was imposed on Africans. This process was violent and brutal. After its consolidation came the elevation of things European to the stature of the ideal, and things African came to be renounced. The power and weight of the state was used to maintain, promote, and perpetuate a class system that privileged Europeans and disadvantaged Africans in education, employment, place of residence, and all spheres of life. Political hegemony supported and concretized economic hegemony, and ideological hegemony was dispensed through the efforts of the missionaries in church and school as well as through the media to reinforce the other forms. By independence, the colonialists were able to ensure the maintenance of the structures of domination that they had constructed through their neo-colonial heirs.

Besides its cultural and intellectual implications, one of the most enduring structural legacies of the colonial period in Africa remains the imposition of the state through a massively violent and destructive effort. If there were ever a valid argument for the universalized oppression of women, the agency that has been most responsible is the state, which is modeled on its Western counterpart. In both its colonial and post-colonial forms, the African state has discriminated consistently against women. The post-colonial African state, continuing the colonial assault, has done a lot of violence to women's struggle for equality, equity, and justice. Hamza Alavi, in his study of Pakistan and Bangladesh, argues that the colonial state was created with an agenda of dominating society; thus, with its strong bureaucracy and military organization it is overdeveloped *vis-à-vis* society. This overdeveloped state, which is built on the culture and thought of the colonizer, then dominates post-colonial society through the use of compulsion and violence. (Alavi 1979) Claude Ake similarly argues that the reality of the state falls short of its idealized form, and for women this is especially true. The facade of what the state ought to be covers numerous ills. The state is an instrument of domination which retains its colonial characteristics; as such, it guarantees the rule of law only for the bourgeoisie. Essentially, the state remains an arena of class struggle. (Ake n.d.)

The understanding that the state is an arena of class struggle explains the practice of tokenism in all former attempts to join the bandwagon of "integrating women into development" both in the West and in Africa. These integrationist attempts have largely benefitted the bourgeoisie, both male and female. To the extent that female members of the bourgeoisie have more privileged access to the state and have not used their advantages to press for gender equity, one cannot attribute the condition of all women to a universal experience of patriarchy. Experiences of patriarchy are mediated by class, status, and degrees of hierarchy:

Robertson and Berger comment on the effects of the colonization of Africa: Foreign domination with its extension into neocolonialism has introduced new class cleavages into African societies, sometimes onto a relatively egalitarian base, sometimes into previously stratified social structures. While earlier patterns of inequality usually intensified during the colonial period, new class systems also have developed in accordance with changing forms of capitalist penetration.Many of these processes of social transformation have been detrimental to women. Their previously dominant role in food production has often been overlooked or ignored in the process of developing new crops and farming techniques, yet there have been fewer opportunities for them in newer capitalist enterprises than for men. This has left disproportionate numbers of women in economically precarious positions at the lower levels of the socio-economic scale (Ake n.d.:9-10).

In an attempt to explain the interaction of state, class, and gender in disadvantaging African women, Fatton accurately attributes African women's lack of power to the blocking of autonomous African women from the nascent ruling class. He also argues that it is impossible for women to attain positions of political power without being protégés of powerful men:

> In Africa, the construction of ruling class hegemony has the effect of conflating male power with class closure. Women are not totally excluded from the ranks of the ruling class, but their quest for status and wealth depends inordinately on aligning themselves with powerful men. In the absence of such alignments, women tend to withdraw from the public arena to build their own parallel and independent spheres of survival. The emancipation of women is thus linked to the struggle against ruling class hegemony; it requires both a feminist and a class consciousness (Fatton 1989:48).

While conceding that African women deploy conventional and unconventional strategies in struggles against male dominance, Fatton is uncritical about the origin of male dominance, and he sweeps aside an account by Christine Obbo as an insufficient defense against male dominance and class oppression. Drawing heavily on Jane Parpart's earlier study on Kenyan women, Fatton reduces all achievements by African women to their dependence on "their father's and/or husband's social status" (Ibid:49). Such reductionism is neither accurate nor supported by empirical evidence. Clearly, patron-client relations in Africa do not affect women exclusively.

The adverse consequences of economic programs which are advocated by multilateral organizations such as the World Bank and the International Monetary Fund [IMF] are the most recent incursions against the autonomy of the African state. These Structural Adjustment Programs (SAPs) introduce policies that complicate the livelihood struggles of people in most African countries. One of the predominant goals of SAPs is to promote the spread of global capitalism by opening African economies to market forces and, by implication, reducing the influence of the state on the economy. The vulnerability of African countries to the vagaries of the international market forces makes them susceptible to the exercise of leverage on the part of the IMF and the World Bank which are forcing the SAPs through. Many studies have documented the deleterious impact of these programs on African women.[4]

The depiction of African women as powerless is not limited to scholarly works. Media reports fortify and support scholarly ideas. Cases in point are several opinion pieces in *The New York Times* by A.M. Rosenthal (1995), and television and radio commentaries.[5] The focus of such reports is the misery, powerlessness, and marginalization of African women. A report in *West Africa* on the situation of African women by Enid Buchanan (1993) asked:

> Why is there such a short flow of women, the likes of Indira Gandhi and Margaret Thatcher, on the leadership scene in Africa when they are so manifestly numerous on the major international forums? African women's presence and influence in senior policy and decision-making positions in their Governments or parliamentary representation is surprisingly negligible. Why? (Buchanan 1993:1070)

Buchanan's answer is that this situation resulted from the heavily male-dominated nature of African society, where:

> the educated and professional woman, no matter how capable, is never considered the equal of her male peers and colleagues. She may be admired, humoured, tolerated ... and if she plays her cards well, she might even make an inroad in her field of activity. But too often, it will be because of "favour," rarely because of her capabilities. It is only in the outside world that she can really shine and be appreciated for her professional value. This explains the number of outstanding women in the international forums. (Ibid:1070)

One wonders how many women of the stature of Gandhi and Thatcher exist in India and Britain, respectively, and how many exist in industrialized countries throughout the world. Switzerland became democratic in 1848, yet even though Swiss women have only very recently become enfranchised, (Rueschemeyer, Stephens and Stephens 1992: 48, 85-87) Switzerland is not pointed out as a country which sits on its women. In May 1977, the percentage of women in the French National Assembly was just 6 percent.[6] No French woman has risen to the level of Gandhi and Thatcher. No women in the U.S. have either. Patriarchy is alive and well all over the world. However, we must bear in mind Joyce Gelb's aforementioned study of feminism and politics in Britain, Sweden, and America, which acknowledges that there are systemic and cultural differences which shape the nature of Swedish, British, and American politics and feminist responses thereto. This is a reinforcement of the need to conceptualize gender as socially constructed. The commonalities among African societies exist and must be taken seriously. However, some have female genital surgeries in common while others do not. Those who practice these surgeries do so for different reasons which cannot be reduced to patriarchy, powerlessness, or false consciousness. Women's agency is also implicated as a cause. My point is that the assumption of African women's ignorance is not a viable analytical tool. To make a truly comparative analysis of the state of the world's women, it would be more accurate to acknowledge that the absence of women from decision-making positions is generalized and to trace that generalization to the internationalization of the Western state through colonialism. Although there were pre-colonial African states, the colonial state provided the foundation for the contemporary African state. The gender bias of the African state is at least partially traceable to its colonial origins.[7]

There is a tendency to attribute class inequalities as well as the inequalities between men and women solely to the persistence of tradition in the face of modernity. However, the inequalities observed in contemporary Africa have deep roots in the continent's colonial history and cannot be studied solely as a product of its pre-colonial past, since that past has co-mingled with colonial inputs. The colonial period was one of state creation, when state power was forcefully imposed on Africans by the colonizing Europeans. Both African men and women were disadvantaged by this process, losing status, property, and power. Since the colonizing Europeans were products of Victorian culture, the subordination of women to men was the norm. This norm was imposed on African society. Wage employment was restricted to men, as were the limited educational opportunities that existed and the authoritative positions in African society. The codification of "native law and custom" also privileged male over female sources of knowledge. It is no wonder that contemporary African women are lacking in decision making positions, just like their Western counterparts. They are all part of the same world system.

In contemporary Africa, the neo-colonial state is the manifestation of all that was wrong with its colonial predecessor. It has neither lived up to the social contract between African nationalist leaders and the people in the anti-colonial struggles nor succeeded in producing its own nationalist agenda independent of the powerful and influential ideas within the world system on the political, economic, and social responsibility of a state to its people. Thus, its agenda reveals a tacit compliance with external interests rather than domestic desires.

Building Knowledge on African Women

Who is the African woman according to Western feminist theory? She is a construct of the imagination of Western scholars, made possible through the misapplication of Western models to African social life. Given the portrayal of these fictional beings in feminist thinking, it is understandable that African women are classified as "the wretched of the earth." How did the African woman of Western feminist thought come about? She is the product of voluminous research which emerges out of the ideological hegemony of Western feminist scholarship. This hegemony results in a distorted view of the world which has a powerful hold on the characterization of the African woman. In this sense, research has become an instrument of domination. (Steady 1979:4) The invention of the African woman as victim is almost inevitable, given her origins in the racial, cultural, and class biases of Western feminism.

Contrary to these analyses, there is evidence that African women held important political, economic, and social positions prior to the imposition of colonialism. It seems likely then that the nature of the colonial and post-colonial state is the most significant variable in determining women's inequality. Moreover, if we accept the assertion that women are disadvantaged all over the world, we have to look to causal factors that are generalizable world-wide as the cause of such inequality. Colonialism and the imposition of the capitalist system on the rest of the world by Western imperialist countries constitute the most logical causal factor. (Ibid:7-8) Contemporary social, political, and economic systems are necessarily shaped by the imposition of capitalism and colonialism and cannot be taken as unadulterated depictions of pre-colonial African life.

Contrary to the negative portrayal of Africa and its women, I argue that African women are multidimensional in terms of their status, class, involvement in politics, social life, and the economy. This conceptualization enables one to understand the existence of powerful as well as powerless women in all spheres of life, and that is the starting point for more meaningful research on the global nature of sisterhood among women. The means through which women gain influence include the ownership and control of means of production; the prestige deriving from the bearing and socialization of children; seniority; the exercise of ritual power and authority; and wealth, which may be inherited or achieved individually. (Mba 1982; Awe 1992; Uchendu 1993; Steady 1979; Coles and Mack 1991:3-26)

Examples abound of the power and prestige of African women. Despite the setbacks they suffered under colonialism, oral tradition suggests that they continued to play an important role in society. To quote Steady on pre-colonial Africa:

> Since production was primarily for use, the question of differential valuation between production and reproduction was not an issue. The basis for valuation of reproduction was more metaphysical and symbolic than purely materialistic. As a result, a woman's role in reproduction often received supreme symbolic value, since it strengthened the human group, ensured continuity of life, and became equated with the life force itself. The bond between the mother and child surpassed all other bonds and transcended patrilineal rules of descent. In patrilineal societies, the structural position of women as those who perpetuated the patrilineage served to modify the undue male control made possible by the strong corporateness of localized patrilineage groups (Steady 1979:7).

There is no allowance for female power not granted by men in Western feminist thinking. Instead of a nuanced approach which recognizes multiple variations in the situation of women, women are presented as a jumbled mass of sameness.

According to the theoretical framework and argument presented here, like women all over the world, some African women are powerful, influential, intelligent, and capable, some lack power and influence and others are more powerful than most men in their society. (Coles and Mack 1991; Awe 1992) Most studies, however, look for the "dog bites man" kinds of cases to reinforce the dominant thinking in the West about the inferiority of Africa and her women.

The idea that women are dependent first on their fathers and then on their spouses along with the idea that they depend on the influence of powerful men to propel them into politics indicates that women are considered jural minors. For Enid Buchanan, African women "are always owned by someone. Generally father, family or husband." (Buchanan 1993:1070) African women can only be owned in the sense of being chattel when considered from the ethnocentric position of the Western scholar. The studies which indicate the autonomy and command of African women over their lives and resources remain overshadowed by the ones which stress negative variables. Some of the more productive studies reveal complementarity among men and women in pre-colonial African society, women as well as men holding positions of power and leadership in all spheres of life. Other studies indicate that contemporary African women have some control over their own fate, though much more needs to be done.

The underlying assumption in most studies on African women is that these women are impoverished, downtrodden, and oppressed as a result of their ignorance. To quote Buchanan once again:

> Given the present situation and status of the African woman, (as legal mi-
> nors) the promoters of African women's rights will have a hard uphill struggle
> to attain their objectives. The obstacle in their paths will be, not only the
> societies that relegate women to their present inferior position, but the very
> women themselves, who unenlightened, are obstinately resigned to their situ-
> ation (Ibid).

Unfortunately, ignorance and lack of enlightenment are neither useful nor productive as analytical categories. To attribute the persistence of these conditions to the ignorance of the African women is to take an arrogant stance of being more capable than they of apprehending and interpreting reality. As Esther Hicks argues:

> Qualifying a given problem as social does not make it so. Infibulation (the
> most extreme form of female circumcision) is a case in point. [for] the vast
> majority of the female population in infibulation-practicing societies, not
> being infibulated would be the social problem (Hicks 1993:1).

Olayinka Koso-Thomas, a Sierra-Leonean medical practitioner, in a book directed at devising a strategy for eradicating female circumcision, makes the typical Western feminist mistake in evaluating the arguments proffered by societies that practice female circumcision (Koso-Thomas 1987:5-9). She rejects the arguments that she enumerates, stressing "the ignorance factor" as being in large part responsible, together with "mystical and ritualistic factors" (Ibid:12-14). To buttress her points, she makes the following statement:

> "Beauty is in the eye of the beholder." The eye that finds the normal female
> genitalia ugly has been conditioned to this perception. Even in those very rare
> cases in which enlargement of the clitoris and labiae occur, to the unbiased
> mind the enlarged organs are never objects of disgust or embarrassment
> (Ibid:10).

But in truth, standards of beauty are only acceptable to Koso-Thomas if they are her own. If African women cling to their traditions and practices, they have to be approached as sentient, rational beings and studied using the same standards as are used in all other studies, not as exotic carryovers from a dim and brutal past. Moreover, if and when there is a shift from this preoccupation with negativity, more useful studies will emerge which avoid the gross over-generalization and under-specificity that exists in much of the literature thus far. These studies will offer a more balanced, multi-dimensional depiction of African women.

The studies of the 1970s are a carryover from the historical tendency to underestimate the extent to which African women were productive members of their societies. In response to the critiques of these studies, present studies tend to overestimate women's ability to generate income under the adverse conditions that are the consequence of SAPs. As with all adverse situations, some individuals profit, but the livelihood of the overwhelming majority is threatened. These individuals are both male and female. The assumption that gender equality will ameliorate the situation of working class women is erroneous because women join the labor force under the same exploitative and alienating conditions as men. Structural constraints often cause a perpetuation of these same conditions by women. (Kanji and Jazdowska 1993:13)

In contemporary Africa, the study of women's responses to SAP is a salient issue precisely because it demonstrates the ongoing struggles of women with ideological, political, and economic inequality. In studying women's responses to SAP, it is possible to analyze the struggles of women to make meaning out of their lives, grapple with difficult socio-economic problems, contest onerous state policies, and make change in their lives. Women's responses necessarily differ according to the objective situation faced, and depend on the opportunities and constraints arising from their class and regional situation. For scholars interested in other issues, the caution is that objectivity is well near impossible, especially in situations where another culture is being studied. The responses we get to questions depend on the questions we ask, which depend on our perspective. Our perspective is informed by our socialization and cultural biases.

What Women? Whose Development?

What women? Whose development? Are pertinent questions when one considers the myriad studies which have emerged to argue for the inclusion of African women in the development process. The UN Decade for Women is an important watershed for the advent of these studies. It became clear during the conferences that commemorated the decade that the ideals and norms of Western feminism were the new standards by which feminists from other parts of the world would be judged. The resistance of Third World feminist delegates to these conferences underlined the inappropriateness of the assumption that identical development standards can be fashioned for all women at all times in all parts of the world. Given this increased attention to development issues and problems by multilateral organizations, it is surprising that the empowerment of even rural women is so elusive. Whose development, then, is the focus of such efforts? Development administration is so top heavy as to make it easy to suggest that the focus of multilaterals is to maintain a steady pool of victims in order to justify their existence.[8]

One of the most significant consequences of the UN Decade is the focus of the Women in Development effort of the international governmental and non-governmental organizations on "the integration of African women in the development process." Beginning in the 1970s, many studies have recommended that development efforts should be directed toward rural women who are disadvantaged *vis-à-vis* rural men and urban women. However, the development efforts that are directed at women suffer from the fatal flaw of manufacturing victims where there exist powerful, vibrant, active human beings. When women's activism, power, and control over their lives is not acknowledged, these efforts create victims. Awa Thiam's critique of mainstream feminist thought as applied to black women is instructive in this regard. Looking back into the decade of the 1970s for variables which imperil the equality of women, she argues:

> Four aspects seem to be particularly striking in their implications for women. The first is the frequently misguided nature of attempts to integrate women into development; the second, the straitjacket which global capitalism has placed on African development via the IMF and its structural adjustment policies; the third, the potential but unfulfilled role of the state in contributing to the transformation of gender relations; and the fourth, the deepening class (and other) divisions emergent amongst women themselves. (Baylies and Bujra 1993:4)

The drive to integrate women into development was revealed to be totally misdirected when it became obvious that women had always been integrated in a multiplicity of occupations and had never been precluded from gainful employment. For Baylies and Bujra, the efficacy of many of the measures supposedly introduced to ameliorate the condition of African women, such as "income-generating" schemes and agricultural innovation, were also questionable (Ibid:4-10). Secondly, when women's economic independence is acknowledged, it is often taken as a negative factor which indicates the shiftlessness of African men. Whereas women are essentially portrayed as beasts of burden, the men are portrayed as lazy and underemployed. (Coquery-Vidrovitch 1997:13-15,26-27) The theoretical frameworks that emerge from this kind of analysis as characterized by Steady fosters "dichotomy, individualism, competition and opposition" (Steady 1979:8).

Following are some crucial questions to ask with regard to Africa: Do the Western feminist models apply? Do African women believe that they are under the oppressive weight of patriarchy?To avoid overgeneralization and the reification of any given experience, research should focus on the multiplicity of ideas that exist among African women, ideas that are necessarily informed by the diverse cultural differences that exist among African ethnic groups. This is a gargantuan task which cannot be undertaken, as has often been done in the past, by studying one group or a fraction thereof and assuming that what is observed applies to all Africans. Hanny Lightfoot-Klein, as indicated earlier, conducted studies in Egypt, the Sudan, Uganda, and Kenya, but talks quite authoritatively about Africa as a whole. (Lightfoot-Klein 1989:1-46)[9] This approach to Africa is problematic because one cannot assert correctly that even within one country, all ethnic groups observe given practices or even that all parts of one ethnic group do. Circumcision, for instance, is not practiced by all Yorùbá -speaking people within Nigeria. Neither should scholars take whatever is observed in Africa as representative of tradition, as though its peoples have been frozen in time.

The task ahead is two-fold. In the first place, the feminist contention that gender is socially constructed must be taken seriously. Doing so necessarily involves the recognition that multiple fabrications of the concept are inevitable. It cannot be reduced to an essentialist, unproblematic definition, and its consequences will differ with variations in time and space. As a first step, then, studies of African women must be clear on the differences that set apart African societies. Of course, biases cannot be totally ruled out, since individual perspectives are shaped by experiences and socialization, but when generalizations are made, they must have a clear eye on reality.

Secondly, as Patricia Hill Collins suggests, Black feminist thought is comprised of specialized theoretical knowledge that is produced through the creative energies of African American women that interpret their lived realities. In other words, Black feminist thought encompasses theoretical interpretations of women's reality by those who live it. The implication of this recommendation for studying African women is that the inequality and oppression experienced by African women cannot parallel those of their sisters in the West. Thus, more African women must use their specialized knowledge to construct their own theories. These too would reveal multiple perspectives, since there is no unified, indivisible African viewpoint. To enrich the cross-cultural debates among all feminist theorists and to erode the presumed Western monopoly on knowledge, Africans in the self-conscious examination of their individual societies must build theories that are not mere replications or confirmations of age-old Western constructions.

The third point is that sisterhood, properly conceptualized, should not be oppressive. It ought not to be a relationship of domination, the privileging of one sister over the other. My appeal to African scholars and activists is to eschew uninformed cosmopolitanism. Uninformed cosmopolitanism is here defined as the proclivity to be uncritical about the acceptance of theories and ideas from the West, and worse, combining this with the wholesale rejection of African social mores as primitive, ignorant, uninformed and brutal. When this is done, African scholars are not only identifying with the oppressor, they are complacent but active participants in the re-colonization of their own people. Our most important task is to self-consciously understand our own societies on their own terms, to "decolonize" our minds from the insidious influence of Western thought, in order to fully apprehend the reality as it is in our societies.[10] African scholars, having been immersed in Western culture, being educated in Eurocentric institutions, particularly on the continent, are all skilled and knowledgeable in Western modes of thought, analyses, assumptions, axioms, and principles. The new research project is that they must become equally skilled in African bodies of thought, which, I argue, have been taken for granted by African scholars, who have vigorously participated in denigrating and delegitimizing them. The beauty of good theory and activism is that the human knowledge pool is broadened and deepened. The West has as much or even more to learn from African societies as Africa has to learn from the West. African scholars owe it to themselves and their societies to forge ahead and create bodies of knowledge that are not only socially relevant, but liberatory.

The duty of an intellectual is not only to record phenomena, but to find hidden meanings and expose them. According to the Yorùbá, *àbò òrò l'à nso f'ómolúwàbí, t'ó bá d'énú è, á d'odindi* [any reasonable, intelligent individual needs only a hint, which is digested, and processed into the whole, or complete knowledge]. The words represented by the acronym FGM can thus not be taken at face value. Words, as some feminists have convincingly argued, can empower or silence. Ironically, feminists also do a lot of analyses which identify and pinpoint instances of women being silenced by patriarchal structures of domination. However, women of color and black feminists such as bell hooks (1984), Patricia Hill Collins (1991), Cade Bambara (1983), and Audre Lorde (1996) have demonstrated the intolerance and/or patronizing attitude that mainstream feminism exhibits toward non-white feminists.[11] Critiques by womanists and black feminists argue that liberal white feminists were complicit or at least tacit in their support of white patriarchy's oppression of women of color and radical feminists. In like manner, Western feminists and activists have used the words "Female Genital Mutilation" to silence those who may hold contrary opinion.

Too often, the feminist research project and feminist social engineering have as a goal the *normalizing* of all women. Feminists present a universalized picture of commonly experienced patriarchy, but when this picture is coupled with the conceptualization of gender as socially constructed, a duality is inserted in feminist thought which creates a fifth column in the corpus of feminist works. In consequence, each concept erodes the other's meaning. If patriarchy is universalizable, all women's experiences should be mirror images of one another. I am convinced that they are not. My mother, brother, sisters, aunts, uncles, grandfather, uncles, and myself all share the same *oríkì-orílè*, the praise poetry with which the Yorùbá honor individuals, both great and small. Each family has its own distinctive *oríkì.* It provides an insight into the past ancestry, inspires, is an example of the skill of orature. Contrary to the assertion by Karin Barber in the book *Oríkì,* (1991) these poems are studied and recited by both men and women. Skill and expertise in this genre are not a function of gender, but of learnedness, being affected by intellectual capacity and quality of training. While for Barber *oríkì* is a woman's genre, one of the few areas that they control, or are allowed to control *oríkì* to the contrary has both male and female experts. One may argue that there is a given corpus of *oríkì* where there is a gender-based division of labor. For example, *ekun iyawo* or brides' lament is only recited by young women at that particular moment when they are in the process of becoming new brides. The question is: what does this symbolize? It symbolizes, most importantly, that there are social norms on desiderata, and thus people, both male and female, conform. Change however, is inevitable. Unfortunately, it is not always positive. Many Yorùbá brides of today, regrettably, have no idea that *ekun iyawo* exists and, where they do, their Christian ethics often generate a condemnatory response rather than warm embrace. This discussion of *oríkì.* is relevant to that on female genital surgeries in at least two respects. First, it illustrates my point that social practices often die a natural death, even without overt external intervention. Second, it underlines the tendency for even the most careful and respected experts to read societies to which they are outsiders wrong, despite spending quite a few years observing the "natives." Outsiders do not have to be those that come from abroad. The indoctrination that is an integral part of the education of most African scholars pushes them toward unseemly cosmopolitanism and homogenizes their perspective in a remarkable way.

For African scholars who consider themselves feminist, there ought to be more exchange of ideas with feminists from the West that problematizes Western-originated ideas rather than privileging them. To the extent that this is done effectively, feminism as a movement–and, indeed, feminist theories– will be enriched, and then we can talk about the possibility of engineering sisterhood. Again, there is much to learn from the work of Fanon in *The Wretched of the Earth.* Of the manicheanism that arises from the colonial situation, Fanon says the following:

> At times this Manichism goes to its logical conclusion and dehumanizes the native, or to speak plainly, it turns him into an animal. In fact,

the terms the settler uses when he mentions the native are zoological terms. He speaks of the yellow man's reptilian motions, or the stink of the native quarter, or breeding swarms, of the foulness, of spawn, of gesticulations. When the settler seeks to describe the native fully in exact terms he constantly refers to the bestiary.... Those hordes of vital statistics, (recall the numbers of the mutilated) those hysterical masses, those faces bereft of all humanity, those distended bodies which are like nothing on earth, that mob without beginning or end, those children who seem stretched out in the sun. That vegetative rhythm of life–all this forms part of the colonial vocabulary. The native ... knows that he is not an animal; and it is precisely at the moment that he realizes his humanity that he begins to sharpen weapons with which he will secure his victory. In the colonial context, the settler only ends his work of breaking in the native when the latter admits loudly and intelligibly the supremacy of the white man's values. In the period of decolonization, the colonized masses mock at these very values, insult them, and vomit them up (Fanon 1963:42-43).

Lightfoot-Klein's book is replete with negative references such as are identified by Fanon above. Some of them have been discussed earlier. I submit that Western feminist pedagogy is evangelism and that, as a social movement, it seeks to dominate Africa by "helping" it. It presents only one perspective and, like patriarchy, which is its focus, it is hierarchical and shares a great deal in common with the colonial project of inculcating Western values regardless of local desires and priorities.

To make sense of the phenomenon of female genital surgeries, we do not need travelogues. We need serious inquiries into why people do what they do, and what the possibilities are for change within the context of their own history. We need socially relevant scholarly activism, particularly among Africans. The African scholarly mind must be decolonized. There are enough pictures of women's genitals floating around, and enough sensationalized media and scholarly accounts of female genital surgeries. These have changed nothing. I submit that even without intervention, social practices for which people have no use die a natural death. This is not to argue against intervention, but to draw attention to the fact that intervention that comes from a lack of respect for those being studied is even more dangerous than doing nothing.

NOTES:

1. Like colonial discourse, these reflect the pre-conceived notions of European superiority and African inferiority of the colonialists and the proliferation of studies that reinforce these notions.

2. For example, the actions of Nigerian women in Aba and Abeokuta during colonialism were informed by the fact that Nigerian women drew upon the sources of power that they had in precolonial times. For a discussion of the role of Nigerian women in the anti-colonial struggle, see Nina Mba, *Nigerian Women Mobilized: Women's Political Activity in Southern Nigeria, 1900-1965*. For a numver of studies which concentrate on studying Hausa women and their role in the 20th century, see Catherine Coles and Beverly Mack, *Hausa Women in the Twentieth Century*.

3. See, for example, Koso-Thomas, op cit. She credits Fran Hosken for making her aware of the importance of the issue of female circumcision and takes an approach that is no different from Hosken's in *Female Sexual Mutilations*, p. xi.

4. See Baylies & Bujra, op cit. for an overview; see also, *Review Of African Political Economy*, #56 (1993).

5. Examples of these are the "Day 1 TV" program on "Female Genital Mutilation"; *Time, US News and World Report*'s sensationalized coverage of the Oluloro case, which is also reported by Timothy Egan in "An ancient ritual and a mother's asylum plea," *The New York Times*, March 4, 1994; *WBAI New York* (Pacifica) Radio's special programming on International Working Women's Day, 1994 and the eve on "Female Genital Mutilation" and A.M. Rosenthal's columns in various issues of *The New York Times*. For representative examples, see "Fighting Female Circumcision," April 12, 1996; "The Possible Dream," June 13, 1995; "Female Genital Mutilation" December 24, 1993; "Female Genital Torture," November 12, 1993.

6. *New York Times* May 28, 1997, p. A1.

7. This was the most significant point made in *Women and the State in Africa* op. cit.

8. See Cheryl Payer (1982) and Ayers (1993) for critiques of development administration.

9. Compare Lightfoot-Klein's social problem approach with the factual approach by Hicks in *Infibulation*.

10. For a clear, and trenchant critique of this tendency, see Frantz Fanon's *The Wretched of The Earth*, and Ngugi wa Thiong'o's *Decolonizing the Mind*.

11. See, for instance, bell hooks, *Feminist Thought: Knowledge, Consciousness, and the Politics of Empowerment;* Cherrie Moraga and Gloria Anzaldua, foreword by Toni Cade Bambara *This Bridge Called my Back: Writings by Radical Women of Color;* Audre Lorde *The Audre Lorde Compendium: Essays, Speeches and Journals.*

WORKS CITED:

Ake, Claude. "Manichaean Dialectics: The State Project and its Decivilizing Mission in Africa." *Paper Presented at the Brookings Institution*, n.d.

Alavi, Hamza. "The State in Post-Colonial Societies: Pakistan & Bangladesh." *Politics and State in the Third World*. Ed. H. Goldbourne. London: Macmillan, 1979.

Awe, Bolanle. "Nigerian Women & Development in Retrospect." *Women and Development in Africa: Comparative Perspectives*. Ed. Jane L. Parpart. Lanham, Maryland: University Press of America, 1989. 313-334.

Ayers R.L. *Banking on the Poor: The World Band and Poverty*. Massachusetts: MIT Press, 1993.

Barber, Karin, *I Could Speak Until Tomorrow: Oríkì., Women and the Past in a Yorùbá Town*. Edinburgh : Edinburgh University Press for the International African Institute, London, 1991.

Baylies, Carolyn, & Bujra, Janet. "Challenging Gender Inequalities." *Review of African Political Economy* 56: 3-10.

Boahen, A. Adu. *African Responses to Colonialism*. Baltimore: Maryland: Johns Hopkins University Press, 1987.

Buchanan, Enid. "Women: Struggle for Change" *West Africa* 1993:1070-1073.

Coles, Catherine & Mack, Beverly. *Hausa Women in the Twentieth Century*. Madison, Wisconsin: University of Wisconsin Press, 1991.

Collins, Patricia Hill. *Black Feminist Thought: Knowledge, Consciousness, and the Politics of Enlightenment*. New York: Routledge, 1991.

Coquery-Vidrovitch, Catherine. *African Women: A Modern History*. Boulder, Colorado: Westview, 1997.

Davidson, Basil. *The Black Man's Burden: Africa and the Curse of the Nation State*. New York: Times Books, 1992.

Fanon, Frantz. *The Wretched of the Earth*. New York: Grove Press, 1963. Longman, 1987 (4th impression).

Fatton, Robert, Jane L. Parpart, and Kathleen A. Staudt, *Women and the State in Africa*. Boulder, Colo.: Lynne Rienner Publishers, 1990.

Gelb, Joyce. *Feminism and Politics: A Comparative Perspective*. Berkeley: University of California Press, 1989.

Giorgis, Wolde Belkis. *Female Circumcision in Africa*. Addis Ababa: UNECA, African Training and Research Centre for Women & AAWORD, 1981.

Hay, Margaret Jean, & Sharon Stichter. *African Women South of the Sahara*. London: Longman, 1987 (4th impression).

Hicks, Esther K. *Infibulation: Female Mutilation in Islamic and North Western Africa*. New Brunswick: Transaction, 1993.

hooks, bell. *Feminist Theory: From Margin to Center*. Boston, Massachusetts: South End Press, 1984.

Hosken, Fran. *The Hosken Report, Genital Mutilation, the Practice and its Prevention*. Minority Rights Network News, 1994..

Hoskens, Fran P. *Female Sexual Mutilations: The Facts and Proposals for Action*. Lexington,

Mass: Women's International Network News, 1980.

Kanji, Nazneen & Jazdowska, Niki. "Structural Adjustment and Women in Zimbabwe," *Review of African Political Economy* 56: 11-26.

Koso-Thomas, Olayinka. *The Circumcision of Women: A Strategy for Eradication.* London: Zed, 1987.

Lightfoot-Klein, Hanny. *Prisoners of Ritual: An Odyssey into Female Genital Circumcision in Africa.* Binghamton: Haworth, 1989.

Lorde, Audre. *The Audre Lorde Compendium: Essays, Speeches, and Journals.* London: Pandora, 1996.

Mba, Nina Emma. *Nigerian Women Mobilized: Women's Political Activity in Southern Nigeria, 1900-1965.* Berkeley, California: Research Series/University of California Press, Berkeley, Institute of International Studies #48, 1982.

Moraga, Cherrie and Gloria Anzaldua, forward by Toni Cade Bambara. *This Bridge Called My Back: Writings by Radical Women of Color.* New York: Kitchen Table, Women of Color Press, 2nd ed., 1983.

Mudimbe, V.Y. *The Invention of Africa: Gnosis, Philosophy and the Order of Knowledge,* Bloomington: Indiana University Press, 1988.

Ngugi wa Thiong'o, *Moving the Centre : the Struggle for Cultural Freedoms.* Portsmouth, N.H.: Heinemann, 1993.

Parpart, Jane L. & Staudt, Kathleen A.,eds. *Women and the State in Africa.* Boulder, Colorado: Lynne Rienner, 1989.

Payer, Cheryl. *The World Band: A Critical Analysis.* New York: Monthly Review Press, 1982.

Robertson, Claire & Berger, Iris, eds. *Women and Class in Africa.* New York: Africana, 1986.

Rodney, Walter. *How Europe Underdeveloped Africa.* Washinton, D. C.: Howard University Press, 1981.

Rosenthal, A.M. "The possible dream. Ending female genital mutilation." *New York Times* Jun 13 1995 p. A25.

Rueschemeyer, Dietrich, Evelyne Huber Stephens & John D. Stephens. *Capitalist Development and Democracy.* Chicago: University of Chicago, 1992.

Sanderson, Lilian Passmore. *Against the Mutilation of Women: The Struggle to End Unnecessary Suffering.* London: Ithaca, 1981.

Serequeberhan, Tsenay, ed. *African Philosophy: The Essential Readings.* New York: Paragon House, 1991.

Schattschneider, Elmer Eric. *The Semisovereign People: A Realist View of Democracy in America.* Fort Worth, Texas: Harcourt Brace Jovanovich College Publishers, 1975.

Steady, Filomina Chioma. "African Feminism: A Worldwide Perspective." *Women in Africa and the African Diaspora.* Ed. Rosalyn Terborg-Penn, Sharon Harley and Andrea Benton Rushing. Washington D.C.: Howard University, 1979.

Stichter, Sharon B. & Parpart, Jane L. *Patriarchy and Class: African Women in the Home and the Workforce.* Boulder: Westview, 1988.

Sudarkasa, Niara. "The 'Status of Women' in Indigenous African Societies." *Women in Africa and the African Diaspora.* Ed. Rosalyn Terborg-Penn, Sharon Harley and

Andrea Benton Rushing. Washington D.C.: Howard University, 1979.

Uchendu, Patrick Kenechukwu. *The Role of Nigerian Women in Politics: Past and Present.* Enugu: Nigeria, Fourth Dimension, 1993.

Walker, Alice, *Possessing the Secret of Joy.* London : Women's Press Book Club, 1992.

Walker, Alice, *Warrior Marks : Female Genital Mutilation and the Sexual Blinding of Women.* San Diego : Harcourt Brace, 1996.

5.
O AFRICA:
Gender Imperialism in Academia

Nkiru Nzegwu

Language and conceptual ideas can be dramatic sites of violence in which the activities, actions, and humanity of others are violated. Psychic liberation begins through resisting the superordinate/subordinate structures and relationships that pathologize and demonize difference. In an attempt to promote the self-(re)membering of subjugated identities, this essay examines the social, psychic, and political effects of the structures of whiteness in academia and the varied forms of gender imperialism that arise from the denials of one's cultural rights and cultural personhood. The examination is detailed because it methodically unravels the link between gender and imperialism, and interrogates the processes by which knowledge is racialized in the construction of hegemonic discourses. A 1988 review of the *Heroic Figures* catalogue by a white female student provides an entrance into the invisible, subtle politics of racial and sexual difference, and to the "silencing" strategies utilized to erase the Other and reinscribe privilege. Hoffman becomes a metaphor through which I argue the case on gender imperialism; for this reason, most of what is said applies also to the hegemonic actions of a large number of white professional women.

The argument is divided into seven major sections. The first deals with the effects of whiteness on the bodies of African professional women in academia. The thoughts generated by a panel on "Resisting Imperialism," presented at the fifteenth annual meeting of the Canadian Society of Women in Philosophy (C-SWIP), provides an entrance into a discussion of the ways participation in the Eurocentric Western structures of privilege fractures and erodes the identities of non-European peoples. In the second section, I establish the link between gender and racial imperialism as I explore the effects of authorial arrogance in the production of knowledge. This leads to a consideration of the mental reversals that facilitate the racialization of knowledge. In this third section, I will examine the process by which knowledge is gendered to enhance the power and privilege of white women. The fourth section looks at the commodification ideology underpinning knowledge production in the structures of whiteness, and the fifth considers, the ways in which the guise of expertise masks ignorance and legitimizes the theoretical reconstruction of culture along lines that inscribe whiteness. I do this by focusing on how a white woman "knowledgeably and sympathetically" offers a white aesthetic scheme for evaluating Ibibio *ekpo*. I shall then examine the epistemological sub-text of her argument to illuminate the political agenda of her position. Since the issue of aesthetic sensitivity and knowledge of the Ibibio artistic scheme are disingenuously raised in the review, in the sixth section I consider the effect of linearity in knowledge construction and raise the issue of language and translation and the relegation of Africa and African perspectives to the margin of art historical discourse. In the seventh section, I conclude by identifying a useful strategy for resisting imperialism and avoiding its manifold psychic and physical mutilations.

> *Oburo mbosi ukwa dalu*
> *ka oga ele,*
> *oburo mbosi o'daa*
> *ka o'le.*

> It is not the day the breadfruit falls
> that it will rot,
> it is not the day it falls
> that it rots.

Toronto 1992

At the fifteenth annual conference of the Canadian Society for Women in Philosophy, a plenary session was organized to explore the ways in which women are dealing with the impact of imperialism in their lives. Titled "Resisting Imperialism," the panel was comprised of "Visible Minorities," the official Canadian expression for "people of color." The three presenters were Haida Moghissi, an Iranian-Canadian political theorist, May Yu, a Chinese-Canadian philosopher, and myself.

At the time of the meeting, Moghissi was in the midst of a grueling anti-racism hearing at Queen's University, Canada. The charges she brought against the Political Science Department, concerning its discriminatory gender and racist policies had sparked an uproar that exposed the subterranean racism of key members of the department. Yu was teaching at a university in northern Manitoba where, as in the rest of Canada, the dominant preference of the department was for white male philosophers, and philosophy was narrowly defined as Anglo-analytic philosophy. As the lone non-white Asian Canadian and the only woman in the department, she was institutionally positioned as a deviant presence, at the receiving end of various institutionalized forms of racist and sexist attitudes. I came to the panel with a weighty baggage of experiences accumulated in social and intellectual encounters in both Canada and the United States, where African women are patronized. Being an African and a woman in these contexts specifically meant being the oppositional other, the antithesis to the deliberative, competent, rational, and civilized white person.

Worried about the negative effects of sharing personal experiences in an imperial structure that had encouraged my exclusion, and knowing of the organizer's opposition to a panel format she had once described as "putting women of color on display," I stoically contemplated my participation. If my political struggle was to disrupt imperialism, guard against its exploitation of my experiences, and resist its racist erasure of my personhood, I had to be alert to its multiple sites and continually changing forms. Since imperialism is coded and skillfully inscribed in Western intellectual and cultural activities, the only way I could do this was by constantly questioning the basis on which I was being invited to participate in events, and by critically evaluating the convener's agenda as well as the operative modalities for selecting the speakers.

Thinking through the terms of participation unleashed long forgotten memories. I recalled having witnessed the exploitative edge of British imperial rule in my impressionable years in Malawi (then Nyasaland). I recalled my father's counsel that one ought to be cautious when solicited to share personal testimonies within imperialist structures. Using the lives of then revolutionary leaders Jomo Kenyatta, Kenneth Kaunda, and Julius Nyerere as examples, he explained that imperialism often legitimizes itself by appropriating the experiences of the oppressed, and then sustains itself by exploiting the power of those experiences. His view of the matter is that if one decides to participate in imperial structures, one must critically study the Kenyan *mau mau's* model of resistance and be alert to the numerous diversionary tactics of imperialism.

I accepted the invitation to the panel because I decided that it was important to confront the sites and processes of gender domination as it affects my

Nigerian, Igbo, female identity in North America. I needed to have a keener understanding of the internal dynamics of the white female variant of imperialism as it manifests in the rarefied air of academia. To fully comprehend what happens when race and class intersect, I deliberately chose the privileged arena of academia as an investigative site to probe the meaningfulness of the slogan "sisterhood is global" and to examine the processes by which it transmogrifies into sisterarchy.

Why gender imperialism? Simply, I wanted to interrogate whiteness as it relates to and is practiced by white women. I know that imperialism defines a hierarchical relation of dominance and subordination between nations and institutions, but I wanted to understand how that relationship also works between elite, racially privileged women and elite, racially disadvantaged women. It was important to question the institutionalized authority and privileges that establish a dyadic mistress/mammy power relationship between white women and women of color in a professional environment. I needed to examine how that relationship influences authorial production of knowledge and what tacit gender images and expectations rule in that setting, many of which I am expected to uphold. Furthermore, I wanted to question the commitment of tenured and non-tenured white women colleagues to the principles of difference and cultural diversity. Were their overtures of friendship genuine, or were they an enticement to subjugation? Were our white sisters serious in their commitment to the principle of difference, or were their assertions merely rhetoric? With past experience as guide, more troubling questions followed. Would they evasively screen out the ugliness of the pain created by their privilege and in the process shut us out? Would they step out of the comfortable locations of racial privilege and work to end that privilege?

It was clear at the outset that gender imperialism would be a most difficult subject to tackle, given its nebulous form. The politically correct postures taken by some of its ardent perpetrators as well as the general denial that white women have power in academia were additional obstacles. The well-entrenched view that white women are victims of patriarchy but never its conscious perpetrators[1] fosters this denial despite the roles of many as gatekeepers of privileges, mistresses of patriarchs, and matriarchs of a new developing canon. Many of our white "sisters" assume that having women of color as friends or having cross-cultural expertise proves their non-racist nature. However, when one moves beyond "politically correct" pronouncements to the realm of deeds, one finds that most privileged white women function either as surrogates of white males who desire to stay above the fray or, having internalized the oppressive structures of whiteness, are themselves engaged in an imperial mission of their own.

Understanding the internal dynamics of imperialism means recognizing the different permutations of its exploitative nature. Imperialism is gendered when the political, economic, and social character of dominance is constructed on racial and gender lines, when white women exploit their racial and institutional privileges to racialize others, to claim advantages, and to assert authority over women of color. Insofar as these women's legitimizing authority derives from the structure of the larger socio-political framework of imperialism and global economics and establishes a racialized relationship of subordination between women, white women cannot absolve themselves of complicity in imperialism and oppression. Their claim to sisterhood is diversionary.

"Occasionally we do more than serve."
–Haideh Moghissi, my Iranian-Canadian co-panelist, upon being "mistaken" for one of the serving staff five minutes before her talk at the 1992 C-SWIP conference in Toronto

"Sisterhood is Global:" Oppression and Identity Mutilations

Working independently of each other, my C-SWIP co-presenters and I responded to the issue of imperialism from the standpoint of personal, specifically located experiences rather than from abstract, experientially disconnected postulates. We each analyzed the implications of imperialism from the specificity of our experiences, knowing that the experiences of other women of color would differ from ours, but would nonetheless illuminate important undeniable commonalities. The breadth of issues raised from our three culturally divergent perspectives underscored the non-monolithic nature of "visible minorities" in Canada. Yet the vast areas of overlap revealed the common effects of imperialism on this culturally diverse population.

Five minutes before this session was to begin, Moghissi was mistaken for one of the serving staff by one of the "progressive" white women at the conference who, from across the room, saw her quietly waiting at the back for people to settle down. She approached and asked Moghissi when the coffee would be replenished.

Unconscious gestures often reveal more about latent attitudes than carefully thought-out actions and intellectual theorizations. Such split-second judgments speak more powerfully than either words and or feminist critical writings about white women's attitudes towards women of color and their perception of them as subordinate in social encounters. Such unmediated instinctual gestures isolate the inferior serving maid roles white women have reserved for women of color and highlight the roles women of color are expected to play within the structures of white imperialism, for example.

When I accepted the invitation, my difficulty in thinking through my panel participation was that it forced me to confront directly what imperialism had done to me in North America: how it forces me to be other than I am, how it assumes that I must be other than I am. Knowing all this, I became even more reluctant to have some white interpreter present my reality. As the late Nwalie Egbuna, the then head of Ikporo Onitsha, had counseled, "avoid them, through their writings and interpretation they have always managed to make us out into monkeys." To avoid misrepresentation, I realized I had to speak, even if in fear. Some of the things I wanted to highlight were best said by me. My voice, my anger, my pain are cognitive acts that must be systematically conveyed; they cannot be captured by someone else, lest they be erased. I searched for words:

> Many things are still painfully difficult in your white system. The pain derives from the forced mutilations, identity destructions, oppressive psychological manipulations that take place each time one functions in your system. Even in this mundane public act of sharing my experiences with you, I still undergo innumerable metamorphosis and translation. First, I have to sublimate my frustrations (*as stilted "civilizing" voices harp: you cannot show your emotions in public, it's unprofessional*). Next I have to suppress large parts of myself and familiar ways of speaking (*as I recall the stiletto whine: wait a minute, could you speak in English? Nobody here understands your language*). Then I have to switch languages and translate my visceral thoughts into cold foreign words that leave out the spirit of my talk (*still I hear: oh, you have an accent. Where are you from?*). The distortions drive me to the processing plant of inhuman, professional power-language (*because you have to write and speak in a "theoretical" way, the way stuffy white males authorized*). And as if all that isn't enough, I have to swallow my anger, and valiantly find some lessons that I could offer the sea of white faces to let you know that I value you, that you are blameless, and that somehow, I made sense of all these senseless mutilations and appreciate the insight it gave me of myself.

Imperialism is implicit in the very structure of western academia and encoded in its processes, in the very production of knowledge. It stipulates a definite logic of being, a certain mode of thought and behavior, and covertly sanctions a definite style of speech, of being, of acceptability, and of propriety. Voice, gender identity, and most especially skin color are discursively dispersed and subsequently marshaled to determine whether one is worthy of speech, of respect, and of even admission.

Within the sacred halls of academia we find the inscriptions of imperialism and racism in the very categories of Rationality, Objectivity, Universality, Truth, and Knowledge. Racialized, they acquire exclusionary force that is utilized in three major ways: to keep people of non-European descent at the gate; to delegitimize what these non-European scholars know and bring to theoretical work; and to pass off as scholarship prejudices, irrelevancies, half-baked truths, and problematic interpretations about others by white scholars. Imperialism in academia works both by refusing to see me, and by refusing to allow me be myself. The variant I am familiar with racializes and forces me to accommodate whiteness by forgetting myself and becoming more like it. Caught in this conflictual web of legitimation, the ideological force of whiteness works through a "silencing" cloak of invisibility. Being invisible, the structure always insists on the vulnerability and "nakedness" of others as a precondition for understanding them. Never revealing itself, the physical and psychic force of whiteness systematically destroys cultures, peoples, and objects in its path without disclosing its varied sites of operation. Being invisible, it is automatically absolved from blame, for you cannot assign responsibility to something unseen, that leaves no trace of its presence.

Knowing all this, I worried. Should I or should I not participate in the panel? True, the audience is composed mainly of progressive white women, but what does that matter? The leopard never changes its spots. Where is the assurance that this occasion will be different, that these liberal middle- and upper-class women will listen? (*Again the intermittent inner voices, this time from a different cultural location: Can you trust? Remember the innumerable occasions in colonial Africa, in the slave plantations of the Americas, in the suffragist movement, in the civil rights movement, in apartheid South Africa, and even in today's multiculturalized social, political, and economic worlds of the betrayal of black women by white women who have professed friendship.*) These memories cautioned me to be less optimistic and less eager to form alliances. Their immediacy was overpowering, especially since I had no equally compelling memory-evidence to refute them.

I was aware of the weighty political dimensions of my task when I accepted the invitation to speak on resisting imperialism. What I didn't anticipate was the extent and depth of the corrosive effect on my body, mind, and psyche. I stopped to count imperialism's numerous inscriptions: bodily mutilations, mental dis-colorations—black skinned, white-minded, alienated voice, internal voices of the advocate constantly pleading the oppressor's case, the yet unexorcised apologetic voices ignorantly accepting and meekly accommodating domination, and on and on. To be really worthwhile, participation in the panel required "truthful-speaking," which in turn required that I completely expose my vulnerabilities and mutilations to the very same structures of whiteness capable of destroying and erasing by means of their invisible cloak.

Things need not be this way, I am told. Those with whom I shared my experiences are not directly responsible for the traumatic condition in which I live. Patriarchy is the problem, they say; but as I look to real-life encounters, I ruefully wonder how to distinguish between the two kinds of women. How do you tell who is the progressive, and who is not? Since all lizards lie on their bellies, how do you tell the one with a bellyache? Since all I see is the white skin, how do I determine the women's intentions? Like the invisible structures of whiteness, these too are concealed.

The more I looked at the structures of whiteness, the more I fathomed the importance and significance of skin. The privilege of skin allows them to be on either side of the divide, to ally with the imperial power structure when it is to their gain. As Third World women discovered in Nairobi at the 1985 Women's Conference, we see them congregate on the side of the institutionally disadvantaged, jostling for leadership roles, insistently explaining their own agenda, stridently advocating for priorities that will inflate their powers. Yes, always exhorting against sexism because it benefits them, never against racism that takes away some of their privileges. When do we find them with us? Don't we find them on the institutionally advantaged side, where life in a melanin-deficient skin is valued more highly than the rest, where racism becomes a statistical index of black people's inability to "pull themselves up by the bootstraps and make a success of their lives?" Living on this North American "black" side where lives, opportunities, interests, expectancies, goals, hopes, and identities are viciously constrained by the loaded criteria of America's social, political, and economic institutions, one lacks locational flexibility. Stuck in an institutionally devalued skin, the stigmatizing structures of whiteness are experienced as the brutal rapier thrusts of exclusion and oppression.

In anger I turned the edge of my talk to the past, present, and future actions of the audience, questioning their intentional and unintentional complicity with the oppressive structures of whiteness. If I perpetually frame questions in ways that stroke their egos, putatively separating them from the white imperialistic structure that crush non-white realities, they win concessions and end up preserving their white privileges.[2] Though I remained vaguely aware that my immediate audience may not necessarily approve of the despotic behavior of their "siblings," nonetheless my voice also indicted these progressive white women with whom I ought to have been establishing alliances. I indicted them for their latent racism, and for that of their absent reactionary "sisters." "Dressed" in white, the differences between the two sets of women blurred; they merged as one as images of power, of mistresses and mammies, flashed through my mind. I saw only the expanding whiteness and the crushing weight of their privilege that goes with it. I felt the enveloping privilege of that cold clammy skin that crushed me.

Living in North America, I know that racial imperialism is not simply a matter of choice, of whether one approves or disapproves of somebody's position. As a perversely normalized part of reality, it is an amorphous, disingenuous power that conceptually stigmatizes, psychologically castrates, and socially marginalizes. Resisting imperialism in academia means resisting cultural death. It means re-visiting sites of resistance to draw sustenance and strength from the works of women who had audaciously shaken their world, women who refused to roll over and die: women like Queen Kambasa of Bonny,[3] the visionary Atagbusi,[4] Iyalode Efunroye Tinubu (Biobaku 1991; Awe 1992:55-71)[5] and Iyalode Efunsetan Aniwura, Omu Nwagboka,[6] Yaa Asantewaa of Edweso, (Aidoo 1981:65-77) Nwanyeruwa, Ikonnia, Nwanedie, Nwugo and the countless participants of the 1929 Women's War in Eastern Nigeria,[7] Olufunmilayo Ransome-Kuti,[8] Margaret Ekpo, Janet Mokelu and Janet Okala,[9] Umekwulu Odogwu, Veronica Uwechia, and Nneka Chugbo,[10] and the Kenyan environmentalist Wangari Maathai. I draw strength from these *odogu* (brave warriors) to examine the dynamics by which the invisible mechanics of whiteness are brought to bear on African scholars.

> *Nne m'agadi si*
> *na oburo mbosi ukwa dalu, ka ona ele*
> *"Echezona," ka 'agulu n'afa*
> *na mbosi ole*
> *anyi ewe ulu ya melu ife.*

> My grandmother said,
> that it is not on the day the bread fruit falls that it will rot
> "Do not forget," is a name we gave a child
> that on the day of reckoning
> we will put the memory to use.

Umekwulu Odogwu, the acting head of Ikporo Onitsha in the 1970s, accounts for her coolness in the face of a provocation by explaining that it is not on the day the breadfruit falls that it rots. *Nwannyiuzo Eze-nwa-oduga*, my grandmother, counsels against hasty responses on the ground that all facets of a provocation need to be carefully explored before framing a response. "Have patience," she always advised, "When you have deepened your understanding of your opposition, set a time and date and then let them know where they have been shortchanged by their *chi* (personal spirit)."

Putting this advice to work, I reflected on an event which occurred long ago that raises interesting questions for gender imperialism or sisterarchy. In this case, intellectual coercion was applied to achieve intellectual subordination. In a scathing review of an essay of mine, I was pressured by a white woman, Rachel Hoffman, to speak in the voice and manner of her own pedagogical training. She compelled me to dwell on "contemporary controversies" which originate from Eurocentric assumptions and recycled anthropological misrepresentations about Africa. This attempt to embroil me in issues that are incidental to me but central to her is a silencing strategy that is employed to preserve Euro-American dominance of the intellectual realm.

I should make abundantly clear that my reflection on Hoffman is not on the person, but on the strategies that she and others like her employ to perpetuate Euro-American vision and pre-eminence in scholarship, and the basis on which they reproduce imperial relations of power. Lest this reflection be taken as a covert attempt to avoid critique,[11] I should add that I do not subscribe to the view that white women scholars have no right to critique the works of black women scholars, or that whatever black women scholars write is necessarily correct. However, while upholding the authorial right of white women scholars to critique, I want to explore the motivational basis of these critiques so as to ascertain what is involved when whiteness critiques the experiences of its marginalized other.[12] Implicated as we are in a racialized global economic structure of dominance, such an investigation is crucial since it ensures that the resultant critiques produced by white women do not conceal a colonizing agenda. While it is true that not all white women's critiques are imperialistic, we have to establish a procedure to weed out hostile, colonizing ones from those that both inform and enrich.

Thus, following the idea that there is something to learn from hostile critiques, I set out to discover who Hoffman is, and was surprised to learn she was just an ordinary graduate student. Having said that, I should add, not polemically, that Hoffman became a very important metaphor for the colonizing attitudes that I and many women of color encounter from white female colleagues in academia as we strive to articulate and bring elements of our cultural, social, and political consciousness to our theoretical work. Although just a student at the time she wrote the piece, Hoffman already exhibited the sorts of imperialistic attitudes that her senior, professionally established white "sisters" display towards women of color. Usually hidden by masks of collegiality, this subterranean attitude becomes evident when the works of women of African ancestry either are virulently and publicly critiqued as naive, as mine was, and then indicted for missing the more (always unspecified) important theoretical issues, or are represented as "descriptive" and in need of being elevated to a theoretical level.[13]

At the time I "met" her on the pages of *African Art*, Hoffman lived in what would be perceived in Nigeria as "God's own kingdom" (the United States of America) and plush Los Angeles to boot. She had reviewed the *Heroic Figures* exhibition catalogue to which I had contributed the essay, "Overcoming Form-Content Tensions in Appreciating African Art Forms" (1988). The *Heroic Figures* exhibition was organized by the Africanist French art historian, the late Jacqueline Fry, for the Agnes Etherington Art Gallery, Queen's

University, Canada. It complemented the Canadian African Studies Association (CASA) conference, whose 1988 theme was "Domination, Resistance and Liberation." By inviting me to submit an article, Fry wanted to make a statement about domination and resistance, namely, that it is by creating spaces to encourage the flourishing of marginalized voices that domination could be defeated.

In choosing my topic, I addressed an attitude repeatedly encountered in North America and which I believe obstructs understanding and appreciation of Africa's art. For some "inexplicable" reason, one finds that what is African is almost always denigrated as illogical and incomprehensible to a broad section of the Canadian and American public.

From my position as an African and one whose culture's artifacts have continually been devalued as "strange, exotic representations" by Western audiences, I believed that if Africans are seriously to challenge the underlying resistance to deeper understanding, we must explore its epistemological basis to determine for ourselves what genuine problems there may be (Boahen 1987; Enekwe 1987; Akpabot 1986). We must ascertain to what degree a resolution of the problem of appreciation requires formal-stylistic and contextual-cultural information. Before accusing the audience of racism, it seemed more prudent first to explore whether or not genuine cognitive problems exist. My analysis led me to conclude that a synthesis is necessary if viewers are to avoid the kind of puzzlement that over-reliance on one component may bring (Flores 1985:27-41).[14] Context is critical, but there has to be a clear idea of the artifact's stylistics and form.

Since two main epistemological approaches, formalism and contextualism, have been the predominant approaches to understanding,[15] an evaluation of the efficacy of both seemed an appropriate place from which to begin demystifying cross-cultural appreciation. In retrospect, I realized that I laid myself open to criticism by adhering to the prescribed number of pages. The problem was not that the crucial argument cannot be made in that number of pages. Rather, the operative modalities of white intellectualism ascribes ignorance to black women. Its criteria of scholastic assessment require black women in academia to prove our knowledge and intelligence each time a white person happens along.

In my ardent desire to engage in a discussion of my culture's artifacts, I had forgotten I was no longer residing in Nigeria, where the intelligence of a black person is taken for granted. I had naively forgotten I was in North America, where the sexist and racially slanted academic environment is one in which white people, particularly men, are taken seriously, even when speaking about things of which they are ignorant (Danto 1988:18-32). In my irrepressible desire to speak, to participate in intellectual discourse, I had forgotten the racial sub-texts and narratives of the arena. I had ignored that African women like myself are not supposed to know, hence should not participate in intellectual discourse without obsequiously paying homage to the white gods and goddesses of the profession. Thus, the required proof of our knowledge in the Western structure of whiteness is our official declaration of our colonial servitude; the cost of our entrance and participation is intellectual and gender enslavement.

In her review, published in 1989, Hoffman was not expecting a philosophical argumentation on any area of African arts. The review's tone was stern. Hoffman reprimanded me for not being "familiar with the current (that is, Western) scholarship"; for failing to "give the reader any real sense of contemporary controversies"; and for producing an essay on themes that virtually every publication in the field for the past twenty years had addressed. According to her, my treatment of the contextualist approach as an outsider's and my "categorical segregation of the formalist/contextualist camps" were all rhetorical devices that were "hardly insightful or innovative." "The form/content dichotomy," she asserted, "does a disservice to the novice [for it] suggest[s] that there are but two angles." As she derisively saw it, my "generalizations are patronizing, a disposition easily discernible by followers of *any* scholarly route." The problem, Hoffman conjectured, results from my "not being trained in art historical method"; the danger she feared is that my "interpretations may misrepresent artistic motivations and compromise artists, authors, and readers alike."

Before ending on the outraged note that the essay is "specious and labored," Hoffman had deprecatorily called it a "'how to' manual for appreciating African art"; she had stated that she "was provoked and insulted by judgments...about [two types of] Ibibio *ekpo* masks" as disgustingly ugly and aesthetically sensitive and appealing; she had dismissed as presumptuous my contention that many Western museum visitors are confused and perplexed by African art; she had consistently underscored the idea that I was a novice, and she had suggested that I was hardly suited to participate in a historical discourse of African art.

Authorial Arrogance in Knowledge Production

When I first read her "Heroic Figure" review in 1990, I had dismissed it, having assumed that Hoffman was an old-time colonial anthropologist indignant that her textual trophies had been ignored. Knowing the politics in the Africanist field and the gate-keeping role of reviews, the haughty outraged voice I heard resonated with the fear of the possible disruption of a dyadic patron/subordinate relationship that prevails in the field. The mannerisms and omniscient tone of the review reflected that of white male gatekeepers who valorize a preferred writing style, and who position "the literature" (from which the writings of a large number of African scholars are excluded) as the only creditable source of knowledge. Having emulated these mannerisms of privileged white male professors, Hoffman projected an image of the expert who, as she also mentioned, is aware of all the main issues in the literature for the past two decades.

Given Hoffman's emphasis on "the literature," an emphasis that treats the written word as the pre-eminent source of knowledge, it was clear that she viewed the lived experiences and orally preserved knowledge of many African peoples as irrelevant. Pre-emptorily positioning herself as the legitimizing authority of both my lived experience and art historical knowledge on Africa, she regally asserts her authority in the field.

Hoffman's imperial response raises important questions about authorial arrogance in the production of knowledge of others' realities, and the role of an imperial power relationship in the subversion of knowledge. Consider her contestation of my claim that many Western museum visitors are often confused and perplexed by the strange African mode of representation. In hastily dismissing it as a presumption, Hoffman unwittingly denied the 1977 findings of a Winnipeg Art Gallery survey of visitors to its African art exhibition which revealed that a significant number of the visitors were indeed puzzled and perplexed by what they described as a "strange" mode of representation (Fry 1979:535-552). That the Winnipeg 1977 findings are neither atypical nor outdated is seen when one enters into a serious discussion with the non-specialist North American audience, and in some cases with members of the specialist public.[16]

As is usual in the dynamics of domination, Hoffman instinctively challenged the validity of my claims by assuming the omniscient role of an expert. Having "placed" me in a position of intellectual otherness, she saw only ignorance in my African female identity and loudly proclaimed that fact. In the process, however, she ignored the social implications of her white privileged identity and the access to certain social arenas it either offered or denied her. Caught by the dominance ideology of white intellectualism, she failed to realize that her authorial identity as a white art historian removes her from contexts where racist questions, narratives, and stories are posed to Africans by the general North American public.[17] Her absence from such arenas signals her "otherness" and "places" *her* out of touch with this cutting edge of the public's racism. Hence, regardless of her breadth of training and mastery of the literature, her white interpretive framework lacks this vital information.

Ironically, in dismissing the validity of my claim, Hoffman perpetuates and directly challenges the existence of racism in North America. Indirectly, the epistemic effect of the challenge is to assert that white people have full knowledge of Africa's cultural artifacts. This falsehood and racialization of knowledge begins because Hoffman hegemonically positioned herself and members of her society as being in possession of all the facts. Within this illusory cognitive terrain, the logic of imperialism and racialized knowledge reconstructs reality to suit a white supremacist view of it. These reconstitutions permit her to disregard the social implication of my African identity and the access it provides to social encounters where depreciatory views about Africa are insensitively expressed. Because she is unwilling to admit and interrogate her own racism as well as that of her culture, Hoffman's white interpretive framework propels her to racialize knowledge and to foolishly oppose any suggestion that white people (including scholars) may be ignorant about Africa's art, culture, and life.[18]

The very suggestion that the viewing public knows calls attention to two false assumptions underpinning the imperial authorial position. The first is that Africa's artistic intentions are transparently simple and can easily be discerned by any white observer, regardless of level of expertise. The second is that such observations correctly reflect the intended artistic rationale. Now, when the Winnipeg case is viewed against these false assumptions, we read Hoffman as saying either that the intended artistic rationale of African artifacts is confusing, or that to say that one does not know (as in the Winnipeg case) is to imply that one knows. To the extent that a contradiction follows in both cases, Hoffman's contestation is not only misguided but incoherent.

Such incoherence is important not because it underscores the implausibility of Hoffman's assertion, but because it points to a backdrop of powerful racial narratives, stereotypes, and assumptions that underpin knowledge production in North America. Even at a time when feminist and postmodernist interrogations are deconstructing and reshaping the mode of knowledge production, these imageries at the heart of whiteness remain exceptionally powerful, fueling the imperialistic need to assert white superiority. In the manner of a self-fulfilling prophecy, white intellectual superiority is proven by bouncing it off the manufactured image of "naive Africans." In like manner, Hoffman exploits the "ignorant African" stereotype to set off her intellectually superior response. Not unlike the white male professor who gave me a lower grade because he "didn't know you did analytic philosophy in Nigeria," Hoffman dismissed my essay on the supposition that the "naive African woman" could not possibly know African art history since she has not been tutored by those whom western scholars (the legitimizing authorities) consider knowledgeable. In short, Hoffman fed off her ignorance to proclaim the ignorance of the "Nigerian sculptor turned philosopher."

White racism is such a normalized fact of North American reality that many do not seem to realize how deeply immersed they are in it, nor how much they manifest the tendencies. It is so much a part of the conceptual apparatus through which reality is perceived and knowledge is produced that white beneficiaries do not care to grasp its oppressive nature fully. Their reluctance derives from the fact that to interrogate racism is to interrogate their very identity, to shake the very center of their normative order, and to forego their privileges.

Gender imperialism is consequently misrecognized because the oppressive attitudes of white women *are* a normal part of that unnamed, colonizing reality. Further complicating the issue is the fact that white women generally mask their power by cleverly blaming the patriarchal order that stigmatizes blacks as deviant. Distancing themselves from its oppressive character, they vilify the patriarchal structure yet gratuitously draw their power, social status, and identity from it. This refusal to acknowledge their complicity in the structure enables them to forget the ways they are advantaged by the system and become partners in oppression. "Forgetfulness" allows them to ignore the fact that the only reason they are institutionally privileged and superior to women of color is that they have been defined as such by the white patriarchal system they spend so much time vilifying.

White women's collusion in patriarchal forms of power and the relation of that power to imperialism is receiving increased attention as African women and other women of color engage in feminist theorizing (Amadiume 1987; Amos and Parmar 1984:3-19; Mohanty, Russo and Torres 1991; Aguilar 1989:338-344; Terborg-Penn 1981:301-315).[19] In these times of critical reexamination of traditional assumptions and structures of knowledge, one way to broaden our understanding of the intersection of racism and sexism is to shift from the exceedingly narrow focus on patriarchy and its articulations to the broader issue of imperialism and its manifestations. Focusing on social contexts of power provides a useful perspective from which to observe the shifting, interlocking nature of racism and patriarchy and the impact of the two in hitherto unexamined sites. Concealed racialized attitudes of domination are revealed in social and intellectual interaction, even as the perpetrators (some of whom are white feminist liberals) have donned their "politically correct" garb. Naturally, what gives them away is the instinctual stereotyping and denial of intelligence to anyone who is not socially perceived as white. That they always assume a divine right of leadership regardless of the inappropriateness of contexts blatantly reveals the underlying imperialist ideology of our white "sisters"[20] and of feminism.

It pays to note that gender imperialism or sisterarchy manifests itself in academia where white women erect barriers to listening to and perceiving their sisters of color. Our "white sisters" adopt a way of hearing without listening; they hear just what they want to. Deploying their internalized supremacist stereotypes, narratives, and images, "our sisters" quickly make judgments about our intellectual capacities and attitudinal behaviors and screen us out. This elimination process is demonstrated by the "progressive" white sister who saw one of the serving staff in Moghassi. Her "white gaze" had automatically projected ignorance, servitude, and incompetence on the Other, clearing the way for her to assert her rights and imperiously demand what she felt was her due.

Racialization of Knowledge: Attitudes of Domination

Ifi Amadiume tells a revealing story of a young white sister whose goal in studying social anthropology was to travel to Zimbabwe to teach the local women how to organize (1987:7). In her desire to fulfil her dreams, our intrepid teacher had pre-emptively constructed a dyadic relationship between herself and her Zimbabwean sisters. Drawing from her affluent First World geopolitical location, she imperiously assigned herself a leadership role through imagining that Zimbabwean women lacked organizational skills. Lost in her narcissistic reveries, she neglected to study Zimbabwean history; hence she missed the vital data that her erstwhile students were veterans of a fifteen-year war of liberation. Through their incredible fortitude, organizational skills, and participatory role in the liberation struggle, Zimbabwean women with their men had successfully wrested independence from the repressive, racist white minority regime of Ian Smith.

Imperialism and oppression are fostered by lack of respect for the history and cultural identity of others. Within academia, this lack of respect persists as a result of a proliferation of pernicious images, notions, concepts, and ideas about Africa that are freely disseminated by elementary and high school teachers, media pundits, museum officials, scholars, and theorists in their characterizations, descriptions, and interpretations of materials about Africa. In one revealing example, E.F. Fair (1993) asked his students, primarily white and middle class, to describe their images and ideas of "Africa" and "African." He received a litany of negative descriptions:

> "Africa" is "a basket case," "jungle-covered," "big game, safari," "AIDS-ridden," "torn by apartheid," "weird," "brutal," "tribal," "underdeveloped," and "black"; "Africans" "have AIDS," are "lazy," "crazy," "savage," "exotic," "sexually active," "backward," "tribal," "primitive," and again "black." (Onwudiwe 1995:5).

The enduring nature of this stock of stereotypical descriptions derives in part from their constant reinforcement in both educational and media settings. As

Ebere Onwudiwe cogently argued, the persistence of these images are not unintentional, since an "abundant body of work in sociology, intellectual history, social psychology, and cognitive psychology of the nature of images and world-views" prove that such images mediate and impact phenomenally on important policy decisions (1995:87).

With this experience as a guide, we can see that dominance manifests itself within academia and feminist circles when white women avail themselves of these condescending images in their establishment of what they take to be African women, and their establishment of what they take to be the appropriate ground rules of social and intellectual interaction. Evidence of this occur in the way African women are automatically constructed as backward, and their progress is represented as depending on the magnanimity and superior intelligence of their white sisters. That Amadiume's intrepid female teacher is a student too, who like Hoffman, underscores the role of academia in perpetuating racialized imperialistic attitudes. The systemic nature of this process undermines the feminist idea of global sisterhood, since the untheorized way in which we are "sisters" is implicated in a mistress/subordinate model of relationship, not in the consanguinal family relationship model with which we are familiar.

At the transnational global level, sisterhood functions as a metaphor for white women's subjugation of Third World women. A further complication of this glossing of the subordinate ideology at the heart of the feminist sisterhood is that we miss how white women's power derives substantially from the same patriarchal ideology that they claim to be subverting. Thus, as beneficiaries of this state of affairs, they need to acknowledge the centrality of the patriarchal structure in their present identity, and to recognize that the professional competence automatically ascribed to them actually derives from racially-based patriarchal privileges. In a situation in which they, rather than African women themselves, are the definers of African women's reality, there is need to name the nature of that relationship, given that it undermines the legitimacy of assertions about the primacy of gender equality in women's solidarity.

Regardless of the anti-racist, anti-patriarchal declarations by our progressive white sisters, many of them regularly perform acts of erasure, "screening out" women of color, effectively dismissing and devaluing the racial, gender, cultural, as well as the authorial identities of these women. It is as mimicry that our intrepid teacher's delusion and Hoffman's adversarial stance are significant. They are emblematic of scores of similar imperial acts in North America, including those used by white men to keep white women from boardrooms. What is most interesting about the formal character of this "screening out" process that Chinua Achebe, the Nigerian literary theorist, referred to as "tactics of evasion" is not just its imperial character, but its pervasiveness in academia. On the one hand, the "tactics of evasion" (including those of white women) signals the racialized denial of legitimacy to non-Euroethnic categories and issues which, from our marginal cultural location, we know to be salient. And on the other hand, it forcefully brings to attention the sorts of flawed issues that are disseminated as knowledge about Africa in academia.

The racialization of knowledge that occurs in these evasive tactics oppressively halts any attempt to re-think colonizing attitudes by devaluing the cognitive worth of issues that arise outside the structures of whiteness. "Screening out" any suggestion that is potentially damaging to the white intellectual normative order, the mental reversals feverishly work to reassert white superiority in knowledge *in a manner that* shores up white authority in the production of knowledge about Africa, and *in a manner that* exploits the image of "the ignorant African" endemic in North America's popular culture. As the Moghissi incident illuminates, the process involves both falsification and then fabrication of the nature, character, and experiences of Others. That such identity reconstructions stereotype and misrepresent people of color is consistent with the desire to foreclose discussions on power and domination. As an essential process in "naturalizing" knowledge as a white experience, the fabrication justifies white control of and dominance in knowledge. It entrenches and normalizes white power, privileges, and world-view, and it normalizes all others as abnormal or deviant. Imperialism thrives on knowledge racialization.

The epistemological difficulties in Hoffman's conception of knowledge notwithstanding, it is also important to highlight the racist elements at play. Because Hoffman and the others she typifies *consciously and subconsciously believe in* and promote only European American interests,[21] priorities, and agendas, they narrowly define knowledge in terms that exclude many interests that African scholars may have but which do not overlap with European American interests. The effect of this "border patrol" is to preclude the free discussion of ideas that are potentially disruptive of the power, dominance, and prestige of patriarchs and their minions. Thus, for this reason, in the white imperialist model on which Hoffman framed her conception, knowledge is *naturally* a fixed hierarchical structure rather than a shifting, reflexive, on-going activity of interrogation and counter-interrogation. Its white intellectual vision *naturally* occupies the archimedean point and issues directives that others ought to follow in the production of knowledge of non-Euroethnic cultures.

In this implicitly racialized cognitive scheme, there is a correspondingly narrow conception of knowledge, of what it does, and of who ought to be the principal spokespeople. Any issue that challenges the structure's prescribed natural order, or threatens its legitimacy and hierarchical order, academically appears as *unnatural* and is subsequently "normalized" as pointless. In addition, the existence of other bodies of literature and experiences are rarely cited and routinely disregarded, a strategy that speaks much more powerfully than words about racialized attitudes and regimentation of thought. Against this background, it is certainly understandable, though not excusable, why a Hoffman would appeal *only* to Western literature and to categories of interpretation and issues of interest to Western scholars to blunt the legitimacy of issues that would be of interest to an African scholar. The appeal is a mechanism that tacitly penalizes deviations from its intellectual norm by ignoring that my scholarly interest could have originated from an alternative body of literature and experiences of which they are ignorant.

It is disturbing, though entirely in tune with the dynamics of imperial power, that globally privileged white women and their men who are desirous to learn about Africa's cultural life come to the inquiry with attitudes of condescension. In a crucial way, they ignore their outsider status and the theoretical importance for African aesthetics and artistic evaluation of deliberative discourses on art in African languages in an intellectual foray of disputations or such printed works as E. L. Lasebikan's "Tone in Yoruba Poetry" (1955), Chinua Achebe's *Things Fall Apart* (1958), Adeboye Babalola's *The Form and Content of Yoruba Ijala* (1966), Okot p'Bitek's *Song of Lawino* (1966), and Ben Enwonwu's "The African View of Art and Some Problems Facing the African Artist" (1968). Racism surfaces when white scholars refuse to engage the reality of African languages and to recognize the existence of another body of literature. Imperialism encourages lack of sensitivity to Africans' concerns and interests and compels white scholars to ignore that their own concerns, processes of documentation, and interpretations might implicitly be colonializing. To be sure, ethical problems are raised by the impact of racism on knowledge and knowledge production, especially when ideas articulated by Africans are appropriated and used without citation by white scholars to frame their own intellectual work.[22]

With Africa as one example, the larger issue of this investigation is that of white women scholars wittingly and unwittingly having a colonial impact on world societies through the globalization of feminist scholarship. If critical re-thinking and self-reflexiveness are absent in their interpretation of African, First Nation, Native American, Chinese, or Latina reality, attitudes of domination will continue to surface, reproduce oppression, and oppressively erase the realities of Others. While disregarding their perspective of power and privilege, and oblivious to their positionality, white women like Hoffman continually invoke a framework of domination which they use oppressively to silence and marginalize. The suspicions of the general Canadian and American public (my students included) that white scholars may, in fact, be engaged in Western aesthetic imperialism have often compelled them to ask for the insider viewpoint of how Africans really relate to their work. Such skepticism is an important step towards examining the outsider status of theorizers of African reality and the ways in which these culturally dislocated theorizations reinforce racist attitudes, reinscribe white dominance, and control definitions of academic scholarship.

Ikwe na aka felu nkpili aka
obulu mgba

When a handshake extends beyond the elbow
it has turned into a wrestling match.

In teaching people to recognize when collegial jostling turns into an aggressive or hostile act, the proverb emphasizes the importance of critically evaluating actions that may first appear to be innocuous. Whatever else it might purport to be, a handshake that extends beyond the elbow, such as Hoffman's review, is definitely not a handshake. When read within the context of the history and politics in African studies and through the racialized lens of American reality, Hoffman's review highlights the invidious stratagems of appropriation that relate to how whiteness is inscribed, and how "subalterns" are forcibly ejected from arenas where discourses of their realities occur. It may seem that this focus on a student is excessive, but it is necessary, since it directs attention to the primary basis on which the dynamics of imperial power enter into knowledge construction and mold the character of individuals in academia. Through it, we see more clearly the connection between white intellectualism and domination, and the way in which gender imperialism exploits and thrives on the patriarchal structures of whiteness.

The stratagem of ejection practiced by scholars in the intellectual structures of knowledge has a converse side: the invasion of conceptual space. In a penetrating critique of the complex epistemological and methodological problems of data-quality control (or ethnographer bias) in anthropological research, Maxwell Owusu (1978) demonstrates how this invasion occurs and its import on scholarship. Using the work of key anthropologists, he showed that lack of familiarity with the phonetic, lexical, and idiomatic expressions of African languages resulted in errors of translation that misrepresented the cultural logic of those societies. Despite Owusu's critique, Africanist art historians continue to reproduce the errors he identified sixteen years earlier, as evidenced in Sarah Brett-Smith's acclaimed doctoral study of Bamana art. Published in 1994 by Cambridge University Press, the book is vitiated by serious translational and interpretive problems. After five years "in Mali working primarily with the Bamana...the Malinke, Bobo, Senufo, Minianka, and Dogon peoples" (1), Brett-Smith mixes up tonal meanings and takes expressions too literally. In his review, Kassim Kone (1996) reveals that she reinterprets "to become impotent" into "to become a woman" (91), a twist that erroneously makes womanhood a defect of malehood. *Manyokolon*, which in the carving context means "detail," is sexualized as "penis" when Brett-Smith relies on Frenchman Gerard Dumestre's interpretation; *Kulukutuma*, which means "rough," becomes "nude"; and *walaki*, ("to remove the bark,") is retranslated into "disrobe" (1994:188). Seemingly oblivious to the tonal variations of *wulu* as "dog" and *wulu* as "penis," Brett-Smith conflates the two homonyms and constructs her Bamana subject, Nyamaton, as using the word "dog" to refer analogically to the "penis" (210). The confusion is stretched to the point of incredulity when, in the endnote, she theorizes that the Bamana think this way about the penis-dog analogy that *she* had constructed (320).

Serious theoretical consequences follow Brett-Smith's obsessive sexualization of the Bamana cultural logic, the most important of which is the injection of the Oedipus complex into the society through conceiving of the earth as a primeval mother and the termite mounds as her sex. Her contention that a new *Komotigi* or *Komo* leader swears "an oath on a red termite mound, and rinses his mouth with a liquid containing seeds found in the fine soil taken from the interior of the mound" (122), offers a picture of a son's access to a mother's vagina, together with the connotation of oral sex. Not only does Brett-Smith turn the entire oath-taking ceremony into a bizarre activity, but she also justifies her conflation of the termite mound and the female vagina—and the representation of the latter as a sacred site—by insisting that "[i]n the Mande world...men take their most profound oath by invoking their mother's sex" (122). But according to Kone, the female sex organ, most especially a mother's, is something that "no Bamana or Malinke man would mention [or think about], even in drunkenness or madness" (1996:91) for fear of "the *nyama* it carries when pronounced by a man" (103).

Kone's many disagreements with Brett-Smith converge on the triple ground of "methodological approach, content, and certain translations and analyses" that Owusu identified sixteen years earlier. The resultant manipulation of meanings, ideas, and cultural logic that occurs constitutes the sort of predatory invasion of African world-view that Owusu raised in his critique of ethnographical practices, and which routinely occurs in the intellectual structures of whiteness after Africans have been ejected from the domain. That a highly reputable press published the book, replete with all its mistranslations and avoidable errors, is a testimony to the ways publishers serve the imperial objectives of the structures of whiteness.[23] To put the problem into context, no press would approve the publication of a manuscript by an African scholar on the art and culture of the United States if it contained a tenth of the errors made by Brett-Smith. It is unimaginable that Cambridge University Press would publish a scholarly study that represents the American world as one in which men routinely swear by invoking the sexual act, and that claims that the United States' presidents taking their inaugural oath by placing their hand on a black book simulates the sexual act.

Another way in which the occupation of Africa's conceptual space is achieved occurs when white scholars project themselves as the interpreters of African societies. Simon Ottenberg, the American anthropologist, did this for over a decade when he styled himself "the sole interpreter of Afikpo Igbo culture," simultaneously identifying the American art historian, Robert Farris Thompson, as the pioneer of the study of African aesthetic consciousness.[24] In both cases Ottenberg strategically refused to call into question the epistemological quality and extent of what he knew, preferring instead to cut off any interrogation as to what he knows. In the first case, this strategy enables Ottenberg to erase his Afikpo collaborators who had guided and taught him what little he knows about the interpretive scheme of their culture, and in the second case, he overlooked the efforts of writers like Lasekan, Lasebikan, Achebe, Oba Laoye Kinni—the Timi of Ede, Babalola, and p'Bitek, who collectively contributed to an understanding of their cultures' aesthetic schemes for more than a decade before Thompson wrote "The Aesthetic of the Cool." (Thompson 1973:41-43,64-67).

In another pathway to conceptual invasion, exhortations about "truth," "objectivity," and "knowledge" in African studies sometimes function as ruses for the enthronement of Eurocentric views that have as their goal the maintenance of an imperial order. While in residence as a postdoctoral fellow at the National Museum of African Art in Washington, D.C. in 1989, I asked one of the curators to introduce me to a leading American scholar of Igbo art who was also in residence at the museum. I was eager to meet this white male scholar who was working on the arts of my people. However, on learning my Igbo identity and the subject matter of my postdoctoral research, this man aggressively interrogated me on the objectives of my form/content essay, implying that it fell short of the appropriate standard of truth, objectivity, and knowledge. He chastised me for failing to rely on the works of a white male anthropologist who had written on the Ibibio. Then, shifting to the topic of my postdoctoral research, spirit manifestation, he demanded to know whether I had ever *seen* a "mask," and whether I had *photographs* of "masks." His line of interrogation suggested that "seeing a mask" and "having photographs of masks" were the elements that constituted good research and scholarship. I responded that I was very familiar with *mmuo* since they were a vital part of *my* everyday reality, and that I could easily obtain photographs from archivists in Onitsha when I needed them. At this juncture, the scholar informed me that *he* had done all there was to do in his investigation of the subject and nothing else could be contributed.

While this exchange preceded my discovery of Hoffman's review, its logic of invasion was powerfully linked to the criticisms of the latter white female colleague. Both attempted to delegitimize orality, erasing the voices of people whose experiences were being appropriated. Both substituted themselves as interpreters, insisting that only the works of white scholars of whom they approved could plausibly be used. Both made much of the fact of the standards of scholarship in knowledge production. And both tried to claim that white scholars have conclusively addressed all the pertinent issues that may be raised. In fact, the close similarity of their operational moves exposes a striking link between gender imperialism and patriarchy, and how white women are ideologically implicated in the structure.

Thus, the centrality of African sites of resistance provides the relevant framework from which to examine, identify, and understand the politics of power inherent in the Western intellectual tradition that white women emulate. Such locations expose the disempowering strategies that are disingenuously employed to assert the center/periphery dyadic logic that preserves the intellectual whiteness of academia.[25] To fully understand the nature of white women's collusion in oppressive forms of power, we must continually look to the broader everyday level of life, in which racialization of knowledge surfaces and precedes its genderization. Prodded on by the multi-tiered educational system and its inherent patriarchal logic, the female of the white species comes to an understanding of herself by modeling herself on, and reflecting the image, of her culture's patriarchs. For this reason, Hoffman's graduate student review captured the power dynamics of appropriation that was played out by the white male in the master/subordinate, center/periphery, metropole/colony encounter at the Smithsonian Institution. It shows her carrying on the tradition of dominance by using the flip-side of patriarchal power, matriarchy.

The masculine/dominance character of white intellectualism is inscribed in the ground rules of academic engagement, which participants often unconsciously reflect. Unfamiliar with my background and perceiving me as a bright-eyed youngster, Hoffman had set about *like the white male expert* to assert her expertise and pre-eminence in the field. Without revealing that she herself was a student, she made much of the fact that I was a doctoral student, hence a junior or a "novice" as she denigratingly put it. Like her white male counterpart, she quibbled that I was not trained in art historical method, hence falsely implying that there is *a* method.[26] Narrowly limiting the possible strategies of resistance, she argued from an imperial matriarch's standpoint that my essay lacked art historical merit since it did not combatively engage the CASA conference theme of resistance and domination. Writing in the authorial power-language of the structure of whiteness, Hoffman invoked a mistress/mammy relationship to chastise me roundly for a "specious and labored work," and for presuming to tell Westerners (that is, white people) how to appreciate African art.

With a slight substitution of "maternal" for "master," Hoffman unproblematically emerges as "mistress and gatekeeper of the canon." In her role as a metaphor of white women's colonizing role, her attack is more interesting for the things it left unsaid and for the sub-text of her narrative. The unvoiced commentary states that in a hierarchically structured white intellectual world, African scholars—especially African women—bring down the quality of scholarship, and hence have no business examining issues that white Africanist scholars have purportedly examined and which they have ruled no longer important or interesting. In fact, people from marginalized territories, if they are to be validated, are expected meekly to follow the linear path charted by white scholars, who have limited language and metalinguistic competence in an African language who are theorizing about African realities in the *metropole*. Ensconced in the global power of their metropolitan vantage point, Owusu's critiques are ignored by white scholars who assume that no theoretical reassessment of the field by Africans could possibly bring any special insight.

In the context of imperialistic power relations, sarcasm functions as a tool of chastisement that guards against revisiting old issues. With sisterhood in the background, the barb in Hoffman's review discursively raise questions about the quality of the opposition's scholarship while obfuscating the carefully orchestrated processes of erasure, of appropriation, of colonization, and of another's conceptual space. This is revealed most forcefully in her essay "Objects and Acts" (1995), in which she grapples with the idea that art objects are "conduits" and "dynamic, complex, independent reservoirs of many types of knowledge and power" (56),[27] and in which, following the anticipated retirement of a group of older white male mentors, she is being jockeyed into a leadership position.

From the opening sentence right through to the end of the essay, she leaves no doubt in readers' minds about the identity of her intended audience, and about her conceptual views of Africa and its peoples. She states:

> For more than two decades, theorists and scholars of African art objects have been *pondering how knowledge of Africa can be gained and through what means an understanding of African material culture might be possible*. To whom does knowledge of Africa belong, and what are the most authentic and useful ways of

interpreting and transcribing such knowledge for future generations of think-ers? In the following...I too ask how we may best further *our* understanding of Africa and its art objects. (1995:56; emphasis mine)

As conveyed by the logical structure of her expression, Hoffman does not see Africans as theorists and scholars of African art, nor are they perceived as part of the coterie of scholars to whom she is addressing her thoughts. That this is true becomes clear once the following questions are asked: "What does it really mean for Africans to ponder about how knowledge of Africa can be gained and through what means an understanding of African material culture might be possible?" Again, what does it mean for Africans to ask, "To whom does knowledge of Africa belong?" Indeed, what does it mean for African scholars to claim Africa as a research specimen, and to talk about it as if it is conceptually remote and inhabited by aliens with whom scholars (they in-cluded) cannot engage in intellectual discussion? In exposing both the incoherency and underlying imperial logic implicit in Hoffman's language, attitudes, and assumptions about her audience, we need to first recognize that the excision of Africans from the intellectual domain is already a foregone conclusion. Surreptitiously performed as it is, its value is that it funds the perverse idea that there are no intellectually accomplished Africans with whom to engage in theoretical discussions.

The perversity in Hoffman's assumptions manifests itself in different ways. Without going into the details, consider the three objectives of her argument: First, "to propose that objects can and do act on us; [second] to inquire how an object can be understood cross-culturally; and [third] to suggest what it is about some objects that may differentiate them as masterpieces" (56). The first objective is basically a hegemonic appropriation of what African artists working in the traditional style have always asserted about a class of their works. With regards to the second objective, the author's perplexity about the prospects of cross-cultural understanding retraces tired old arguments that falsely represent African culture as so complex as to be incomprehensible. (While we should note that this justifies for Hoffman why Africans cannot be theoretically engaged as equals, it is remarkable that Africans, in turn, never seem to manifest this problem of cross-cultural understanding that so se-verely tasks the cognitive ability of some American scholars). Lastly, although cast as a legitimate theoretical question, Hoffman's search for criteria whereby to identify masterpieces is driven not by theoretical issues, but by the mon-etary interests of Western collectors concerned with assigning higher value to the objects in their collections.

Cultural appropriation of others' realities, as performed by Hoffman in her essay, is the proof of imperialism. Just as in 1884-1885, imperial relationships are constructed when white theorists and scholars simulate artificial dialogues and controversies on African art after having excluded Africans' views and theorizations about their reality. Evidence of this colonial act emerges in Hoffman's treatment of the ideas of Ibrahim Poudjougou, the Dogon sculptor. In appropriating Poudjougou's statement, Hoffman detaches it from its framework of ideas and assumptions from which its meaningfulness and signification are derived. Relocated to its new environment in America, Poudjougou's culturally dislocated statement is subjected to a battery of readings from ideas gleaned from critical theorist Barbara Hernnstein Smith, sociologist Grant McCracken, Paul Feyerabend, anthropologist Michael Connerton, and philosopher Maurice Merleau-Ponty. In this contrived world, in which only the views of scholars of European descent matter, no attempt is made either to engage the works of any Malian sociologist, anthropologist, historian, critical theorist, or philosopher, or to rely on Dogon explanations. Effectively shorn of its cultural reading, Poudjougou's ineluctable comment becomes a malleable object to be stroked, squeezed, teased, inserted into, and withdrawn from European and European American theories in acts of intellectual masturbation.

Commodification and Power

In *African Perspectives in Colonialism*, Adu Boahen, a leading African historian, contends that economic factors were the most decisive of the forces propelling the colonization of Africa (Boahen 1987:31-32). Imperialism, he argues, had commodification as its goal; it achieved its objective by injecting laissez faire mercantile ideology into its various sites of operation.

Having become the dominant ideology of the world following its acceptance as the definitive feature of modernism and of the capitalist "Free World," mercantilism was read into the intellectual domain in ways that transformed theories, ideas, and knowledge into commodities that could be appropriated, possessed, and traded. In the manner of C. B. McPherson's possessive individuals, scholars became proprietors of their ideas and theories, retaining an inalienable right over them (1962:55) and "owing nothing to society for them" (2). As theories became valued items, they became commodities to be acquired, accumulated, and exchanged for authorial "wealth," namely, intellectual authority. Within this possessive market ideology—ideas, theories, hypotheses—everything is a commodity, everything has market value, everything is available for acquisition, nothing is sacred. As in the present global economic reality, Africa is positioned as an arena for raw materials to feed the intellectual factories of whiteness.

Unbridled market competition spawns monopolies that subvert individuals' and cultures' control of their resources and powers. Relentlessly striving for market control, the monopolistic impulse facilitates the oppressive foreclosures of competing arenas of discourse as a way of preserving control. Within this framework, authorial wealth is accumulated by setting one's self up as *the* expert. Of critical importance in intellectual commodification and its underlying acquisitive spirit is the surreptitious silencing of competing voices, especially those with the power to unmask the privilege. Commodification stipulates what "subalterns" from previously colonized societies can and cannot discuss and critique. It does this by defining a relation of ownership and control over appropriated experiences. The inherent possessiveness of this relation further fans the exploitative desire for control, which in turn fuels the need for dominance. The effect of intellectual commodification, as Trinh Minh Ha rightly observed about anthropology in *Woman Native Other*, is that it "creates a conversation of 'us' with 'us' about 'them'... a conversation in which 'them' (Africans) is silenced" (1989)·

By untangling the colonizing attitudes and processes at play in the West, one comes to understand the reasons for the linearity of Western thought and scholarship. One learns that old, longstanding stereotypes and prejudices about Africa's material culture still drive the intellectual engine and generate much of today's Africanists' art historical controversies. Spinning on the axis of tradition, Western scholars and theorists still puzzle about how to understand Africa and its material culture; they discover that assumptions of tribality still haunt their intellectual imagination; they find that collectors' search for masterpieces directs their research agenda and museum exhibitions; and they see that ritual rather than creativity still assigns value to collections. In fact, a close reading of Adrian A. Gerbrands' history of African art studies (1990) and a grasp of the central issue of Joseph Cornet's "African Art and Authenticity" and Sidney Kasfir's "African Art and Authenticity: A Text with a Shadow" (1992) reveal the strikingly close parallel between old research questions and new ones, indicating that genuine progress has not exactly been made (1990).

The enormous power differential in the positions of those at the center/metropole and those at the margins/colonies has a corresponding impact on the sorts of issues that are perceived to be of interest to members of the two oppositional worlds. It is generally the case that what is important to the marginalized, the dispossessed, and the oppressed is hardly ever important to the centered, affluent imperialist. For while the marginalized may want to challenge the conditions of their marginalization, the imperialist is concerned with covering up such investigations: first by diversion, pointing out how much they have done to help, and second, by creating a tightly patrolled arena in which the marginalized voice is alienated and silenced. The Nigerian archeologist Ekpo Eyo knows this well: as the former director of the Nigerian Museums, he constantly encountered such condescension in the international arena. He recounted that the exhibition, *Treasures of Ancient Nigeria: Legacy of Two Thousand Years*, which the Nigerian Museum organized in 1980, was conceived partly to challenge the imperialistic idea that "one race has a monopoly on creativity over time and space" and partly to expose the falsity in the idea that Europeans were the inventors of art by showing that the "early history of (Nigerian) art is coterminous with the early phase of Greek art" (1990:113).

The refusal by white intellectual structures to acknowledge that Africans can have legitimate concerns that differ from whites' research priorities is the final stage in the racialization and total domination of knowledge. In a plantation-type framework, only whites are deemed intellectually competent to articulate the important theoretical issues in scholarship. This bars Africans from participating in the arena where production of knowledge about their own cultural objects is taking place. Relegated to the sidelines, their role is limited to mindlessly shouting approbations or to providing raw materials for white intellectual consumption. That the rich aesthetic insights in the writings of Babalola, Achebe, and Lasebikan, that Bamidele Arowogun passed on to Lamidi Fakeye, that Acholi elders bequeathed to p'Bitek, that are sometimes discussed at age-grade meetings, or that Poudjougou's Dogon culture provides in comprehending his statements are never seriously validated, while white intuitions about African artistic schemes are privileged, speaks to a politics of delegitimation that rejects Others' conceptualization of their own realities.

So when a Hoffman goes to Mali for three to six months of "field trip" to discover the aesthetic categories of Dogon art objects and "to investigat(e) the mechanisms through which... outsiders might know and come to understand this entity" (1995:56), I see another Mungo Park come to "discover" the hidden secrets of the "dark continent." When she voraciously collects "raw" materials for investigation, I see a multinational conglomerate exploitatively accumulating Third World resources for First World comfort. I see another confirmation of the "center-periphery economic doctrine" in which countries on the periphery (the colonies) supply the center (the *metropole*) with its conceptual raw materials. When she clinically examines Dogon artists and ponders to whom knowledge of Africa belongs, I see a Conradian Marlow in the Congo seeing people who "howled and leaped...and made horrid faces" (106). When she spins out her interpretations of Dogon art object scripted through the interpretive categories of Western cultural reality, I see the dumping of intellectual toxic waste that is fast obliterating Africa's categories of interpretation. I see a process of investigation that, unlike the scientific logic of discovery, proceeds from a negative focal point and is implicated in the assumptions and legacies of colonialism. I see a scholarship in which Africans have been and are still being judged as sub-human.

O uwa mebi
bu na onye ilo benarilu ndi nwe ozu na akwa

It is a sign of a world gone awry
that the outsider cries louder than the bereaved.

In "The Race for Theory," Barbara Christian describes narrative forms, stories, riddles, and proverbs as forms of theorizing employed by "people of color (who) have always theorized" (1987:52). She characterizes this theoretical mode of speaking as "[p]ithy language that unmasks the power relations of (our) world" (52). In the African world of which I best know, we say that the world has gone to ruins when an outsider cries louder than the bereaved. We never call it hypocrisy; we tactfully save the hypocrite's face.

So, when a white American-Africanist scholar feels insulted and provoked at an African's unflattering description of some cultural artifacts, it is not just a charge of misrepresentation on *the African's* part, it is a public proclamation by the white scholar of his or her all-knowing vision. Since the issue of authorial knowledge is central to this investigation of gender imperialism and since the structure of whiteness projects itself as having a special understanding of African art and culture, it is time to examine how white imperialism works through its interpretive scheme to override Africa's aesthetic schemes.[28]

Consider the intended artistic objective of the category of *ekpo* masks I described as disgustingly. Within the Ibibio aesthetic universe, these works are consciously made to be ugly, hideous, and frightening. Given this aesthetic ideal, carvers liberally employ facial contortions that evoke congenital cranial deformities and other deformities like leprosy. These aberrant features are referentially located in the societal category of ugliness, and are stigmatized as horrendous, undesirable, and taboo. When these ugly types of *Ekpo* figures are smeared with *uto* (a ritual paint that is deemed to have magical properties) and then viewed against the juridical power and executioner role of *Ekpe Ikpa Ukot* (Man's Leopard Society), the visceral effect resonates at the psychological level (Umoetuk 1985:40-56; 1985). They instill psychic terror which, depending on the location of the observer, may be real or feigned. Within this sociohistorical scheme, the appropriate aesthetic response of revulsion indicates recognition of the awesome persona of the *Ekpo* spirit; it marks respect for the underlying artistic, political, and social significance of the *Ekpo* institution.

A white scholar's umbrage in seeing these works characterized as "disgustingly ugly" can only derive from a conceptual scheme that blunts the fierce history of *Ekpo* obliterates the social implications attached to facial distortions, and obfuscates the function of the principle of ugliness in Ibibio art. Thus, unconscious of its theoretical implications, a Hoffman-type outrage is proof that one is employing a culturally inappropriate aesthetic reference frame. The utilization occurs because the evaluator has illicitly substituted a Western scheme for the appropriate Ibibio aesthetic scheme. The substitution goes unnoticed because the response is carefully positioned as sensitive and generous—in short, "politically correct." From an African location, however, the response is brilliantly evasive. Its hollowness rings through the conceptual shift that emasculates the *Ekpo's* power, and thus transforms it into a passive, nonthreatening object. The castration severs the *Ekpo* from its rich sociological history and relocates it within the white aesthetic framework, where it becomes a wooden object of visuality that meets with Hoffman's "sensitive" response.

The replacement of Ibibio artistic intentionality with a white aesthetic scheme underpins Hoffman's denial of the ugliness of *Ekpo*. The inscription of white aestheticism onto the Ibibio aesthetic scheme automatically subverts the creativity of *Ekpo* and transforms Africa's cultural artifacts into benign objects to be viewed with maternal familiarity and benevolence. That Hoffman's feelings of insult really derive from an inappropriate gaze is revealed when we challenge her inability to confront, grasp, and respect the aesthetic implication of ugliness and its role in fashioning the *ekpo's* identity. For one so concerned about the welfare of *Ekpo*, Hoffman seems not to know that to describe such *Ekpos* as "disgustingly ugly" is not to put them down but to validate their aesthetic ideal. It is to recognize their mystique, and to understand that they derive from the exploration of the principle of ugliness that aims to terrify. That Hoffman needs to be *told* that is proof that she never accorded aesthetic primacy to the Ibibio scheme. Had she done so, Hoffman would have acknowledged the history and executioner functions of *Ekpo*, recognized that in the Ibibio creative scheme, ugliness embodies an ambiguous element which, in the evaluative realm, presents a positive review as a "negative" evaluation. (This sort of aesthetic ambiguity resonates in African-American culture's use of "bad" to describe something pleasing or good; or in Onitsha where to compliment *Oganachi* [Spirit/mask] aesthetically is to underscore its intense ugliness.)

In the larger context of imperialism, knowledge reversals occur as white scholars and theorists impose a truncated vision of reality onto Africa's cultural landscape. Imperial relations of power (by no means restricted to African art history) are invoked as Western notions of art and creativity are mapped onto African views of it.[29] The result of this colonizing inscription is the obliteration of Africa's categories of thought—in short, the intellectual bleaching of Africa's aesthetic landscape.

The Sub-Text, the Stories, the Narratives

In the arts, the theories of Africanists (white scholars for whom Africa is merely a place of study) sometimes serve as organizational tools of difference or of homogenization for white aesthetic imperialism. This allows them to inscribe Western attitudes on African art *even as they publicly defend that art.* Like the-outsider-who-sees-through-the-nose (Yoruba proverb), Hoffman conveniently imagines that a "negative" description of an *Ekpo* by a non-Ibibio Nigerian is symptomatic of ethnic bias. Rather than question the limitation of *her* "acclaimed insight" and received racialized knowledge, Hoffman projects out her ignorance and indicts me for *tribalism.* Convinced she has uncovered the root of the problem, she introduces my ethnic background and promotes the idea that my comments are *tribally* motivated: that "judgements rendered by Nzegwu, herself an Igbo, writing about Ibibio *Ekpo* mask" cannot be trusted. It is instructive to note that the problem of misunderstanding never arises for the imperialist in the metropole; it is always reserved for the periphery, the dominions, the *tribes*, the marginalized, the subaltern.

The tribalizing strategy of Hoffman's review, also employed by other white scholars in academia, illuminates the "divide and rule" tactics of imperialism. During European colonization of Africa, the concept of tribality was divisively deployed to accentuate Africa's ethnic differences, and to promote distrust among the different ethnic groups. Hoffman's red herring shift to ethnicity is a classic obfuscation move that follows that tradition. In the late 1980s, in which it was deployed, it appealed to the media images of Africa's horrific *tribal* conflicts and "black-on-black violence." The violent inter-ethnic strife, surreptitiously invoked, becomes the wedge that "proves" the existence of unresolvable Igbo/Ibibio hostilities and proves that Africans cannot legitimately comment on each other's art. (*Sub-text: As members of opposing tribes, they lack objective distance. Only we—white imperialists—can comment because we lack ethnicity, we are beyond such tribal pettiness.*)

The ulterior motive behind the deployment of the concept of tribality is, of course, the regulation of intercultural critiques between Africans. By problematizing ethnic differences, the immediate and relevant experiences that Africans may bring to discourses on African art and to the evaluation of white scholars' writings are delegitimized. This enables Western scholars to present their white intellectual intuitions as objectively neutral knowledge and to offer their aesthetic scheme as the best possible standpoint from which to understand and interpret African art.

The insidious assumption that Africans cannot objectively engage in intercultural critique[30] has long allowed Western scholars to epistemically privilege their field notes and diaries and the sometimes misleading interpretations that follow therefrom. Further, the assumption enables the deflection of damaging critiques by African scholars, by casting these critiques as inherently problematic. Many white scholars of African art recurrently employ that tack to conceal the cultural paucity of their "knowledge" and to preserve the legitimacy of their misrepresentation, while validating their privileged location in the white intellectual structure of knowledge. Allusions to torrid *tribal* animosities allows these white Africanist scholars and trainee-scholars like Hoffman perversely to emerge as benevolent masters and mistresses, virtuously "protecting" Ibibio art from a "vicious" Igbo assault.

When Yoruba describe the outsider as one-who-sees-through-the-nose, they emphasize the wide discrepancy between things as they are culturally constituted and the incredulous interpretations of the outsider. In promoting the idea of cultural difference, white female colleagues like Hoffman subversively relegate experientially informed knowledge of Africans to the sidelines and restore the centrality of Western constructions of African art. More fundamentally, they establish their authorial legitimacy by constructing themselves as "intimate outsiders," in the process reconstructing Africa's social landscape to accord with their view. Reading Nigeria's history from Hoffman's *tribalized* adversarial reference frame, one gets the impression that Igbos and Ibibios live in mutually exclusive homelands, that they are in perpetual conflict, that *Ekpo* performances are restricted to Ibibio areas, and that Igbos are uninformed about *Ekpo* performances so there is nothing they could possibly offer. Interestingly, this white reading of Ibibio art takes place against a corollary reinterpretation of Nigeria's historical reality to accord with a false, anthropologized, ahistorical Africa.

Living far away on the West Coast of the United States and anxious to exploit Igbo otherness to Ibibio culture, Hoffman and other white women like her are often unwilling to accept their thrice-removed otherness. Striving to legitimize her expertise, Hoffman seems unable to grasp that my otherness to Ibibio culture is radically different from her Western otherness and the conceptual chasm it entails. She refuses to see that there are important overlaps in the cultural experiences of Igbos and Ibibios which she does not share. Some of these derive from cultural similarities, our colonial experience, our Nigerian history and identity, and the forging of inter-ethnic friendships and scholarly collaboration between the two groups.[31]

Although I am an Igbo, the modern Nigerian reality in which I was raised was one in which these two ethnic groups shared the same administrative structure up until 1968. Even as I remember the formidable presence of Dr. Nnamdi Azikiwe, Michael Okpara, and Kingsley Mbadiwe, I remember too that it was the time of Margaret Ekpo, Eyo Ita, N.U. Akpan, H.U. Akpabio, E.O. Eyo, Udoma Udo Udoma, Francis Ikpeme, and many others. As part of the political and economic unit known as the Eastern region, members of both groups lived and worked in each others' geographical area.[32] *Ekpo* performances were prominently featured in the annual festival of the arts as well as during Christmas, New Year, and Easter festivities in places like Aba, Port Harcourt, Degema, Onitsha, Enugu, Lagos, Ibadan, and Okitipupa. Although some performances were primarily geared towards entertainment,[33] any Igbo child knew enough about *Mmanwu* (spirits) from the cultural logic of his or her own lived reality to know that an *Ekpo* is a spirit, and to adopt the proper gestures of respect. Most importantly, as part of our pre- and post-independent Nigerian history, and in addition to our everyday lived experiences and oral cultural history, we learned about the Man Leopard Society.

Africa's complex histories and cultures always appear unproblematically simple to those in the *metropole*, whose perspectives are uncritically informed by a linear evolutionary model of cultural development. Although Hoffman and others like her will quickly distance themselves from this charge of anthropologized, ahistorical reading, the outrageous ideas they feel compelled to assert and defend give them away. To attain scholarly adequacy, white Africanist art historians, like Hoffman, would need to discard the fictitiously timeless lens of their anthropological training and integrate the concept of historical change in their analyses. A prolonged period of lived experience, as Barry Hallen (a white American philosopher who lived in Ife for over fifteen years) found out, is required to arrive at some informed understanding of the cultural practices before participating in meta-aesthetic conversations.

Harold Garfinkel, the interactionist social psychologist, explains why embeddedness in cultural practice is critical (Garfinkal 1972:1-30). His experiments revealed that the observer approach (of the sort favored by white Africanist art historians) is necessarily a disengaged perspective that is ill-equipped to discern the rationale and motives of actions. The flaw in the observer approach is that it relies on intuitionism to make sense of phenomena that are outside the scope of its interpretive framework. Consequently, attempts to understand an observed culture in terms of the observer's familiar scheme subverts the logic of the observed actions and compels the outsider "to see through the nose." In a corollary study, Garfinkel notes that it is by becoming a participant, immersing oneself in the experience as a member of the studied unit that the alienating barrier is breached. To the extent that an insider perspective is a revelatory one that yields the significance and logic of an artistic scheme, it is critical to an understanding of the artistic significance of any culture's art. Thus, no equivalence exists between "the literature" of reconstructed textual readings and the lived experiences of people in a culture whose mode, production, and transmission of knowledge is orally structured.

Asi na etiye nwata aka odudu
egosiya mmee

It is said that when one hits a child to swat a gnat
as evidence, one is obliged to present a bloodied palm

As the proverb demonstrates, evidence is critical in establishing motive and proving that one acted responsibly and prudently. If one missed the gnat, then one must be able to show the insect in flight. Where evidence cannot be adduced, or where it fails to match the act, one lacks the socially validated basis to justify the good intent of an act.

In the wake of Hoffman's review, I have spent time examining the historical context of privilege in which anthropological theories and methods were constructed. I also considered the charges made by leading African scholars against white scholars who appropriate Africa's material culture and eliminate the African voice in their writings. I recall that Enwonwu made the charge in "Problems of the African Artist Today," Enwonwu 1956:177-178) contending that "the science of anthropology has...been used to create an intellectual barrier which makes it extremely difficult for most Africans to be considered qualified to play an important part in the development and preservation of their native art." I remember Chinweizu, Onwuchekwa Jemie, and Ihechukwu Madubuike declaring they were *bolekaja* (come down let's fight) critics and stating that *Towards a Decolonization of African Literature* was written out of a need to combat the "stale, sterile, stifling" effect of Eurocentric categories on the literary arts of contemporary Africa.

As the memory reel unwound to the *Foundation of Nigerian Traditional Music*, I remembered Akpabot wondering how John Cage could seriously be credited with discovering indeterminacy in music when the Birom (Nigeria) musicians of the *kara* flute ensemble have been playing random music for most of their history. I recalled Enekwe's affront as he argued in *Igbo Masks: The Oneness of Art and Ritual* that the fluid non-specificity of the Igbo dramatic mode was being devalued because it failed to fit the radically different European model. In *Hope and Impediments*, I watched Achebe demonstrate how Conrad's *Heart of Darkness* "fortifies racial fears" by erasing the humanity of Africa. As the reel raced to the end in "The Future of African Art Studies: An African Perspective" (1990), Rowland Abiodun asserts that Westerners' ignorance about Africa's aesthetic categories results from their inability to proficiently speak any African language and to enter the conceptual universes of discourse.

At the end of this long recollection, I revisited Hoffman's indictment that I am out of touch with "the literature" and its "contemporary controversies." I wondered which literature she had in mind: the writings of African scholars which may be more relevant, or the writings that issued from the structures of whiteness? I then remembered the exclusion of Africa's conceptual schemes in canonical literature, I thought about colonialism as I recalled the proverb, and I wondered what gnat Hoffman was striving to kill.

While working on the essay, "Overcoming Form-Content Tensions in Appreciating African Art Forms" (1988), it was not my objective to examine the depths of what white scholars of African art really know about the artistic and aesthetic schemes of the various African cultures. In a spirit of good will and as a mark of respect to them for having chosen to work in this area, I accepted whatever they claimed to know. Knowing that most African societies preserve their artistic and aesthetic concepts in an oral mode, I did not believe it was important to disclose that very few white scholars proficiently understand the phonetic, lexical, and idiomatic meanings of Africa's tonal languages, nor have lived in the societies long enough to acquire the requisite deep-level mastery of the concepts and categories for critical understanding.

Intent on drawing our attention to how whiteness is reproduced in historical interpretation, Boahen once said that when the tiger controls the telling of history, we should remember that the historical account is the tiger's story, never ours. Boahen's parable cogently highlights the fact that whiteness is reproduced in historical interpretation, because narrators typically strive to impose their vision on the world. A.E. Afigbo caught G.I. Jones at this when he examined the latter's assertion that there is "little weaving or dyeing of cotton cloth [in Igboland except where introduced or borrowed from Igala or Yoruba]." (Afigbo 1984:58). Not only was Jones's assertion unsubstantiated by oral tradition (and even by European travelers' journals), but also it lacked factual basis. The falsehood was concocted by colonial officers' in their intense distaste for the Igbos during the early days of colonial rule.

As those who reside at other centers of life and who have heard Western scholars interpret their reality know, Boahen's observation and Afigbo's discovery speak succinctly to the sort of distortions that white inscriptions create in their reconstruction of Native Canadian, Native America, African, African American, and Chinese realities. If such narratives are imperialistic and offensive, as Boahen and Afigbo indicate, it is because they say nothing about us, our actions, our lives, or our reality. Imperialism emerges in the substitution of Africans' voices for the narrator's Eurocentric voice. This voice emerges powerfully in Michael Crowder's *The Story of Nigeria*, making it a white reading of Nigeria's history; Gerbrands' "History of African Art Studies"

(Gerbrands 1990:11-28) is a story about the presence of an European anthropologist in African art; and Herbert Cole's *African Arts of Transformation* is similarly a white center-periphery survey of the continent's arts.

While recommending that scholarly focus be shifted from the present anthropological bent to an art historical axis, Abiodun revisited the twin problems of an anthropological-outsider perspective and non-African scholars' lack of proficiency in an African language (1990). His preliminary insider analysis of Yoruba aesthetic categories showed up the work of white Africanist scholars as lacking the necessary cultural understanding needed to formulate an appropriate reference frame for art historical analyses. Reminding scholars that the discipline deals with art forms in oral societies, Abiodun insisted, as did Robert Rattray too (Owusu 1978:323), that acquisition of the relevant language and metalanguage proficiency would greatly expedite access to the knowledge repository of African societies, and is critical to understanding the aesthetic and formal elements of art in Africa. The suggestion of the two scholars (one Nigerian, the other British) offers a relevant path to white scholars and theorists to effectively redress the sort of speculative interpretation they have been engaging in that leaves Africa out of the equation.

The problem of language, as revealed by Kone's critique of Brett-Smith's study, is a problem of conceptual erasure in which the humanity of others is distorted. The critical shortcomings of much of white scholars' writings on Africa and its art occur at the very intersections of language and translation, calling into question the competence of scholars and their compliance with the requisite standard of scholarship. In art history in the United States, doctoral students (including Africans) must satisfy two language requirements, especially in their area of specialization, before commencing their study. For those whose area of study is Europe, fluency in the relevant language of the society is crucial.[34] This, however, is hardly the case in African studies, where many European and American Africanist scholars have attained positions of prominence without ever having passed a proficiency test, or achieved conversational fluency, in any African language. In the global intellectual arena, where African scholars and theorists are competing from a position of triple disadvantage (financially, linguistically, and technologically), the requisite standard of scholarly work is waived or lowered for white Africanist male and female scholars so that they can function in the field.

Such affirmative action measures for whites limits academic progress in African art scholarship. Take the case of Hoffman, who defines Dogon culture as an area of study, yet fails to speak the language. Easily absolved from satisfying the language requirement, the imperialist scholar now pressures illiterate sculptors to step outside their own familiar linguistic and cultural scheme if they are to be written about. Working with informant/translators (many of whom are unreliable), she excuses her inability[35] to speak the language by contending that "Dogon languages and dialects are many" (1995:91). This classic imperialistic complaint ignores that the burden of language learning is being shifted on to the Dogons and that, for serious scholarly work to be done, language acquisition is crucial since it is the medium in which Dogons express their views, histories, philosophic ideas, social values, norms, and practices. Moreover, Hoffman ignores the fundamental epistemological problems of an informant-dependent mode of research and the data-quality control it creates in her chosen methodology: "At the start of each interview, I would ask the sculptor his preference: to work through an interpreter or to speak directly to me in French. In almost all cases, the sculptors spoke some French and preferred to speak directly to me" (1995:91).

The epistemological problems identified by Owusu cannot be solved by simply shifting the burden of language-learning to another, or by blithely assuming that a subject's limited French will not negatively affect data-collection. Most troubling in this disingenuous maneuver to avoid learning the language of her primary area of research is that Hoffman presents her tainted material as respectfully collected and then tries to avoid culpability in distorting Dogon culture by representing Poudjougou's (the sculptor with limited French) verbal expression as "eloquent" (91) and having him assert reassuringly that his "Dogon is as poor as my French" (91). Noteworthy in this elaborate performance of language-learning avoidance is that the central problem of data degradation is covered up by passing off tainted materials as respectfully collected and replacing questions of methodological rigor by appealing to an interviewee's eloquence. Hardly addressed at all is the fundamental issue of transmogrification of meaning that comes in part from Poudjougou's limited French vocabulary–particularly from his inability to translate complex cultural concepts and ideas into French–and from the triple process of translating from Dogon to half-baked French (Poudjougou), from half-baked French to standard French (Hoffman), and from standard French to English (Hoffman).

Writing Out Africa

Lack of proficiency in the relevant language and metalanguage of discourse results in flawed interpretations about Africa's material reality. Without admitting to the fact, Western researchers typically rely on their cultural categories of interpretation to make sense of a different reality without ascertaining whether or not there are conceptual overlaps in the observed phenomena. At one level, the utilization of inapplicable cultural categories, rooted in Western epistemological order, seriously calls into question the relevance, veracity, legitimacy, objectivity, and rationality of the resultant interpretations, the proceeds of which still make interesting reading. At another level, as Paul Tiyambe Zeleza underscored, the occurrence of such theorizations in African studies is "a reflection of relations of dominance of Africa by the West [since it] enhances the capacity of Western scholars for intellectual accumulation, appropriation, and domination in African studies" (1994).

Important theoretical questions emerge when the white cultural poltergeist inhabiting the interpretive framework problematizes Africa's values, history, and philosophic logic and degrades the level of theoretical interpretation. An instance of this occurred when Brett-Smith constructed Bamana and Malinke men as swearing their most profound oath on their mother's sex (1994:122). If after five years of research Brett-Smith is still subject to such outrageous interpretations, there is need to reassess the issue of language waivers and the relevance of language-learning. In such badly theorized work as Brett-Smith's and Hoffman's, culturally informed Africans can easily note the slippages and shortcomings of Africanist scholarship because we can detect the geo-cultural displacement of our center to a marginal position, as Kone did in the work of Brett-Smith. Unlike outsiders, who most need to acquire cultural competence, informed Africans do not need to ponder with the anthropologist the process by which they gain a knowledge of Africa, just as informed United States citizens do not stop to inquire about the process by which they know United States culture. Indeed, as Ayo Bamgbose demonstrated in his etymological analysis of the concept of Olodumare, deep cultural knowledge is required, a substantial part of which comes from knowledge of social history, the syntactical rules of language derivation, the logic and philosophic concepts of the society, and the different dialectal shifts of the language (1971).

It is relatively easy to hear the hollow sound of otherness in the speculative interpretations. Residents at the social margins of life in North America are intimately aware of the theoretical limitations of canonical literature that fall below acceptable standards of scholarship in representing their cultural experiences. Unlike most African scholars, few white scholars (women included) ever bother sufficiently to "enter" the metanarrative level of discourse of the African thought worlds they are reinterpreting. Like the perpetual tourist, they stand at the cultural doorway, casting fugitive glances, seeking quixotic materials to use in framing Africa with the next trendy theory or hypothesis. Because they never really grapple with the specific cultural logic presented to them, their views and occassional interpretive accounts say more about the totalizing discourse of imperial epistemologies and interpreters than about the phenomena and peoples being described.

Remembering the colonial legacy of 19th-century anthropology and the Cold War legacy of African studies programs in the United States, Africans need to acknowledge the heavy political and emotional investment at work in securing the foundation of the white normative order in area studies. Eva Cockcroft's article, "Abstract Expressionism, Weapon of the Cold War," highlights the intimate connection between art/culture and the United States foreign policy during the Cold War Era,[36] and the formidable role of the Rockefeller Foundation in transforming art/culture into an effective political instrument of global change. As Cockcroft argued, this political relationship resulted in the establishment of area studies programs in select American universities to provide policy makers with the necessary information on the emergent nations of Africa and Asia as part of the United States global defense against communism. Initially provided by some peace corps volunteers who later became Africanist scholars and theorists, the much-needed information generated numerous publications on the histories and cultures of diverse African nations. Since the African Studies program was primarily designed to provide information for the political objectives of the United States, the orientation of materials collected, the emphasis of interpretation, and scholars' accountability for the knowledge produced had to accord with America's perception of and centrality in the world. That knowledge *qua* knowledge was not the overriding objective of American research in Africa explains why the recovery of Africa into the American intellectual imagination invoked the hegemonic center-periphery relationship of United States imperialism.

In light of this narrative, it is instructive that Suzanne Preston Blier's account ignores the significance of this political relationship of the discipline to the State and to its Cold War objectives in shaping the agenda and direction of the area studies program. In the essay "African Art Studies at the Crossroads: An American Perspective" (1990), she constructs a benign apolitical history of the development and growth of African art studies in the United States in which the discipline vigorously flourished under the energy and dedication of a few highly motivated liberal white scholars. Yet, as Cockcroft makes clear, the imperialistic goal of the Cold War entered into the character and structure of the programs and created a U.S.-centered view of the world. In different programs, scholars (unwittingly or wittingly) lent themselves to the realization of America's global objectives, which converged with their personal objectives to become the definers and experts of diverse regions of the world. Reinforcing Cockcroft's analysis are historians Keletso Atkins, John Higginson, and Atieno Odhiambo, who shed greater light on the history of African Studies in the United States. According to them:

> [t]he decolonization of European empires in Africa, coming as it did during

the height of the cold war, posed new challenges for America's conception of its 'national security.' Policy makers demanded background and up-to-date information on the emergent nation-states of Africa. Hence, African studies was constructed by an alliance of academics, private foundations, and government agencies. It is this relationship that nurtured the growth in African history and African studies in the United States in the 1950's and 1960's, not Africanists on the 'fringes' of the civil-rights struggle with 'sympathy for the underdog. (Keletso, Higginson and Odhiambo 1995).

At the very least, a historicized, accurate reading of the creation of African Studies programs at leading research universities in the United States provides an answer to the sort of culturalist questions that are of interest in the field: e.g., how do "we" understand Africa? Do Africans have a notion of art? Are African masks produced by the community or by individual artists? Are the artists named or do they remain nameless? What are their names? An accurate narrative of the history of the discipline should facilitate an understanding of the ways race and Cold War politics converged to construct the foundations of the discipline, define the paradigms of research, and establish who are considered worthy of speaking. Wielding enormous power and influence as chairs of departments, as jurors for exhibition and research proposals, as architects of African art programs in universities, and as editors of journals and reviewers of article submissions were white male scholars (many of whom spoke no African language) who set the research agenda and defined publication orientation and priorities in light of their own knowledge, understanding, biases, interests, and prejudices. That today Africans have problems with the prevailing paradigms of the discipline is not because they are intellectually inferior, but because the paradigms were not designed to substantively address issues of knowledge, but rather to reflect American intuitionisms about Africa and the sorts of knowledge white America thinks should be produced.[37]

Thus, in African art studies, in particular, and African studies in general, gender imperialism interweaves with cultural imperialism as white women curators, scholars, theorists, and researchers, uphold the America-oriented paradigms of knowledge that invidiously erase African realities. Privileged over their African American counterparts, the white female students of these white male scholars succeed both by being drawn into the inner circle of these mentors and by upholding the imperial epistemologies and methodological style of their mentors. Parlaying individuality for trooper-identity, they play the politics of the discipline, adopting the hierarchical position of power and privilege accorded to them in the program. In their role as gatekeepers of the status quo, many of these white female scholars (many of whom do not speak any African language) effectively control the interpretation of African reality by corralling discourse into the "house of canons," where research questions are set by transmogrified interpretations.

The importance of this canonical edifice is that it provides a means to subvert the legitimate basis on which the outsider/insider dichotomy is marked. By covering up the cultural location and identity of the theorist, it is easier to persuade the skeptic that all interpretations are the same and that there is no distinction in the level of knowledge between Africans and white Africanist scholars. Placing all scholars (African and non-African alike) on the same cognitive level of cultural knowledge undermines the basis on which Africans have critiqued Africanists' misinterpretations. In attempting to assert that any interpretation of African cultural reality is valid, it purports to state that there is no cultural reality outside of the descriptions and interpretations of the scholars. This attempt to collapse the very important distinction between reality and interpretations of it strives to render of equal heuristic value both flawed outsider interpretations and accurate insider interpretations.

And Is It "Art"?

The argument of the limitations of an outsider's interpretation is being made not on the grounds of cultural origin, but on the basis of the quantity and quality of knowledge. In an earlier work (1985), I defended the theoretical position that, in principle, Western aesthetic theories are relevant for the understanding of African art. As cognitive tools with transcultural possibilities, I argued that the problem of ascription or of mapping Western values onto African culture can be avoided by clarifying the implicit aesthetic and artistic terms to rid them of their misleading connotations. Effectively, what this means is that concepts and categories *can* be used transculturally *provided* that one is aware of their ideological baggage and is careful enough to prevent the transfer of potentially distorting ideas. Whether or not this procedure will yield significant insight is a problem which interpreters have to deal with, in deciding to apply their pet theories. My main concern was to undermine the legitimacy of the idea that theories can be dismissed simply because of their cultural origin. The possibility that knowledge or theories can be produced in diverse geographical locations must be defended, since such theories can have useful application outside their cultural limits. Other relevant grounds of dismissal must be established, and these must be made on epistemic or methodological grounds. If theories emerge from and discursively work within a racialized and imperialistic context of power, depending on the sort of use to which they are put, their heuristic value and epistemic efficacy may be compromised in significant ways that curtail the applicability of the theory.

If the image of expertise is to be assertively projected, Hoffman and others like her–given their facile knowledge of African languages, cultures, and realities–need to defend their claims before Africans. Before this begins, there is a need to reconcile the inconsistencies in their positions, especially the idea that the question about what is art in Africa is resolved, following the acceptance by Western scholars of African material culture as art. It must be remembered that the claim of Western acceptance of African artifacts as art is highly contentious. In the first place, what do these Western scholars understand to be art in these artifacts? Do their views on the matter overlap with those of the indigenes? Why is the status of African artifacts as art pre-emptively made to depend on "its acceptance as art by Western scholars"? Why has Hoffman ignored the Africans' own views on the matter? Moreover, what are the various African societies' artistic and aesthetic categories?

In the racialized context of U.S. imperialism in which knowledge about Africa is being produced, it pays to challenge interpreters on their utilization of Eurocentric paradigms, especially the exclusive deployment of the Western definition of art as the operative model against which other cultures' artistic universes are to be understood. Since this deployment is an enthronement of the culturally specific European views about art, it violates the idea of art as a genus or category. It provides untenable grounds for representing Africans as lacking a notion of art simply because their notion of it does not correspond to that of Europeans. So, to make the status of African artifacts as art dependent on "its acceptance as art by Western scholars" is to engage in artistic imperialism.

Another problem in unequivocally assigning cognitive primacy to Western scholars' views is that many Euroethnic scholars who have written about African art–Janson, Susan Vogel, Arthur Danto, G.I. Jones, Jacques Maquet, Robert Plant Armstrong, Herbert Cole, to mention a few–consider African artifacts as art not in the creators' own sense but rather in the Western sense of it (Armstrong 1966:137-146; Danto 1988:18-32; Janson 1993; Jones 1984; Maquet 1986; Vogel 1988). In fact, they are on record as saying that Africans do *not* have a conception of art, a matter contested by Aniakor, Abiodun, and Enwonwu,[38] to mention a few. Since the question of artistic intentionality is central to determining the status of a work of art, and since white Africanist scholars, as a rule, lack proficiency in an African language to accurately map out the society's conceptualization of its art, how are we sure that what these scholars aver is African art counts as such for Africans?

Such problems of misinterpretation arise most urgently in exhibitions organized by the Museum for African Art, formerly the Center for African Art, New York, and the National Museum of African Art, Washington, D.C., where Africans' views on art are routinely ignored. To the regular multigenerational, multicultural American audience, conceptual displacements go unnoticed because viewers lack the requisite frame of reference to detect the interventions. Notwithstanding the avowals of respect by some white female curators/art historians, their representation of African cultural life and notions of art and creativity are freely predicated on and presented in terms of Western views of them. These representations are excused on the grounds that the artifacts have undergone a metamorphosis through cultural dislocation and must be apprehended as art exclusively in the Western terms.

But what is really implied when a society's conceptualization of its art is overridden and exhibitions are used to perpetuate this view? In *Secrecy: African Art that Conceals and Reveals*, an exhibition organized by the Museum for African Art, the curator, Mary Nooter, claims to take cultural legitimation very seriously.[39] The level of her seriousness is measured by her claim that in regards to how Westerners understand African art, any interpretation is permissible since cultural representations are never "objective" presentations of "facts" (4/5). This idea of cultural respect and legitimation is further stretched to the limit when she represents herself as a Luba initiate and contends that in Africa "the substance of secrets proves less important than the boundaries they set up and the privileges that ownership imply" (1993:20). The effect of this can be seen in the chosen mode of display.

Treating sculpture as the appropriate category for the visual apprehension of multimedia assemblages, Nooter places the severed wooden heads of *gelede, sowei,* and *dan* on stands for public display (this is not unlike demolishing Michelangelo's statue of *David* and displaying only the head or the genitalia as the work of art). By this act, she reinforced the flawed view that a culture's artistic vision could be overridden with impunity. At the other extreme, a talisman-covered Bamana hunter's shirt, an *nkisi nkondi* ritual object, masks, and an *Ekpe* association emblem are presented as aesthetic objects coding secret knowledge and power without considering the closely related question of whether they would treat as art objects a New York hunter's orange cap, broken crucifixes, torn up torahs, chalices of Catholic mass rituals, and the Masonic seal and Judaic ritual paraphernalia.

The conferment of cognitive pre-eminence to Western interpretations rather than to those of Africans themselves speaks to the participatory role of white women in maintaining and preserving imperialistic structures. Why is it that Africans' views on the matter so rarely count?[40] Why is it that our sacred objects are in private collections in the West? Why are they represented as *art* objects while the West's are represented as *sacred* objects? Why is it that the creative vision underlying the construction of *gelede, sowei,* and *dan* is constantly overridden by the Eurocentric view of what constitutes art? Do we emasculate the sculpted heads of spirits? Do we treat a dirty, ragged, amulet-covered hunter's tunic as art? Why do white female curators and art historians, like their male counterparts, assume that the aesthetic value of the works is dependent on the aesthetic sensibility of their own Western framework? Why do they assume that the African perspective is peripheral rather than central? And why do they feign helplessness when the vital objects of our cultural norms and institutions are violated? The lapses speak powerfully to colonizing representation, to the production of imperial relations in knowledge, and to white women's collusion in the process. The lapses are important precisely because they reveal latent attitudes of dominance and subordination of Africa.

The basis on which African art forms were historically "included" in art historical discourse and in museums is one in which form and content were separated, and the conceptualization of African art as art took place within the conceptual structures of white aesthetics. This explains why the multimedia assemblage that is the "Mask" is hardly ever exhibited and why only the sculpted face/head is exclusively the focal point of white aesthetic attention. It is true, as Hoffman pointed out, that the form/content debate has been around for over twenty years. But as we all know, ever since the intervention of white modernist artists (Picasso, Derain, Modgliani, Klee, Matisse, Moore) and theorists (Roger Fry and Clive Bell) in highlighting the formal elements of African artifacts, the form/content debate as it spilled over from anthropology into cubism (Rubin 1984:1-79; Paudret 1984:125-175) and finally into African art history has centered on issues that do not interrogate the cultural location of speakers. Nor has it sufficiently questioned the basis of the assumptions utilized in the identification and evaluation of Africa's artifacts.

Again, as Hoffman already knows, nowhere in the literature in the last ninety years has this form/content debate been examined for its perspectival implications.[41] So, to contend as she did that the issue has been dealt with following "the acceptance by Western scholars of African material culture as art" and by virtually every literature in the last twenty years is radically to misread the literature. It is also radically to miss the pertinent point that an acceptance by the West of Africa's art does not imply the acceptance of Africans' conceptions of art, philosophy, beliefs, or artistic expectations. The form/content issue remains that of understanding African art on its own terms, not the Eurocentric acceptance of Africa's artifacts as art.

The fundamental differences in the cultural identities of the imperially marginalized and imperially privileged are revealed in the treatment of Africans' authorial objectives as unimportant. The Euroethnic failure to understand why Africans would want to re-examine the form/content tensions in art not only confirms whites' location on the privileged side of the divide, but also proves their inability to comprehend the trauma of the colonial experience and the reluctance to have the defects of white intuitionism exposed. As people who do not share nor live Africa's cultural and metaphysical reality, yet copiously write about its products, white Africanist scholars do not appreciate the importance of re-tracing old grounds and reopening old issues. Because they have not experienced colonization, they cannot seem to understand our need to unravel the twisted legacies of colonialism or our concern to determine where whiteness was inscribed[42] or to see how trendy theories and "contemporary controversies" are essentially oppressive.

Furthermore, in African art studies, white imperialism cannot evade the methodologically pertinent issue of cultural location by contending that the characterization of the contextualist's approach as an outsider's perspective and the formalist approach as an insider's perspective is a rhetorical device. It is not enough to conceal the white-centered basis on which African material culture has been interpreted for the past twenty years by dismissively claiming that "few, if any, scholars of African art...would call themselves purists of either (contextualist or formalist) schools" (Hoffman 1989). The issue is not what white scholars of African art want to call themselves or one of how they want to position their writings. At issue is the nature of understanding, the nature of the epistemological approaches that have been chosen to facilitate understanding of Africa's cultural realities, and the efficacy of the approaches that historically have offered ways to appreciate these realities.

As Chinweizu, Jemie, and Madubuike rightly argued, effective decolonization entails the deployment of an African reference scheme in the production of literary works that *must* speak to that audience. The politics of language, as Abiodun constructed it, requires that interpretive analysis occur within the framework of a culture's philosophy of arts and creativity, just as it is done in the West, and as Babalola did with Ijala poetry. Michael Echeruo correctly argued that Africa and its interests must be at the center, not the periphery (Echeruo 1991:135-145). Unless one has lived the experience of Africa's social life and experienced the effect of its colonialism, it is difficult to hear how hollow many Euroethnic interpretations sound, or to perceive the erasure of Africa's cultural identity in Africanist art historical literature. Henry Drewal's desire to see a "balance between the generation of data and its analysis, synthesis, and interpretation" is timely if the discipline is to be turned around (Drewal 1990:49-50).

Oburo mbosi ukwa dalu
ka o'na ele,
oburo mbosi o'daa
ka o'le.

> It is not the day the breadfruit falls
> that it will rot,
> it is not the day it falls
> that it rots.

My mind swirled as garrulous voices relentlessly queried: *Why accuse Hoffman of imperialism? Didn't she merely do what was required of her? Aren't reviews meant to be critical and tough? Why should she be held accountable for the way the system works? Isn't that inconsiderate? Aren't you asking for special privileges? We think your critique is too emotional and subjective...much too emotional. It is downright petty!*

I looked up and saw Iyalode Tinubu, the political power of old Eko and Abeokuta, a strong and vocal opponent of British rule, the woman who rallied the Egbas to repulse the Dahomey army in 1864 and who a year later financed the Ikorodu war. Beside her was the "Lioness of Lisabiland," Olufunmilayo Ransome-Kuti, the <u>odogu</u> who dared the might and power of the Alake of Abeokuta, who plucked the corrupt man from the throne and freed Egbas from tyranny. Striding about with growing impatience, Umekwulu Odogwu, the indomitable head of Ikporo Onitsha, who fought the East Central State government that tried to erase women, strikes the hollow sacred bowl of her office. She bellowed: What are you sniveling for, child? We've rescued you from oppression so you could get to work, what are you now waiting for? Don't let us beat that servility out of you! You're here worrying about one who has no regard for you. Have you lost your mind?

Ever since the historical encounter of African women and white European/ American women, the former has had to consider and work for the welfare of privileged white mistresses. Under imperialism, the terms of interaction have always been those from which reciprocity was excluded. African women were constructed as monstrously black, dumb, and disease-laden by the colonial system. By contrast, the white wives of plantation owners, empire-builders, and colonialists were perceived as kind and good intentioned, hence were protected and promoted at the expense of African women. In the American context, "Ain't I a woman," directly speaks to the history of this supremacist erasure in the United States.

Our white female colleagues and feminist "sisters" must learn that solidarity is not built on other women's backs, with people of color relegated to the subordinate status of servers and cleaners. They need to learn from strategists the art of being at one with others if they seek a viable women's movement. In the turbulent politics of colonial Nigeria, women like Olufunmilayo Ransome-Kuti emerged to fight for women's equality, recognizing that no woman is empowered when another is in bondage (Fig. 5: *The Lioness of Lisabiland*). Refusing to define women's needs from her advantaged class position and from her ethnic identity, (Mba 1992:133-148) Ransome-Kuti articulated the needs of the poor, non-literate market women from the radical position of economically poor women. She understood the significance of the immense cultural diversity in Nigeria, and realized that it was foolhardy to assume that all women's realities and sufferings were the same as or identical to hers. She perceptively grasped that women's collective interests can be advanced by working for the empowerment of economically disadvantaged women and by acknowledging that sexist manifestation differs along class and cultural lines.

Reflecting on the politics of the American feminist movement from this historical angle, and considering the issues that are deemed important to fight over, one cannot but understand the disenchantment and reservation of women of color towards feminism. Time and again, painful experiences have shown them that feminist exhortations of solidarity are essentially colonizing, usually carefully pitched to further white women's careers, because they define the needs of women from the racial and class location of relatively privileged middle- and upper-middle-class white women.

In "Race and Essentialism in Feminist Legal Theory," Angela Harris (1990:581-616) demonstrates how this works in the respected writings of Catharine MacKinnon and Robin West, even as the two claim to acknowledge African American women in their discourse. Harris' critical reading uncovers that even as MacKinnon takes a positive anti-racist stance on rape, a resilient essentialist strand in her thinking enables her to seemingly include, while excluding, the experiences of African American women in her discussions. Harris' analysis of rape from the perspective of African American women shows that MacKinnon's representation of rape completely erases the radically different history of African American women and, most annoying, minimizes the ignominious history of White America's sexual abuse of African American women. Though unintentional, MacKinnon's erasure exposes how feminism becomes a metaphor for indifference, for white women's devaluation of African American women's experiences by refusing fully to acknowledge the different histories and identities. It reveals white women's commitment to gender equality as largely narcissistic.

Harris' recovery of African American women's history demonstrates again that gender imperialism is played out in academia through white women's inscription of African American women's views, experiences, and selves into interpretive frameworks. Indulging in the myth that sisterhood is global, that women's experiences are shared and the same, they refuse to acknowledge the exploitative dimension of their history in enforcing and reproducing social, economic, and cultural imperialism. Their failure to listen, their reluctance to see that different class and cultural experiences yield other sets of concerns and options, leads them to impose their vision on matters of which they do not entirely understand. Exposure is avoided by exercising the privileges accorded to them by the white patriarchal structures and reducing the experiences of African, Native American/Canadian, African American, Caribbean, and Hispanic women to raw, uninterpreted data.

Patricia Monture, the Mohawk lawyer, has eloquently described the implicit brutality in the racist erasure of others' reality and personhood in which even feminists participate (Monture 1986:159-170).[43] Her reflective reminsciences show that the material is put to work to benefit white women's intellectualism and power. The outrage, she feels, is not just that one is constantly belittled and then ridiculed for feeling the pain inflicted, but that one is callously shoved aside as these experiences are appropriated for the white intellectual order. The value of Monture's work is that she shows how the erasure of "owners" of "experiences" allows the latter to be treated as "raw materials" and recouped without the attendant pain into a sanitized mode. Rendering the Other faceless and voiceless neutralizes the biting edge of the experiences and, in most instances, inflates the socio-political power and privileges of Euroethnic users of such narratives. Trendy theorizing occurs as white theorists, feigning ignorance of the racist side of their power and privileges, spin their yarn, well insulated from the impact and pain of racism. This prompted Monture to ask: "[W]hen are those of you who inflict racism, who appropriate pain, who speak with no knowledge or respect when you ought to know how to listen and accept, going to take hard looks at yourself instead of at me? How can you continue to look to me to carry what is your responsibility" (168)?

Thinking about race and gender politics in the new climate of multicultural America, it is clear that middle and upper-middle class white women must take responsibility for their actions and the hegemonically-derived privileges of their locations. Equally, African women must interrogate the basis of their own subjugation in the larger global economic structure, just as white women must examine racial privileges and their unintended complicity in global exploitation. For middle, and upper-middle-class African women in particular, transformatory change begins when they empower themselves by empowering their less educationally, less economically, and less socially advantaged sisters.

Monture's uplifting message is that gender imperialism will be overcome when racialized women assertively speak and concertedly work towards checking the exploitative actions of their white female colleagues. To achieve this, they must learn from their histories, from their mothers, and from their sisters who fearlessly worked to neutralize oppression. Ransome-Kuti constituted such a model. Uniting the middle-class Yoruba women with the economically poor Egba Yoruba women, she forged a powerful movement that challenged the oppressive taxation structure and policies of the colonial administration. The radical platform of her movement was that no woman can be truly free while another is dispossessed. Although relatively insulated by her class position from the oppressive policies of the Egba Native Authority, she nevertheless strategized and worked with rural and market women to articulate their response. In solidarity, she demonstrated with them until both the oppressive taxation and the corrupt Alake of Abeokuta were removed.

The importance of this grass-roots mobilization for contemporary African women is that it provides evidence of their activist history as well as a working model of effective action. Well aware of the resourcefulness of women, Ransome-Kuti succeeded by building effective coalitions across religious lines, with supportive men's groups and other social organizations in the town until the generated groundswell resulted in the abdication of the Alake. Quite remarkably in this movement, the leaders astutely did not project their own interests: they refused to patronize economically disadvantaged women, and did not erase them by regarding their own privileged reality as shared by all. Unlike Western feminists, she knew that radical social change is achieved principally by working to transform the conditions of poor rural women, and that gender equality comes from acknowledging class, religious, and cultural differences, even as coalitions are built on commonalities in women's lives and experiences.

Feminism notwithstanding, a significant number of middle- and upper-middle-class white women in academia are oppressors, either as surrogates of white males (if they lack institutional power) or as on a colonizing mission (if they are institutionally privileged.) The driving need to share in the pay-offs of a structure that long privileged white men has increased their fear of competing for "leftover" resources they have come to expect as naturally theirs. Academic imperialism, the imposition of the white ideology of reality in academia, interweaves with gender imperialism to preserve the Western intellectual status quo. It is true, as feminists have loquaciously argued, that white women are institutionally disadvantaged in relation to white males, hence occupying a subordinate position in academia. But, as Monture pointedly reminds us, "we are [still] talking about White people, *all* White people" living in a privileged white world. Though these women might appear as victims in the patriarchal power relations of North America's society the issue is not their victim status. At issue is their manipulation of their racial status (that derives from patriarchal power) to absolve themselves from seriously interrogating racism. At issue too is their obstruction of the professional advancement of women of color.

Proudly speaking about the strengths of her Mohawk tradition, heritage, and culture, Monture highlighted the re-vitalizing, healing character of a lifestyle that respects the world and others' identity. Imperialism, the ideology of disrespect, will be vanquished only when we learn from and respect the histories, cultures, and identities of others. Catherine Nweze, a Nigerian female politician, vociferously protests disrespect and erasure by loudly and colorfully serving notice: "Ekwelum? Ekwerom! Ana me kick!" [Did I accept? No, I didn't! I'll keep kicking (resisting)!] Resisting imperialism means loudly protesting, in the activist manner of "Béère" (Ransome-Kuti's nickname) and Kate Nweze, the oppressive practices that nurture and sustain domination and erasure. It involves resisting the homogenizing force that compels me to be other than I am, to mimic its voice, to speak its power-language. Liberation means finding myself, recovering my voice, my language, my culture, and adopting the laconic poetic mode of speech where:

inu, abulu mmanu eji esuli okwu

proverbs, become the oil for coating words.

As proverbs smooth the path, sensuous, abstract, dynamic, and revelatory words spiritedly flow in open-ended riddles, narratives, and dreams while ideas cartwheel, twisting and turning as they roll along.

NOTES

1. I do not mean to imply that some white women are not victims. I am mainly objecting to the essentializing way of treating them all as victims, even when it is clear that many are conscious oppressors.
2. If you ever wondered why the greatest beneficiaries of affirmative action programs are white women, here's the answer.
3 According to E.J. Alaoga, Queen Kambasa was the first woman ruler of Bonny, Nigeria and the one who unified Bonny into a nation-state. She is believed to have ruled Bonny in 1500. A.D. Alaoga, "Queen Kambasa of Bonny," in *Nigerian Women in Historical Perspective*, Bolanle Awe, ed. (Lagos: Sankore/Bookcraft, 1992), 27-35.
4. Atagbusi was an 18th-century *isi ada* of Ogboli Eke village in Onitsha. As a venerable seer and priestess, she forecasted the coming and establishment of a European trading mission in Onitsha. Sensing the turbulent impact of these visitors on the socio-cultural life of Onitsha, she initially opposed the establishment of the trading posts. She met the first wave of traders at the Niger River bank, offered them charmed bananas, whereupon the traders lost interest in the strategic site of Onitsha and moved across the river to the low-lying town of Asaba, where they set up their

headquarters. Atagbusi is venerated as a major deity in Onitsha. Her shrine is on the banks of the River Niger.

5. Iyalode Tinubu lived between 1805 to 1887. She was a politically powerful woman and an immensely wealthy trader in Eko (Lagos). She was a strong and vocal opponent of British rule. Her influence over Oba Kosoko and his son, Oba Dosumu, so annoyed the British Consul that he imprisoned her husband and forced the Oba to expel her to Abeokuta. During the Dahomey assault on Abeokuta, she obtained guns and rallied the Egbas to repulse the Dahomey army in 1864. Iyalode Tinubu also financed the Ikorodu war of 1865.

6. Omu Nwagboka was the last Omu of Onitsha. She went down in history as the female ruler who led an all-women boycott of their social duties to make the point that women were socially indispensable, and therefore were not to be trifled with or ignored.

7. These women, Nwanyeruwa, Ikonnia and Nwanedie, played a very prominent role in the war against the fiscal policies of the British colonial government. They opposed the taxation of women on the ground that there was a severe decline in women's income (a result of the 1929 economic crash), and that they were already carrying a disproportionate weight of the family needs. It is true that the war was also directed at the patriarchal ideology of British government, which had devalued and erased women. Igbo women lacked the requisite official organ to voice their concerns and protect their interest in the new political order.

8. Olufunmilayo Ransome-Kuti is famed for mobilizing and leading Egba women against the excesses of the Sole Native Authority and the Alake of Abeokuta, one of the most powerful Yoruba kings. The women's rallies, sit-ins, and public demonstrations brought Abeokuta to a standstill, and forced the abdication of Alake Ademola. It is a testimony to her organizational skill, leadership and courage, and to the political power of Egba women that they succeeded in dethroning the Alake where all others had failed.

9. Ekpo, Mokelu, and Okala were three of the most prominent women politicians of Eastern Nigeria. Ekpo was the president of NCNC Women's Wing in Aba.

10. Odogwu, Uwechia, and Chugbo were the leaders of Ikporo Onitsha (Women-of-Onitsha Organization) between 1974 to 1979. Following the excesses of the Obi of Onitsha, they led the entire Onitsha community in ostracizing Obi Ofala Okagbue for three years. For over two years they were arrested, roughed up, and harassed by the police and agents of the then East Central State government for leading a counter-government. Ikporo Onitsha was protesting the government's revocation of their traditional powers and its takeover of Onitsha market, an arena that is customarily under the jurisdiction of women. Their protest was directed against the economic and political emasculation of women. The lasting achievement of this group of women was the resuscitation and revamping of the ancient political structure of Ikporo Onitsha for contemporary life.

11. As an Isiokwe (Onitsha), I am engaged in that which comes most socio-culturally—contestations and disputations—and as an analytic philosopher, reexaminations, critiques and interrogations are my disciplinary task. Thus, this interrogation should not be seen as a means of avoiding critique but of centering the grounds of debate.

12. This is an African response to the bewilderment of white women in Marilyn Frye's workshop who are unable to see the relation between liberalism and imperialism. See *The Politics of Reality: Essays in Feminist Theory*. Other responses have been given by such black women writers as bell hooks, *Talking*, and Carole Boyce Davies, "Feminist Consciousness and African Literary Criticism" in *Ngambika: Studies of Women in African Literature*.

13. This means running the ideas through some fashionable theory that in most instances do not have much relevance to the African phenomena under analysis.

14. Toni Flores identified the problem of contextualists as being the problem of inadequate emphasis on the visual form and formal elements. The problem of the formalist side is that its descriptions are dislocated when one lacks a knowledge of their context.

15. I am taking anthropological oriented approaches such as structuralism, poststructuralism, and Boas' particularism to constitute a contextualist approach. Also included would be Marxist approaches. By a formalist approach, I mean the typical art historical method that begins and revolves around the formal features of the works as is found in modernism, baroque, renaissance, and so on.

16. I've done this in Ottawa, Toronto, Kingston, Washington D.C., and Binghamton. The general public in these places simply do not know much about the stylistics of African art.

17. This audience comprises professionals, business people, managers, graduate and high school students, school children, homemakers, the unemployed. In short, ordinary folks from all spectrums of the society.

18. An eminent progressive white male scholar with an impressive list of publications once lectured me that sex discrimination exists in Africa because "while watching the Discovery Channel on television I saw this scene of some tribe in Africa dancing, and only the men got to dance while the women were at the edge of the circle clapping." The absurdity of his proof never struck this man who, ordinarily, is most circumspect about what he would plausibly claim to know. Yet what is most striking is not his ignorance, but his willingness to hang it out for public display simply because he was talking to an African woman.

19. I owe this observation to Julia Emberely, one of the 1992-93 Fellows of the Society for Humanities, Cornell University.

20. It is singularly disturbing to witness this in operation at conferences where such white female scholars take it upon themselves to "elevate to a theoretical level" African women panelists'discussion. Other occasions exist when our white female sisters are theorizing about the experiential reality of women in some parts of Africa seemingly oblivious that some members of the audience are the very people being described. The shock expressed when challenged is proof that they never really expected the erased women to speak out.

21. This helps explain why it is rarely problematic to find a well-received scholarly book on African women by an all-white cast of writers. On occasion one may find that a token black woman scholar is thrown in to establish the editor's openness. Consider the unlikely scenario of a book on white American women by an all-black African cast of writers. The fact that such a scholarly book, would not be published by any

reputable press in the United States raises disturbing questions about the control of theoretical representation of African women in America, and reveals the extent to which celebrated books by white women on African women are highly problematic.

22. The politics of citation is most commonly observed in the works of white scholars who will deliberately refrain from citing the works of African scholars, thereby claiming the idea for themselves. Africans are cited only when not to do so is perceived as gauche, or when the African scholar is absolving the West through holding up Africa and its culture to a higher standard of morality. In contrast, Africans foolishly cite the works of white scholars even when what is being supported is an everyday fact of their reality. For example, some Yoruba scholars have been known to cite Parrinder's or Bascom's statement that Yorubas believe in Olodumare, something they already know. As can be seen, white scholars are reluctant to reference black scholars because doing so will acknowledge the intellectual acumen of African scholars. African scholars, by contrast, subserviently reference white scholars as proof of their scholarship.

23. Given the epistemological issues raised by Owusu, the distortion of African conceptual categories is further facilitated by the publishing industry's failure to subject manuscripts written by white scholars to competent African scholars for review as is done to African authors writing about the culture of Europe and its diaspora.

24. See "Response by Simon Ottenberg" in *African Art Studies: The State of the Discipline* (1990), 125-136. African literary writers have long been engaged in articulating the features of diverse communities' aesthetic consciousness. In the area of arts, the paper Ben Enwonwu presented at the 1st Negro Arts in Dakar, Senegal in 1966 is particularly relevant. Since African art is multidisciplinary, further readings on the aesthetic consciousness of Nigerian ethnic groups can be found in the writings of Onuora Nzekwu, who from the late 1950's wrote extensively on the aesthetic consciousness of various ethnic groups for *Nigeria* magazine. Also, the novels of Achebe (I have *Things Fall Apart* [1958] and *Arrow of God* [date] in mind) give an account of how Igbos operated in their aesthetic scheme. p'Bitek's *Song of Lawino* (1966) provided a rich comparative account of the Acholi aesthetic scheme and the synthesis that resulted with colonialism. The critical writings of Ngugi wa 'Thiong'o, who in urging a shift to African aesthetics, articulated the features of the aesthetics of the Gikuyu. The works of Fagunwa, Amos Tutola *The Palm-Wine Drinkard* (1953), and Duro Ladipo, including the verbal and written commentaries and reviews to those works, deal with Yoruba aesthetics in a deeper, more profound way; the works of Babalola (1966); Lasebikan (1955). Uche Okeke began his challenge to colonial education in the late 1950's from the basis of his Igbo aesthetics (works are to be found in his Asele Institute), and Obiechina on Igbo art and aesthetics. That these writings are not easily available in America, and have no reason to be, does not justify a theoretical exclusion. If anything, it indicates research sloppiness.

25. That they systematically occur in African studies, in general, and African art history studies, in particular, is a revelation of the colonized state of the discipline.

26. For evidence that there is no one method in the field, see Adrian A. Gerbrands, "The History of African Art Studies" and Henry Drewal, "African Art Studies Today". Drewal uses the term "eclecticism" to characterize the wide variety of recent approaches in the field. What Drewal failed to acknowledge is the ties of these "eclectic"

approaches to contextualism and formalism, and the extent to which their prescription for artistic and aesthetic understanding are based on the primacy of cultural information over the form. The artistic elements are generally lost because the analyses, as Rowland Abiodun points out, lack an understanding of the indigenous notions of art.

27. I found this line of exploration very interesting given that in 1992 I had curated an exhibition, *Celebrating African Identity: Politics and Icons of Representation*, at A-Space, Toronto, and wrote accompanying catalogue, in which this theme of art works as "conduits of memories" and repositories of knowledge was elaborated. The difference in the two lines of argument is that while I set the reading of objects as conduits of memories within the context of the cultural history of the artists and their societies, Hoffman invoked the theories of several European and American scholars to understand a Dogon sculptor's comment that objects have power, hence can act.

28. The importance of James Clifford's radical critique (1990 and 1991) of the foundations of anthropology is that it not only reconfirmed what African scholars have said about anthropological practice, but also revealed the hierarchical power dynamics underpinning interpretive insight, and pinpointed how, and the areas where, the white cultural lens of the interpreter/translator displaces that of the culture/object of study. Hoffman's erasure of the Ibibio aesthetic scheme reveals the dynamics of the process.

29. The essays of Susan Vogel, "Introduction," and Arthur Danto, "ART/artifact" in *ART/artifact* (New York, The Center for African Art, 1988) provide instructive reading. Also see Robert Armstrong "Guineaism" in *Tri-Quarterly* 5 (1966): 137-146; Vogel, 12-17 and Danto, 18-32.

30 This is a classic move that whites make when they find Africans discussing each other's art. They arrogate to themselves the right to discuss the art of any culture even when they lack adequate knowledge about it, and arrogate themselves the right to cut off our conversations and fault our judgement by introducing issues of objectivity. Susan Vogel exemplified this position when she maternally denied the Ivorian master-carver Lela Keuakou the right to comment on the works of other African ethnic groups. David Rockefeller, on the other hand, was given carte blanche to voice his personal opinions and biases, and treat the works in his personal collection as if they represented the best that Africa has to offer. See Susan Vogel, *Perspectives: Angles on African Art*.

31 At the time of writing the essay, I was living with an Ibibio woman, with whom I had attended the same primary school in the former Eastern Nigeria. Part of our coping strategies in Canada's educational institution involved reading and commenting on each others' papers. Interestingly, she read the paper Hoffman found so offensive and wasn't taken aback at the description of some *ekpo* masks as disgustingly ugly.

32. They still do so today even after the political restructuring of the country.

33. For further adaptations of the *ekpo* routine in entertainment, see Meki Nzewi, "New Directions For Dysfunctionalized Art Forms: Prospecting the Ekpo Routine".

34. Africans too who are studying French, German, or Spanish art have had to satisfy

this requirement to participate in the intellectual discourse of their chosen area of study.

35. I do not think Hoffman is unable to learn the language. Having demonstrated her ability to learn French, it is clear that the problem here is not one of incapability, but of willingness.

36. This helps to explain why the National Museum of Art, Washington D.C. was founded by Warren Robbins, a retired foreign affairs officer, and only later acquired by the Smithsonian Institution.

37. A classic example of this colonizing act is performed by Blier in *African Vodun* (1995) published by University of Chicago Press. In this book, Blier hopes to use the *bocio* and *bo* to map the interconnection between art, psychology, and power among the Fon in the Republic of Benin and Togo. Acknowledging the difficulty in researching the *bocio* and *bo*, given that her questions were "frequently met with silence" (20), Blier stated that "many features of this tradition remain obscure to me" (20). Notwithstanding this epistemic blockage, she goes on to assert categorically that this evasiveness "is because the works themselves are not meant ever to be "understood"...but instead remain enigmatic and obscure to local residents and foreign observers alike." In her view, this "does not reflect an arbitrary desire to hide or cover the work's hidden ("secret") meanings from foreign (or local) audiences, but rather has grounding in the highly personal psychodynamic roles these objects play in local communities" (20).

38. It may correctly be said that Western skepticism about the existence of an African conception of art was what spurred Rowland Abiodun into his investigation of the Yoruba aesthetic universe. See Chike Aniakor, "The State of Igbo Art Studies and Ben Enwonwu "The African View of Art and Some Problems Facing the African Artist".

39 For a more extensive critique of *Secrecy*, see the exhibition review in *American Anthropologist* (March 1994): 227-229.

40 These museums may charge that they often consult the views of African scholars and museum officials in the organizing of these exhibitions. It is pertinent to stress, however, that the consultation always presupposes the legitimacy of the exhibition ground rules. African art will never be allowed to subvert institutional guidelines and speak in its own voice.

41 The anthropological outsider perspective raises such questions as: how are the objects used? In what context? In which rite, ritual, or ceremony? An indigene who comes asking such questions will be given a dressing down for the lapses in knowledge. The formalist outsider perspective focuses on why-questions such as: why the ugly and the beautiful? Why is the head bigger than the torso in representation? The formalist indigene approach is an evaluative-comparative mode. Here knowledge of the context and form are presupposed as they evaluate the merits of the object, play, performance in terms of the indigenous criteria of artistic excellence.

42 One would suppose that feminists could appreciate this need, but they don't because it raises the issue of white women's complicity in the oppression.

WORKS CITED:

Abiodun, Rowland. "The Future of African Art Studies: An African Perspective." *African Art Studies: The State of the Discipline*. Washington D.C.: Smithsonian Institution, 1990: 63-89.

Achebe, Chinua. *Hope and Impediments*. New York: Anchor Books/Doubleday, 1989.

——, *Things Fall Apart*. London: Heinemann, 1958.

Afigbo, A. E. "Oral Tradition and the History of Segmentary Societies." *Perspectives and Methods of Studying African History*. Ed. Erim O. Erim and Okon E. Uya. Enugu, Nigeria: Fourth Dimension Publishing Co. Ltd., 1984: 54-63.

Aguilar, Delia. "Third World Revolution and First World Feminism: Toward a Dialogue." *Promissory Notes: Women in the Transition to Socialism*. Ed. Sonia Kruks, Rayna Rapp, and Marilyn B.Young. New York: Monthly Review Press, 1989. 338-344.

Aidoo, Agnes Akosua. "Asante Queen Mothers in Government and Politics in the Nineteenth Century." *Black Women Cross-Culturally*. Ed. Filomena Chioma Steady. Cambridge, MA: Schenkman Publication Co., 1981. 65-77.

Akpabot, Samuel Ekpe. *Foundations of Nigerian Traditional Music*. Ibadan: Spectrum Books, 1986.

Alaoga, E.J. "Queen Kambasa of Bonny." *Nigerian Women in Historical Perspective*. Ed. Bolanle Awe. Lagos: Sankore/Bookcraft, 1992.

Amadiume, Ifi. *Male Daughters, Female Husbands*. London: Zed Books Ltd., 1987.

Amos, Valerie, and Pratibha Parmar. "Challenging Imperial Feminisms." *Feminist Review* 17 (1984): 3-9.

Aniakor, Chike. "The State of Igbo Art Studies." *Nigeria Magazine* 54, no.1 (1986): 9-17.

Armstrong, Robert Plant. "Guineaism" *Tri-Quarterly* 5 (1966): 137-146.

Atkins, Keletso, John Higginson, and Atieno Odhiambo. "The Significance of Race in African Studies." *The Chronicle of Higher Education* (7 April 1995): B3.

Awe, Bolanle, ed. *Nigerian Women in Historical Perspective* (Lagos: Sankore/Bookcraft, 1992).

Babalola, Adeboye. "Ijala Poetry among the Oyo-Yoruba Communities." *Oral Poetry in Nigeria*. Uchegbulam N. Ed. Abalogu, Garba Ashiwaju, and Regina Amadi-Tshiwala. Lagos: Nigeria Magazine Publications, 1981: 3-17.

——. *The Form and Content of Yoruba Ijala*. Ibadan: Oxford University Press, 1966.

Bamgbose, Ayo. "The Meaning of Olo.dumare: An Etymology of the Name of the Yoruba High God." *African Notes* 7, no.1 (1971): 25-32.

Biobaku, S. *Egba and Their Neighbors*. Ibadan, Nigeria: University Press Plc, 1991.

Blier, Susan Preston. *African Vodun: Art, Psychology and Power*. Chicago: University of Chicago Press, 1995.

——"African Art Studies at the Crossroads: An American Perspective." *African Art Studies: The State of the Discipline*. Washington D.C.: Smithsonian Institution, 1990, 91-118.

Boahen, A. Adu. *African Perspectives on Colonialism*. Baltimore: The John Hopkins Press,

1987.

Brett-Smith, Sarah. *The Making of the Bamana Sculpture*. New York: Cambridge University Press, 1994.

Chinweizu, Onwuchekwa Jemie, and Ihechukwu Madubuike. *Towards The Decolonization of African Literature*. Enugu: Fourth Dimension Publishers, 1980.

Christian, Barbara. "The Race for Theory." *Cultural Critique* 6 (Spring 1987): 51-63.

Clifford, James. "On Collecting Art and Culture." *OUT THERE: Marginalization and Contemporary Cultures*. New York: The New Museum of Contemporary Art and The MIT Press, 1991. 141-169.

————. "Histories of the Tribal and Modern." *DISCOURSES: Conversations in Postmodern Art and Culture*. New York: The New Museum of Contemporary Art, 1990. 408-424.

Cockcroft, Eva. "Abstract Expressionism, Weapon of the Cold War." *Artforum* 12, no. 10 (June 1974): 39-41.

Cole, Herbert. *Icons: Ideals and Power in the Art of Africa*. Washington D.C.: Smithsonian Institution, 1990.

Cornet, Joseph. "African Art and Authenticity." *African Arts* 9, no.1 (1975): 52-55.

Crowder, Michael. *The Story of Nigeria*. London: Faber and Faber, 1962.

Danto, Arthur. "Artifact and Art." *ART/artifact*. New York: The Center for African Art, 1988. 18-32.

Davies, Carole Boyce. "Feminist Consciousness and African Literary Criticism." *Ngambika: Studies of Women in African Literature*. Ed. Carole Boyce Davies and Anne Adams Graves. Trenton, New Jersey: African World Press, 1986: 1-23.

Drewal, Henry John. "African Art Studies Today." *African Art Studies: The State of the Discipline*. Washington D.C.: Smithsonian Institution, 1990. 29-62.

Echeruo, Michael. "From Transition to Transition." *Research in African Literature* 22, no.4 (1991): 135-145.

Enekwe, Onuora. *IGBO MASKS: The Oneness of Ritual and Theatre*. Lagos: Nigeria Magazine, 1987.

Enwonwu, Ben. "African View of Art and Some Problems Facing the African Artist." *1st World Festival of Negro Arts*. Paris: Society of African Culture/UNESCO, 1968. 417-426.

———— "Problems of the African Artist Today." *Presence Africaine* 8-10 (June-November 1956): 177-178.

Eyo, Ekpo. "Response by Ekpo Eyo." *African Art Studies: The State of the Discipline*. Washington D.C.: Smithsonian Institution, 1990. 111-118.

Fagg, William. "Introduction." *The Art of West Africa: Sculpture and Tribal Masks*. New York: The New American Library and UNESCO, 1967. 5-24.

Fair, E. F. "War, Famine, and Poverty: Race in the Construction of Africa's Media Images." *Journal of Communication Inquiry* 17 (1993): 5-22.

Flores, Toni. "The Anthology of Aesthetics." *Dialectical Anthropology* 10.1-2 (1985): 27-41.

Fry, Jacqueline. "On Exhibiting African Art." *The Visual Arts: Plastic and Graphic*. Ed. Justin M. Cordwell. The Hague: Monton Publishers, 1979. 535-552.

Frye, Marilyn. *The Politics of Reality: Essays in Feminist Theory*. Trumansburg, New York:

Crossing Press, 1983.

Garfinkel, Harold. "Studies of the Routine Grounds of Everyday Activities." *Studies in Social Interaction*. Ed. David Sudnow. New York: The Free Press, 1972. 1-30.

Gerbrands, Adrian A. "The History of African Art Studies." *African Art Studies: The State of the Discipline*. Washington D.C.: Smithsonian Institution, 1990. 11-28.

Harris, Angela. "Race and Essentialism in Feminist Legal Theory." *Stanford Law Review* 42 (1990): 581-616.

Hoffman, Rachel. "Objects and Acts." *African Arts* (Summer 1995): 56-59.

———. "HEROIC FIGURES." *African Arts* 22, no.2 (February 1989): 22, 24, 27.

hooks, bell. *Talking Back*. Boston: South End Press, 1989.

Janson, H. W. *The History of Art*. New York: Harry N. Abrams Inc., 1993.

Jones, G. I. *The Art of Eastern Nigeria*. Cambridge, rpt. 1984.

Kasfir, Sidney Littlefield. "African Art and Authenticity: A Text with a Shadow." *African Arts* 25, no.2 (1992): 41-53, 96-97.

Kinni, Oba Alaiyuyeluwa Adetoyese Laoye. "On the subject of Yoruba drum music." *Odu* 7 (1959).

Kone, Kassim. "Review of *The Making of Bamana Sculpture: Creativity and Gender*." *African Arts* (Spring 1996): 90-91.

Lasebikan, E. L. "Tone in Yoruba Poetry." *Odu* 2 (1955).

Maquet, Jacques. *The Aesthetic Experience: An Anthropologist Looks at the Visual Arts*. New Haven: Yale University Press, 1986.

Mba, Nina. "Olufunmilayo Ransome-Kuti." *Nigerian Women in Historical Perspective*. Ed. Bolanle Awe. Ibadan: Sankore/Bookcraft, 1992. 133-144.

McPherson, C.B. *The Political Theory of Possessive Individualism*. London: Oxford University Press, 1962).

Minh Ha, Trinh. *Woman Native Other*. Bloomington: Indiana University Press, 1989.

Mohanty, Chandra Talpade, Ann Russo and Lourdes Torres, eds. *Third World Women and the Politics of Feminism*. Bloomington: University Press, 1991.

Monture, Patricia. "Ka-Nin-Geh-Heh-Gah-E-Sa-Nonh-Yah-Gah." *Canadian Journal of Women and the Law* 2 (1986): 157-170.

Nooter, Mary. *Secrecy: African Art that Conceals and Reveals*. New York: Museum for African Art, 1993.

Nzegwu, Nkiru. "Exhibition Review." *American Anthropologist*. 96, (1994): 227-229.

———. "Overcoming Form/Content Tensions in Appreciating African Art Forms." *Heroic Figures*, Kingston, Canada: Agnes Etherington Art Center, 1988. 5-13.

———. "Are Western Theories Relevant for the Understanding of African Art." *The Reasons of Art*. Ed. Peter McCormick. Ottawa: University of Ottawa Press, 1985. 173-177.

Nzewi, Meki. "New Directions For Dysfunctionalized Art Forms: Prospecting the Ekpo Routine." *Nigeria Magazine* 53, no.3 (1986): 38-51.

Onwudiwe, Ebere. "Images and Development: An Exploratory Discussion." *The Journal of African Policy Studies* 1, no.3 (1995): 85-97.

Ottenberg, Simon. "Response by Simon Ottenberg." *African Art Studies: The State of the Discipline*. Washington D.C.: Smithsonian Institution, 1990. 125-136.

Owusu, Maxwell. "Ethnography of Africa: The Usefulness of the Useless." *American Anthropologist* 80 (1978): 310-334.

Paudrat, Louis. "The Arrival of Tribal Objects in the West: From Africa." *"PRIMITIV-ISM" in 20th Century Art*. New York: The Museum of Modern Art, 1984. 125-175.

p'Bitek, Okot. *Song of Lawino*. Nairobi: East African Publishing House, 1966.

Rubin, William. "Modernist Primitivism: An Introduction." *"PRIMITIVISM" in 20th Century Art*. New York: The Museum of Modern Art, 1984. 1-79.

Terborg-Penn, Rosalyn. "Discrimination Against Afro-American Women in the Woman's Movement, 1830-1920." *Black Women Cross-Culturally*. Ed. Filomena Chioma Steady. Cambridge, MA: Schenkman Publication Co., 1981. 301-315.

Thompson, Robert Farris, "Aesthetic of the Cool." *African Arts* 7, no.1(1973): 41-43, 64-67.

Tutola, Amos. *The Palm-Wine Drinkard*. New York: Grove Press, 1953.

Umoetuk, Okon U. "Body Art in Ibibio Culture." *Nigeria Magazine* 5, no.2 (1985): 40 56.

Vogel, Susan Mullin. "Introduction." *ART/artifact*. New York: The Center for African Art and Prestel Verlag, 1988. 11-17.

______. *Perspectives: Angles on African Art*. New York: The Center for African Art and Harry N. Abrams, 1987.

______. *Aesthetics of African Art: The Carlo Monzino Collection*. New York: The Center for African Art, 1986.

Zeleza, Paul Tiyambe. "African Studies and the Disintegration of Paradigms." *Africa Development* 19, no.4 (1994): 179-193.

6.
ALICE IN MOTHERLAND:
Reading Alice Walker on Africa and Screening the Color "Black"

Oyèrónké Oyewùmí

"Let the jury consider their verdict," the King said, for about the twentieth time that day.
"No, no!" said the Queen. "Sentence first—verdict afterwards."
Lewis Carroll, Alice in Wonderland

In the imaginary worlds frequented by Alice, the sentence always precede the verdict. And so it is that when mother Africa, without due process, was arraigned in the international court of Euro-American opinion, mama could not be anything else but guilty and guilty as presupposed. Africa's fancied accuser was none other than the "Blameless Vulva,"[1] which was presumed innocent. I am, of course, referring to African American feminist writer Alice Walker's assault on Africans in the guise of an evangelizing mission to eradicate female circumcision in "Africa."[2]

In 1992, Walker published *Possessing the Secret of Joy*, a novel in which she purports to document the social practice of female circumcision in "Africa." The novel is presented as part fiction and part fact; one could call it "factitious." By the end of the book, however, there is no doubt that, for Walker, the story must be read not as a work of imagination but as a call to arms. In her final chapter, she addresses the reader and produces some "real" facts and statistics to undergird her tale of horror. Playing the evangelist, she even promises to use a portion of the royalties from her book "to educate women and girls, men and boys about the hazardous effects of genital mutilation" (Walker 1992:285). How much more reality-based can one get?[3]

Following *Possessing*, Walker collaborated with film-maker Pratibha Parmar on a film documentary accompanied by a book titled *Warrior Marks: Female Genital Mutilation and the Sexual Blinding of Women*. The book provides an account of the making of the movie, which depicts in a visual medium what is alleged in the novel. The objective of this paper is to interrogate Walker's representation of Africa in both *Possessing* and *Warrior Marks* (the book), examining the images of Africa presented and the strategies used to ground the picture. It is my contention that Walker's claim of consanguinity with Africans notwithstanding, she is best read within the context of Western imperialism in relation to Africa and the narcissism or navel-gazing of contemporary American life.

In the first part of the paper, I will show that Walker affirms the age-old Western tradition of inventing Africa, in the process, I try to discern what new contribution she is making. In the second part of the paper, I will unpack the concept of blackness and also the category of race, which is one of the tropes in these writings. Walker deliberately cultivates race as a central category and then problematizes it by her oppositional representation of Africans and African Americans. A thorough understanding of Walker's project, neuroses, and concerns requires an investigation of her positioning *vis-à-vis* "blackness" and motherhood.

From the outset, it should be clear that this paper is not about the social practice of circumcision in some African cultures, because I do not believe that this is Walker's primary interest. To introduce a cliché, if there were no female circumcision in some parts of Africa, Westerners would have invented it. Such a development would be nothing new; in the past, they have been known to create persons, events, and customs that affirms their voyeuristic and groin-centered preoccupations with Africa. Remember that from 1810 to 1815, Saartje Baartman (also called Sarah or the "Hottentot Venus"), a twenty-five year-old Khoi-San woman from Southern Africa, was exhibited in many parts of Western Europe; only her death in 1815 put an end to this spectacle. (Gilman 1985: 111-2) Saartje Baartman had been exhibited to present to European audiences a so-called anomaly they found riveting: her protruding buttocks. The alleged large size of her labia and nymphae, labeled the "Hottentot apron," was also of immense fascination in scientific circles. For most Europeans who viewed her, Saartje Baartman existed only as "a collection of sexual body parts." (Ibid:88)

In 1993, almost two centuries later, Walker collaborated with Parmar on a film to expose African women's genitalia as an anomaly. Walker's African woman, like her foremother Saartje, is nothing but a collection of sexual parts, this time mutilated to boot. It must be remarked that though Saartje was displayed for European consumption because her parts were *hyper-sexual* from a Western perspective, the African woman today is displayed for the *hypo-sexuality* caused by her presumed missing parts. The bottom line (pun intended) is that whatever the realities of Africa and African bodies, they are liable to be exhibited to soothe the Western mind/body of its sexual predilections *du jour*. This course of events is nothing but a demonstration of the unequal power relations that have continued to structure the association between Westerners and Africans since the fifteenth century. Walker is just the latest writer in a longstanding Western tradition that employs stock images and ideas about Africa. These portrayals are not informed by African realities; instead, they reflect the mind of the writer and the Western culture of which she is a part.

The medium may have changed, but the mindset and concerns remain the same. Up until the 1920s, Africans were routinely exhibited in European zoos and natural history museums, as part of their "exotic" collections. By the 1920s, these exhibitions had been replaced by film. With the development of cinematic technology, exhibitors did not have to bring whole villages of Wolof or "Ashantee" to Paris and Vienna, as they had done in the past; now villages could just be filmed *in situ* and the images brought back to the West. (Gilman 1985:88) This is precisely what Walker attempts to do in *Warrior Marks* (the movie). The theme of the project is really Alice's Odyssey; focusing on the mid-life phase of her lifelong journey to find herself against the background of an American culture that is increasingly and unashamedly narcissistic. Consider this navel-gazing statement from *Warrior Marks* in which Walker is both the speaker and the addressee:

> Happy Birthday my little wondrous brown body that has its period and is trying to get through (or begin) menopause–hence my insomnia! You have carried my spirit well. I honor you and love you and vow I will continue to care for you with all the love I have found waiting for myself in my heart. (Walker 1993:50)

Clearly, the preoccupation is always with exhibiting bodies, whether it is African bodies or "my little wondrous body."[4] Precisely because Euro/American discourse of the social, is somatocentric in that what is believed to undergird social hierarchies, privileges, identities, and ultimately social interest derives from the body.

A well-known European custom prescribes that, at her wedding, a bride should wear:

> something old,
> something new,

something borrowed,
something blue.

My analyses of Walker's writings on Africa are inspired by the themes suggested in these couplets, although not necessarily in this order. The imagery of marriage invoked here draws attention to the marriage of convenience between Western imperialist traditions and the ideas of Walker, an African-American woman who belongs to a group that has borne disproportionately the brunt of these racist practices. The image of a marital union also highlights the unhappy marriage of feminists of different hues—Western feminists and those from Africa, Asia, and Latin America at one level; and, at another, the presumed alliances among a hodge-podge of women homogenized into the categories "Third World Women" and "Women of Color." These alliances are predicated on the idea that people with similar body parts and pigmentation must have a common interest. But a common biology is not a common interest. Humans are cultural beings and culture cannot be wished away in favor of biology. If this variety of people are homogenized, it is not their bodies which make them the same, but their common histories of colonial oppression. On the other hand, it could be the result of the Western cultural perception that they are as a group distinct from Europeans and are therefore homogeneously, systematically discriminated against. At yet another level, the allusion to marriage draws attention to the notion that in the United States children can now divorce their parents. In the writings that are analyzed here, we see Walker attempt to divorce both her real mother and her symbolic mother, Africa, on account of a perceived betrayal.

SOMETHING OLD: WESTERN IMPERIALIST TRADITIONS AND THE INVENTION OF AFRICA

Africa has been central in Western discourses of difference and degeneration. For centuries, Europeans have envisioned and written about Africa mainly in terms of Otherness, a vehicle for articulating what the West is not. Of course the classic statement of this belief is Joseph Conrad's *Heart of Darkness*. This intellectual tradition owes much to a vision of society as being a reflection of the physical bodies to be found in it. Because Africans were seen to be physically different from Europeans, who presented themselves as the norm, certain ideas and images were deployed to enunciate what Europeans perceived as the pathologies of difference. Africans were by no means the only group upon which Europeans pinned the badge of difference; European women, the urban poor, Jews, and Native Americans were similarly labeled. African women in particular, however, appear to represent the ultimate Other, combining in one category a racial and sexual Otherness with a special role as the "Other's Other," at least from the point of view of the European males who authorized these images.

In this regard, Sander Gilman's work shows the various modes of figuration of Otherness[5]; they invoked, including the reduction of the Other to body parts along with projections of hyper-sexuality and bestiality. In the nineteenth century, for example, when Saartje Baartman was exhibited in Europe, she was in the charge of an *animal trainer* and was viewed as no more than a collection of sexual body parts. After her death, George Couvier, the dean of French biologists, dissected her genitalia; the remains are still on a shelf in the Musee de l' Homme in Paris. After a tour of the museum, historian of science Stephen Jay Gould observed that "no brains of women, ... nor any male genitalia grace the collection" (Gilman 1985:270). It is equally noteworthy that there were no European female genitalia in the collection; the three jars containing female genitalia were labeled *"une negresse, une Peruvienne, et la Venus Hottentotte"* (Ibid:20). Given the premise of genetic research, it is curious that no samples of European female genitalia were on display for comparative purposes. Feminist purveyors of global sisterhood–a sisterhood based on a common genitalia–would do well to note that even apparently similar body parts have different histories and locations. It is similar histories and common interests, and not body parts, that should be the focus of alliances.

Nancy Stepan explains the Victorian mindset that created the gory exhibits in this Paris museum:

> Of all the boundaries between peoples, the sexual one was the most problematic to the Victorian mind. In the area of racial thought, there had been since the earliest of times a prurient interest in the strange sexual customs of alien peoples, especially the African. Did African women, for instance, mate with the great apes who came out of Africa? Were the sexual organs of Africans larger than those of whites? Did a tropical climate encourage an unbridled sexuality that resulted in promiscuity? It was not surprising that anthropological accounts of strange peoples provided a surrogate pornography for Europeans. (Stepan 1985:104-105)

Walker's *Possessing* and *Warrior Marks* are best read within the Western imperialist tradition in which "the black whether male or female, came to represent the genitalia." (Gilman 1985:109) In that discourse, African female genitalia are also highlighted as proof of African sub-humanness.

In the nineteenth century, the newly emerging discipline of *anthropologie* focused almost exclusively on the study of humans in their physical forms and the ways in which physical characteristics dictated human behavior. "In France more than in any country, anthropology took a definitive turn towards physical anthropology" (Cohen 1980:219). The setting of some scenes of Walker's novel *Possessing* in France is not accidental. Part of the French *mission civilisatrice* in Africa from the sixteenth century onwards, like Walker's evangelizing mission at the closing years of the twentieth century, was carried out in the Senegambian region of West Africa. Walker's indebtedness to French *anthropolgie* is quite apparent in the construction of her fictional characters and in her claims about Africans in general, African women, and the practice of female circumcision. In fact, one of the main characters in the novel is a French anthropologist whose apparent mission is to save Africans from themselves. He is presented as the missionary "Pierre, who has said he wants to be the first anthropologist to empower and not further endanger his subjects" (Walker 1992:230). This messianic, French anthropologist comes complete with the Western gaze. Tashi, the African woman, is hypnotized by his omniscient eyes and she alleges that, "it was those knowing eyes, with their appraising look, that, from as far away as an undergraduate dormitory at Harvard, saw into me. Even into my dreams" (Ibid:163).

Walker also employs an enduring trope in Western writings: the representation of Africans as animal-like. Consider our introduction to Tashi, the protagonist of the novel:

> Tashi was standing beside Catherine, her mother, a small swaybacked woman with an obdurate expression on her dark lined face, and at first there was only Tashi's hand—a small, dark hand and arm, like that of a monkey, reaching around her mother's lower body and clutching (Ibid:7).

Compare this to the observations of the French scientist Cuvier about Tashi's foremother Saartje Baartman more than a century and half earlier: "When she was alive, her movements were brusque and capricious like those of a monkey... I have never seen a human head more resembling a monkey's than hers." (Cohen 1988:239) Similarly, Berenger-Feraud, the chief medical officer of colonial Senegal, and a nineteenth-century French colonizer of Africa, asserted that "the angle formed by the pelvic bone or backbone of Wolof women is such that it looked more natural for them to be walking on all fours than to walk upright as bipeds" (Cohen 1980:241). Walker echoes this racist idea in her depiction of Tashi. In one of the sessions with her psychoanalyst, Tashi recounts that in her dream, "The first thing I drew was the meeting of my mother with the leopard on her path.... But I drew, then painted, a leopard with two legs, my terrified mother with four" (Walker

1992:54).

There is even a literary precedent for this interchangeability of Africans and animals. In 1863, a novel titled *Five Weeks in a Balloon* by Jules Verne, published in Paris, contained dialogue revealing the author's belief about the close resemblance between Africans and monkeys:

> "There was an attack!" said Joe. "We began to think we were besieged by the natives."
> "They were only apes, fortunately," replied the doctor.
> "At a distance the difference is not striking, my dear Samuel."
> "Not even when you are close," said Joe (Cohen 1980:243).

Walker takes up this bestial imagery using the depiction of the beast of burden arguably, the dominant image of the African woman today. Elsewhere (in this volume), I have argued that the belabored image of the overworked African woman complements the image of African men as lazy and indolent in traditional Africanist discourse. Walker works this image at various points in *Possessing,* but one of the most striking instances is in Tashi's description of her mother:

> And there was my mother, trudging along the path in front of me, her load of groundnuts forcing her nearly double. I have never seen anyone work as hard as my mother, or pull her share of work with a more resigned dignity... I studied the white rinds of my mother's heels, and felt in my own heart the weight of Dura's death settling upon her spirit, like the groundnuts that bent her back. As she staggered under her load, I half expected her footprints, into which I was careful to step, to stain my own feet with tears and blood (Walker 1992:16).

In *Possessing,* the representations of pathology are equally central. Olivia's observations about Tashi's state after the circumcision are telling enough:

> It now took a quarter of an hour for her to pee. Her menstrual periods lasted ten days. She was incapacitated by cramps nearly half the month. There were premenstrual cramps: cramps caused by the near impossibility of flow passing through so tiny an aperture as M'Lissa had left, after fastening together the raw side of Tashi's vagina with a couple of thorns and inserting a straw so that in healing, the traumatized flesh might not grow together, shutting the opening completely; ... There was the odor, too, of soured blood, which no amount of scrubbing, until we got to America, ever washed off (Ibid:65).

Of course, today no depiction of disease and sexual pathology would be complete without AIDS, a disease that is perceived to collapse together degenerate people and degenerate behavior. The Olinkans, Walker's fictional Africans, are afflicted with AIDS, a disease which she believes is spread primarily through circumcision. Both AIDS and female circumcision, then, serve as convenient vehicles for articulating centuries-old European stereotypes about Africa.

A discussion of this image-making would not be complete without consideration of the rhetorical strategies used to put them in place. One particularly glaring strategy, like the images described above, does not originate with Walker. This strategy is what I call the villagization of Africa, the assertion of the powerful myth that Africa is a homogeneous, unitary state of primitivism in words and deeds. This myth is part of the traditional discourse of inventing Africa and over the years has proved undiscardable despite the diversity of African nations, cultures, and societies. African philosopher Paulin Hountondji appropriately named this myth Unanimism. Its primary assumption, he explains, is "primitive unanimity with its suggestion that in primitive societies—that is to say non-Western societies—everybody agrees with everybody else. It follows that in such societies there can never be individual beliefs or philosophies but only collective systems of belief" (60). Thus Walker in *Warrior Marks* writes condescendingly about this person/thing called Africa: "To be in Africa. To realize Africans are doing OK, basically, if they'd just stop hurting themselves. And that I love Africa. That Africans have time and space. . . Africans really should be able to be wise, not just clever or smart" (Walker 1993:50).

Similarly, in *Possessing* she miniaturizes Africa by stereotyping: "The Mbele camp was a replica of *an African village*" (Walker 1992:43). And yet another passage reads, "The operation she'd had done to herself joined her, she felt, to these women, whom she envisioned as strong, invincible. Completely woman. *Completely African*" [my emphasis] (Walker 1992:64). What is a typical African village, and indeed who or what is this typical African that embodies Africanness, given a varied and various continent of peoples, cultures, and countries? It is this unanimist perception that enables this wholesale homogenizing and miniaturizing of such a vast and diverse continent. How and why does female circumcision, which is not practiced by many African cultures, become the defining characteristic of Africanness? Are the Luo of Western Kenya, for example, not African then because they circumcise neither males nor females? What about the two Ijo communities of Amakiri and Ebiama in southeastern Nigeria, in which both groups claim the ethnic identity of Ijo but only one group practices clitoridectomy? Consider this reaction of a group of Suku from Zaire to the idea of female circumcision as reported by an anthropologist:

> When I once mentioned to a group of Suku that in some parts of Africa
> women are "circumcised," the information was greeted with disbelief and
> hilarity. One person who had literally fallen on the ground with laughter, asked
> in jest whether women in these places also impregnated women (Kopytoff
> 1990:83).

Why should infibulation and clitoridectomy be lumped together as one cultural practice? Consider this discussion of female circumcision in Amakiri,
where premarital sex is not frowned upon, and in which "before a girl finally
settles down to a permanent partner and marital proceedings are initiated, she
frequently bears a child" (Hollos and Leis 1989:124).

> Becoming an adult Ijo is *bound up with pregnancy* [my emphasis]. In Amakiri
> there is an added contingency to attaining adulthood—circumcision—which is
> avoided on Ebiama. In the former community, *women are circumcised in the
> seventh month of gestation*, which is the first step in the ritual process toward the
> attainment of full adult status, culminating in later life in a coming out cer-
> emony (Ibid: 125).

Clearly, the practice as described for the Ijo has nothing to do with maintaining virginity; rather, it is a prenatal rite to ensure the safety of the child and the
fertility of the mother and the earth. It is apparently unlike infibulation as it
has been described for Sudan and Somalia, where it appears to be associated
with the preservation of virginity, a tenet that is associated with adherence to
the two world religions: Islam (in this specific case), and Christianity.

In researching socio-cultural practices, context-specificity is important.
Interpretations of circumcision or any other issue, for that matter, cannot be
generalized from one place to the other, because, although the practice may
appear similar, its underlying meaning and function may be different. Consequently, using the Kikuyu[6] example or the Dogon[7] meaning of the practice to
interpret other societies makes no sense whatsoever. The practice must be
interpreted within the cultural and historical context of each society; we have
to see how it functions and fits in with other institutions before we can begin
to make any kind of assessment or judgment about its purpose or meaning.
The point is that very little research on circumcision has been done within the
whole cultural context of specific communities. Thus, many of the claims
that are being made are based on Western assumptions and studies of a few
groups, which are then applied to other African groups to prove Western
ideologies. Such generalizations are baseless in reality and yield very little useful
information.

Undoubtedly, the deployment of a unanimist perspective of Africa is
exemplified by Walker 's insistence on creating an African language despite

the fact that there are at least one thousand African languages in use today; hers is a fictional language in which she blends the vocabulary of one language with that of another and even manufactures some more words. This creation of a supposed "African" language underscores the fictional nature of Walker's Africa.

Another method Walker employs to ground her misconceptions is what I refer to as a process of exceptionalizing. Used positively or negatively, it is the stock in trade of cultural outsiders; once the observer has made up her mind about a person, a practice, a group or phenomenon, nothing else changes the perception. Instead, all contrary evidence is made into the exception that proves the invented rule. The following passage from *Warrior Marks* about the "state of womanhood" in the Senegambia shows Walker's determination to paint only a negative picture.

> There's no such thing as a woman having a quiet moment on the beach alone. Or anywhere else, for that matter. Women are routinely followed, yelled at, harassed on the street. I can't help but connect this behavior to genital mutilation: the acceptance of domination, the lack of a strong sense of self one sees among women here. Or, conversely, there will be *occasionally* an extremely loud brash woman, like the one who pressed us to buy her wares with such vigor that she ran us out of her stall. *These are the women whose pent-up anger seems to be a powder keg* [my emphasis] (Walker 1993:53-54).

Likewise, Nancy, one of Walker's disciples in the film-making party, observes that Gambian women dress in beautiful, colorful fabrics, which she contends are a creative reflection of the women's pain (Ibid:10). Obviously, Gambian women, the object of this instance of negative exceptionalizing, cannot win. Because Walker and her group are bent on painting only a negative picture of Africans, they will create this negative picture regardless of what these African women say or do.

In contrast, Walker uses the method of positive exceptionalizing in *Possessing* not for Africa, but to maintain the civilization that Europe represents from her standpoint. She suggests that Marquis de Sade, the French man from whose name and behavior the word "sadism" was denied, is not representative of French culture. Pierre and his French mother Lisette discuss his uniqueness in French culture:

> "In France there are no instruments of torture beside the bed."
> "And the Marquis de Sade?" I asked.
> "Thankfully, only *one* man, she said, and thankfully not in *this century*. She laughed. And thankfully not beside *my bed*" (Walker 1992:140).

SOMETHING BORROWED: FEMINIST EVANGELISM[8] AND "VICTIMOLOGY"

Western feminists, as heiresses to the imperialist tradition of at once demonizing and saving Africa from itself, have been no less active in refurbishing the old images of Africa; they added new dimensions, including a more gender-specific elaboration of these myths about Africa. Imperial feminism had discovered its social mission. Walker has borrowed from this neo-Western feminist tradition in her project of "saving Africa." Although in her earlier writings Walker had articulated the concept of "womanism" (Walker 1985) derived from African-American culture as a black version of women's self-determination, her approach in relation to Africa offers no departure from the representation of African women in the larger Western feminist discourse.

The denial of female agency, better known as feminist victimology, is one of the hallmarks of feminist writing, and its foundations must be sought in the beginnings of Second Wave feminism in the United States. Because of feminisms connections to the Civil Rights movement, there arose a need on the part of liberal white women to exculpate themselves from the blame of having participated with their men in the ignominious historical processes of genocide, slavery, and colonialism. Claiming powerlessness and the status of victims, they could deny their own agency. However, the source of the lack of agency attributed to African, Asian, and Latin-American women is different. At the global level, the lack of agency attributed to women of these societies is a function of the unwillingness of Western women to accord them humanity. Instead, they have been reduced to chattel. A number of scholars have written about this ethnocentrism but none more eloquently than Marnia Lazreg when she writes on Algerian women. She admonishes researchers:

> To take intersubjectivity into consideration when studying Algerian women or other Third World women means seeing their lives as meaningful, coherent, and understandable instead of being infused "by us" with doom and sorrow. It means that their lives like "ours" are structured by economic, political and structural factors. It means that these women, like us are engaged in the process of adjusting, often shaping, at times resisting and even transforming their environment. It means that they have their own individuality; they are "for themselves" instead of being "for us." An appropriation of their singular individuality to fit the generalizing categories of "our" analyses is an assault on their integrity and on their identity (Lazreg 1988:84).

Walker's interpretation of female circumcision is founded on the idea that it is authorized by patriarchy for the benefit of men and for the sexual control of women. Despite the dominance and centrality of females in performing the rites of circumcision as she describes it for Gambia, she insists that it is a "patriarchal wounding." She claims that her own "visual mutilation" helped her "to see the ways in which women are rather routinely mutilated in most parts of the world" (Walker 1993:267). One should ask the question, the routine mutilation of women by whom? It is curious that in the larger debate on female circumcision in the United States media, instances of mothers who take the initiative to circumcise their daughters despite the objection of the fathers, are not interpreted as examples of female self-assertion and/or defiance of patriarchal authority. Instead, such women are often projected as having succumbed to community pressure, the community of course being defined as male-created. It should be understood that, just like men, women are participants in the creating of cultures and in the constitution of community standards for good or ill.

A more recent development can be seen in the emergence of scholars and writers like Walker who claim to fall into the nebulous category of Third World Women and women of color, non-Euroethnic women who have now stepped into the high heels of their European sisters to speak for and about women from other regions of the world–women of which they know nothing and with whom they have few common interests. Homogenizing concepts like "Third World women" and "women of color " and even "Black women" are used to erase cultural specificities, but also, and more importantly, to mask regional and class privileges undergirding the global system. Often these categorizations function as yet another opportunity to elevate one group at the expense of another. It needs to be understood that representation cannot be on the bases of pigmentation or a common collection of body parts, but on the commonality of interests, recognizing that interests are dynamic and situational. It is a fallacy to think that common interests can be discerned just by color, and it is a mistake to act as if groups and group interests are cast in stone.

Many Western women continue to maintain their patronizing attitude towards different groups of non-Western women, upholding a "We've come a long way, baby"[9] posture to underscore what they consider their superior achievement in liberating themselves from the shackles of patriarchy. As I have pointed out elsewhere, the advantages enjoyed by Western women in the global system have nothing to do with womanhood, whatever that may be. Rather, these privileges are due to the benefits they enjoy as a racial group and to the dominance of their countries in the global capitalist system. When Walker declined to pay the Gambian woman film consultant her due, she defined herself as a black woman who did not have the same resources as her American compatriots who had earlier made a documentary in Gambia.

She writes, "Well, we are black women, and our resources are not the same as those of the American television network, which is upper-class white and male (even though a white woman had come to make the documentary)" (Walker 1993:41). Her claim is disingenuous because she conveniently forgets that, black or not, the fact that she is an American has contributed largely to her ability to engage in this kind of project in Africa. Walker may or may not have the same advantages as the white American male and female filmmaker (although I believe this to be debatable in this instance, at least), but, pigmentation notwithstanding, she is clearly not in the same position as the African women whose genitalia she insists on making the topic of discussion in American living rooms and coffee shops, and the victim *du jour* of some Women's Studies courses across the United States. In fact, she is simply exploiting purported racial consanguinity to practice capitalist exploitation American style.

On the issue of female victimhood and male agency, it is disturbing to see how African female prostitution is perceived in contrast to male prostitution. Walker registers her objection to female prostitution when she mentions a place in Dakar called "Le ponty, a place of prostitution. It looked like a very sleazy sandwich shop, and Deborah and I left after a few minutes. The thought of prostitution is always horrible, but the thought of genitally mutilated prostitutes was more than I could tolerate." (Walker 1993) She is, however, silent on male prostitution. Parmar, her collaborator, is more explicit. She claims that the young African prostitutes were eyeing Walker and her group and "suspected them of horning in on their territory. Their clients are white men, tourists who come to Africa specifically to have sex with African women. It is so sad that these women must resort to prostitution as a means of survival" (Walker 1993:143). Regarding, the same phenomenon amongst males, Parmar merely observed, "We have noticed many older white women tourists accompanied by young Gambian men. Interesting" (Ibid: 200). Clearly, for her, African male prostitution is acceptable. And just as clearly, this is a case of gender discrimination.

In contrast, a recent report on sex tourism in Gambia paints a disturbing picture particularly in regard to its prevalence. A white, female senior citizen from England who had had numerous sexual encounters with young Gambian male prostitutes had this to say:

> You don't ask for sex, but the men seem to know you want it. They say things like, "would you like to see the real Africa?" It's all very discreet. I had four different boys that holiday and the best sex I ever had. I came back a new woman. It was very empowering as a woman to be able to have my pick of a bunch of beautiful men (*Marie Claire* 1994:69).

Walker had stated that one of her goals in doing the documentary was to explore "the likelihood of a connection between AIDS and female circumcision?" Clearly, prostitution fits very well into this theme. Why, then, does she not seize the opportunity of white men and women cavorting with Africans (male and female) to explore the transmission of AIDS transglobally? One cannot over-emphasize the role of prostitution in disease transmission when one takes into account the numbers of sexual partners encountered. Take, for example, the variety of European women encountered by a Gambian male prostitute, a veteran of the sex trade.

> I've fucked all sorts since then, all nationalities. The British like rastas, and they like to drink before they do anything. They're kinder than the Swedish, who just want to get a black man. The old women need you to like them; you have to fuss over them and spend a lot of time to give enjoyment. I don't like condoms because they leave no feeling. *I'm not worried about AIDS-I trust myself.* [My emphasis] (Ibid:18).

Between Walker's Africa, and the "Africa" unveiled by the male prostitutes, will the real Africa(s) please stand up? Both Parmar and Walker are silent about another very visible aspect of sex tourism in Gambia, the preying of white men on young boys *a la* Philippines and Thailand. For a person who is concerned about saving Africa's children and saving the continent from an alleged AIDS genocide, Walker's silence on this issue of male prostitution is deafening and suggest a sexist perspective which assumes that boys will be boys and girls will be victims. Females do not have a monopoly on victimhood, nor males a corner on agency. If salvation is indeed an issue, then all victimized children are in need of it.

In many feminist writings, the universe of female oppression is created by a failure to acknowledge the ways in which some societal institutions and practices victimize males. I am at a loss to understand why the periodic patriarchal blood-letting euphemistically known as civil wars, world wars, and regional wars which in many societies have victimized more directly the male population have not received adequate feminist attention and vituperation. Too often, feminist analysis of circumcision and other social practices fails to pay attention to how they may impinge on males and other social groups. For instance, one reason young male prostitutes in Gambia give for their line of work is that they are required to provide for their families despite the fact that there are no other jobs available.

SOMETHING NEW, SOMETHING BLUE: MOTHERHOOD AND THE AFRICAN-AMERICAN SEARCH FOR AFRICA

> Negro women, the doctor says into my silence, can never be analyzed effectively because they can never bring themselves to blame their mothers.
> Blame them for what? I asked.
> Blame them for anything, said he (Walker 1992:19).

Motherhood is an especially appropriate theme for the elucidation of Walker's mission in Africa. On the issue of motherhood, Walker sings the blues. Historically, many African Americans have portrayed Africa as the motherland. Africa is seen as mother, sometimes as the mother who allowed her children to be sold into slavery. Although by and large, her sin is, portrayed as one of omission, she remains the mother nonetheless. With regard to the other parent, the picture appears different in that America—the father—is presented as one who refuses to acknowledge Africa's children who have been rendered bastards as a result. W. E. B DuBois' elucidation of the two souls of black folks—the Negro and the American—echoes this theme of dual cultural parentage. Along the same lines, literary scholar Henry Louis Gates called America the surname in the appellation African Americans. (Gates 1992) In short, they are mama's baby, papa's maybe, to borrow a phrase from African American scholar, Hortense Spillers. One should note that in addition to being the symbolic father, in reality the slave master's institutionalized rape of black women during the period of slavery resulted in the reproduction of labor and capital in the form of unacknowledged children who were exploited as slaves. It is this tension between Africa as mother and America as the abusive patriarchal father that has been one of the central themes of the African-American experience.

Walker has, however, successfully reversed this formulation in her representation of Africa as the guilty, evil mother and America as the father who fell into sin because of her. "White is not the culprit this time," she writes in *Possessing* (Walker 1992:106). Walker readily identifies with the father in her portrayal of America and Africa in binary opposition of the Self and the Other, respectively. The America of *Possessing* is hardly recognizable as the place of pain and sorrow that many other African American writers through the years have projected in their accounts. Raye, the African American psychoanalyst, explains to Tashi, the troubled African woman in the novel, why she had asked her dentist to mutilate her gums as a way of empathizing with Tashi's pain of circumcision: "Don't be mad, because my choosing this kind of pain is such a puny effort, … in America this is the best I can do" (Ibid:132). Is this what America really looks like? In sharp contrast, let us look at Cornel

West's portrait of America, which he described as a nihilistic place characterized by "the collapse of the meaning in life" (West 1992:9). West further notes that "the tragic plight of our [American] children clearly reveals our deepest disregard for public well-being. About one out of five children in this country lives in poverty, including one out of every two black children…. Most of our children are neglected by overburdened parents and bombarded by the market values of profit-hungry corporations (West1992:12).

In yet another move to paint a rosy picture of the West in contrast to Africa, Olivia the young African-American woman in the novel lied that "nobody in America or Europe cuts off pieces of themselves" (Walker 1992). To the contrary, consider the observations of feminist scholar Kathryn Pauly Morgan on the prevalence of mutilations among American women:

> I believe we need a feminist framework to understand why breast augmentation, until recently was the most frequently performed kind of cosmetic surgery in North America ("New Bodies for Sale") and why, according to longevity magazine, 1 in every 225 adult Americans have elective surgery in 1989. We need a feminist analysis to understand why actual live women are reduced or reduce themselves to "potential women" and choose to participate in anatomizing and fetishizing their bodies as they buy "contoured bodies," "restored youth" and "permanent beauty." In the face of a growing market and demand for surgical interventions in women's bodies that can and do result in infection, bleeding, embolisms, pulmonary edema, facial nerve injury, unfavorable scar formation, skin loss, blindness, crippling, and death, our silence become a culpable one (Morgan1991:28).

Given the situation as described in the preceding quote, the label "mutilating culture" which Walker uses to describe African cultures is obviously applicable to North America as well. She did not have to go to Africa to find mutilation and pain, or even to find children in need of a savior, for that matter. What is remarkable also in Walker's account of pain is the emphasis on only physical pain as primary, as if this were the only dimension or even the most profound kind of pain. This unidimensional focus on the body speaks to the aforementioned somatocentricity in Western approaches to humanity and society.

In a most disturbing fabrication of history, attempting to apportion blame for the Atlantic Slave Trade and the oppression of slavery in the United States, Walker makes the claim that Africa had taught America about violence:

> Many African women have come here, said Amy. Enslaved women. Many of them sold into bondage because they refused to be circumcised, but many of them sold into bondage circumcised and infibulated. It was this sewed up

woman who fascinated the American doctors who flocked to the slave auctions to examine them, as the women stood naked and defenseless on the block. They learned to do the procedure on other enslaved women; they did this in the name of science. They found a use for it on white women (Walker 1992:188).

These claims at best display Walker's abysmal ignorance of the history and sociology of slavery and of circumcision as a world-wide practice which did not exclude Europe and America.

Walker writes that her African foremother must have been sold into slavery because she refused to be mutilated. In her relentless efforts to force a marriage between incompatibles, she equates circumcision of women with slavery: "I recognized the connection between mutilation and enslavement that is at the root of the domination of women in the world" (Walker 1992:139). She lumps slavery and circumcision together again in her interview with Parmar during the making of the film: "I want to ask them [African women] what custom made it possible for me to end up on another continent, in the USA? We have been separated by a custom similar to genital mutilation, a custom of slavery" (Walker 1993:280).

It is only in the light of the connections she makes between female circumcision and slavery that one can make sense of the nonsensical question that she poses to African American singer Tracy Chapman on Goree Island in Senegal. In the proverbial manner reminiscent of rearranging the deck chairs as the *Titanic* sinks, she asked the singer the following question: "Here we are sitting on the steps of what is called the House of Slaves, and I wondered what you have been thinking about and what you have been feeling about genital mutilation" (Walker 1993:345). The House of Slaves is a monument of remembrance to all the enslaved Africans taken to the Americas, whether they were men, women, or children. For many of these Africans, circumcision was not a custom, and for some it must have been. These facts notwithstanding; it was certainly not an issue at the "door of no return" to the motherland. From Walker's standpoint, Africa is the origin of slavery and even Western misogyny. In keeping with the time-honored Western tradition of demonizing Africa, diseases, pathological behavior, and all bad things in the West are supposed to have originated in Africa.

Still, Walker's gripe against the mother, her palpable anger and unhappiness with mothers, cannot be fully explained by the symbolism of Africa as motherland; at the heart of her pain and anger is the betrayal that she believes she has suffered by her own mother. For Walker, the personal is indeed political and then again personal. She connects her mission in Africa to the fact of a childhood accident which resulted in the loss of an eye, an accident for which she blames her mother. Regarding the accident, she explains,

One day after the birth of my own daughter, I confronted my mother. My father had died, never speaking to me about what happened. After my injury, in fact, he completely withdrew. His own mother had been shot to death when he was eleven, by a man who claimed to love her; *maybe the sight of my injury pained him, maybe not* [my emphasis]. In any event, this is something I will never know (Walker 1993:16).

Even here, we see that she is willing to give her father the benefit of the doubt. But with regard to her mother, this is what she had to say:

My mother asked me to forgive her. She and my father had of course purchased the gun that shot me. *It was she, in particular, who had been in love with "shoot- 'em - up" Western cowboy movies* [my emphasis]. She hadn't considered the consequences of buying my brother's guns (Ibid:17).

Clearly, nearly four decades after the accident, and a quarter of a century after her mother begged for forgiveness, Walker has not forgiven her mother–if indeed an apology is the appropriate response.

But why is Walker so hard on her mother, and why is her father so easily exonerated? The answer may lie in the construction of black motherhood in American culture and the special relationship between mothers and daughters among African Americans. Audre Lorde, the late black poet, elaborates the importance of this mother/girl-child relationship in her discussion of a black woman who was grieving because of the death of her mother:

"The world is divided into two kinds of people," she said, "those who have mothers and those who don't. And I don't have a mother anymore." What I heard her saying was that no other Black woman would ever see who she was, … I heard in her cry of loneliness the source of the romance between Black women and our mommas. Little Black girls, tutored by hate into wanting to become anything else. We cut our eyes at sister because she can only reflect what everybody else except momma seemed to know–that we were hateful, or ugly, or worthless, but certainly unblessed. *We were not boys and we were not white, so we counted for less than nothing, except to our mommas* [My emphasis] (Lorde 1984:159).

In this light we can only imagine the devastating effect on Walker of her mother's supposed betrayal. Who was to give "poor Alice," the motherless child, any sense of worth? We are then not surprised at her denunciation of her mother. Walker readily admits that the unfortunate experience of losing an eye and the negative feelings about her mother's culpability motivate her. It is this personal experience that she projects and imposes on Africans, using it to interpret the practice of female circumcision. Consequently, she collapses together female circumcision—a rite of passage often collectively experienced—with an aberrant personal childhood accident:

> Children place all their love and trust in their mothers. When you think of the depth of the betrayal of the child's trust, this is an emotional wounding, which will never go away. The sense of betrayal, the sense of not being able to trust anyone, will stay with the child as she grows up. I think that is the reason why in a lot of the cultures that we are talking about, there is so much distrust and dissension, and so much silence. (Walker 1993:274)

Apart from the narcissistic nature of her engagements, Walker's facile imposition of her American experience on Africans also stems from the misguided notions in regard to a homogeneous and ontologizing race that subsumes Africa under a regime of blackness. I do not to deny the fact that the enslaved persons who were brought to America were Africans or that many aspects of African values were retained by African Americans. Rather, I merely want to make the point that, despite their African origin, for African Americans, the specificity of the history of capitalist slavery, resistance, and the continuing struggle against racism in the United States are crucial to their self-definition. In their experience in the United States, "blackness" has become a trope for inscribing and describing their history and culture. Significant as it is, the experience of African Americans should not be projected as an essential black experience which defines Africans and all other peoples of African descent in the same way across time and space. Any such attempt constitutes, at best, African American solipsism and, at worst, a fabrication.

Above all, such homogenizing usage represents an unquestioned acceptance of Western biological determinism, which purports that social hierarchies, group interests, and solidarity are a function of genetic considerations. According to this line of reasoning, Africans and African Americans, because of their similar skin pigmentation—blackness—experience the world in the same way and have the same interests regardless of history, social situation, geographical location, and even the issue under consideration. It is not shared pigmentation, however, but shared histories and locations that actually undergird group interest and solidarity. Any assumption to the contrary is nothing but biological-foundationalist thinking which Cornel West has termed racial reasoning, i.e., "an understanding of the black freedom struggle as an affair of skin pigmentation and racial phenotype" (West 1993: 38). Elaborating on the meaning of blackness in the United States, law Professor Patricia Williams asserted that black is also a "designation of those who had no place else to go" (Williams:1991:124). This is hardly an aspect of blackness that one can impose realistically on Africans; it amounts to self-dispossession if we embrace it. "Blackness" whatever the complexity of its history and meaning in the United States, is certainly not what being black means in Nigeria or many other African countries, for that matter; if anything, it has little meaning in terms of situating people in social hierarchies, and it has no predictive value whatsoever as to who goes to school or prison, who gets a job or who doesn't, who lives where, and even who marries whom, or who gets rejected. This situation may change in the future given the on-going racializing process of the global system; but it is not inevitable. Neither is the outcome going to be totally predictable, unidirectional or identical to the African American situation, as it has been commonly understood.

Walker throws history and culture to the wind when she situates female circumcision within the tortured relationship she shares with her mother—a filial relationship whose construction underscores the impossible expectations of African American motherhood in a racist society in which the mother is blamed for the sins not only of the patriarchal fathers but for those of "Uncle Sam" himself. The reality of female circumcision as it is practiced in some African cultures bears no resemblance to Walker's imaginings, which are motivated and shaped by a deep, personal crisis occasioned by her mother's perceived betrayal. The problem is heightened by racism—the bane of American society.

Moreover, it is a retrograde, self-defeating step for Africans to treat their skin pigmentation as something to be explained. In the United States, projecting "black" as a marginalized category of Otherness in relation to "whiteness," which is taken as the norm may be unavoidable. In most parts of Africa, black is the norm, white is the mark of otherness. African American Nobel laureate Toni Morrison (1992) reiterates the value of taking blackness for granted when she writes that she "got titillated" through reading African novelists like Chinua Achebe:

> They did not explain their black world. Or clarify it. Or justify it. White writers had always taken white centrality for granted. They inhabited their world in a central position and everything nonwhite was other. These African writers took their blackness as central and whites were the "other" (Morrison 1992:73).

The approach of these contemporary African writers is a natural outgrowth of living in a society where everybody looked like you. The following example reiterates my point. Mungo Park the British explorer of the river Niger recounts his visit to Bondou in West Africa. The royal women who had never seen a white person were fascinated by his appearance. According to Park:

> They rallied me with a good deal of gaiety particularly on the whiteness of my
> skin and the prominence of my nose. They insisted they were *artificial*… The
> first they said, was produced when I was an infant, by dipping me in milk.
> They insisted my nose had been pinched everyday till it acquired its present
> *unsightly* and *unnatural* conformation [My emphasis] (Davidson 1964:364).

For the Royal women of Bondou, black was the norm; therefore, Parks'
white skin had to be explained and accounted for. In contrast, in the writings
of many African Americans, blackness is represented as a "condition" that
has to be examined and explained in an effort to normalize it. As DuBois
noted, the major characteristic of the African-American experience is what he
calls a "double consciousness… this sense of looking at one's self through the
eyes of others" (DuBois 1995:45). He was, in my view, also referring to an
Othering and marginalization of the self. More recently, African American
literary critic Henry Louis Gates articulates this problem of Otherness very
clearly in his memoirs titled *Colored People*. He stated that "one of the most
painful things about being colored was being colored in public around other
colored people, who were embarrassed to be colored and embarrassed that
we *both* were colored and in public together" (Gates 1994:xiii). In using "colored" as an adjective (colored people), Gates appropriately captures the lack
of agency, and the loss of agency and self-definition that seem to characterize
the African American experience. "Being colored in public"–this phrase succinctly shows that the active coloring process is in the hands of whites, not the
black people who are being colored by a white (con)artist.

From my perspective as an African, the appellation "black" is the category created by the outsider looking in. It is a category of the "Other"; as
such, it should be resisted as a term of African self-definition. Consequently,
to use "black" to qualify movements, events, or processes on the African
continent is to elevate Western visions and yield African self-definition to
outsiders. Along these lines, Africa is Africa; the term "black" Africa, which is
sometimes used to designate parts of Africa, is an aberration. This is so because Africa by definition is associated with people of a particular pigmentation; the "black" should be taken for granted as it is in much of the continent.
Qualifications such as North Africa or Arab Africa or even white Africans
should be introduced and used to describe other groups that have come
much later to share a continent which in origin is associated with people of a
darker pigmentation. Since it is still considered preposterous to talk about
white Europeans, despite the historical and large presence of other racial
groups in Europe, I do not see why black should be used to qualify Africans
in Africa, their place of origin.

Thus, constructions such as "black women of Africa" are not acceptable.

Women of Africa are simply women of Africa, Arab women, and white women who claim Africa should be identified as Arab or North African and white African women, respectively. For African Americans, however, having had a different history, a specific type of racialized experience, being referred to as black now carries the undertone of inevitability and may indeed have other more positive connotations that are obviously made in North America. Black power as a defiant, resistant, and activist concept and movement comes readily to mind. The fact that blackness is the fundamental social identity of African Americans is a product of the American experience. During the period of European colonization in Africa, white was the category of Otherness. Whites are a minority on the African continent. The fetishization of color cannot be the starting point or end of African self-articulation.

SOMETHING BLUE: COLORISM, THE DIFFERENT SHADES OF PREJUDICE

Finally, let us turn to an analysis of what is new that Walker contributes to the genre of Western imperialist writing on Africa's "colorism." Even as she claims some essential consanguinity with Africans, she problematizes that connection in the way in which she uses the binary Self/Other framework to construct Africans and African Americans. She does this effectively in her deployment of color in a process that is best described as colorism. In an earlier essay, Walker herself decried this behavior in African American social life, as the "prejudicial or preferential treatment of same race people based solely on their color" (Walker 1983:290).

The way in which every character in *Possessing* is color-coded suggests the importance of shades of blackness for Walker and indeed their role in putting people in their place in African-American culture. Let us begin with *Warrior Marks*, where Walker found it necessary to insert herself in this color scheme. On her birthday during the filming of *Warrior Marks*, she sends herself the congratulatory message quoted earlier in this essay: "Happy Birthday, my little wondrous brown body" (Walker 1993:50). Many of the people whom she encounters during this project are situated in a color scheme. Thus Efua Dorkenoo, the Ghanaian head of a London-based organization is described as "richly brown" (Ibid:26). The Yoruba priestess she meets in London came in "black and glowing" (Ibid: 28). Aminata Diop, the Malian woman, is said to have "bronze skin." The Ghanaian writer Ayi kwei Armah is described as "very dark, all African," whereas Julius an African American resident in Senegal is very light, African American. In describing a meeting with Ayi kwei Armah, she writes "into his tender black arms I went" (Ibid:68). Why the color of his arms is necessary to an understanding of the action is not clear at all, but Walker takes it for granted that such information is necessary. Moreover, the fact that she does not explain what brown, bronze, black, or light means shows that she assumes we are all privy to this African-American obsession. She is mistaken: dark brown, light, black black, and high yellow–relative to *what,* I must ask?

With regard to the fictional characters in *Possessing,* colorism as a mark of identity is significant: Catherine, Tashi's mother, has a "dark lined face" and Tashi herself has "a small dark hand" (Walker 1992:7). Olivia's skin is mahogany, whilst Tashi's is ebony (Ibid:23). Benny, Tashi's retarded son, is a "radiant brown" (Ibid:56). Raye, the African-American psychoanalyst, has "brown skin, the color of cinnamon." Did we need to know the shade of Raye's skin to judge her competence as a psychoanalyst? Need I go on? The fact that Walker's painstaking descriptions of color do not represent a mere description of the rich variety of shades of African complexions, becomes more apparent as she betrays her discomfort with blackness, by using it to separate Africans and African Americans.

Walker's obsession with color is very much in line with her identity as an African American and the negative images attached to blackness in American culture in spite of the heroic efforts captured in the 1960s slogan "I'm black and proud." Consider Audre Lorde's own experience of colorism:

> Somewhere I knew it was a lie that nobody else noticed color. Me, darker than my two sisters. My father, darkest of all. I was always jealous of my sisters because my mother thought they were such good girls, whereas I was bad always in trouble. "Full of the devil," she used to say… They were *good-looking,* I was *dark.* Bad, mischievous, a born troublemaker if there was one (Lorde 1980:149).

In what way does good-looking contrast with dark? In the African-American context, as we can gather from Lorde's experience, family members are routinely ranked and graded in a color scheme. Accordingly, Henry Louis Gates presents his maternal uncles:

> The Colemans were a colored people…. Uncle Jim or Nemo, was slightly reddish, … Ed was lighter than Jim, still reddish … Charles had dark skin, … Raymond was a saturated reddish-brown color, … He had the kinkiest hair and was the darkest, which was a source of pain for him for much of his life at least. And the Black is Beautiful movement didn't seem to help him all that much. David had the lightest skin of all (Gates 1994:58).

Acquaintances, community leaders, and indeed each person is located in a color hierarchy. Again, Gates gives a colorful description of the church leaders in his hometown of Piedmont in West Virginia; "Reverend Mon-roe's predecessor, Reverend Tisdale was tall and fat, greasy and black, and his highly powdered, light complected wife played the piano too" (Ibid:117).

> Reverend Mon-roe was a nice guy, medium-brown-skinned, with a not bad
> grade of hair, ... His wife was blue-black, actually kind of purple, ... I'd heard
> about blue-black Negroes and had never actually seen one up close till the
> Mon-roes came to our church. (Ibid:116).

Apparently, the "nice guys" are always brown or the brown guys are always nice.

Consequently, it comes as no surprise that Walker visualizes herself as brown. Similarly, she defines African Americans as brown in relation to Africans, who are said to be black. Witness the contrasting colorization of Ghanaian writer Ayi Kwei Armah, who is described as "very dark, all African," whereas Julius, an African-American resident in Senegal, "is very light, African American." Or the contrasting description of Tashi the Olinkan as ebony and Olivia as mahogany. This construction is not without deeper meaning, given that color is not to be taken lightly (pun intended); in African-American culture, it must be decoded in all its layers. The "improvement" of the race signified by the alleged browning /lightening/whitening of African Americans is what enables Walker to think that now they/she can play the role of saving Africans from whatever problems she so designs. Tashi, the protagonist of *Possessing*, understands the irony here, when she exclaims to the African American Olivia "And the nerve of you, to bring us a God someone else chose for you!" (Walker 1992:23).

According to W. E. B DuBois, the problem of the twentieth century is that of the color line, but for Walker and many of her compatriots, it is actually a problem of the color-shaded lines—many lines, many colors, not just black and white. From an African perspective, the problem with Walker and some of her compatriots, is that, as with their American Express cards, they do not want to "leave home without it."[10] It (racism) is one of their precious exports.

In this review of Walker's writing on female circumcision, the objective has been to tease out the intricate threads of underlying imperialist thinking. I have shown how she follows the traditional Western cultural imperialist patterns of objectifying, demonizing, and homogenizing Africa, and her debt in this regard to the racism of nineteenth-century French "*anthropologie*." I have also demonstrated how she combines this with the imperialist varieties of Western feminism and African American solipsism.

This elaborate edifice of imperialist writing is also articulated as a personal experience in her diatribe against her mother over a childhood accident. Unquenched by apologies made a quarter of a century ago, her anger is channeled under the guise of a perfectly legitimate and time-honored tradition of interrogating Africa about its role in the Atlantic Slave Trade, unleashed with a fury so blinding that it consumes all rational discourse. Thus she invents, exceptionalizes, pathologizes, and colorizes. At no stage does she, as a writer or self-styled explorer, remove from her eyes the scales of pre-conception.

The value of her work at the global level, however, is that it demonstrates the limitations of the categories of gender, race and color as common denominators within the struggle for African self-determination. It also teaches Africans to be wary of assumed consanguinity of purpose in a doctrinal sisterhood which does not respect diversity—not of bodies, but of history, social locations and group interests.

For Africa, ultimately, the issue is not Walker; if not Alice, it could be Leroi, Andrew, Peter, Paul, or Mary. The real issue is the unequal power relations between the West and Africa that is constituted by and makes possible the continued exploitation of Africa economically and psychically. It is this hierarchical relationship that enables the invented discourse of African primitivism to continue, especially in its latest highly sexualized and invasive form. I, for one, would admonish that Africans must continue to face Mount Kenya[11] and Kilimanjaro, not the Alps or the Rockies or even the Himalayas of Third Worldism. Genuine cross-cultural dialogue can only take place when different peoples have equal access to modes of production and the means of representation and constitution of knowledge.

NOTES:

1. The novel is dedicated "With Respect and Tenderness To the Blameless Vulva."
2. Africa is put in inverted commas to call into question the homogenization of the continent which is suggested by the usage. Female circumcision is not a continent-wide practice.
3. The first time I heard Ms. Walker read from her novel *Possessing* was at U. C. Berkeley, on April 23, 1992. It was at a benefit concert titled *Risin' Up Live*, staged to draw attention to incidents of genocide world-wide. She chose to speak about what she termed "self-genocide" (as opposed to genocide perpetrated by imperialists) and used female circumcision as the main example of such a practice.
4. For a documentation of American exhibition of African, see Ota Benga: The pygmy in the zoo by Phillip Verner Bradford and Harvey Blume. New York: St. Martin Press, 1992.
5. In April 2002, Saartje Baartman's remains were finally handed over to South African authorities for return and burial in South Africa.
6. In *Facing Mount Kenya*, Kenyatta elucidates the institution as practiced by the Kikuyu in Kenya. Ngugi Wa Thiongo's account in *The River Between* is also based on the Kikuyu experience.
7. French anthropologist, Marcel Griaule recorded the Dogon meaning of the institu-

tion in his book *Ogotemmeli*.

8. This term is borrowed from Okome in this volume.

9. I have substituted "we" for You in the Virginia Slims cigarette advertisement targeted at women in the U. S. The slogan is actually "You've Come a Long Way, Baby."

10. Here, I am alluding to the American Express corporation's popular slogan "Don't leave home without it" meaning their credit card.

11. The point here is that Africans must look at themselves and the world starting with themselves. Africa should always be at the center of African concerns and productions.

WORKS CITED:

Achebe, Chinua. "An Image of Africa." *Research in African Literatures* 9:2 (1978).

Asante, Molefi. "Racing to Leave the Race: Black Postmodernists Off-Track." *The Black Scholar* 23:3-4 (1993).

Caroll, Lewis. *Alice in Wonderland and Through the Looking Glass.* New York: Barnes and Noble Classics, 1992.

Chamberlain, Edward J., and Sanders Gilman. *Degeneration: The Dark Side of Progress.* New York: Columbia University Press, 1985.

Cohen, David. *French Encounters with African.* Bloomington: Indiana University, 1980.

Davidson, Basil. *African Past: Chronicles from Antiquity to Modern Times.* New York: Grosset and Dunlap, 1964.

Du Bois, W.E.B. *The Souls of Black Folk.* New York: Signet/Penguin Books , 1995.

Gates, Henry L. *Colored People: A Memoir.* New York: Alfred A. Knopf, 1994.

_____. *Loose Canons: Notes on the Culture Wars.* New York: Oxford University Press, 1992.

Gilman Sanders. *Jewish Self-hatred: Anti-Semitism and the Hidden Language of the Jews.* Baltimore: John Hopkins University Press, 1986.

_____. *Difference and Pathology: Stereotypes of Sexuality, Race, and Madness.* Ithaca, New York: Cornel University Press, 1985.

_____. *On Blackness Without Blacks: Essays on the Image of the Black in Germany.* Boston: G. K. Hall, 1982.

Gould, Stephen. "The Hottentot Venus." *Natural History* 91 (1982): 270-277.

Griaule, Marcel. *Conversations with Ogotemmeli: An Introduction to Dogon Religious Ideas.* New York: Oxford University Press, 1965.

Hollos, Marida and Philip Leis. *Becoming Nigerian in Ijo Society.* New Brunswick: Rutger's University Press, 1989.

Hountondji, Paulin. *African Philosophy: Myth and Reality.* London: Hutchinson University Library for Africa, 1983.

James, Stanlie and Abena Busia. *Theorizing Black Feminisms: The Visionary Pragmatism of Black Women.* New York: Routledge, 1993.

Kenyatta, Jomo. *Facing Mount Kenya.* New York: Vintage Books, 1965.

Kopytoff, Igor . "Women's Roles and Existential Identities." in *Beyond the Second Sex.* Edited by P. G. Sanday and R. G. Goodenough. Philadelphia: University of

Pennsylvania Press, 1990.

Lazreg, Marnia. "Feminism and Difference: The Perils of Writing as a Woman on Women in Algeria." *Feminist Studies* 14:1 (1988): 81-107.

Lorde, Audre. *Sister Outsider: Essays and Speeches.* New York: The Crossing Press, 1984.

Marie Claire (a magazine)., United Kingdom Edition. May 1994, no. 69.

Morgan, Kathryn. "Women and the Knife: Cosmetic Surgery and The Colonization of Women's Bodies." *Hypatia: a Journal of Feminist Philosophy* 6:3 (1991).

Morrison, Toni (1994). "Chloe Wofford Talks About Toni Morrison." *New York Times Magazine.* September 11, (1994).

Oyewumi, Oyeronke. *Mothers not Women: Making an African Sense of Western Discourses on Gender.* Ph. D. Dissertation submitted in the Department of Sociology, University of California, Berkeley (1993a).

Sanday, P. G. and R. G. Goodenough. *Beyond the Second Sex.* Philadelphia: University of Pennsylvania Press, 1990.

Spillers, Hortense. Mama's Baby, Papa's Maybe: An American Grammar Book." *Diacritics* Summer 1987.

Stepan, Nancy. "Biological Degeneration: Races and Proper Places." *Degenera tion: The Dark Side of Progress.* Ed. Edward J. Chamberlain and Sanders Gilman. New York: Columbia University Press, 1985.

Walker, Alice. *Warrior Marks: Female Genital Mutilation and the Sexual Blinding of Women.* San Diego: Harcourt Brace, 1993.

______. *Possessing the Secret of Joy.* New York: Pocket Books, 1992.

______. *In Search of Our Mother's Gardens: Womanist Prose.* San Diego: Harcourt Brace Jovanovich, 1983.

West, Cornel. *Race Matters.* Boston: Beacon Press, 1992.

Williams, Patricia J. *The Alchemy of Race and Rights: Diary of a Law Professor.* Cambridge: Harvard University Press, 1991.

7.
POSSESSING THE VOICE OF THE OTHER:
African Women and the 'Crisis of Representation' in Alice Walker's *Possessing the Secret of Joy*

Nontsasa Nako

"…the fact of being biologically or culturally African neither guarantees nor necessarily permits any sort of purely authentic "African" reading, in relation of total oneness with its text or with Africa itself … The question thus becomes a practical one of establishing guidelines for a kind of reading that lets the Other talk without claiming to be possessed of the Other's voice."
— Christopher Miller's "Theory of Africans" (Miller 1987:282)

I open with a quote from Christopher Miller because it pinpoints one of the issues that plague feminist politics today, that of speaking about, for, or to, the Other. This is because even if feminism requires some women to speak on behalf of others, such acts of representation are fraught with problems in that who speaks and who is spoken about or for has depended largely on other categories such as power, race, class and sexuality. Indeed much of what has been written about mainstream feminism's privileging of experiences of white middle-class women as experiences of all women, and its assumptions about all women who are not white and middle-class, has had a lot to do with representation; that is how mainstream feminists, often homogenized as Western feminists have represented themselves and Others. Indeed some self-labeled Third World theorist such as Chandra Mohanty, Uma Nayaran, Cherri Moraga and Gloria Anzaldua[1] have emphasized the importance of recognizing the ethnographic diversities of different women's realities as intersections of race, class, power and sexuality continue to create problems for categorizing of gender. They have also pointed out the dangers of ignoring the historical, cultural and political contexts when formulating theories about women. But even if we feel that such criticisms of mainstream feminism's omissions have run their course, the politics of solidarity persist within feminism, the need to institutionalize difference still exist.

In her essay, "The Problem of Speaking for Others" Linda Alcoff, identifies two widely accepted claims relating to speaking for others (Alcoff 1994). The first one concerns the relationship between location and speech; that the position from which one speaks affects the meaning of his or her speech. Therefore where one speaks from "has an epistemically significant impact on that speaker's claim and can serve either to authorize or disauthorize one's speech"(Alcoff 1994:287). This is perhaps the reason why most critics tend to leave their identities and locations visible. One example is Chandra Mohanty in her introduction to a volume of essays by Third World women, where she writes: "I [also] write from my own particular political, historical, and intellectual location as a third world feminist trained in the U.S., interested in questions of culture, knowledge production, and activism in an international context" (Mohanty 1991:3).

Whether such acts of self-identification are always possible is debatable, as it is now commonly understood that identities are fluid and always shifting. But it is clear that such acts are necessary, because for instance, in Mohanty's case, by foregrounding her position within the category Third World women she ensures that the meaning of what she says is not separated from the conditions which produced it. She also acknowledges the difference within Third World women, and this anticipates her definition of Third World women as "imagined communities of women with divergent histories and social locations"(Mohanty 1991:4).

The second claim that Alcoff identifies is that power relations make it dangerous for a privileged person to speak for the less privileged because that often reinforces the oppression of the latter since the privileged person is more likely to be listened to. And when a privileged person speaks for the less privileged, she is assuming either that the other cannot do so or she can confer legitimacy on their position. And such acts, do "nothing to disrupt the discursive hierarchies that operate in public spaces" (Alcoff 1994:287). Most of the criticism against mainstream feminism has pivoted on these two claims. First of all, that when Western women speak simply as women, without specifying their location, (white middle class women) the meaning of what they say is often misunderstood and taken out of its context as representing all women. And second, that when Western feminists take up the cause of Third World women they reinforce the subjugation of Third World women by denying them the right to articulate their own problems.

Indeed these two claims inform Alice Walker's attack of feminism in her oft cited womanist essay, "One Child of One's Own." Walker's argument in this essay is that by excluding black women and continuing to speak on their behalf white women are subjecting black women to the same kind of chauvinism they decried in patriarchal structures. She writes scathingly of white women's appropriation of the term woman for themselves; and points out that as they are now claiming the name woman for themselves; "Then Black women must perforce be something else" (Walker 1983:376). And this appropriation does not end with the name only, but moves beyond, to the bodies of black women, she continues; "white women feminists, no less than white women generally, cannot imagine black women have vaginas. Or if they can, where imagination leads them is too far to go"(Ibid:372). In the same essay she upbraids Patricia Meyer Spacks for excluding writings by black women in her book *The Female Imagination* on the grounds that she [Spacks] like Phyllis Chesler, is "reluctant and unable to construct theories about experiences [she] hasn't had" (Ibid). Walker's rejection of this argument implies that white women can and should represent black: "Perhaps it is the black women's children, whom the white woman – having more to offer her own children,…- resents…. She fears knowing that black women want the best for their children just as she does. Better then to deny that the black woman has a vagina" (Ibid:374).

It is clear from this then that such acts of representations have dangerous consequences for those represented, not only because of the images they circulate about them but also because of the part they play in preserving the status quo. Thus as Walker points out, in speaking of "the female imagination" rather than "the white female imagination" Spacks excludes black female imagination, and invalidates black women's experiences.

Ironically though, the criticism that Walker levels at Spacks and white feminist scholars, is pretty much the same kind of criticism that has been leveled at her for her novel *Possessing the Secret of Joy*. The main charge against Walker has been that of cultural imperialism. That her depiction of Africa and Africans is beholden to her Western hegemonic heritage as an American rather than the African self she claims in the novel.[2] Her response to such criticism, it can be argued, is just as disingenuous as Spacks' in its tenuous linking of the past to the present. Where Spacks claims the Brontë sisters, Walker claims her slave "great-great-great-great grandmother."[3] Again the problem with the representations by both women is their location, where they locate themselves in relation to the other they seek to portray. But to return to Walker, the accusation of cultural imperialism relates to her two mutually exclusive positions of "being possessed of the Other's voice" and simultaneously locating herself as the vessel by which the Other gains voice. The first claim obscures Walker's ideological upbringing, allowing her to judge and moralize about what she views as African culture, from an inside position. And the second casts her as a philanthropic Westerner who intervenes on the other's behalf.

Walker deploys three strategies to deal with this contradiction the first is by displacing her imperialist reading onto another text. The novel foregrounds its politics through the use of Mirellia Ricciardi's autobiography, *The African Saga*. Walker's novel derives its title from the following lines in Ricciardi's text: "With the added experience of my safaris behind me, I had begun to understand the code of 'birth, copulation and death' by which [the Africans] lived. Black people are natural, they possess the secret of joy, which is why they can survive the suffering and humiliation inflicted upon them" (Ricciardi 1981:147).

The inscription of Ricciardi's words as the author's in the novel's opening epigraph: "There are those who believe Black people possess the secret of joy and that it is this that will sustain them through any spiritual or moral or physical devastation" (Walker 1993:ii). This sets the scene for textual appropriation and confrontation which demands that the reader read Walker's texts against such texts as Ricciardi's. The implicit irony of Walker's words foregrounds the author's reading of Ricciardi's text, and makes clear her intention to interrogate Ricciardi's discourse and, to paraphrase Mikhail Bhaktin's, to populate it with her intention. Indeed later in the novel Tashi and Mbati, the novel's African characters read Ricciardi's novel, setting up a *mise en abyme* in which the reader reflects on the novel about characters who reflect on a novel. The fact that the characters read Ricciardi's text towards the end of the novel emphasizes the novel's indictment of Ricciardi's text. The reader, having witnessed the events the characters go through in *Possessing the Secret of Joy* is drawn into the text to question, along with the characters, Ricciardi's words.

Mbati stares at me blankly. I return her look.

But what *is* it? I ask. This secret of joy of which she writes. You are black, so am I. It is of us then that she speaks. But we do not know (Walker 1993:255).

This kind of reading serves to authorize Walker's speech, to locate her firmly on the side of the colonized. The reader is invited to join Walker in trying to see beyond texts like Ricciardi's, to question along with the characters the motive for dissemination of such images about the Africans. When Tashi asks, "Why don't they just steal our land, mine our gold, chop down our forests, pollute our rivers, enslave us to work on their farms, fuck us, devour our flesh and leave us alone? Why must their write about how much joy we possess?" (Walker 1993:256).

It is up to the intrepid reader to recognize in this lament traces of a similar statement by the most credible critic of colonialism, Franz Fanon, when he suggested that: "Colonialism is not satisfied merely with holding people in its grip and emptying the native's brain of all form and content. By a kind of perverted logic, it turns to the past of the oppressed people, and distorts, disfigures and destroys" (Fanon 1995:154).

And perhaps attribute the same credibility to Walker. Against Ricciardi's white colonialist reading, Walker's credentials are established. But despite Walker's recognition of Ricciardi's colonialist position, Walker also succumbs to the same colonialist discourse, in that her representation of Africans, like that of Ricciardi and other colonialist writers, evinces her obsessions and pathologies as a representing subject rather than the Africans she is attempting to represent. What she tells us about Africa and Africans relates to her experiences, her "added safaris." Her reading of African women and their bodies evinces the same kind of ethnocentrism she decried in white feminist scholars. With her representation of the African woman's body, she does not account for the different meanings that different cultures attach to the body. Her reading of African women's bodies is informed by her Western culture and its privileging of the body.

Thus Walker's position when she reads female circumcision[4] as genital mutilation is what Uma Nayaran has called the colonialist stance because she "reproduces a Western tendency to portray Third World contexts as dominated by the grip of "traditional practices" that insulate these contexts from the effects of historical change" (Nayaran 1997:49). This kind of representation highlights the role of the enlightened Westerner in the African's salvation. As Trinh T. Minh-ha reminds us: "The invention of needs always goes hand in hand with the compulsion to help the needy, a noble self-gratifying task that also renders the helper's service indispensable. The part of the savior has to be filled as long as the belief in the problem of endangered species lasts" (Minh-ha 1989:89). Thus Walker creates a position of power for herself, from which she can save the benighted Africans from themselves.

The second strategy that Walker employs is that double-consciousness. Walker employs what seems to be one of the most democratic narrative strategies by incorporating as many voices in her text as she possibly can. The novel is a polyphonic text made up of stories from different characters in the form of recollections, letters and perhaps diary entries. The narratives of the different characters are meant to complement, complete and sometimes contradict each other, allowing for as many perceptions about female circumcision as possible. Thus reading the novel requires the reader to participate in the narrative by completing some of the narratives, and deciding on which of the narrators are reliable and which are not. However the multiplicity of voices is a stylistic device and does not offer divergent perspectives, while the narrative is fragmented, the story is thematically monolithic. The characters never fundamentally contradict each other but move toward a more integrated vision.

But the text does maintain a double-voice, symbolized by Tashi's bi-cultural-ness but because the double-voice of the text is structural rather than thematic, it does not disrupt or undermine the colonial stance of the text. Tashi's bi-cultural-ness is crippling rather than enabling. The two identities exist within the same text, but one is subjected to the worldview of another. The Western worldview is the yardstick with which everything is measured. Take for instance the scene that most critics return to again and again in the novel. Olivia tries to dissuade Tashi from undergoing female circumcision, and Tashi asks her: "Who are you and your people never to accept us as we are? Never to imitate any of our ways? It is always we who have to change" (Walker 1993:21). Most critics have ignored or missed the rhetorical nature of Tashi's questions and have read more into this scene than there really is, for instance that the novel is making a case for cultural autonomy (Turner 1992). If that is so then the case is very weak, for instance the whole section of the narrative is laced heavily with irony. There is no doubt that the Tashi who now recalls this event recognizes the error of her ways, as she can say things like "I had in my mind some outlandish, outsized image of myself" (Walker 1993:20) or "I was crazy. For why could I not look at her" (Ibid:21) Tashi's recollection of the event anticipates her rejection of the sentiments she utters. Tashi eventually turns away from her "outlandish" image of her self and embraces instead Olivia's image of her.

The double-consciousness of the text also allows Walker to explore all the consciousness of the characters, albeit selectively. Thus M'lissa, the most vilified character in the novel, gets her token say as a circumciser, but we need to ask, if it's M'lissa or her author who is asking, "but who are we but torturers of children?" (Walker 1993:210) By trying to contain two opposing views in one narrative Walker only manages to subject one worldview to another. This is because she uses language, discourse and epistemic modes of Western culture to nullify even the possibility of such things in Africa. The Africa she creates, like the Africa of the colonialists has no language, no people, no ideology and is instead what Achebe calls "a place of negations" (Achebe 1988:2). The lack of a frame of reference for the Africans is one of the most limiting aspects of the novel.

For instance in her classic essay, "Can the Subaltern speak" Gayatri Spivak emphasises the role of ideology in subject constitution. Thus robbed of any way of representing themselves African women like Tashi are totally dependent on Walker for their salvation. However she reads female circumcision from her Western culture and speaks out against it just as other Western feminists have done. And her motive, like Frans P. Hosken, Mary Daly and Hanny Lightfoot Klein is to save African women from "ritualized atrocities" (Daly 1978:155). And just like them she wants to name what she believes to be taboo. She depends on these writers for the language and discourse with which to represent these women. But unlike these writers Walker aligns herself with the women she hopes to rescue in her fiction and in the process conceals the extent to which speaking for African women empowers her as an African American. In speaking about and for African women Walker does nothing to disrupt the hegemonic hierarchies, but rather reinforces them because she acts as a legitimating presence who facilitates discourse on a taboo subject. Furthermore, central to Alice Walker's corpus is the Black women's [read African-American] struggle for self-definition against the evils of sexism, classism and racism. As Barbara Christian (1985) suggests in *Black Feminist Criticism*, Walker's struggle focuses on the "struggle for black people, especially black women to claim their lives." Christian characterizes this struggle as a form of rebellion,

> Her willingness to challenge the fashionable belief of the day, to re-examine it in the light of her own experiences of dearly won principles that she has previously challenged and absorbed. There is a sense in which the "forbidden" in the society is consistently approached by Walker as a possible route to truth (Christian 1985:82-3).

Possessing is continuation of that struggle. Africa and the Africans serve merely as a backdrop, a convenient vehicle for her to play out her mode of contrariness and to confront the forbidden in her society.

Finally the third strategy that Walker deploys in her novel is essentialism. She relies on an essentialist differentiation between Africans and African Americans. Tashi is an African woman who suffers emotional and psychological trauma as a result of what Walker terms genital mutilation. Tashi is portrayed as a "true" or authentic African woman, who by the novel's end attains the hybrid identity of an African American. She becomes an outsider in Olinka after murdering M'lissa and she remains an outsider in America even after marrying Adam because of her remaining tie to Africa, symbolized by her "mutilation." Tashi's authenticity is placed against Olivia's much more complex identity as an African American growing up in Africa. With the two characterizations the notion of irreducible, fixed identity is promulgated because despite growing up in Olinka, and learning Olinka culture, Olivia and Adam are "essentially" American. The same is true for Tashi who grows up around the American missionaries but retains [to her detriment Walker would have us believe], her "essence." It is only after Tashi leaves for America that she learns the nature of her subjugation. While this claim depends on the essentialist notion of identity, that is a true African self that can be recovered, the two constructions of black womanhood are never reconciled in the novel. African American women and African women are represented as different and all the negative stereotypes of black womanhood are projected to African women. African American women like Raye, Olivia are portrayed as strong, assertive and independent. In contrast to African women like M'lissa, Nafa/Catherine who are either timid over-worked slaves in the latter case or witches who are nothing "but tortures of children" in the former

In conclusion, then I would say that I cannot come to total conclusions about the common experiences of Black women. I hope with my reading of Alice Walker I have demonstrated that if our concerns continue to be pre-scribed for us then we will hardly get anything done. Indeed, the fact that I am preoccupied with Walker's text, her omissions and misreadings, rather than getting on with the urgent task of defining for myself who I am and what my purpose is, is a testament to the unequal power relations that we are trying to address. Thus, Walker's incessant wailing over the blameless vulva is distracting most of us from the work we need to do. Unfortunately we do not have the luxury of ignoring it in hope that it will go away, but have to address it lest it drowns out whatever else we have to say as African and Black women.

NOTES:

1. See for instance Mohanty's classic essay "Under Western Eyes" Uma Nayaran's *Dislo-cating Cultures* and *This Bridge Called My back: Radical Writings by Radical Women of Color* eds. Gloria Anzaldua and Cherri Moraga.

2. See for instance Oyeronke Oyewumi's "Alice in Motherland: Reading Alice Walker on Africa and Screening the Color "Black"" in this volume and Margaret Kent Bass "Alice's Secret."

3. See Walker's rebuttal that "Spacks never lived in nineteenth-century Yorkshire, so why theorize about the Brontës?" p.372 and her assertion that Slavery gives her the rights to represent African women as she is speaking for her "great-great-great-great grandmother who came here [to America] with all this pain in her body" in Alice's Walker's Appeal, an interview with Paula iddings *Essence* July 1992 p. 60.

4. I use the term female circumcision rather than female genital mutilation, the term most preferred by the opponents of this practice, because it is value laden. And I also do not use genital surgeries which I feel is too clinical and elides the coming of age pathos of this practice. And finally because, as the many cases of deaths and penile

mutilations have shown in South Africa, male circumcision is not always "just a removal of a bit of skin" *(The Color Purple,* 202].

WORKS CITED:

Alcoff, Linda "The problem of Speaking for Others" in *Feminist Nightmares: Women at Odds: Feminism and the Problem of Sisterhood* Eds. Susan Ostrov Weisser and Jennifer Fleischner. New York and London: New York University Press, 1994.

Achebe, C *Hopes and Impediments: Selected Essays 1965 – 1987.* Portsmouth: Heinemann, 1988.

Anzaldua, G. and Moraga, C. Eds. *This Bridge Called my Back: Radical Writings by Women of Color.* New York: Kitchen Table: Women of Color Press, 1983.

Christian, Barbara. *Black Feminist Criticism: Perspectives on Black Women Writers.* New York: Pergamon Press, 1985.

Daly, Mary. *Gyn/ecology: the Metaethics of Radical Feminism.* Boston: Beacon Press, 1978.

Fanon, Franz. "On National Culture" in *Postcolonial Studies: A Reader,* eds Bill Ashcroft and Gareth Griffiths.. London: Routledge, 1995. ch. 23.

Lightfoot-Klein, Hanny. *Prisoners of Ritual: an odyssey into female genital circumcision in Africa.* New York: Haworth Press, 1989.

Miller, Christopher. "Theory of the Africans: The Question of Literary Anthropology" in *Race", Writing And Difference* eds. Henry Louis Gates Jr. Chicago: University of Chicago Press, 1987.

Minh-Ha, Trinh, T. *Woman, Native, Other: writing postcoloniality and feminism.* Bloomington: Indiana University Press, 1989.

Mohanty, Chandra Talpade. "Cartographies of Struggle: Third World and the Politics of Feminism." In *Third World Women and The Politics of Feminism* Eds. Mohanty, C. Trusso, A, Torres, L. Bloomington: University Press, 1991, I-47.

——— "Under Western Eyes" in *Third World Women and The Politics of Feminism* Eds. Mohanty, C. Trusso, A, Torres, L. Bloomington: University Press, 1991.

Narayan, Uma. *Dislocating Cultures: Identities, Traditions, and Third World Feminism.* New York And London: Routledge, 1997.

Ricciardi, Mirella. *African Saga.* London: Collins, 1981.

Walker, Alice *Possessing the Secret of Joy.* New York: Vintage Books, 1993.

——— *In Search of Our Mother's Gardens: Womanist Prose.* New York: Harcourt Brace Jovanovich, 1983.

Spivak, Gayatri "French Feminism in an international Frame," *In Other Worlds.* New York: Methuen, 1987.

——— Can the Subaltern Speak" in *Marxism and the Interpretation of Culture.*London: Macmillan, 1988.

8.

THE LITTLE FOXES THAT SPOIL THE VINE:
Revisiting the Feminist Critique of Female Circumcision[1]

L. Amede Obiora

The title, "*The Little Foxes That Spoil the Vine*," is a biblical juxtaposition of images of beauty and destruction. The imagery in the title speaks of how ill-conceived strategies to end female circumcision may undermine rather than further feminist goals. More precisely, it is invoked by the author to capture the insidious and far-reaching negative implications of well-meaning efforts to stem the practice. Within a broader historical and sociological context, the article traces the emergence of the Western feminist campaign against female circumcision in order to illuminate the limitations of its reductionist approach to a deeply embedded cultural phenomenon. Primarily informed by Alice Walker's best-selling novel, *Possessing the Secret of Joy*, the critique emphasizes the subversive dangers of studied sensationalism. Enunciating the virtues of contextualized analysis and bottom-up solutions, derived in collaboration with (not in alienation of) grassroots initiatives, the article calls attention to the need for connections between altered perceptions, material empowerment, and social change.

Ugoye had earned a name for herself as a professional mourner. On the occasion of the death of Okoye, she came prepared, mindful that the important corpse would attract a company of dignitaries. Her performance at the funeral was so spectacular that all attention was diverted to her. In fact, some condolence visitors mistook her for the principal bereaved and sought to console her. Although in her mind Ugoye was merely fulfilling her calling, her performance wrought something of a mess and all but defeated the purpose of her presence there. Had it not been for her misconceived agenda, Ugoye's participation could have been quite welcome and enriching. Instead, however, she succeeded only in exacerbating the grief of the bereaved family members. And for generations, the lore of the proverbial mourner has come to stand for a lesson in moderation and discretion.

The question of female circumcision has recently received considerable adverse publicity in the West. Due to the alleged prevalence of the practice in Africa, wide-ranging efforts have been orchestrated against it under the guise of redeeming the integrity of the African woman. In material respects, the controversy surrounding this practice mirrors the lore of the proverbial mourner described above. I was first exposed to the scandalized tone and exaggeration which surrounds western discourse on female circumcision when a co-participant at a 1990 legal education seminar at Stanford University referred to the practice. My initial wincing reaction to the allegation of mutilation rapidly escalated into rage. Although I had been born and raised in Africa, I found what I heard at this conference very hard to believe, and thus conducted a preliminary survey which confirmed that "genital mutilation" was not a figment of someone's imagination. Perplexed and troubled, I read and reflected, agonized, and engaged in extensive discussions about the practice. My reaction eventually metamorphosed from suspicions like "The West is at it again," and "These African men!" to questions like "What is the evidence?" and "What is at stake?" Through my research, I have come to realize that part of my discomfort stems from the problematic terms of the discourse, and the ideology of exclusion resplendent in its vanguardistic tone, as well as from the preoccupation with criminalization as the pre-eminent strategy for eradicating the practice.

In this article, which is informed by a panoramic survey of a barrage of literature on female circumcision in Africa, I critique the limitations of certain Western feminist protestations against the practice. To illustrate the shortcomings of this literature, I focus upon Alice Walker's work in the area, especially her critically acclaimed novel, *Possessing the Secret of Joy*, which depicts the life of a child, Tashi, who was alleged to have been betrayed by her mother and by a culture which subjected her to "genital mutilation." (Walker 1992)[2] Although this article explores and deplores aspects of the anti-circumcision campaign, my purpose is not to refute the underlying feminist vision and purpose of the campaign; to do that would be tantamount to "throwing out the baby with the bath water."

Part I of the paper outlines certain aspects of the epistemology and praxis of Western feminism which help to frame the problem under review. In Part II, I take up Walker's works, using them to illustrate the drawbacks in the campaign against female circumcision. In the final part of the article, I focus on the means of reorienting discourses about female circumcision in a manner that will attenuate the problematic posturing. I argue that female circumcision is not simply a problem to be solved, it is also a complex cultur-ally-embedded critical act which signifies continuity and meaning, and ex-presses fundamental social values. Therefore, conventional ways of dealing with it are worth reconsideration. Further, I suggest that the peculiar facts, circumstances, and settings of the practice call for a multi-pronged strategy which would entail international commitment while at the same time giving centrality to local initiatives.

Background

To the credit of feminism, the world has become more sensitized to prob-lems that are of particular concern to women. Prior to the inception of concerted feminist activities, problems of women were marginalized and occluded due to the sheer force of patriarchal prejudice. With a view to remedying this bias, feminist theory and practice give centrality to the experi-ences, consciousness, and perspectives of women. Feminism emerged in opposition to patronizing and paternalistic politics predicated on phallocentric misconceptions of women's "nature" and "best interests."[3] Feminist critique seeks to redeem women's voices and realities from the eclipsing of male-controlled social discourses and institutions.[4] Insisting that no one community of norms is astute enough to trump the variegated values and standards of human experience, feminists argue that the male ideal oppresses, disempowers, and renders the "other" invisible.[5] To counter the pressure on women to uncritically adopt male standards, feminism validates the significance, strengths, values, and positive functions of women's experiences and perceptions. Be-cause it grows out of direct experience and consciousness, feminism empha-sizes context and the importance of identifying personal experience and claim-ing it for one's own.[6] As a mode of analysis, feminism rejects elitism and vanguardism, recognizing that people are imbued with transformative ca-pacities and are best situated to champion their own revolutions.[7]

Nevertheless, whether out of arrogance or for fear of fracturing the base for mobilization, feminism sometimes manifests a tendency which be-trays the partiality of its makers. In this mode, it entertains a party line that muzzles voices which do not echo mainstream sentiments. By assuming that women are a determinate group with interests and desires identical to those of its "prima donnas," feminist inquiry's once inspirational evocation to liber-ate a balanced reality risks deteriorating into the suppression of difference and re-enacting the self-same evil that it confronts in patriarchy.[8] Even if sincere, certain feminist strategies point up the hypocrisy inherent in profess-ing high-sounding principles of global sisterhood and the politics of experi-ence while meting out a double standard that reinstates the very silencing and stigmatization of women which feminism was supposed to challenge.

Owing to their attraction to essentializing categories, their unconscious attachment to stereotypes, and their participation in a culture in which power is enforced by dominance over definitions and truth claims, these feminists renege on the principal insights that animate their initiatives: insights about the problems of unstated reference points and about how privileging a particular experience obscures difference and situatedness.[9] Although challenging patriarchal paradigms of power and knowledge has been a key item on the feminist agenda, the actions of these feminists compromise the *raison d'être* of feminism when, in its name, they betray the ground-level realities of women and resurrect processes that pawn the actual interests of women under the guise of protecting them. To the extent that they recuperate transgressions which they traditionally identify as patriarchal, these feminists bring home the paradox that no politics remains innocent of that which it contests.[10]

Several women of color have aired sentiments which serve as a corrective to questionable feminist inclinations to structure power relations in terms of a unilateral and undifferentiated source (read as male) and a cumulative reaction to power (read as female). Contrary to dominant conceptualizations of gender differences as fixed and essential, these women of color, among others, acknowledge gender as a multi-faceted and dynamic social phenomenon which is constituted by and constituting of the experiences of race, class, culture, and other attributes of subjective identity. While in the interest of political mobilization, strategy, and rhetoric, it may be expedient to minimize the divergence of these experiences, they cannot be subsumed to a grand scheme. In many instances, the commonalities of women from different backgrounds are discernible only insofar as they are defined in relation to men. Once this preliminary comparison is accomplished, however, the complex heterogeneity of their objective realities becomes both obvious and urgent[11].

Audre Lorde poignantly captures the gravamen of the issue in one of her writings. Alluding to the disparate distribution of the benefits and burdens of patriarchy, Lorde explains that to imply that all women suffer the same oppression simply because they are women, "is to lose sight of the many varied tools of patriarchy. It is to ignore how those tools are used by women without awareness against each other."[12] (Lorde 1984:66). bell hooks makes the point more bluntly, stating that the idea of a "common oppression" is a corrupt platform which disguises and mystifies the fact that women are divided by sexist attitudes, racism, class privilege, and a host of other prejudices.[13] Juxtaposing the (re)presentation of Third World women as ignorant victims of barbarous sexual practices with the discursive self-representation (not necessarily material reality) of Western women as enlightened and liberated, other commentators delineate the imperialistic roles and interests of certain Western feminist elites.[14] In a similar vein, but with particular reference to scholarly definitions of African womanhood, Filomina Steady extrapolates from the "expert" undertakings and manipulation of data by some of these feminists to underscore her submission that the exploitation of Africa has not been restricted to the historical extraction of natural and human resources.[15]

Relational feminists have vigorously argued that, in comparison with men, women are more attuned to contextual specificities and averse to undue universalizations, or that they are more likely to resist the temptation to trump the practicalities of everyday life in the quest for abstract justice.[16] The record shows, however, that this is not always the case. Some feminist activists have been exempt neither from wide-eyed propagandism nor from purposeful paternalism.[17] Especially in situations of inequalities of power, many of these activists (apparently convinced that they are indispensable and beyond reproach) have turned deaf ears to constructive criticisms of their insights and approaches. (Griffin 1982:273) Armed with unverifiable dogma and exuding a dessicated passion reminiscent of the patriarchal power which they condemn, it is not unusual for such feminists to arrogate to themselves prescriptive rights. Rather than exploring how to transcend the inherent limitations of their pre-ordained prescriptions, they prefer to derive the impetus for campaigns which may be ultimately premature by "preaching to the choir."[18] As long as the actions of these activists replicate some of the fundamental flaws of "patriarchy," they compromise and render feminist ideology ostensible.

On the level of fundamental feminist principles, it goes without saying that vehement opposition to any practice that is detrimental to the interests of women is valid, if there is credible evidence to establish the existence and detriment of such a practice. Hence, where it is shown that severe forms of female circumcision jeopardize the health of girls and women, there is a *prima facie* case for reform. However, it must be noted that the relative strength of the case against female circumcision is apt to be undermined by nihilistic and ethnocentric radical campaigns. These campaigns are engineered by activists who indulge in inexcusable exaggeration, denigrate other legitimate points of view, and co-opt or insist on controversial postures. Although female circumcision is a social practice with health consequences, in order to portray it as indefensible, the bulk of these campaigners resort to decontextualized depictions that fail to illuminate the social dimensions of the practice. Many of the studies on circumcision upon which they rely fall short of the standards of feminist and scientific scholarship. They are rife with broad generalizations, poverty of analyses, dearth of evidence, and a host of other limitations which render them questionable.[19]

Female circumcision is a diverse set of practices. Women are circumcised at different ages, depending on the locality. Some women, like Tashi in Alice Walker's novel, appropriate the practice as a form of self-assertion; others may be circumcised when they are under-age and relatively unmindful of the implications of the practice. In some instances, the circumcision may involve just a symbolic piercing or the removal of the hood of the clitoral prepuce; in other instances circumcision may mean the thorough excision of the clitoris. One hardly gets a sense of these differences from reading popular feminist accounts of the practice. The various forms of circumcision and their gradations of harm are conflated as "mutilation"; the entire continent of Africa, despite its complex heterogeneity, is reduced to a single research site. Further, the emphasis is on children, as if they were the sole subjects of the practice, whereas, in reality, the ages of the circumcised vary from place to place.[20]

In lieu of rigorous, systematic and substantiated analyses, many of the contestable studies on female circumcision in Africa settle for hearsay anecdotes which are embellished with speculative and titillating commentary. Typically, the anecdotes only capture the worst-case scenarios; they also blur various forms of and motives for the practice. In the 1970s when the international campaign against female circumcision was just beginning to gather momentum, some nascent French feminist sponsors relied on the anecdotal despair of a child of ten years as their determinative evidence.[21] Reliance on anecdotal evidence is understandable given the reticence and surreptitiousness surrounding the practice in some places. However, this does not warrant the arbitrary manipulation and parade of spiced anecdotes as absolute fact. Generalizing from such anecdotes to the entire population of women undergoing the procedure is akin to estimating or predicting the incidence of strep in a pediatrician's office from the number of children who come in complaining of sore throat.

The shoddiness of much of this work on circumcision is exemplified by the level of ignorance exhibited in Pratibha Parmar's designation of Ngugi Wa Thiong'o as Nigerian. (Walker and Parmar 1993: 214).[22] Ironically, Ngugi, an icon of African literature and activism, and Parmar are both Kenyan-born, and Parmar's Kenyan identity tends to be invoked to underscore her familiarity with Africa. Pratibha Parmar's blunder occurred in her report on the making of *Warrior Marks*, a documentary film which drew extensively (if not exclusively) from selectively solicited and compensated informants and volunteers. The representativeness and reliability of information derived from a minute and arguably stage-managed sample of respondents with overt political agendas and economic interests are open to question. Even Parmar grew exasperated with the mercenary overtone of the endeavor.[23] Accordingly, she lamented that at least she had never depended as much on the contacts and commitments of "people whose motives [she is] not always comfortable with" for her other films.[24] Nonetheless, she proceeded to rely on the uncorroborated information of the very characters that she had castigated as dubious. To complicate matters, it appears that Parmar, consonant with the saying that "[s]he who pays the piper calls the tune," stymied candidness and pre-determined the structure and outcome of the exchange, while paying lip-service to the goal of fostering candid reflections about circumcision.[25]

Social Architecture, Cultural Imperialism or Literary Aesthetics?

The furor in the US over female circumcision, where it has taken on the prominence of a *cause célèbre*, is hardly surprising. There is always something or the other which American women feel bound to take up on behalf of the women world-wide, in much the same way as their government sees itself as the world's police (Charles 1994:1138).[26]

Third World women have become the subject matter of many literary and artistic endeavors. Our traditional native cultures are displayed as the artifacts of "primitive" peoples and we are dealt with as a political issue, rather than as flesh and blood human beings (Smith 1980:48).[27]

As an African-American woman in white patriarchy, I am used to having my archetypal experience distorted and trivialized but it is terribly painful to feel it being done by a woman (Lorde 1984:67-8).[28]

When the axe came into the forest, the trees said the handle was one of us.

Much has been written about the conceptual and ideological reservations that Third World women and women of color harbor against the approaches and political priorities of white, Western feminists. The literature problematizing the imperialist propensities and modalities of Western feminists of all racial and ethnic origin are especially pertinent to my analysis. In particular, the conceptualization of Western feminism as a mindset which is neither racially nor geographically specific is instructive. The works of Alice Walker, especially *Possessing the Secret of Joy*, illustrate this point.

Walker maintains that she does not write just to tell stories because her work is at once political and personal. But *Possessing the Secret of Joy*, raises political questions and concerns that Walker fails to address.[29] To begin with, it is difficult to reconcile her purported humanitarian motive with her monolithic construction and equation of female circumcision to her own personal and cultural context. Her devoted projections of values are of questionable ecological relevance. Commenting on the literal ramifications of Walker's propagandist posturing, Max Davidson notes that, unfortunately, Walker dotted her i's and crossed her t's just a little too assiduously for the good of the story (Davidson 1992: H2). Along similar lines, Carol Anshaw asserts that Walker, in service to her agenda to shock, imposes her voice on her characters and leaves little to the reader's imagination (Anshaw 1992: C3). On a pragmatic level, it bears mention that being a rebel with a cause—no matter how laudable the cause—does not justify inciting a rebellion which risks a backlash that would redound exclusively on the lives of other persons.

Although Walker validates her involvement in the campaign against female circumcision on grounds of her love for her African roots, her work is peppered with contemptuous remarks about things African.[30] Of graver concern is the fact that her angle of vision and unmonitored biases reinforce imperialistic impulses which reify Africa as the morally bankrupt antithesis of the West.[31] Anyone with an inkling of the images of Africa in the Western media knows the continent's perverted depiction as a jungle inhabited by human beings who are hardly distinguishable from beasts.[32] As far back as the nineteenth century, Henry Stanley postulated that Africans were the "link sought between the average modern humanity and its Darwinian progenitors, and certainly deserving of being classified as an extremely low, degraded, almost bestial type of humanity" (Stanley 1913:274-5).[33] When Walker introduces the heroine of her novel, Tashi, and her imaginary African tribe, she deliberately feeds off truncated and oppressively racist objectifications by describing her as having monkey-like hands (Walker and Parmar 1993:3).[34]

In one of the many reviews of the novel, Jennifer Mitton observes that its most blatant flaw is that Walker's fictional Olinkans, created to stand for Africans in general, end up unlike anyone anywhere and leave the reader with a vague and stereotyped vision of present-day Africa (Mitton 1992: H11). This view is echoed by another writer who remarked that "[a]n American of European descent, passing himself off as an expert on Europe, is not likely to make up a pan-European language and meld Germany, France, Russia, Spain and Albania into one country. But Walker does not know enough to have the faintest notion of her fraudulence as an Africanist" (Grenier 1992:G64).[35] Also, in portraying Petit Pierre, a partial product of white blood, as the fountain of knowledge and a paragon of virtue, while depicting the black child as an imbecile, Alice Walker resurrects the time-worn and discounted assumption that race is the principal determinant of capabilities.[36] Another interesting case in point relates to Walker's failure to explore the possibility of some connection between Tashi's mental predicament and her husband's infidelity. She attributes Tashi's degeneration into a psychotic state solely to her circumcision, leaving out the possibility that her husband's infidelity was a contributing factor. By collapsing the complexitites of causation into a single factor, she condones the infidelity. Interestingly, on the other hand, she condemns polygamy.

In her rendition about Tashi's sister, Dura, who died prematurely at the hands of a circumcisor, Walker writes that when Dura was a toddler, she had picked up a burning twig that protruded from the fire and attempted to put it into her mouth. It stuck to her lip and "she cried piteously, her arms outstretched, looking about for help the twig, ashen, finally dropped away, having burned through the skin. But did [the] mother or a co-wife leap to gather the crying child in her arms?" It stands to reason that heeding the heart-rending scream of an injured child is a spontaneous instinctual reflex for many in the human society. More so, no one who appreciates the value of children in the African world-view could question whether the child was rescued.

Tashi, though Walker has rooted as an African, is entirely Eurocentric. Because of her precarious entanglement in a clash of religions and cultures, she becomes predisposed to psychosocial disturbances. In fact, it appears that she resorts to the procedure of circumcision in an effort to resolve the turmoil. Her crisis escalates when she "erases her African self by accepting how Americans judge, smell, see, and treat her, metamorphosing into a pluri-conscious African-American, devastated by her difference" (Ogunyemi[37] in this volume). (Dis)located in the suggestively pristine West, she is compelled to come to terms with her life primarily by probing motive and memory through introspection and analysis (Jersild). However, unequivocal empirical evidence of the emotional security which prevails among many African children would suggest that had Tashi stayed within her native culture, she might have found a modicum of the affirmation and sanity which utterly eluded her in the individualism, narcissism, and racism of the West.[38] Of particular relevance are the findings of Hanny Lightfoot-Klein, who, incidentally, is one the few references upon which Ms. Walker relies. Reading Lightfoot-Klein's report of the unanimity of local psychiatrists about the unflinching support for children, one cannot escape the contemplation that Tashi's alienation from her culture was a major factor in her unhappiness (Boddy 1989). After an extensive study of female circumcision in Sudan, a perplexed Lightfoot-Klein observed "the general aura of serenity and balance that [the Africans she encountered] far more commonly exude than a lot of Western women."[39]

For all of her investment in symbolism, Walker's obsession with a single understanding of female circumcision obscures its other dimensions.[40] Suggesting that the practice is a sadistic venture thoroughly enjoyed by privileged spectators, Walker declares, "it's unbearable to me to think there are little girls in Africa today being held down by their mothers and aunts, deprived of parts of bodies they don't even know they had, with papa proud as punch sitting outside" (Holt). Accepting that the practice is susceptible to flagrant abuse, it is conceivable that such factors as the relative power of the collective of women, belief and value systems, and the multiplicity and interdependence of social relationships, significantly check the extent of abuse. It is probably as an instrumental measure which lends itself to the expression of social values relating to sexuality, fecundity, maturity, and solidarity that the custom has come to gain a foothold.[41] Insinuations of pre-meditated and misogynistic intent to harm, mutilate, and deliberately impair the circumcised female-child or woman over-simplify the issue and run the risk of thwarting change-oriented endeavors.[42] It is one thing to blame a mother for the plight of her daughter; it is another thing to probe the reason for her apparent "connivance." Less strident scholars, those not given to summary pontifications about complex issues, who have truly considered the motivations of the average mother whose daughter is circumcised, find that she is typically a loving and well-meaning woman who pursues the practice out of concern for her daughter and in sincere belief of its benefits and necessity.[43] As Boulware-Miller points out, dwelling exclusively on the risks involved in circumcision overlooks its mitigating psychological, social, and economic benefits.[44] Even in *Warrior Marks*, a more sensitized Walker concedes that women circumcise their daughters because they want to ensure their future well-being or ability "to marry and at least have a roof over her head and food" (Walker and Parmar 1993:227).[45]

Despite fleeting intimations of the courage and agency of African women, of how they made a way out of no way, Walker goes to great lengths in portraying them as passive pawns of male transactions.[46] In *Warrior Marks*, she states that African women are routinely followed, yelled at, and harassed on the street by men who look at their bodies as if they were meals, and that the women seem so joyless and oppressed, with downcast eyes and stiff vertebrae, and are frequently abused by fathers, brothers, and husbands (Walker and Parmar 1993:53,69). Elaborating, she writes: "I can't help but connect this behavior to genital mutilation: the acceptance of domination, the lack of a strong sense of self one sees among the women here" (Ibid: 53-4). Walker's proclivity toward generalization and selective amnesia is evident when one juxtaposes this remark against Pratibha Parmar's recollection: "it was the very image [of proud African women who hold themselves with a noble majesty that speak of their determination and hope that] Alice had described when she'd said she wanted to be filmed with African women celebrating their strength" (Ibid: 144,185). It is the same Alice Walker who compares the passive African woman of her imagination with the occasional "extremely loud, brash woman, like the one who pressed us to buy her wares with such vigor that she ran us out of her stall. These are the women whose pent-up anger seems to be a powder keg" (Ibid: 53-4). In the same stroke of the pen, she denigrates the assertive as well as the seemingly passive. It appears that, for her, African women are damned if they do and damned if they don't.

In an interview, Paula Giddings anticipated the main criticism against Alice Walker and sought to prod her to articulate the basis for her intervention as a Westerner in the cause of African women (Giddings 1992:59). Walker retorted that slavery intervened and that she was speaking for her great-great-great-great-grandmother "who came to America with all this pain in her body" (Ibid: 60). She said: "when Africans get in trouble, they call on everybody" and that "[t]hey don't have a leg to stand on, so they better not start hopping around [her]" (Ibid). On the issue of sexuality, she pontificated that genital mutilation, as she calls it, makes her wonder about "everything [she has] been taught about African women, that they are 'hot' and 'lascivious'" (Ibid: 62, 102). More lucidly, she subsequently alluded to the reality of human interdependence, but, instead of developing this cogent thought, she digressed into a fantasy in which she equated her novel to a psychoanalytic healing device or a mirror which illuminates areas that are not readily observable, such as the posterior of an assessor (Ibid: 102). Finally, in her standard refrain about her own visual mutilation and miserable childhood (which often sent her scurrying off to the woods for solace), she maintains that even though it is extremely difficult for women to blame their mothers, they must begin to confront their mothers' complicity in their distress (Ibid: 62).[47]

In her remark about African dependency, Walker introduced but forfeited an opportunity to situate and address the underlying power dynamics of her own intervention.[48] Her comment about the lasciviousness of African women is obviously gratuitous. The support provided by African familial and communitarian orientation is well-documented, and challenges Walker's correlation between her personal flights to the woods and her perceptions of the plight of African children (Walker and Parmar 1993:42-3). In reductively extolling blame and the "couch approach," (Hughes 1993; Bloom 1987) she loses sight of the possibility that these may well be culturally specific rather than universal methods of conflict resolution. Perhaps some (non-Western) cultures are more oriented towards conciliatory understanding and less obsessed with finger-pointing. Indeed, in Igbo land, one way of instilling the preferred value of conciliation in children is by dramatizing the irony of finger-pointing. The irony lies in the fact that when finger-pointing, only the thumb and/or index finger points at the indicted; the remaining three fingers are bent toward the finger-pointer, as if beckoning her to acknowledge her complicity.

In Gidding's interview with Walker, the "how dare this American judge us" which Giddings considers the crux of the criticism against Walker is not without merit. However, it pales in light of other criticisms. Walker's controvertible authority for her own representation is peripheral to the issue of actual *mis*representation which, for example, manifests itself in her crass disrespect of the world and lives of African women. Respect and sensitivity will not necessarily valorize the social assets of the subjects of a scholarly or literary endeavor: they are merely threshold indicators of goodwill. In other words, showing respect for the African women she has chosen to discuss would be more helpful in establishing Walker's good intentions than it would be in altering the material conditions of the women. Yet this respect and sensitivity is absent in many aspects of her work.

Additionally, Walker's claim to be vindicating her African forebear who was doubly-victimized by circumcision and the transatlantic slave trade is speculative (Giddings 1992: 58). But for the assertion of Tashi's fictional psychoanalyst who hypothesized that African female slaves introduced Western doctors to circumcision, there is little documentation of the mutilation of the genitals of slave women. Chattel slaves were purchased for breeding purposes, *inter alia*. In light of the intensity of racism in the antebellum era, and slave dealers' yearnings to inculpate exotica, it is unlikely that an "anomaly" which debilitated the reproductive and productive capacities of slaves and thereby interfered with the slave owners' investment in them would have gone down in history without comment.[50] Despite the rape of African women institutionalized in plantation slavery in the New World.

Walker assumes that female circumcision pre-dated the slave trade, that it was practiced in the particular locality from which her putative forebear hailed, and that this forebear had the severe form of the operation. In fact, the date of origin of the practice is unknown and its frequency, in terms of form and geographic location, remain largely unresolved and in need of further research.[51] Besides, one cannot imagine that Walker's forebear, if she was circumcised, perceived circumcision as the quintessential manifestation of patriarchal oppression most worthy of vindication, as opposed to the plethora of indignities and fundamental dehumanization of slavery (Walker and Parmar 1993: 48).[52]

In this sense, Walker's isolation of circumcision as a *cause célèbre* is analogous to a legend which emanates from the village of Ugoye, the proverbial mourner whose *faux pas* appeared in the preface of this critique. Oral tradition has it that during the colonial era, the Catholic church established a presence in the village. On one dry harmattan day, a wildfire razed the mission. The resident Reverend Father, who from popular description bore a striking resemblance to Sigmund Freud, was badly burned. He died shortly thereafter. During his tenure, this Father had worked his way into the heart of every child in the village. These children were particularly fond of what they saw as the sage's awe-inspiring navel-length beard. When news of the devastation and death reached the children, they were dumbstruck. The one child that recollected himself looked the harbinger in the face and gasped: "Did I hear you say that Father was burnt to death? Ewoo-o-o, was his beard burnt too?" Obviously, the child seemed more concerned about the father's beard than about the extensive damage to persons. The child's prioritization of and fixation with the Reverend's beard parallel Walker's preoccupation with the conjecture that her great-great-grandmother's clitoris was missing when she disembarked on the shores of America from a slave ship.

Implications of Respect for Meaningful Social Architecture

There are many people who consider [Third World] dwellers marginal, intrinsically wicked and inferior. Such a Manichean attitude is at the source of the impulse to "save" the "demon possessed" Third World, "educating it" and correcting its thinking according to the [savior's] own criteria. [The savior] can never relate to the Third World as partners, since partnership presupposes equals, no matter how different the equal parties may be. Thus, "salvation" of the Third World by the [savior] can only mean its domination (Freire 1970: 213).

We were admonished more than once by the African panelists to eschew the insensitivity and arrogance [of] the "Desert Storm approach." [One white woman was asked what right she had to be on the panel.] She went on to explain that 14 years ago, while wandering through Egypt, she had discovered the practice of genital mutilation and suddenly found her "purpose in life" (Eichman 1992: 48).

The overwhelming majority of the [people] believe that it is the secret aim of those who attack this centuries-old custom to disintegrate their social order (Kenyatta 1965: 263).

I would advise you to tackle this problem very carefully. From generation to generation, customs tend to disappear. I myself blackened my lips, but our children have categorically refused to do that, and I am convinced that the same thing will happen with circumcision (Walker and Parmar 1993: 330).

Female circumcision has been a standing source of conflict between the West and Africa. Ample evidence that previous abolition efforts have not appreciably changed the situation serve as an inescapable corrective to delusive inscriptions of alien paradigms and modalities of change. The platform of the United Nations World Conference on Women which was held in Beijing in 1995 positioned female circumcision alongside a host of other practices which it condemned for inhibiting the advancement of women. The Beijing initiative reinforced the pressure on governments to confront the issue. However, in the face of continued ignorance about why the practice persists in places such as Burkina Faso, Kenya, Sudan, Britain, Sweden, France, Switzerland, and Italy where it has been criminally prohibited, legislative endeavors in other jurisdictions will be prone to the same abortive fate.[53] Various non-criminializing approaches have also been espoused. For example, although conventional medical and ethical standards prohibit the unnecessary removal of tissue from female genitals, physicians in some jurisdictions do perform less invasive versions of the procedure.[54] In 1993, Canada became the pioneer country to recognize gender persecution as grounds for asylum. Since then, however, only a couple of women have successfully secured asylum on the basis of female circumcision (Gunning 1994-5; Reuben 1996; Farnsworth 1994; Thompson 1994). The potential flaws in these approaches will not be uncovered, nor will they succeed until the practice of female circumcision is understood in all of its complexity.

For historical reasons, a preponderance of Africans are averse to other-defined and imposed priorities or patterns of cultural chauvinism which masquerade as a sense of moral responsibility of the enlightened to save the benighted.[55] Replete with pedestrian broadsides, tensions, and contradictions, some radical Western feminist efforts against circumcision are ripe to re-enact mistakes of the past. These efforts not only run the risk that their legitimacy and effectiveness will be undercut; they may also tragically erect walls between women, and even burn nascent trans-cultural bridges.[56] Rather than locating their campaign against circumcision as part of a progression of indigenous struggles against the practice,[57] the stalwarts of the problematic efforts tend to arrogate to themselves patronizing prerogatives that divert attention from the reality at issue.[58]

The usurping of African initiatives is a throwback to missionary and Eurocentric views which explain events and developments only in terms of an external frame of reference.[59] A variant of this manifests itself when opposition to circumcision is attributed to the frustration of the foreign-educated African elite. Awareness of the hazards posed by some forms of circumcision to the health of women is not peculiar to the educated elite. If the reports on circumcision have any modicum of validity, one would think that a reasonable proportion of the affected women are not oblivious of their plights.[60] Even base beasts are capable of perceiving danger. If self-preservation is a basic instinct, it stands to reason that the value and utility attached to circumcision are predicated on its burdens not exceeding its benefits. Like human beings who have a limited threshold for pain, a culture cannot afford to subscribe to and sustain a practice that threatens its very existence; to do that would be to create the conditions for its own extinction.

Notwithstanding its excesses and poverty, there are clearly some merits to aspects of the campaign against female circumcision. Where there is *well-founded* evidence that the practice causes harm, the custom should be challenged.[61] The issue becomes how to identify and execute the responsibilities of relevant communities to attenuate the danger of harm.[62] Corollary issues revolve around the logistics of change. A nagging consideration concerns the role of outsiders in directing change. This issue raises several questions: What is in the best interest of the affected population of women? Who decides what constitutes "best interest?" Who decides this? Further, is "best interest" as obvious and as simple as it seems or are there latent and unintended consequences of change? Can an outsider be so arrogant as to assume that she is omniscient or omnipotent enough to unilaterally appropriate a lead role and articulate a viable reform agenda?

The salience of these questions is compounded for the feminist community by feminist discourses which generate profound skepticism about the ability of a select constituency to "know" what is in the interest of others (Spelman 1988; Lugones and Spelman 1983; King 1989; Hawkesworth 1989). A close reading of this literature reveals the hypocrisy behind the rhetoric of global sisterhood which is not informed by consistent practice. For example, the feminist concept of sisterhood eschews hierarchy and implies an alliance that is actively forged, not merely theorized or assumed into existence. Additionally, an understanding of the concept suggests that it is only a person with a vested interest in the status quo who assumes that she can project, top-down, a course of action on a perceived subordinate.[63] An unscrupulous outsider may exploit power differentials and violate the lives of the women by refusing to understand their realities, and instead impose her culturally mediated and specific definitions of reality on the group she intends to "save." But whether that will take her far in resolving the matter at hand is most improbable. A compelling insight into the inadequacy of such attitude is offered by bell hooks. Insisting that the structures and dynamics of domination seldom castrate so-called subordinates, hooks illuminates the resilence of their agency and their potent refusal to uncritically swallow the definition of their reality which is put forward by the dominant.[64] Indeed, even Alice Walker is not unmindful of the agency and resilience of women.[65] About twenty years ago, she delivered a speech at Radcliffe called "In Search of Our Mothers' Gardens," eulogizing mothers who persevere in life, in spite of the many obstacles that threaten to stifle and destroy their creativity.[66] To discount long-standing traditions of agency, power, and strength among African women is to risk stalling progress and constructive dialogue *vis-à-vis* female circumcision.[67]

Among the Ewe of Ghana, a proverb states that, "because a stranger has big eyes does not mean that she sees everything." The Chinese, on the other hand, counter that distance lends enchantment to the view. These seemingly opposed world-views are reconciled by Richard Wright, who points out that while an observer who is too close to a subject may suffer a blurred vision, the one who stands far away may have the benefit of detachment, but runs the risk of neglecting salient issues.[68] Wright's comment does not just articulate the essence of a balanced perspective; it also subtly extols the virtues of complementarity and cooperation. In organizing for change, effectiveness is better guaranteed if the change is actually perceived as necessary by the people at the grass roots level.[69] The value of change which is meant to improve their lot must be judged largely from their own point of view (Galt and Smith 1976; Lee 1959). Because they are more familiar with the dynamics of and the conditions for meaningful change than outside experts, they are best suited to engineer and spearhead enduring reform.

The relevance of this discussion for female circumcision is that no substitute exists for the involvement of the women who provide the impetus for the practice. Consequently, it behooves feminist crusaders to steer clear of absolutist dogma in favor of more collaborative schemes and strategies.[70] A crucial element in this approach is the development of connections with the affected population, tapping into the indigenous perspectives about the rhythms of change, and conceding to local women the right to take the lead in identifying their needs and formulating their solutions. If female circumcision is their everyday reality, it is inconceivable that it could be eradicated without their input. Radical approaches that covertly or overtly shun these women bode ill for enduring change and reduce reformist efforts to little more than intellectual masturbation.[71]

In order to make the discourses of reform relevant to the ground-level realities of women in cultures that perform circumcision, the material bases of the practice of circumcision, as well as the consequences of the push for eradication, must be addressed. Superficial expressions of solidarity and reductive conceptualizations which are disinclined to address the issue in the context of the secondary allocation of resources to women's education, economic participation, health care, etc., lose sight of the need for a response that embraces the issue in its totality. Meaningful analysis of the practice of female circumcision by feminist scholars who situate the practice in a broader developmental context is a laudable step in the proper direction. Achola Pala's remarks about the problems posed by misconceived research processes that are incongruent with the structural dimensions of the very realities that they purport to address are insightful. She writes:

> I have visited villages where, at a time when the village women are asking for better health facilities and lower infant-mortality rates [pipe-borne water and access to agricultural credit], they are presented with questionnaires on female circumcision. There is no denying that certain statistical relationships can be established between such variables … [however,] a statistical relationship per se, which can be exercised as an academic exercise, does not necessarily constitute relevant information or a priority from the point of view of those who are made the research subjects (Pala 1977: 10-1).

The unfortunate approach that Pala identifies is exemplified by Alice Walker. Walker reports that female circumcision is performed with rusty razors, tin can tops, shared pieces of unwashed glass or a sharpened stone's edge. Nevertheless (and in spite of her reputation for asking big questions), (Ansa 1992) she neglects to engage the rudimentary questions of why such crude implements are used and why infection from the grotesque procedure she describes has not escalated to frightfully decimating proportions. Her expectation is probably that the graphic details she divulges speak for themselves. They may, but what they say is a matter of interpretation and, for some, a site for value-laden opinions (Obiora 1996). What is clear, however, is that female circumcision is a delicate and risk-ridden procedure. In spite of the descriptions of the operation by researchers, namely, that this delicate procedure may be performed by an elderly woman of dimming vision and that the unsanitary conditions may contribute to the spread of AIDS and other communicable diseases, many feminists are vehemently opposed to clinicalization. To Walker and others who would settle for nothing short of prohibition, "in hospital" is not the answer.[72] However, clinicalization, while not without its own risks, may resonate with many women in the cultures that engage in female circumcision, at least, to the extent that a forum change attenuates the risk of mutilation, morbidity, and mortality, *inter alia*.[73]

Walker may have come to terms with the conflicting priorities of outside and indigenous campaigners when she realized that she could not show her film from village to village as planned because many had "absolutely no audio-visual facilities. Barely, sometimes, drinking water" (Walker and Parmar 1993: 82).[74] But the most vivid depiction of the conflict is contained in the passage where she writes:

> In the middle of this I was stunned to hear Madame Fall, our host, ask me to buy them a refrigerated truck. Having seen some of the splendid gardens the women have, I realize this is just exactly what they need to get their produce to market; still, I assured her that a whole refrigerated truck is a bit out of my range and the film's budget. Maybe I could contribute a couple of tires? (Ibid: 73).

Her inability to respond with sensitivity to the request betrays her lack of appreciation of the correlation between circumcision and structures of underdevelopment. Her skillful but parochial extraction of a single aspect of a complex problem often led her to discrepant and derisive conclusions. Although she repeatedly alludes to the socio-economic realities of the women,[75] she fails to explore the socio-economic implications for the change she posits, and offers little if any guidance regarding the actual process of implementing change.[76]

Female circumcision is on a continuum with a series of ceremonies which clarify and preserve social principles, roles, and continuity (La Fontaine 1972). While the practice is deeply entrenched in the social matrix, it is not unyielding.[77] Scholars have found that customs like circumcision express a fundamental contradiction: although they are conserving and conservative institutions which derive force from the real or apparent antiquity and sanctity of tradition, they provide simultaneous opportunities for flexibility and are accommodating to evolving social circumstances (La Fontaine 1972: Obiora 1996). However, an ill-conceived reform campaign runs the risk of playing into the hands of radical nationalists (Fanon 1963:180; Kenyatta 1965). When a people undertake a struggle against an imperialist onslaught, the significance of tradition can change (Fanon 1963: 191). Adherence to the hard core of the contested custom, regardless of its risks to segments of the population, becomes interpreted and glorified as faithfulness to the spirit of the nation and as a refusal to submit (Obiora 1996; Obiora 1994: 217). Moreover, if the practice is culturally significant, uncategorical prohibition is likely to banish it into clandestine operation, much like the prohibition of abortion (Obiora 1994). In the case of circumcision, impediments to effective enforcement, such as a lack of will to enforce and an absence of appropriate enforcement structures are compounded by the cultural embeddedness of the practice and by the fact that it is, as Pratibha Parmar puts it, deeply fossilized in women's psyches.[78] The distinctive feature of legal symbolism in this instance is the clear and present potential for loss of lives. The lessons of past prohibitionist efforts behoove us to proceed with circumspection and to critically reflect on other alternatives (Obiora 1994).

NOTES

1. I am indebted to Kofi Agawu, Nitya Iyer, Martha Jackman, Jesus, Ron Krotozynski, Yuri Kuwahara, Obioma Nnaemeka, and Oyeronke Oyewumi for their respective roles in the making of this article.
2. Alice Walker, *Possessing the Secret of Joy*. I also discuss Alice Walker and Pratibha Parmar, *Warrior Marks: Female Genital Mutilation and the Sexual Blinding of Women,*

and Parmar's documentary film of the same name.

3. See Mary E. Hawkesworth, "Knowers, Knowing, Known: Feminist Theory and Claims of Truth".

4. See Helen Cixous, "Sorties" in Elaine Marks and Isabelle de Courtivron, eds., *New French Feminisms: An Anthology*; Ellen C. Du Bois, et al., "Feminist Discourse, Moral Values and the Law: A Conversation (The 1984 James McCormick Mitchell Lecture; Elizabeth Fox-Genovese, "The Personal is Not Political Enough"; Alison M. Jagger, *Feminist Politics and Human Nature*; Alison M. Jagger, and Susan R. Bordo, *Gender/Body/Knowledge: Feminist Reconstructions of Being* and; Sallyanne Payton, "Releasing Excellence: Erasing Gender Zoning From the Legal Mind"; Diane Polan, "Toward a Theory of Law and Patriarchy," in David Kairys, ed., *The Politics of Law: A Progressive Critique*.

5. See Jane R. Martin, *Reclaiming a Conversation: The Ideal of the Educated Woman*; Katherine T. Bartlett, "Feminist Legal Methods".

6. See Martha Minow, "Feminist Reason: Getting It and Losing It"; Deborah L. Rhode, *Justice and Gender: Sex Discrimination and the Law*.

7. See Nancy Hartsock, "Fundamental Feminism: Process and Perspective".

8. See Susan Griffin, "The Way of All Ideology," in Nannerl O. Keohane, Michelle Z. Rosaldo, and Barbara C. Gelpi, eds., *Feminist Theory: A Critique of Ideology*; Elizabeth Spelman, *Inessential Woman: Problems of Exclusion in Feminist Thought*; Elizabeth Spelman, "Theories of Race and Gender: The Erasure of Black Women".

9. See Maren Lockwood Carden, *The New Feminist Movement*; Minow, *op. cit.*

10. See Lasch, Christopher, *The Culture of Narcissism: American Life in an Age of Diminishing Expectations* ; Spelman, "Theories of Race and Gender" *op. cit.*; Minow, *op. cit.*; Sir Carleton Kemp Allen, *Law in the Making*; Fox-Genovese, *op. cit.*; Adrienne Cecile Rich, *On Lies, Secrets, and Silence: Selected Prose, 1966-1978.* p. 306.

11. Compare Frantz Fanon, *The Wretched of the Earth.* p. 174.

12. Lorde is echoed by Jane Flax who observes that if gender is not recognized as a social relation, it is difficult to identify the varieties and limitations of different women's powers and oppressions: cited in Bartlett, *op. cit.* p. 876.

13. Zeroing in on the racial dimension, hooks notes that white women who daily exercise race privilege may not have a conscious understanding of the ideology of white supremacy and the extent to which it shapes their behavior and attitudes towards women unlike themselves. See bell hooks, *Feminist Theory: From Margin to Center.* p. 54.

14. See Chandra Talpade Mohanty, "Under Western Eyes" in Chandra Mohanty, Ann Russo, and Lourdes Torres, eds., *Third World Women and the Politics of Feminism*; Ifi Amadiume, *Male Daughters, Female Husbands: Gender and Sex in an African Society*; Nawal Sadawi, *The Hidden Face of Eve: Women in the Arab World*; Trinh T. Minh-ha, *Woman, Native, Other: Writing Postcoloniality and Feminism*; Tiffany R Patterson and Angela M. Gilliam, "Out of Egypt: A Talk with Nawal el Sadawi".

15. The politics of publication and exploitation of power that resound in Steady's

critique call to mind the tale of a child who, upon reading several expeditions in which the hunter prevailed over the lion, asked the father why the hunter was always triumphant. The father answered that it will be that way until the lion learns to write. See Filomina C. Steady, "Research Methodology and Investigative Framework for Social Change: The Case for African Women,".

16. Feminism has traditionally exposed and denigrated the tendency to represent reality in exclusionary and absolute terms as the defining feature and forte of the patriarchal order. See Martha Minow and Elizabeth V. Spelman, "Passion for Justice". p. 53; Bartlett, *op. cit.* p. 849; Mary Field Belenky, et al., *Women's Ways of Knowing: The Development of Self, Voice, and Mind.*

17. These feminists renounce animating feminist insights and convey the impression that only the pool of players, not the game or its dynamics, has changed. See Spelman, *Inessential Woman, su op. cit.,* for a chronicle of instances of feminist assumptions of a unitary, homogenizing and fixed standard for "women's experiences". See also hooks, *op. cit.,* and Angela P. Harris, "Race and Esentialism in Feminist Legal Theory," in Katherine T. Bartlett and Rosanne Kennedy, eds. *Feminist Legal Theory: Readings in Law and Gender* for incisive criticisms of the broken promise of feminist method.

18. The metaphor of the choir describes here an audience of moral elites who are conditioned for the spectacular and who see eye to eye with the exponent of the view in question. See Carden, *op. cit.* p. 46.

19. See L. Amede Obiora, "Bridges and Barricades: Rethinking Polemics and Intransigence in the Campaign Against Female Circumcision". Fran P. Hosken, the author of a series entitled The Hosken Report, which has been the "bible" for some "jihads" against circumcision has been indicted in this respect: Obioma Nnaemeka, *Reporting Fran Hosken* (work in progress discussed with author).

20. This general obfuscation regarding female circumcision is comparable to a 1993 Olympic advertisement which featured representatives of *specific* countries in the West with one African, collapsing a continent into a single a country.

21. Diana E.H. Russell and Nicole Van de Ven, eds., *The Proceedings of the International Tribunal on Crimes Against Women.* p. 151.

22. It is also interesting that the map of West Africa reproduced on the inside front cover of the 1996 Harvest Book edition of *Warrior Marks* is inaccurate. For example, it omits Nigeria, Africa's most populous nation.

23. Complaining about the haranguing of her local aide, Bilaela, who wanted to know when she would be remunerated for her assistance in setting up interviews and visits to the villages, Parmar writes, "Right away, I sensed that something didn't feel right about Bilaela." Walker and Parmar, *op. cit.* p. 162, 167. It was this same Bilaela that brought in a New York television agent who had previously enlisted her help and remunerated her for her stand against circumcision. As reported by Parmar, "Stephanie had somehow found out that Bilaela was working with another film crew to make a film about female genital mutilation, and was pressuring Bilaela not to cooperate with us. We heard Bilaela say that she had not given the American crew an exclusive and therefore felt free to work with us." *Ibid.* p. 162.

24. Parmar is scandalized by what she perceives as her contacts' capitalistic disposition, as if such a disposition were abnormal, and without pausing to ruminate on what their actions say about their material realities or about the possible tainting of the information they volunteered.

25. Walker and Parmar, *op. cit.* p. 96. On several occasions Parmar expressed her disgust for the practice to her paid informants. In so doing, she did a disservice to the foregrounding of African women's voices of anger, analysis, resistance, and self-determination which she claimed to be one of her fundamental guiding principles. *Ibid.* p. 109.

26. Smith, Barbara, "Racism and Women's Studies" *Frontiers* 5 (1) (1980) 48. The balance of power, which is related to the world economic divide, vests Westerners with the discursive privilege of acting as theory-smiths or producers of knowledge. See Paulin Houtondji, "Daily Life in Black Africa: Elements for a Critique," in V.Y. Mudimbe, ed., *The Surreptitious Speech: Presence Africaine and the Politics of Otherness 1947-1987* (Chicago: University of Chicago Press, 1992) 344; Robert Thornton, "Narrative Ethnography in Africa, 1850-1920: The Creation and Capture of an Appropriate Domain for Anthropology" *Man* 18 (3) (September 1983) 502.

27. Lorde, *op. cit.* p. 67-8. Lorde wrote this passage deploring the history of errors of white women who are unable to hear black women's words, or to maintain dialogue with them. She notes that women-identified women cannot afford to repeat these same old destructive and wasteful errors of recognition. *Ibid.* p. 69.

28. This is found in the preface to Walker, *op. cit.*

29. Paul Tilzey, "All the Marks of an Identity Crisis"; Toni Y. Joseph, "Alice Walker the `Womanist' Says Joy Lies in Universal Healing".

30. Evidently she has no qualms about manipulating and shifting identities which she construes at her convenience. See Chikwenye Okonjo Ogunyemi, "Ectomies: A Treasury of Fiction by Africa's Daughters," in this volume.

31. Several essays in this volume draw upon Walker's missionary intervention to point out the overt and subliminal racist parallels between the contemporary and colonialist discourses about Africa. *Ibid.*

32. Stereotypic images of Africa run the gamut from that of "Merry Africa," a place where noble savages frolic unmolested, to that of a dark continent of unbridled savagery. Images that inhere in the circumcision campaign are inspired by the latter model.

33. Mary Kingsley characterized the African as being on the "border-line that separates man from anthropoid apes." Mary H. Kingsley, *Travels in West Africa, Congo Francais, Corisco and Cameroons.* p. 458.

34. See Walker and Parmar, *op. cit.* p. 3. Walker's complicity in the production and perpetuation of racist stereotypes is at odds with the concern expressed by her film collaborator, Pratibha Parmar: "How can I create a sensitive and respectful representation of a people and a continent who have historically been grossly misrepresented? How can *Warrior Marks* begin to challenge the cultural imperialist imagery of Africa and Africans, as perpetuated in Hollywood films like *Out of*

Africa? Ibid. p. 94.

35. Even the *tsunga* tends toward a language of therapy shaped by contemporary Western dialogue, with its presiding metaphor of the lost inner child: Devon Jersild, "Walker: Baring a Terrible `Secret'".

36. See Philip D. Curtin, *The Image of Africa; British Ideas and Action, 1780-1850.* p. 29; Charles Darwin, *The Descent of Man and Selection in Relation to Sex.* See also Christopher L. Miller, *Theories of Africans: Francophone Literature and Anthropology in Africa.* p. 295. Compare with revisionist claims that "hybrids" are not as inferior as "uncrossed negroes." Robert Knox, *Races of Men.* p. 190.

37. According to Ogunyemi, Tashi is an exemplar of Trinh Minh-ha's "woman, native, other."; Minh-ha, *op. cit.*

38. Compare Lasch, *op. cit.* Toubia, among others, records that the psychological consequences of the practice among immigrants differ from those indigenous communities where the practice is prevalent: Nahid Toubia, "Female Circumcision as a Public Health Issue". p. 714. See also Sally Poivoir, "Alice Walker Tackles Challenging Task in `Possessing'".

39. For Lightfoot-Klein, Africans (Sudanese to be precise) are a remarkably peaceable, mutually supportive, generous, deeply devout people, who are inexplicably happy in their desperately poor, monotonously barren, harsh, and bleakly arid land: Hanny Lightfoot-Klein, *Prisoners of Ritual: An Odyssey into Female Genital Circumcision in Africa.* p. 149.

40. In her opinion, it has "everything to do with control with curbing women's sexuality early and keeping them docile and undemanding." Cited in Patricia Holt, "Scars of a Beloved Culture". Elsewhere, she records her surprise and curiosity in seeing women in a "mutilating culture" gyrating in "exaggeratedly erotic [dances] sticking out their tongues and with their eyes rolled back, presumably in ecstasy." Further, one of her interviewees, "big Mary," curtly informed her that "[m]y sex life is perfectly satisfactory, thank you very much!" See Walker and Parmer *op. cit.* p. 71, 44. Nevertheless, Walker fails to re-think or modify her "catch-all" claim that circumcised women are sexually deprived. The interviewee's response is affirmed by several studies, including Lightfoot-Klein who reports a similarly forceful response by an infibulated Sudanese woman. In the words of the woman, *"a body is a body,* and no circumcision can change that!" Lightfoot-Klein, *op. cit.* p. 25.

41. In different communities female circumcision may be performed for varying reasons, including as an integral element of rites of passage, to prepare for parturition, for contraception or fertility, for aesthetics or socialization, for purification and sacrifice, or to reinforce community bonds. See generally, Obiora, *op. cit.*

42. Kay Boulware-Miller, "Female Circumcision: Challenges to the Practice as a Human Rights Violation". Compare with Thelma Awori, "Women's Fear? For African Women Equal Rights Are not Enough,". It would seem that the closer the Africa woman is to tradition, the more seriously she takes her responsibility for her children. Motherhood slavishly inclines her to make the ultimate sacrifices for them.

43. See M.B. Assaad, "Female Circumcision in Egypt: Current Research and Social

Implications". These women are mischaracterized as "prisoners of ritual" for their rational choices: Lightfoot-Klein, *supra* note 46.

44. Boulware-Miller reports that in a bid to spare their beloved children the stigma and "social ostracism" that attach to nonconformity and difference, mothers make a superficial cut when pressured by their daughters: *op. cit.* See also Alison T. Slack, "Female Circumcision: A Critical Appraisal". Badri found an unexpected incidence of high school students indicating that they forced their parents to have them circumcised: Amna Elsadik Badri, *Female Circumcision in the Sudan: Change and Continuity*.

45. Walker contradicts or refutes the premise for the suggestion that men do not marry uncircumcised women. She observes that circumcision prevails in foreign countries like Holland, Britain, and the United States, where women are not bound to marry men who favor circumcision. Walker and Parmar, *op. cit.* p. 229. The claim is also inaccurate insofar as it holds that women in circumcising cultures are economically dependent on their husbands. Marriage is often more a necessity for socio-cultural affirmation and acceptance than a financial insurance. There is no definitive correlation between circumcision and low female status. See Obiora, *op. cit.* Given the availability of historical data which suggest that European patriarchy and colonialism eroded the traditional power and autonomy of African women, the relatively low status of women in the contemporary society cannot be simply attributed to circumcision. See Ester Boserup, *Women's Role in Economic Development*, and Mona Etienne and Eleanor Leacock, eds, *Women and Colonization: Anthropological Perspectives*.

46. Pursuant to Joan Smith's question of why "Alice Walker, who is so moved by Tashi's story, is unable to portray her as anything more than a dolorous puppet?" one is inclined to respond that a more empathetic portrayal requires a subtlety and insight not much in evidence from a novelist who dedicates her book "With Tenderness and Respect To the Blameless Vulva" and sacrifices character and plot to the imperatives of polemic. See Joan Smith, "Genitally Does It".

47. *Ibid.* p. 62. Walker frequently emphasizes the similarities between the practice of circumcision and her visual mutilation which made her childhood lonely and miserable. In *Warrior Marks*, she talks about how she found comfort in running into the woods. Walker and Parmar, *op. cit.* p. 16-19, 267.

48. Identifying a dependency does not constitute proof of the lack of the intrinsic worth of the supposedly dependent. Walker's failure to make this distinction seems to lead her to replicate the imperious negation of her research subjects' attributes of humanity.

49. I also wondered about the role of food, particularly "sweets," in the African woman's life. Perhaps the overweight women one sees so frequently, are still feeding "sweets," to the little frightened and dishonored child inside in an effort to "reward," her for her loss and to make her forget. I suddenly remembered that my own mother, after I was shot and delirious from pain and fever, cooked an entire chicken just for me.

50. For an intriguing discussion of fetishization of African women's sexual organs, with Saatje-je Baartman, the "Hottentot apron," as a focal point, see Oyewumi, *op. cit.* It has been said that people who exploit others tend to emphasize the animal

rather than the human elements of their victims because it eases their consciences. See Ugboaja Ohaegbulam, *Towards an Understanding of the African Experience from Historical and Contemporary Perspectives*. p. 4. Compare with Montesquieu: "it is impossible for us to suppose these creatures to be men, because, allowing them to be men, a suspicion would follow that we ourselves are not Christians." Montesquieu, *The Spirit of Laws*.

51. Ritual is a process; as opposed to being an immutable timeless essence, it evolves over time. What remains far more constant is the symbolic and ideological content of the ritual. See Victor W. Turner, *The Forest Symbols: Aspects of Ndembu Ritual*.

52. With her penchant for flippancy, Walker also quips about the chill she experienced upon the thought that "for many African women this ritual of circumcision is the only real link they have with their ancient African-Egyptian heritage." Walker and Parmar, *op. cit* p. 48.

53. In a companion piece, I have explored the challenges of various prescriptives against female circumcision. Obiora, *op. cit*. In 1995, there was a motion in the Canadian House of Commons to amend the Criminal Code to specifically criminalize the practice. See William Gold, "Women's Concerns on March". This proposal did not universally resonate with Canadian feminists.

54. The College of Physicians and Surgeons drafted a policy barring doctors in Ontario from assisting with the procedure. See "Canada: Policy on Female Genital Mutilation".

55. This aversion is not just attributable to nationalism and traditionalism. It is also related to the fact that many Africans have witnessed many broken promises and false prophecies stemming from interventionist "savior complexes" and they are worse off for it. The aversion has fostered the development of a long-standing and pervasive tradition of resistance to imperialist insurgency which dates back to the days of the maiden encounter. That a particularly wild and domineering species of grass has been called Eliza, after Queen Elizabeth II, among the Oguta Igbo is a testament of this attitude of caution, scepticism, and opposition.

56. It is ironic that in their efforts to implement their vision of societal transformation, some feminists have ended up aggravating the self-same grievances that they seek to eradicate. See Carden, *supra* note 8 at 46. In the course of condemning a New York Television crew that paid for a circumcision in order to have a live recording of the procedure, Pratibha Parmar admitted that it is easy for filmmakers to become a part of the problem even while trying to resolve it. See Walker and Parmar, *op. cit*. p. 162. Parmar obviously was oblivious of her own blunder.

57. African activists and scholars are making concerted efforts to address the problems posed by female circumcision. The strategies of some involve frontal assaults parallel to Walker's approach. Others, even when they advocate prompt prohibition, are less confrontational. For more than a decade, one NGO predominated by Africans, the Inter-Africa Committee on Traditional Practices Affecting the Health of Women and Children (IAC), has engaged in elaborate information campaigns targeted at health professionals and traditional birth attendants, government officials, media specialists, and community leaders. See Claude Welch, *Protecting Human Rights in*

Africa: Roles and Strategies of Non-Governmental Organizations. p. 87-8. By far, however, the unsung heroes of the indigenous movement committed to eradicating circumcision and poverty among women come from rural constituencies who defy innumerable odds, deny high ceremony and visibility, but pursue their agenda single-mindedly and diligently. Locally resident, they are apt to avoid alienating postures and polarizations, and to strive instead to enlist broad-based support by organizing their activities around issues that reflect the basic needs of women and the larger interests of their communities. The members of these constituencies are the life-line of public awareness-raising programmes which have made organizations such as the IAC famous. Pratibha Parmar realized that she had mistakenly thought that Africans were doing nothing about female circumcision prior to her visit to Africa to film *Warrior Marks*. See Walker and Parmar, *op. cit.* p. 242.

58. In this vein, it should be noted that bell hooks argues that white feminists are not yet free of the type of paternalism endemic to white supremacist ideology when they see themselves as providing black women with "the" analysis and "the" program for liberation. See generally, Hooks, *op. cit.*

59. Adu A. Boahen, *African Perspectives on Colonialism* (Baltimore, Md.: Johns Hopkins University Press, 1987) p. 62. The absurdity of this Eurocentrism is most apparent with Alice Walker who even denies nature credit for its endowments. Commenting on the scenery in Ougadougou, the capital of Burkina Faso, she writes that "the French, planted lots of trees, which shade the wide boulevards" Walker and Parmar, *op. cit.* p. 81.

60. Support for this line of thought comes from an unlikely source, Alice Walker's *Possessing the Secret of Joy*. In the novel, Tashi's sister, Dura, had bled to death. Mindful of this, Tashi reacted violently to the sight of blood. As a child, "she played in such a way as to take no risks and even learned to sew in an exaggeratedly careful way, using two thimbles." Walker, *op. cit.* p. 8-9. If one death could make such an impression on a child, how much more the untold hardship and deaths that are alleged to flow from circumcision in a village.

61. See Richard A. Wasserstrom, ed., *Morality and the Law.* Does evidence of harm warrant undifferentiated paternalistic attacks? Several critics maintain that unlike an adult, a child lacks the capacity to give an informed consent. See Scilla McLean and Stella E. Graham, *Female Circumcision, Excision and Infibulation: The Facts and Proposals for Change.* p. 10. Ordinarily, parental consent is a prerequisite for surgical procedures performed on minors. However, there is authority for the view that parental consent is not absolute, but that it is confined to treatment in which there is a demonstrable element of benefit to the child. See Isabelle R. Gunning, "Arrogant Perception, World-Travelling and Multicultural Feminism: The Case of Genital Surgeries"; K. Hayter, "Female Circumcision — Is There a Legal Solution?". Practitioners of female circumcision believe in its benefit. Moreover, as Boulware-Miller reveals, polar invocations of the rights of children conflict with the parents' desires to rear their children in accordance with their culturally moulded perceptions of what is in "the best interest of the child." See Boulware-Miller *op. cit.* p. 155.

62. It is important to note that the notion of harm is relative. For an overview of the

debate between universalists and relativists, see Alison Dundes Renteln, *International Human Rights: Universalism Versus Relativism*; Peter Schwab, ed., *Human Rights: Cultural and Ideological Perspectives*; Rhoda E. Howard, *Human Rights in Commonwealth Africa*; and Warren Weinstein, "Human Rights and Development in Africa: Dilemmas and Options". p. 173. The relativity of cultures is underscored by Gloria Steinem who asserted during a panel discussion in New York that "[j]ust as African patriarchs have fashioned a brutal practice that would ensure the virginity of their brides, the `spirit-killing regimes of male dominance' in the West rob women of their `reproductive rights' by seeking to outlaw abortion." See Eichman, *op. cit.* There is a good chance that abortion is as abhorrent to a woman with a strong pronatalistic orientation as circumcision is to Ms. Steinem. In fact, some women practice circumcision to enhance their fecundity.

63. Critical theorists demonstrate that dominating a discourse is an effective means of exercising, protecting and perpetuating the privileges of power: those who have power can do the talking; those who lack power must do the listening. See L. Amede Obiora, "Of the Female in American Legal Education". Similarly, Carol Gilligan opines that "if you have power, you can opt not to listen. And you do so with impunity." See DuBois *et al.*, *op. cit.* p. 62.

64. See hooks, *op. cit.* p. 90, 93. Elizabeth Janeway designates the phenomenon as the power to disbelieve. According to Janeway, the exercise of this personal power is an act of resistance and strength: Elizabeth Janeway, *Powers of the Weak*.

65. The resilience of victims, or rather victors, of apparent domination also resonates with Labi Siffre's song, *(Something Inside) So Strong*, (Empire Music Ltd./Xavier Music Ltd., 1986) especially in the stanza that begins: "[t]he higher you build your barrier, the taller I become." Interestingly enough, Siffre's song was the concluding score in the film, *Warrior Marks*. See also, Walker and Parmar, *op. cit.* p. 186.

66. See Walker and Parmar, *op. cit.* p. 20. However, Walker juxtaposes these nurturing and creative mothers with the betraying African mother who connives "in the literal destruction of the most crucial external side of her [daughter's] womanhood: her vulva itself." *Ibid.* p. 21.

67. Lorde considers African female bonding to be the epitome of love and female solidarity. Lorde, *op. cit.* See also the forward of Adrienne Rich's *Of Woman Born*, in which she says that most of us first know love, tenderness, and power in the person of a woman.

68. Richard Wright, "Introduction: Blueprint for Negro Writing", in Addison Gayle, Jr., ed., *The Black Aesthetics*. p. 333, 341. See also Obioma Nnaemeka, "Bringing African Women into the Classroom? Rethinking Pedagogy and Epistemology," in Margaret Higonnet, ed., *Borderwork: Feminist Engagements with Comparative Literature*. p. 301.

69. Even Awa Thiam, reputedly no stranger to provocative iconoclasm, was forced to interface with the existing order by the frustrations she suffered otherwise. See Walker and Parmar, *op. cit.* p. 286.

70. The authors of a recent article note that effective intervention takes place within a complex communicative web and that culturally responsive intervention is made in

a voice that engages the "Other" as an equal interlocutor. Arguing that interventions are assertions of legitimacy (what actions are appropriate), standing (who has the appropriate status to carry out intervention), and authority (who has the power to intervene), they conclude that culturally responsive efforts to address problematic practices necessarily involve constructing the analysis and subsequent intervention in ways that are at once honest and respectful. Sandra D. Lane and Robert A. Rubinstine, "Judging the Other: Responding to Traditional Female Genital Surgeries".

71. In *Possessing the Secret of Joy*, Tashi communes with Carl Jung, an African-American woman therapist, and with the son born to her husband's French paramour in order to relieve the concomitant psychosis of her clitoridectomy. However, *it is her own action* — the nemesis of M'Lissa the circumcisor — which precipitates her ultimate recovery. See Tina Ansa, "Taboo Territory".

72. Adverse effects from the less extensive forms of female circumcision, ritualistic *sunna* and excision, are usually less severe. However, the requisite skill, surgical tools and knowledge of anatomy, necessary for performing the operation with a minimum of pain may be lacking. Medical data indicate that *sunna*, is relatively safe if performed under proper conditions. Edna Adan Ismail, "Statement on the Practice of Infibulation". p. 21.

73. In Somalia, for example, the National Committee on Female Circumcision recommended that sunna circumcision be encouraged and performed in hospitals. Other African authorities have made similar recommendations. In Holland, the Somalis usually turn first to the Dutch medical and social welfare personnel. If refused, they carry out the circumcision themselves, often in a very unhygienic and harmful manner. Henrietta Boas, "Problem of Female Circumcisions in Holland". Some efforts to institute a forum change have not been totally successful in convincing some women who are committed to infibulations to embrace modified forms of the practice. There is also some indication that certain practitioners in the medical setting, motivated by selfish economic interests, accommodate the preferences of these women, instead of striving to sensitive and prevail on them to accept less severe procedures. See ECOSOC, Report of the United Nations Seminar on Traditional Practices Affecting the Health of Women and Children; and ECOSOC, Study on Traditional Practices Affecting Women and Children: Final Report by the Special Rapporteur, Mrs. Halima Embarek Warzazi.

74. Walker and Parmar, *op. cit.* p. 82. Then, idiosyncratically, she added "None that we foreigners could drink. It is the poverty of Africa that stays with me, along with the bright spirits of African children". *Ibid.*

75. For example, in the interview with Giddings, Walker alleges that "at night all the women go in, like chickens. There are no windows, they lock the door — practically nail it shut. There is no air. That's how they sleep. It almost killed me to see women in Kenya and other places who actually have grooves in their foreheads from carrying heavy loads." Giddings, *op. cit.*

76. Parmar was equally remiss. She remarked: "It was hard to believe that Banjul is the capital city of the Gambia. There are few paved roads; consequently everything is dusty. Many people live on the streets." Walker and Parmar, *op. cit.* p. 166. Yet she

neglected to analyze the connection and to provide a structural context for her documentary. Ironically, she is more concerned that nobody stops to think of the reality (of circumcision) behind "the usual ethnographic stereotypical images of bare-breasted African women staring into the photographer's lens, images that create exotic other, images of availability for the white male tourist," without realizing how she re-enacts the stereotypes. *Ibid.* p. 199.

77. Beneath the similitude of traditional entrapment seethes an active current and favorable disposition to other concepts of human existence and potentialities. The shifting social base, attitudes and standards; the erosion of rigid ceremonials as well as the tenuousness of the power structure and of the authority of tradition that lent force to the practice, all pose a real threat to its sustenance and perpetuation.

78. The precedent for condonation on grounds of "extenuating circumstances" was established in a recent decision of the French court which suspended the sentence of parents who were convicted for circumcising their daughters. If a court so far removed geographically and ideologically from Africa is prepared to be lenient, one can imagine the attitude of African courts. See the extensive discussion of this case in Francoise Lionnet, *Postcolonial Representations,* p. 154.

WORKS CITED:

Allen, Sir Carleton Kemp. *Law in the Making.* Oxford: Clarendon Press:, 7th ed. 1964.

Amadiume, Ifi. *Male Daughters, Female Husbands: Gender and Sex in an African Society.* London: Zed Books, 1987.

Ansa, Tina. "Taboo Territory". *Los Angeles Times* Book Review 4., July 15, 1992.

Assaad, M.B. "Female Circumcision in Egypt: Current Research and Social Implications", in *Seminar on Traditional Practices Affecting the Health of Women and Children in Africa.* Alexandria, Egypt: WHO/EMRO Technical Publication, 1982.

Anshaw, Carol. "The Practice of Cruelty Alice Walker Inveighs Against Ritual `Circumcision' of African Women" *Chicago Tribune,* June 21, 1992.

Awori, Thelma. "Women's Fear? For African Women Equal Rights Are not Enough," *Unesco Courier,* March 1975.

Badri, Amna Elsadik. *Female Circumcision in the Sudan: Change and Continuity.* Omduran, Sudan: Ahfad University College for Women, 1984.

Bartlett, Katherine T. "Feminist Legal Methods" *Harvard Law Review* 103 (4), 1990.

Boahen, Adu A. *African Perspectives on Colonialism.* Baltimore, MD: Johns Hopkins University Press, 1987.

Boas, Henrietta. "Problem of Female Circumcisions in Holland". *The Jerusalem Post.* May 10, 1992. Features; "Women: Dutch Government Ends Debate on Circumcision Proposal" *International Press Service,* November 11, 1992.

Boddy, Janice. *Wombs and Alien Spirits: Women, Men, and the Zar Culture in Northern Sudan,* Madison: University of Wisconsin Press, 1989.

Bloom, Alan D. *The Closing of the American Mind,* New York: Simon and Schuster, 1987.

Boserup, Ester. *Women's Role in Economic Development,* London: Allen and Unwin, 1970.

Boulware-Miller, Kay. "Female Circumcision: Challenges to the Practice as a Human Rights Violation". *Harvard Women's Law Journal* 8, 1985.

Carden, Maren Lockwood. *The New Feminist Movement*, New York: Russell Sage Foundation, 1974.

Charles, Marilynne. "An Open Wound". *West Africa*, June 27-July 3, 1994.

College of Physicians and Surgeons "Canada: Policy on Female Genital Mutilation". *WIN News,* 18 (2), 1992.

Cixous, Helen. "Sorties" in Elaine Marks and Isabelle de Courtivron, eds., *New French Feminisms: An Anthology*, Amherst: University of Massachussetts Press, 1980.

Curtin, Philip D. *The Image of Africa; British Ideas and Action, 1780-1850*, Madison: University of Wisconsin Press, 1964.

Darwin, Charles. *The Descent of Man and Selection in Relation to Sex*, New York: D. Appleton, 1874.

Davidson, Max. "Genital Interest Defines a Rising New Genre — The Below the Belt Story" *Sunday Telegraph.*, October 18, 1992.

Du Bois, Ellen C., et al., "Feminist Discourse, Moral Values and the Law: A Conversation (The 1984 James McCormick Mitchell Lecture)" *Buffalo Law Review* 34, 1985.

ECOSOC. Report of the United Nations Seminar on Traditional Practices Affecting the Health of Women and Children, Quagadougou, Burkina Faso, 29 April - 3 May 1991. E/CM.4/sub.2/1991/48, June 12, 1991.

ECOSOC. Study on Traditional Practices Affecting Women and Children: Final Report by the Special Rapporteur, Mrs. Halima Embarek Warzazi. E/CN.4/sub.2/1991/6, July 5, 1991.

Eichman, Erich. "The Cutting Edge: Alice Walker's New York, New York Book Party". *The National Review,* 45 (15), August 3, 1992.

Etienne, Mona and Eleanor Leacock, eds, *Women and Colonization: Anthropological Perspectives*, New York: Praeger, 1980.

Fanon, Frantz. *The Wretched of the Earth*, New York: Grove Press, 1963.

Farnsworth, Clyde H. "Canada Gives a Somali Refuge from a Genital Rite". *New York Times,* July 21, 1994.

Fox-Genovese, Elizabeth. "The Personal is Not Political Enough" *Marxist Perspectives* 98. Winter 1979-80.

Freire, Paulo. "The Adult Literacy Process as Cultural Action for Freedom". *Harvard Educational Review,* 40 (2), 1970.

Galt, Anthony H. and Larry J. Smith. *Models and the Study of Social Change*, Cambridge, MA: Schenkman Pub. Co., 1976.

Giddings, Paula. "Alice Walker's Appeal". *Essence* 23 (3)., July 1992.

Gold, William. "Women's Concerns on March". *Calgary Herald*, August 11, 1995).

Grenier, Richard. "No `Joy' for the Reader" *The Washington Times*, July 29, 1992.

Griffin, Susan. "The Way of All Ideology," in Nannerl O. Keohane, Michelle Z. Rosaldo, and Barbara C. Gelpi, eds., *Feminist Theory: A Critique of Ideology*, Chicago: University of Chicago Press, 1982.

Gunning, Isabelle R. "Arrogant Perception, World-Travelling and Multicultural Feminism: The Case of Genital Surgeries". *Columbia Human Rights Law Review,* 23 (2), 1992.

Gunning, Isabelle. "Female Genital Surgeries and Multicultural Feminism: The Ties that Bind; the Differences that Distance" *Third World Legal Studies* 17 (1994-95) 37; *In re Fuziya Kasinga* 35 I.L.M. 1145, 1996.

Harris, Angela P. "Race and Esentialism in Feminist Legal Theory," in Katherine T. Bartlett and Rosanne Kennedy, eds. *Feminist Legal Theory: Readings in Law and Gender*, Boulder, CO: Westview Press, 1991.

Hartsock, Nancy. "Fundamental Feminism: Process and Perspective" *Quest: A Feminist Quarterly* 2 (2), (Fall 1975).

Hawkesworth, Mary E. "Knowers, Knowing, Known: Feminist Theory and Claims of Truth" *Signs: Journal of Women in Culture and Society* 14 (3) (Spring 1989).

Hayter, K. "Female Circumcision — Is There a Legal Solution?" *J. Soc. Welfare and Family Law* (1984).

Holt, Patricia. "Scars of a Beloved Culture". *The San Francisco Chronicle*, June 21, 1992.

hooks, bell. *Feminist Theory: From Margin to Center*. Boston: South End Press, 1984.

Houtondji, Paulin. "Daily Life in Black Africa: Elements for a Critique," in V.Y. Mudimbe, ed., *The Surreptitious Speech: Presence Africaine and the Politics of Otherness 1947-1987*, Chicago: University of Chicago Press, 1992.

Howard, Rhoda E. *Human Rights in Commonwealth Africa*, Totowa, NJ: Rowman & Littlefield: Totowa, 1986.

Hughes, Robert. *Culture of Complaint: The Fraying of America*, New York: New York Public Library:, 1993.

Ismail, Edna Adan. "Statement on the Practice of Infibulation," in *Seminar on Traditional Practices Affecting the Health of Women and Children in Africa*. Alexandria, Egypt: WHO/EMRO Technical Publication, 1984.

Jagger, Alison M. *Feminist Politics and Human Nature*, Totowa, NJ: Rowman and Allanheld, 1983.

Jagger, Alison M. and Susan R. Bordo, *Gender/Body/Knowledge: Feminist Reconstructions of Being and Knowing*. New Brunswick, London: Rutgers University Press. 1989.

Janeway, Elizabeth. *Powers of the Weak*. New York: Knopf, 1980.

Jersild, Devon. "Walker: Baring a Terrible `Secret'" *USA Today*, July 17, 1992.

Joseph, Toni Y. "Alice Walker the `Womanist' Says Joy Lies in Universal Healing" *The Atlanta Journal and Constitution*, June 10, 1992.

Kenyatta, Jomo. *Facing Mount Kenya: The Tribal Life of the Gikuyu*. New York: Vintage Books, 1965.

King, Deborah. "Multiple Jeopardy, Multiple Consciousness in the Context of a Black Feminist Ideology". *Signs: Journal of Women in Culture and Society,* 14 (1) (1989).

Kingsley, Mary H. *Travels in West Africa, Congo Francais, Corisco and Cameroons.*, New York: The Macmillian Company, 1897.

La Fontaine, Jean S. ed., *The Interpretation of Ritual: Essays in Honour of I.A. Richards*, London: Tavistock Publications, 1972.

Lane, Sandra D. and Robert A. Rubinstine, "Judging the Other: Responding to Traditional Female Genital Surgeries". *The Hastings Center Report,* 26 (3) (1996).

Lasch, Christopher. *The Culture of Narcissism: American Life in an Age of Diminishing Expectations*. New York: New York, 1978.

Lee, Dorothy. *Freedom and Culture*, Englewood Cliffs, NJ: Prentice-Hall, 1959.

Lightfoot-Klein, Hanny. *Prisoners of Ritual: An Odyssey into Female Genital Circumcision in Africa*, New York: Harrington Park Press, 1989.

Lionnet, Francoise. *Postcolonial Representations*, Ithaca, NY: Cornell University Press, 1995.

Lorde, Audre. "An Open Letter to Mary Daly," in Audre Lorde, *Sister Outsider: Essays and Speeches*. Trumansburg, NY: Crossing Press, 1984.

Lugones Maria C. and Elizabeth V. Spelman, "Have We Got a Theory for You! Feminist Theory, Cultural Imperialism and the Demand for `The Woman's Voice". *Women's Studies International Forum,* 6 (6) (1983).

Martin, Jane R. *Reclaiming a Conversation: The Ideal of the Educated Woman*, New Haven, CT: Yale University Press, 1985.

McLean, Scilla and Stella E. Graham. "Female Circumcision, Excision and Infibulation: The Facts and Proposals for Change." *Minority Group Report,* no. 47. 1980: 7.

Miller, Christopher L. *Theories of Africans: Francophone Literature and Anthropology in Africa*. Chicago: University of Chicago Press, 1990.

Minh-ha, Trinh T. *Woman, Native, Other: Writing Postcoloniality and Feminism*, Bloomington: Indiana University Press, 1989.

Minow, Martha. "Feminist Reason: Getting It and Losing It" *Journal of Legal Education* 38 (1-2) (1988).

Mitton, Jennifer. "The Fundamental Question: Why is the Child Crying" *The Toronto Star*, August 25, 1992.

Mohanty, Chandra Talpade. "Under Western Eyes" in Chandra Mohanty, Ann Russo, and Lourdes Torres, eds., *Third World Women and the Politics of Feminism*, Bloomington: Indiana University Press, 1991.

Montesquieu. *The Spirit of Laws*, Anne M. Cohen, Basia Carolyn Miller, and Harold Samuel Stone, eds. Cambridge, MA: Cambridge University Press, 1989.

Nnaemeka, Obioma. "Bringing African Women into the Classroom? Rethinking Pedagogy and Epistemology," in Margaret Higonnet, ed. *Borderwork: Feminist Engagements with Comparative Literature*, Ithaca, NY: Cornell University Press, 1994.

Ohaegbulam, Ugboaja. *Towards an Understanding of the African Experience from Historical and Contemporary Perspectives*, Lanham, MD: University Press of America1, 1990.

Obiora, L. Amede. "Bridges and Barricades: Rethinking Polemics and Intransigence in the Campaign Against Female Circumcision" *Casewestern Law Review* 46 (1996) (forthcoming).

Obiora, L. Amede. "Of the Female in American Legal Education". *Law and Social Inquiry,* 21 (1996).

Obiora, L. Amede. "Reconsidering African Customary Law". *Legal Studies Forum,* 17 (3) (1994).

Pala, Achola O. "Definitions of Women and Development: An African Perspective". *Signs: Journal of Women in Culture and Society,* 3 (1) (1977).

Patterson, Tiffany R. and Angela M. Gilliam, "Out of Egypt: A Talk with Nawal el. Sadawi" *Freedomways* 23 (3) (1983).

Payton, Sallyanne. "Releasing Excellence: Erasing Gender Zoning From the Legal Mind"

Indiana Law Review 18 (3) (1985).

Poivoir, Sally. "Alice Walker Tackles Challenging Task in `Possessing'". *Houston Chronicle*, June 21, 1992.

Polan, Diane. "Toward a Theory of Law and Patriarchy," in David Kairys, ed., *The Politics of Law: A Progressive Critique*, New York: Pantheon Books, 1982.

Renteln, Alison Dundes. *International Human Rights: Universalism Versus Relativism*, Newbury Park: Sage Publications, 1990.

Reuben, Richard C. "New Ground for Asylum: Threatened Female Genital Mutilation is Persecution". *A.B.A.J.,* 36 (1) (1996).

Rhode, Deborah L. *Justice and Gender: Sex Discrimination and the Law*, Cambridge, MA: Harvard University Press, 1989.

Rich, Adrienne Cecile. *On Lies, Secrets, and Silence: Selected Prose, 1966-1978*, New York: Norton, 1979.

Russell, Diana E.H. and Nicole Van de Ven, eds., *The Proceedings of the International Tribunal on Crimes Against Women*, Millbrae, CA: Le Femmes Pub., 1976.

Sadawi, Nawal. *The Hidden Face of Eve: Women in the Arab World*, London: Zed Press, 1980.

Schwab, Peter. ed., *Human Rights: Cultural and Ideological Perspectives*, New York: Praeger, 1979.

Siffre, Labi. Song: *(Something Inside) So Strong.* Empire Music Ltd./Xavier Music Ltd. 1986.

Slack, Alison T. "Female Circumcision: A Critical Appraisal" *Human Rights Quarterly,* 10 (4) (1988).

Smith, Barbara. "Racism and Women's Studies". *Frontier, s* 5 (1) (1980).

Smith, Joan. "Genitally Does It". *The Independent*, October 18, 1992.

Spelman, Elizabeth. *Inessential Woman: Problems of Exclusion in Feminist Thought*, Boston: Beacon Press, 1988.

Spelman, Elizabeth. "Theories of Race and Gender: The Erasure of Black Women" *Quest: A Feminist Quarterly* 5 (4) (1982).

Stanley, Henry M. *In Darkest Africa or the Quest, Rescue, Retreat of Emin, Governor of Equatoria*, New York: Scribner, 1913 [c1890].

Steady, Filomina C. "Research Methodology and Investigative Framework for Social Change: The Case for African Women," in Association of African Women for Research Development, *Seminar on African Women: What Type of Methodology*, Darkar: Senegal, 1986.

Thompson, Allan. "Genital Mutilation Illegal, Copps Says". *Toronto Star*, October 4, 1994.

Thornton, Robert. "Narrative Ethnography in Africa, 1850-1920: The Creation and Capture of an Appropriate Domain for Anthropology" *Man* 18 (3) (September 1983).

Tilzey, Paul. "All the Marks of an Identity Crisis" *The Independent*, October 31, 1992.

Toubia, Nahid. "Female Circumcision as a Public Health Issue". *New England Journal of Medicine* 331 (11).

Turner, Victor W. *The Forest Symbols: Aspects of Ndembu Ritual.* 1967.

Walker, Alice. *Possessing the Secret of Joy*, New York: Harcourt Brace Jovanovich, 1992.

Walker, Alice and Pratibha Parmar. *Warrior Marks: Female Genital Mutilation and the Sexual Blinding of Women*, New York: Harcourt Brace Jovanovich, 1993.

Wasserstrom, Richard A. ed., *Morality and the Law*, Belmont, CA: Wadsworth Pub. Co., 1971.

Weinstein, Warren. "Human Rights and Development in Africa: Dilemmas and Options" *Daedalus,* 112 (4) (1983).

Welch, Claude. *Protecting Human Rights in Africa: Roles and Strategies of Non-Governmental Organizations*, Philadelphia: University of Pennsylvania Press, 1995.

Wright, Richard. "Introduction: Blueprint for Negro Writing", in Addison Gayle, Jr., ed., *The Black Aesthetics*, Garden City, NY: Doubleday, 1971.

9.

ECTOMIES:
A Treasury of Fiction by Africa's Daughters

Chikwenye Okonjo Ogunyemi

"Ife di oku ga ju oyi." (What is hot will cool.)
—Igbo Proverb

"Igi a run 'we." (The [cut] tree will leaf.)
—Yoruba Proverb

"Some Western women like to build and promote their careers by going to the Third World and doing research work and becoming scholars.... This sort of neo-colonialism in the name of feminism has to go."

–Nawal El Saadawi, Interview with Patterson and Gilliam, 1983

"As far as I am concerned, I am speaking for my great-great-great-great-grand-mother who came here with all this pain in her body.... In addition to her children being sold, she being raped ... she might have been genitally muti-lated. I can't stand it! I would go nuts if this part of her story weren't factored in. Imagine if men came from Africa with their penises removed. Believe me, we would have many a tale about it."
–Alice Walker, Interview with Giddings, 1992

"[T]here are a number of African women who are leading the battle against female circumcision, but many resent what they feel to be the sensationalistic nature of the campaign by many First World feminists."
–Cheryl Johnson-Odim 1991

I.   CUTTING EDGES

Ectomy, *verbum horribile,*[1] is conventionally excised to operate solely as a suffix in the thesaurus, as if to curtail its dreaded power. I wish to counter this subordination by restoring it to its original position as a word in Greek, to initiate the healing process paradoxically conjoined with surgery. Whether ectomy is performed under (an)esthetics or not, for palliative measures or control, it is pivotal in current gender and cultural wars. Literal, figurative, or psychological, ectomy is at the cutting edge in theorizing oppression, particularly in colonial, postcolonial, and feminist discourses.

In my reading of the African literary world, I will focus on the theoretical and political implications of ectomy. By ectomy I mean excision, particularly female circumcision: the mild form is clitoridectomy and the more radical clitoral erasure with stitching is infibulation. Two African novels—*Efuru* by Nigeria's Flora Nwapa (Flora 1966) and *Woman at Point Zero* by Egypt's Nawal El Saadawi (El Saadawi 1975) —and a short story, "The Collector of Treasures" by South Africa/Botswana's Bessie Head (Head 1977), will provide a basis for a vaginal discourse. They present African women's silent struggle against oppression as ongoing on several fronts, local and international. Two American texts depicting the African world, Alice Walker's novel, *Possessing the Secret of Joy* (Walker 1992), and Hanny Lightfoot-Klein's account of infibulation in the Sudan, *Prisoners of Ritual: An Odyssey into Female Genital Circumcision in Africa* (Lightfoot-Klein 1989), can stand in for a clitoral discourse. These two works serve as counter-response to the earlier African texts, suffused as both are with a missionary impulse. Though both sides focus on eliminating these unnecessary surgeries, their political methods and agenda are divergent, generating some rancor in which we tend to lose sight of the common goal. Many women from the North are seen by some African scholars as anachronistically imperious, external agents who try to control their less privileged stepsisters from the South to enforce attitudinal changes. Silent and silenced subjects, women from the South remain largely unheard. The insistence that we think and fight alike in spite of cultural, political, and economic differences generates an impasse that complicates feminist and postcolonial theoretical positions.

With the increasing recognition of *Efuru,* the battleground has become more bloody. As Africa's first international novel written in English by a woman, *Efuru* represents a historical breakthrough; Nwapa guardedly internationalizes local critique of clitoridectomy, legitimizing the subject in gender discourse, thereby engendering many a tale about it. In tackling the notion that female circumcision is at the center of reproductive economy, she deconstructs precolonial myths about clitoridectomy as biologically essential to forestall barrenness and esthetically enhancing for nuptials. Evolving under women's diminished circumstances within colonialism, her protagonist, Efuru, confronts older women whose complicit role in reproducing patriarchy by organizing and performing clitoridectomies disturbingly institutionalizes the procedure. The first woman in fiction to resent going under the knife and to prove its uselessness, Efuru heroically comes to "grips" with her clitoridectomy, moving beyond motherhood and wifehood to establish a distinguished career as a trader. Endowed with cultural and spiritual authority and dignity, she serves as a model for "new" women who work within, not outside, the system, determined to transform it from inside. They resist the postcolonial African patriarchy that had latched onto the preclusive colonial heritage which displaced some equitable, precolonial gender arrangements.

In the ongoing struggle, ectomy metaphorically signifies the ostracizing of women, particularly the reluctance to include their novels in African curriculums. Fiction serves as an important site for counterdiscourse, yet the sociopolitical and economic marginalization of African women, specifically female castration, prevents the majority of women from speaking out openly on sexuality and hegemony. Ectomy, figuratively speaking, mimics discursive fields where man is pitted against woman. Besides gender, older women regulate young women, thereby creating a generational conflict that validates the doctor/midwife's professional authority over women. A few women oppress the majority of women presumably to benefit the sons, ensure women's chastity, and control reproductivity.

Shifting to the global arena, ectomy embodies the unrelenting attempt of women from the North to determine all women's agenda. They invariably skirt crucial concerns surrounding global economics that impoverish women from the South and keep them under, turning the adventurous into unwelcome, international nomads. It is remarkable how many feminists gloss over the repercussions of the debt crises (excisions mandated by structural adjustment programs which Third World women find more crippling than circumcisions) and large-scale graft, institutionalized by many African leaders, who are aided and abetted by the North for northern advantage.[2] This oversight angers many African scholars who see poverty as pivotal in aggravating many ills in Africa, including female circumcision, physical and mental.

As clitoridectomy and the more severe version, sometimes referred to as pharaonic infibulation, are rituals traditionally shrouded in secrecy, we are reading the African world in the dark. What is clear is that the procedure crystallizes transformations and exclusions, developing into a powerful metaphor in fiction. This fiction derives from ancient tales from a cultural imaginary that links the continually shifting fates of animals and deities with the metamorphosing worlds of humans. Such fiction and ectomy form part of the postcolonial, liberating counterdiscourse. As such, ectomy represents a hidden wound, scar, or void, gradually being exposed, hence the silences and gaps in the telling by African women writers. Kronik reminds us that "Today, gaps speak as loudly as presences, and no story is complete without its absences" (Kronik 1992:9).

Women undergo ectomy for several reasons: to ensure a sound economic base for marriage; to make a living through sex work, as in prostitution and modelling (Overall 1992:709); to enhance beauty; to improve health and hygiene; to guarantee chastity; to effect control. Ectomy involves cutting open, exposing, cutting out, making vulnerable, leaving a physical and emotional scar on woman. As a survival strategy, some women mimic men, exposing them also to castration.

Acknowledging her wound or scar marks a turning point in woman's itinerary. Surgical intervention, whether in African infibulation, Asian foot binding, or Western anesthetized versions, makes women walk crookedly. This deviation from the straight and narrow is akin to prevaricating (etymologically *praevaricatus* means to walk crookedly), that is, to seek refuge in lying. Lying down for men, ectomied women cannot or do not have the will to run. To cope with their untenable situation, many may deny their pain, while some may experience pleasure in pain, or, in a theoretical context, others may adopt a defensive stance for political and ideological reasons. In such a milieu, heterosexual and global feminist relations become invasive, bloodying old, African wounds. Consequently, celibacy and the inability or refusal to reproduce emerge in fiction as forms of resistance, especially as some of the women, like Efuru and Firdaus, produce texts instead of the more desirable children.

Cultural determinism, therefore, becomes the focal point of the politics of ectomy: To cut or not to cut? The mind boggles at Western medical culture's playing on women's bodies: hysterectomies, oopherectomies or ovariectomies, salpingectomies, episiotomies, mastectomies, breast implantations or reductions, abortions, cesarean sections, and the numerous cosmetic, though often debilitating surgeries, which include "face lifts, nose reconstructions, tummy tucks, liposuction, skin peels" (Balsamo 1992:214). The vocabulary is daunting. Anne Balsamo concludes that "For some women, and for some feminist scholars, cosmetic surgery illustrates a technological colonization of women's bodies; for others, a technology women can use for their own ends" (Ibid:226).

A cross-cultural problem arises from such a technological colonization. Intriguingly, in Walker's *Possessing the Secret of Joy,* the African-American Olivia lies to the African Tashi, who is determined to undergo the Olinkan cosmetic surgery of infibulation for ideological reasons. Olivia states, "I told her nobody in America or Europe cuts off pieces of themselves" (Walker 1992:ix).

This lie is still told and believed in the West, while Walker denounces African ectomies in her current political agenda. Its voyeuristic focus on infibulation, which she criminalizes in the phrase "genitally mutilated,"[3] and fetishizes it, and perhaps unintentionally presents as the already overexposed Africa, as Other, is troubling. Equally disturbing are the pointed questions Hanny Lightfoot-Klein poses (through interpreters) to informants about their sexuality in her anthropological journey through Sudan in *Prisoners of Ritual.* We must remember that many African women are reluctant to talk about their sexuality, even considering it taboo. This situation is further complicated by the awkwardness of carrying on a forbidden conversation with a foreigner through a mediating interpreter. The result, a reluctant text, rides roughshod across racial, cultural, religious, and language barriers and lacks intimacy, jeopardizing authenticity.

Foucault cautions about abstractly representing sexuality, insisting that "What is at issue ... is the overall 'discursive fact,' the way in which sex is 'put into discourse'" (Foucault 1978:11). With its condescending overtones and American avid curiosity about African sexuality, Walker's open campaign to stop infibulation in "Africa" cannot but conjure the ghosts of imperialism, particularly as many African spokespersons navigate through the perilous waters of the tabooed subject coming to it through indirection. Further, many would rather confront the more pervasive issue of crippling postcolonial, international capitalism that engenders women's abject poverty with chain-reactions, hindering development in all parts of Africa. Poor women tenaciously cling to the few sites of power they can still call their own; infibulation uncannily burgeons into a prerogative.

While we squabble intellectually far from the complexities of Africa, cut off the voice of the survivor, or, fail to learn from a critique of her text, or, as Ngugi wa Thiong'o so dramatically points out, wallow in the absurdity of our fictions of an "English-speaking ... African peasantry" (wa Thiong'o 1986:22), the problem of the politics of representation remains unresolved. Examining a similar postcolonial dilemma, Chakravorty Spivak problematizes the issue of representing the subaltern:

> And I don't think, really, that we will solve the problem today talking to each other; but, on the other hand, I think it has to be kept alive as a problem. It is not a solution, the idea of the disenfranchised speaking for themselves, or the radical critics speaking for them; this question of representation, self-representation, representing others, is a problem. On the other hand, we cannot put it under the carpet with demands for authentic voices; we have to remind ourselves that, as we do this, we might be compounding the problem even as we are trying to solve it. And there has to be a persistent critique of what one is up to, so that it doesn't get all bogged down in this homogenization; construct-

ing the Other simply as an object of knowledge, leaving out the real Others because of the ones who are getting access into public places due to these waves of benevolence and so on. I think as long as one remains aware that it is a very problematic field, there is some hope (Spivak 1990:63).

With no clear signals as to what to do, ectomies, literal, figurative, and psychological, proliferate. Writing in blood and bloody writing are distinct traits of a violent colonial and postcolonial heritage. Encoded in African myth, legend, storytelling, and history is another violent heritage important to theorizing ectomy within postcolonial counterdiscourse.

In another context, what Spivak says about the practice of *sati* is useful here in considering female circumcision:

> Obviously I am not advocating the killing of widows.... In the case of widow self-immolation, ritual is not being redefined as superstition but as *crime*. The gravity of *sati* was that it was ideologically cathected as 'reward,' just as the gravity of imperialism was that it was ideologically cathected as 'social mission.' [Edward] Thompson's understanding of *sati* as 'punishment' is thus far off the mark.... (Spivak 1988:301).

In some African contexts, female circumcision is cathected as "religious ritual" and in the feminist context as savage amputation, with Walker grossly misreading it by equating it to her kinsman's wounding of her eye. This dichotomous reading returns us to nineteenth-century positions between Africa and the West. As if in response, in June 1997, Egypt's lawmaking body reaffirmed the legitimacy of female circumcision, presumably to avert the onslaught from the North against Islam. Just as some African women feared that there would be a backlash following aggressive, alienating, Walkerian maneuvers, and they, therefore, opposed her un-African style, we have predictably lost some ground surreptitiously gained by African women.

I envision ectomy as a trope to express such loss and the excision, the cutting off, the exclusion, attached to woman's destiny. Also, clitoridectomy/infibulation by sadomasochistic women, literally and symbolically enacting the rape of woman, highlights the complexity of women's politics, even as it comments on women's varying thresholds of pain (Lightfoot-Klein 1989:140-41) and the possible uses of suffering. As Saadawi, a psychiatrist, frames it:

> Masochism, or the pleasure of pain, was thus a protective device, by which the human being tried to rid her or himself of an overpowering feeling of guilt, saying in effect, 'Yes. By practicing sex I am guilty of sin, but I make atones for my sin by experiencing this almost intolerable pain, in which I even discover some pleasure' (Saadawi 1982:150).

Radical operations on the male body indicate some women's attempt to extend the pain across gender lines, drawing attention to reverse "symbolic clitoridectomies." Spivak uses this phrase aptly to capture the universal nature of the problem of women's subordination (1981:181; 1990:10). The phrase emphasizes women's failure to come to "grips" with and "grasp" the true nature of gender positions in order to change traditions that keep them under (1990:41).

In a different take, Paula Bennett grapples with literary traditions in her article, "Critical Clitoridectomy: Female Sexual Imagery and Feminist Psychoanalytic Theory" (Bennet 1993). My work on a contrasting tradition complements hers, as I deal with clitoral erasure in black women's fiction, an area which she does not cover. The struggle to restore the clitoris to its primacy in literature is a Western project, as convincingly delineated in Bennett's repudiation of constricting Freudian and Lacanian theories that negate the clitoris. Naomi Schor wonders about analogous distinctions when she asks, "[H]ow can one hope to distinguish between the 'vaginal' and the 'clitoral' schools of feminist theory? And what is to be gained by adopting this distinction?" (Schor 1981:213), concluding that French feminists "have tended to valorize the vaginal form of jouissance" (Ibid:215), Americans the clitoral. Clitoral erasure as a colonial or postcolonial construct is a missing part of the theoretical puzzle.

Ectomy effects physical and mental transformations, centering on suffering even as it structures the living of a harsh life. It ensures minuscule and major attitudinal changes with a deep-seated mode for grappling with brutal reality. I wish, therefore, to contextualize and historicize ectomy by delving into African myth and storytelling. I will also examine figurative uses of language and the three African texts, then, explore Walker's construct, to see how women make meaning out of their lives, steeped in the pain and senselessness of selective exclusion. The transformative powers of ectomy help in tackling negative scenarios; they encourage the survivor and her support system to revise a terrible situation and to create new meaning, thereby generating a fresh text that enables women not only to protest, but, ultimately, to *act* in their own interest.

II   DISMEMBERED HISTORIES AND PAINFUL GEOGRAPHIES

Isis, the Egyptian nature goddess, wisely resolves her curious relationship with her brother-spouse, the underworld god Osiris. Patently self-serving, in spite of her sisterly devotion and surgical expertise, she painstakingly pieces together Osiris' dismembered body parts, only to discover that his treasure, the part usually covered, is missing. That void cancels the nuptial aspect of their relationship, moving her from the subordinate, "missionary position," as

Spivak would have put it (Spivak 1990:41), to the superordinate position of celibate healer and prolific mother. The primal *penidectomy* helped to establish a verbal treasure trove, part of the discourse on excisions.

In his reading of sexuality, Freud insists that "the female child becomes a woman when her clitoris acts like a chip of pinewood which is utilized to set fire to the harder wood" (Mernissi 1987:39). This image of erasure of the private parts by conflagration, with its hint of pedophilia, is perhaps tenable in cold, Victorian Europe. Tropical Nigeria presents an alternative.

One Yoruba myth relates how Olure, the first woman, sat with her thighs wide open while the macho technocrat Ogun, the orisa pathfinder, was cutting a fallen tree that had prevented her from continuing on her primeval journey to Earth. A chip of wood flew into her private part, causing her discomfort. Requesting that Ogun remove it, he promptly did so, after securing her hand in marriage. His surgery left a circumcision scar. During intercourse, the impatient Ogun cut off the tip of his penis to hasten dissemination of his seed (Beier 1980:36). Circumcision and a painful camaraderie thus became mutually ritualized as a nuptial necessity that enhances conception.

Olure, obviously, had no maternal guide to teach her that a woman must never sit with open thighs. Ineluctably, she learns this elementary lesson painfully through circumcision, and her thighs bind her to Ogun. The clitoris then came to be considered as an unnecessary growth to be surgically removed for health, and even esthetic, reasons. Clitoridectomy becomes a mark of femininity, erasing anything that detracts from woman's beauty, health, or the performance of her traditionally encoded role as wife and would-be mother. Since beauty is in the eye of the beholder, and woman never sees this part of her body except through reflective mediation, woman's treasure becomes regarded as trash.

Also, deeply etched in the West African psyche is the 13th-century, Malian narrative about the legendary Sunjiata and his enemies, popularized by the griot:

'Never tell all to a woman,
To a one-night woman!...

The woman is not safe, Sumamuru.'...
Sumamuru sprang towards his mother...
And came and seized his mother....
And slashed off her breast with a knife, magasi!...
She went and got the old menstrual cloth....
'Ah! Sumamuru!' she swore....
'If ever your birth was ever a fact,
I have cut your old menstrual cloth!' (Okpewho 1992:297-8).

Sumamuru, the Susu usurper of Sunjiata's throne, is predictably undone by the "one-night woman," once his mother, the queen mother, cuts up her menstrual cloth, the source of the powerful juju she used to keep her son enthroned. Mastectomy performed angrily on the breast that suckled the aggressor is unforgivable and punishable. In this *menage-B- trois*, it pays to heed the mother and forgo intimacy with "a one-night woman."

This phrase captures the temporariness and insecurities of wifedom, echoed in a popular calypso song by the Trinidadian Lord Kitchener, who would rather save his drowning mother than his more readily replaceable wife. The implied, serial drowning of islandized women, who, inexplicably, cannot swim to save themselves, comments deeply on women's perceived dependence. Self-serving, masculinist sons will save their complicit mothers, while wives may flounder.

Deep-rooted convictions are hard to dislodge. In these worlds of African peoples, domestic systems with their intrigues, contradictions, and even misogyny open up a Pandora's box which has figurative implications that require investigating.

III   FIGURATIVE USES OF LANGUAGE

Although the vagina and uterus have always been at the core of men and women's sexual transactions, these anatomical parts are rarely mentioned in African women's discourse. In this context, this essay would be considered unusually crude. However, folk wisdom acknowledges that almost everybody enters the world kissing the mother's vagina. The subtext in women's fiction stems from this point. Figuratively, Africa, with her Somalian horns, is represented as uterine, ruptured by the children who emerged from her, cut off from the progressive world and drained by a lack of necessities which she learns to do without. Literate and illiterate are part of the polarization created by colonialism. This and other forms of divisions enable indigenous elitist groups to continuously mimic the draining colonial power structure to their personal benefit. Postcolonialism (internal and external) is, therefore, ectomic; it atrophies, enabling indigenous institutions and invigorating intercourse in the subjugated world. With its military might and international connivance, it controls opposition and, in the process, renders African worlds more dependent and impoverished. The physical and psychological ectomies resulting from the slave trade and its progenies, colonialism and postcolonialism, unfortunately remain unaddressed as Africa meanders on.

In an attempt to address these issues internationally in order to enable West Africa to recuperate, Nwapa undertakes to discredit female circumcision by showing how painfully unnecessary it is. In tackling the politics, economics, and the biology of this surgery, she presents *Efuru* as an allegory of Anglo-African relations and of the inability to read astutely and move into modernity. However, the ability to read intelligently the political narratives of clitoridectomy, which Nwapa diplomatically refers to as "bath," is clearly demonstrated by Efuru and her othermother, Ajanupu."Bath" echoes the Igbo original while stressing the "hygienic" and "beautifying" aspects in woman's nuptial preparations (see also Zainaba 1990:67) in a clearly oppressive atmosphere. Gradually, Efuru grasps the ramifications and retreats from the battle zone of marriage that replicates a colonial union. She shrewdly embraces the water deity, Uhamiri, the traditional female spiritual principle that guarantees emotional, political, and economic independence.

Efuru's development is cautionary. Even as older women deny the pain of bath, Efuru feels it, expresses her dis-ease, then comes to understand its ironies and symbolic function. Her bath is a political turning point for Efuru as a woman, since the older women inform her that clipping is every woman's destiny. Bath becomes a symbol of female suffering, a metaphor for the pain of marriage, whilst the clitoris, as filthy object, becomes a metonymy for woman. Bath prepares woman in her role as soother in marriage and moisturizer in the sexual act, facilitating man's journey to seize his pleasure. Cleansing, lubricating, and pleasure-giving are all aspects of the bath used to express Nwapa's perception of marital complexity and a woman's role, which progressively enslaves her.[4] The colonial subtext is clear: Efuru fails to benefit from her two marriages and her life becomes living proof that female circumcision is null, as it does not facilitate birthing children.[5] She gains independence through female support, the sororal chord linking this novel with *Woman at Point Zero*.

IV   FEMALE CIRCUMCISIONS AND DISRUPTIVE ORGASMS

Economics, psychology, and ethics feature in Saadawi's grappling with female circumcision in *Woman at Point Zero*. This auto/biographical novel explores clitoridectomies, physical and psychological, of two professional women—one a condemned prostitute (the oral narrator, Firdaus), the other, a privileged doctor and author (Saadawi/her alter ego, the scribal narrator). Firdaus is circumcised when she becomes sexually curious, questioning her mother about her paternity and exploring her budding sexuality with a boy. In a perversion of motherhood as seen by the child, the mother organizes the circumcision, performed by women. Though the intent is to maintain female purity, Saadawi undermines the body politic by turning the circumcised Firdaus into a prostitute, who refers to wifehood as prostitution without pay. As a "body machine" (Saadawi 1975:94), the prostitute walks the streets, constantly in motion. The bed, the invisible and unmentionable center of the harem, turns into an open, restless workplace.

Firdaus experiences a disruptive form of pleasure in defying society. With her heightened sensibilities, she experiences orgasmic thrills from mundane events, such as eating without a male critically watching her. She derives deep pleasure in the financial independence of tearing up money as paper and in plunging a knife into her pimp. How then does the society police a circumcised woman whose orgasms have been transferred to other sites? This challenge is met by imprisoning and executing Firdaus. Never to be bested, Saadawi has her talk her talk, refuse to beg for her body, and she is executed and goes off to a Muslim paradise, true to her name.

Thus, the oral telling of her story is inspirational and climactic, metaphorically impregnating the writer, Saadawi, who reproduces a textual body. In a recycling of the body, Firdaus' postmortem disappearance is cancelled by Saadawi, a receptacle for Firdaus' seminal story, whose "dissemination" is out of Firdaus' control (Busia 1992:98). After gestation, she gives birth (in writing) to the already dead Firdaus–a postpartum reappearance in the writing of the telling. Though the narrating body is usually quick, in this novel, writing turns the two narrating bodies into textualized bodies. Firdaus' body is a colonized site occupied by patriarchy and its allies, but her body is also transgressive, struggling for independence. Inevitably, there are casualties on both sides. Do these textual casualties figure in the objective world? For relief, Saadawi intersperses the mortuary culture with birth imagery; with the narrative structured like nestling dolls, the prison-tomb turns into a quickening womb.[6]

With its privileging of the spoken word, *Woman at Point Zero* mocks the reading process, even as the protagonist's oral narrative is written down by her new mother, Saadawi. Firdaus carries around her diploma, really useless, as nobody bothers to read it to employ her, a step that might have saved her from humiliating sex work as wife or prostitute. Earlier, she attempts to decipher the shrouded text in the eyes of her traitorous mother, who, unceremoniously, arranges her clitoridectomy in an effort to silence her and to prevent her from knowing and being known. Ironically, in an ethical disarray, Firdaus has had sexual encounters prior to her clitoridectomy, in spite of which she comes to know and be known, with a vengeance, as wife and prostitute.

The circumcised daughter notes the cessation of a particular type of sexual pleasure, as she is peremptorily launched into adulthood. Pain and pleasure, now transferred to other sites, mingle with memories as the business of adult life relentlessly proceeds. Firdaus reads herself reflected in people's eyes–the zero-ness, the blankness, the stares that mean no good to a woman. She reflects on male secrets. As picara, she journeys restlessly, escaping one form of oppression only to fall into another, garnering knowledge through the labyrinths of the female condition. She solves an enigma when it gradually dawns on her that woman can modify inexorable laws, even those of mathematics and the female/colonial condition.

Having survived, *negative* signs of female oppression proliferate; the symbolic, multiple stabbing of her pimp lands her in prison, in a stasis, the median point zero, where she meets Saadawi. Though battle-fatigued, Firdaus cannot rest; she must venture into the *positive*, to the left of zero, while still at the center of matters. The blank paper she fails to write upon demonstrates that though she has the will to tell her story, writing is not her way.

Saadawi places female circumcision in a psychiatric context, underscoring the missing clitoris as a rupture—emotional, sensual, and political. In psychologizing the situation, she places it in an African context, as she turns the women's meeting not into a doctor/analyst-analysand relationship, but into a mind-emptying session with a live teller and a listener acting as a Marabout, both seated on the floor, solidly grounded (Mernissi 1996:21-31). In a collaborative effort that cleverly resolves the problem of representation posed by Spivak, Firdaus, as survivor, gains a voice, albeit a disembodied one. Her orature metamorphoses into literature through the intervention of a ghost-writer, stressing the need for unity and understanding between women in the face of hostile forces: the ubiquitous "they." While Firdaus is in prison, both produce what Henry Louis Gates categorizes as a "talking book"; Firdaus and Saadawi conjure up a uterine symbol from prison as void. Firdaus is resurrected when the book is born after her execution.

This novel records the workings of an agency that ensures survival, subversive hope, transformation, potential, and the surreal matter which cancels marginalization. The writer becomes analogous to the medicine-woman, catalytically unleashing the verbal facility to enthrall the reader. As fiction, the text is conceptualized as a fervent prayer enunciating an acrimonious life, a healing, a great expectation even as it is the great expectation.

V   VANGUARDISM OR THE DISPOSABLE MARRIAGE

Literacy also plays an important part in Head's "The Collector of Treasure": How do we educate the next generation? What are they to read? One answer here is *penidectomy*, a woman's removal of the penis, no longer as the phallus, the sign of nature's bounty, but the sign of irresponsibility and sexual oppression. That horror which Walker merely imagines, Head had already transmuted into a text for the young son in the story to decipher.

The celibate Dikeledi, the estranged wife suffering from psychological clitoridectomy, recovers to perform fatal surgery on her husband Garesego in order to heal the next generation. This extreme unction is precipitated by

Garesego's refusal to pay their son's tuition and his mortifying insistence on his nuptial rights though he had long abandoned his family. After he washes and feeds at his wife's expense, he falls into a deep sleep, naked and with his thighs wide open, escaping into limbo from his duties as father and husband. Dikeledi turned priestess, surgeon, and midwife, silently performs her ritual. As man-slaughterer and author, she calmly reads the bloody scene she has created with the stroke of a knife, turning her husband's "treasure" into trash. She then asks their son to call the police to come and look at this revision of the ancient text of marital discord, with the wife acting an unspeakable role. Once in the penal colony, Dikeledi knits, producing priceless clothes, even as she draws the women together into a close-knit community paradoxically provided for by men. Her husband gone, her neighbors take care of her children in the more conducive atmosphere she has helped to create for them.

From these three African texts, clearly colonialism with its changing phases/faces is kept in place by guerrilla wars. Woman, acting in extremis, counters clitoral excision with *penidectomy*; counters the exclusion of women with ostracizing men; counters the psychological destruction of women with emasculating and murdering men; counters the marginalization, isolation, and imprisonment of women with communion, collaboration, and the freedom to create. A systematic cancelling goes on, reproducing whole women. The resulting texts are silent declarations of emancipation by women, who, like their countries through which they continuously travel, have seized their independence at an extreme price. Their stories parlay feminist and postcolonial discourses.

To clarify the African trope in the contemporary setting, clitoridectomy signifies misogyny; it represents, metonymically, the displaced female condition which demands reinstatement. Each of the women fights to change her situation without prioritizing clitoridectomy since, diagnostically and from myth, it merely is a symptom of an accelerating loss of women's rank and place in life. For the three protagonists, education is central to the bringing about of attitudinal changes; to be effective, they must start from individual female agency rather than having agency imposed from without. It is therapeutically vital for each afflicted woman, by her action, no matter how minuscule, to say no to her unspeakable situation for a healing to begin.

VI   AN AMERICAN RESPONSE

Walker shifts the discourse in *Possessing* by privileging infibulation or "genital mutilation" as the female problem. She politicizes the female condition by uncovering a presumably representative African vulva, locating it centrally for open, rather than covert, reading. Her position as a successful American writer permits her to disclose with impunity that which the Africans consider taboo.

She then launches a para-imperialist[7] project to stop infibulation by address-ing an American audience with an African problem, miniaturizing Africa to make her work manageable.

Why have the governments of Mali and Sudan, two countries still prac-ticing pharaonic infibulation (Lightfoot-Klein 1989), failed to eradicate it even though it is illegal? Why were the delegates to the UN decade for women and other women's agencies unable to stop it? Why do women infibulate and submit to infibulation? Why do some American feminists fetishize infibula-tion? For a writer moving across the boundaries of fiction to include activ-ism, these urgent issues ought to be addressed. As Linda Alcoff and Laura Gray explain in discussing the tactics for survivors of sexual assault, "The key point here is that disclosure and repression are mutually reinforcing, so as to constitute a single economy of discourse" (Alcoff and Gray 1993:269). In other words, the African women's taciturn tales of resistance engender more explicit Western tales that tend to missionize.

Significantly, though the white American Lightfoot-Klein desires that in-fibulation be eradicated in Sudan, she comments:

> What surprised me most ... is not the degree of mental pathology they [the women] manifest, but the general aura of serenity and balance they far more commonly exude, especially in the outlying areas. They appear to be far more balanced and emotionally healthy than a lot of Western women. (Lightfoot-Klein 1989:149)

What then are the implications of the missionary undertaking to stop infibu-lation without addressing the root causes? To make "serene" African women paranoid to satisfy Western ideology? Or, in this age when a child can divorce an irresponsible parent, to continue the colonial parent-child relationship that has retarded Africa's development? With the unfolding tragedy of the colo-nial experiment and the unmitigated evil of many postcolonial interferences, the West has lost the moral right to criticize Africa and must struggle to make up for lost time, or to attempt, at this late hour, to impose well-intentioned changes which can only be misconstrued as hegemonic.

Despite her being black, Walker's "humanist" project inevitably operates in this imperialist context. Launched with media fanfare, *Possessing* was ig-nored as a novel as Africa's most private parts were unveiled to an uncom-prehending American audience. Such tactics are transgressive and potentially disruptive particularly at a time when the United States was ambivalently car-rying out a mission of mercy in a Somalia that needed it but did not want it from Americans. A Yoruba response to Walker's verbal conduct would be *"Ko m' oro so,"* (S/he doesn't know how to talk), that is, in an African context, or "*O la 'ro mo 'le*," (S/he slapped the word on the ground), problematizing the cultural gap, the politics of speech, misreading, mis-communication, and mis-timing. However, there is obviously no wisdom in retreating into silence, in ignoring onslaughts Walker bills as "loving" (McHenry 1992:10).

Bafflingly in consonance with aspects of the Bell Curve that later generated furor in some intellectual circles, Walker presents her protagonist, Tashi, as the infibulated woman par excellence–a mad, stupid, rootless, idle, malodorous shuffler, with a mentally retarded offspring; she is totally dependent on Americans and Europeans for the basics of existence. This image of the black woman as victim may be a ploy to wrest some power from a guilt-ridden white public, for the imperialism that destroyed Tashi's community is the root cause of her desperate situation. The strategy differs from the survival methods which have sustained women in Africa in the face of centuries of inexorable oppression. Though Walker's intention is to end a "savage" custom to institute postcolonial discourse, the critique unwittingly has the imperious overtones Africa knows only too well. The West, as usual, determines the plan of action, because it controls the purse strings. The resentment this generates is palpable in the Egyptian reaction, which I already mentioned, and in one Ewe oral poem that ridicules the notion of colonial dependency:

> A baby is a European
> *he cares very little for others:*
> he forces his will upon his parents.
> A baby is a European
> *he is always very sensitive:*
> the slightest scratch on his skin results in an ulcer (Chinweizu 1988:xxiii).

This poem leads Chinweizu, in his project to decolonize African literature, to conclude that it "quietly mocks the haughty, aloof behaviour of the European colonizers in Africa. Though ... informed by accurate observation of the parties being compared, and though it subtly and cleverly makes its point, it cannot hope for an unbiased, artistic appraisal from Eurocentric and blancophile academics" (Ibid:xxvi). Tashi emerges from this protracted quarrel: with her acquired Euro-American sensibility and outsiderness, she is crippled on all fronts and provides titillating reading of "Africa" to an insatiable American public.

Having discovered the vulva ironically during Columbus' quincentennial celebrations, Walker puts it on the geoliterary map, while theorizing on reading, refusing to read, failing to read well, and linking these with what she perceives as African women's "dead eyes" and their habitual waffling and shuffling. Shuffling from infibulation, rape, unsatisfactory sex, depression, leg injury, visible and invisible ankle chains of slavery, prison, marriage, mental asylums, and unfulfilling professions seems to be increasingly the black woman's destiny. It results in not keeping pace with others who travel footloose, a point that ironizes Lightfoot-Klein's "odyssey" through the Sudan, studying and incorporating the narratives of infibulated women, who, one may infer, are unable to walk freely and can never reciprocate by studying her. Shuffling comments on the deliberate slowness in accomplishing imposed duty, the necessity to be connected with the solidity of the earth, the wariness over the unevenness of the terrain to be traveled, the waffling at the scant choices at bewitched *cross*roads. In spite of these limitations, fables involving the legendary, slow tortoise lead one to believe that all will be well; the fast runner and the slow walker will each arrive at their destination. This hope induces many to act positively, even when faced with death, for death is not necessarily the worst fate.[8]

While the women in the three African texts act radically and successfully rid themselves of their male oppressors, Tashi, like Lightfoot-Klein's Fahtma (Lightfoot-Klein 1989:132-136), remains perpetually disoriented. In a matrophobic move, she eliminates the old woman M'Lissa, whose agency, though sadomasochistic and secured at the expense of other women, is not the root of women's predicament in Olinka. This turn in the plot to tackle woman as oppressor, though fascinating, leaves unscathed the racist imperialists, the sexist Olinkans, Tashi's adulterous husband, Adam, and her American voyeuristic obstetricians, significant sources of Tashi-Evelyn's physical and emotional pain.

As a black mother, protective of her abused, fictional African daughter, Walker exercises her writerly prerogative, then slides into a propaganda overkill. Reading her reading of Africans reading their culture, she unwittingly plays the role of the anthropologist, whom Trinh T. Minh-ha describes as gossiping about the native (1989: 67-68). Tashi's story is hardly African, but Western with its Judeo-Christian background, and Tashi-Evelyn serves as an exemplar of Trinh's "woman, native, other." Falling into the Du Boisean paradigm that prioritizes issues of the color line, Tashi erases her African self by accepting how Americans judge, smell, see, treat her, and metamorphosing into a pluri-conscious African-American devastated by her difference.

Now imprisoned in American culture, Tashi-Evelyn appears to suffer an identical fate partially endured by the African women characters. Efuru long exists in the prison of marital tradition but breaks out of its constrictions to embrace a spiritual sisterhood. Dikeledi escapes the prison of patriarchal marriage only to spend the rest of her productive life jailed, though she continues to resist by producing clothes and knitting together an audacious women's prison commune. Firdaus walks out of her marriage and, after a picara's existence, she experiences prison as solitary, designed to break the hardened criminal desperate for communication; she subverts this by speaking out her story. Tashi, cut off from both American and Olinkan societies on ideological grounds, ends in jail in an apocalyptic vision of the vast, African continent as a dystopian prison peopled by "criminals" and AIDS patients waiting to die. To Lightfoot-Klein, women are prisoners of ritual; ironically, this includes herself, Walker, and the fictional Tashi.

Prisons (and courts) have always been a colonial and postcolonial bastion to contain dissidents. In *Possessing,* as in Soyinka's *The Man Died,* the reader, faced with the political complexities, is forced to read and *write* between the lines, dialoguing with past texts by writing between the pages in a renewed vision of author-reader collaboration. The forty-three blank pages [9] interspersed within the numerous sections of *Possessing* are not simply a waste of paper (an act that appears forest-unfriendly in this environmentally conscious era), but a reminder of this rapprochement between author, reader, and their commitment to activism in, at least, quarreling about the tale.

Conscious of this, Walker focuses on the nature of reception by dealing with letters written or received belatedly, unanswered, or answered without addressing critical issues raised by the addressee. These complications symbolize the lack of communication or the missed and mis-communication between author and reader, Africans and African-Americans, white and black women, women and men.

Global feminism, basking in the sunshine and moonshine of an incipient international rapprochement, detects oppression in the form of a limping woman. In *Possessing,* M'Lissa, named after the androgynous Dahomean deity Mawu (female and the moon part) Lisa (male and the sun part) (Herskovits 1967:101), is larger than woman. Unlettered yet discerning, a powerful male with her knife yet a powerless female with her limp, a force in the local gerontocracy yet helpless with the limitations of old age, M'Lissa authenticates the contradictions inherent in African female power, exhumed through this mythical horror (s)mothered or, rather, buried in our mothers' gardens.

African-American bitterness against Africans for participating in the slave trade mixed with the joy at the successful outcome of their sojourn in America is reminiscent of the biblical Joseph's auspicious stay in Egypt. It pays off in a love-hate dynamic. A few of America's powerful writers inflict excisions on Africa, which is continually negated in Western discourse. Some of Phillis Wheatley's and Countee Cullen's ambivalent verses, Richard Wright's *Black Power,* which ridicules Kwame Nkrumah and the Gold Coast's attempts at instituting Ghanaian independence, are echoed in *Possessing.* The latest addition in the hostile tradition is Keith Richburg's controversial account of his travels: *Out of America: A Black Man Confronts Africa* (1997). The fictional Tashi replicates the actions of these literary giants: an African turned African-American returns to Africa to avenge past wrongs—on the wrong party.

Does not Walker deliberately set up opposition within the counterdiscourse of women's postcolonial writing, listening to her sisters while arguing against them? Does she not act, perhaps unwittingly, the imperialist? Without any doubt, "The coercive stance that one must tell, must join a support group, or must go into therapy is justly deserving of the critique Foucault offers of the way in which the demand to speak involves dominating power and an imperialist theoretical structure …This is … doubly the case when it is an expert, therapist, or 'well-meaning' outsider who demands of the survivor that she speak" (Alcoff and Gray 1993:281; Foucault 1978:61)–in an alien voice. This opposition in the women's counterdiscourse psychologically circumcises many Africans who resist.

VII   COMPLEMENTARY DISCOURSES

In reply to a question posed by Lightfoot-Klein to an infibulated woman, "Are you able to enjoy sexual intercourse?" she declares irrepressibly "*A body is a body,* and no circumcision can change that! No matter what they cut away from you–they cannot change that" (Lightfoot-Klein 1989:25-26). This cryptic answer cues us in to the widespread philosophy of defusing crises, adaptability, survival, even seizing pleasure, in the face of pain.

Bennett confirms the informant's answer in theoretical terms: "As these and other theorists … insist, female sexuality, like female pleasure, is multiply sited. It presents, therefore, multiple ways in which it can be constructed–as well as experienced–by individual women" (Bennett 1993:238). American clitoricentricity complements the African shift to the vaginal and uterine; all reveal multiple ways of knowing and experiencing sexuality. Where clitoricentricity privileges abortion or matrophobia in order to enhance personal growth, the vaginal and uterine gravitate toward multiple maternal sources to care for the community. In other words, the postcolonial Madonna, with or without the child, is preoccupied with nation building, as embodied in many African women writers' critique of politics as usual. The apparent obsession with motherhood in some African texts indicates women's desire to return from the deprived periphery to participate in a busy center, sometimes vicariously through their offspring, in rebuilding the nation and thereby sharing communal power. Marianne Hirsch explains an analogous plot psychoanalytically: "Women writers' attempts to imagine lives for their heroines which will be different from their mothers' make it imperative that mothers be silent or absent in their texts, that they remain in the prehistory of plot, fixed both as objects of desire and as examples not to be emulated" (Hirsch 1989:34). Matricide, absent mothers, offensive mothers-in-law, and complicit older women are signifiers of a traumatic mother-daughter relationship and the devaluation of women in male-dominant societies.

However, Saadawi's literary project is imaged as laboring to give birth to Firdaus; Dikeledi's desire to further her child's education leads to crime as analogue of sacrifice; Efuru concerns herself with her own and her community's spirituality. These are community-oriented rather than individual projects that entail sacrifices on women's part. Women's policing of themselves for communal benefits thus has overtones of martyrdom. Walker deconstructs this, referring to it as "psychological circumcision," for men misread women's survivalist tactics (see Mernissi's attack of Freud and Aqqad 1987:33). In short, the fact that some African women see themselves as extensions of mother earth[10] in their nation-building role bedevils gender politics, as they sacrifice their own pleasure.

Walker's position is similar to Bennett's reading of the clitoral symbology in 19th-century, white women's poetry. The proliferation of tiny, hard objects in this poetry celebrates their subversive insistence on individual sexual pleasure. This differs markedly from the vaginal symbology of the African women writers under consideration. Prevalent waterways (the phallic symbol of the brown Niger flowing into the blue lake in *Efuru,* the unending streets and the green Nile in *Woman at Point Zero*) with the protagonists traveling on or near them at crucial points in their crises, mark this difference. Waterways are productive, uterine, labyrinthine, cleansing, healing. Firdaus' and Efuru's constant moving around, one as a prostitute, the other as a trader, duplicates the life of the rivers.

Dikeledi's journey to prison by road in the desert terrains of Botswana is also long, if uneventful. Engaged in national recuperation to counter her psychological clitoridectomy, she enables people to acquire treasures that help improve the quality of their lives: as house builder, she is building the nation; as seamstress, she creates by piercing fabrics, cutting and stitching like the surgeon or midwife who incises to heal.

In a contrary direction, the clitorocentric Evelyn (Americanized Tashi) is preoccupied with the frightening tunnel and termite hill, cock and hen, a binary system that defines her ambivalence. She throws stones at her stepson, Pierre (penis), who reminds her of her clitoral erasure. In answer to M'Lissa's question about what an American looks like, Evelyn replies revealingly: "an American looks like a wounded person whose wound is hidden from others, and sometimes from herself. An American looks like me" (Walker 1992:208). As an American, Evelyn prevaricates about her situation yet knows she is prevaricating, creating the need for the analyst, a Western professional many Africans do not use.

For illustration, the psychological clitoridectomy experienced by Efuru spans the space of two marriages. Her first husband openly disrespects her when he fails to come for communal mourning at the death of their daughter, Ogonim, who was greatly treasured for being an only child. He deserts Efuru for a less competent woman. The ultimate insult is his silence. Efuru rebounds by remarrying, and her new husband Eneberi appears more solid than the first. The elation, however, is short-lived since Eneberi sets up a polygynous household to produce the children the "barren" Efuru cannot. He, too, without any explanation, fails to turn up for an important funeral, this time Efuru's father's. Though he is jailed for an undisclosed crime, Efuru stands by him. Soon thereafter, Eneberi falsely accuses the sick Efuru of adultery; her surrogate mother, Ajanupu, pestle-whips and hospitalizes him. This violence liberates Efuru. Using the instrument that enslaves and pulverizes seeds for culinary purposes to liberate is enthralling. Uhamiri the water goddess restores Efuru's female power, which men want to destroy by inflicting deep psychic wounds.

Head also explores a similar notion. "The Collector of Treasures," like most of her works, has some autobiographical touches. Head zeroes in on Dikeledi's psychic wound caused by male absence in her life. Named for being born after her father's death, Dikeledi means tears; like Head, who was born after her father had disappeared, she is saddled with a lecherous husband. To Head, Garesego's indifference to his family represents postcolonial irresponsibility. To restore a modicum of order, Dikeledi undertakes guerrilla warfare, performing a lethal *penidectomy* that gives her some dignity and the children a new lease on life.

Like her two African contemporaries, even in the bleakness of the psychological clitoridectomy, Saadawi still clings to some hope. Dealing with intricate systems of oppression, she transcends zero-ness only to make it a point of departure thought her framing of the book. An umbilical relationship is maintained in this twice-told tale—a talking text, framed by an introduction by a self-absorbed writer-psychiatrist who is soon to become enchantingly other-involved by the closing pages of the text. Saadawi moves beyond excisions, hastening toward the emotional healing of the writer and storyteller, the reader and the listener, of this harrowing tale of sexploitation.

Similarly, the idea of "psychological circumcision" trenchantly captures the devastating effects of black women's circumscription in American society. The shuffle and malodorous stigma announce the African-American woman's difference. Reminders of racist reactions to Negroes and negative responses to "unclean" women, Tashi's odor and anatomical difference set her apart. As if on the auction block, the highlight of Tashi's immigration into the United States occurs in the *labor* room where she becomes an anomaly, gazed at by the curious, clinical eye. Objectification precipitates a birth—Tashi's split into at least six personalities, the different faces of black Eve in America. Lynne Tatlock captures the essence of Western woman's dilemma in the labor room, and so Tashi's, thus: "The vaginal speculum quite literally marks the fissure in these traditional prohibitions rent by the intrusion of early modern male practitioners into the birthing room; it also serves symbolically to legitimate the male medical gaze, the right of medical men to examine the interior of the female body and thus to know what the female patient herself does not know" (Walker 1992:757). Matters worsen during Tashi's technologically assisted labor when the sophisticated instruments brain damage her son, causing Benny's retardation.

Benny cannot hold a candle to Petit Pierre, Adam's outside child by the French Lisette. Unlike Benny, Pierre was born into the loving arms of family midwives, who helped Lisette achieve an orgasmic, Kristevan birth. Pierre develops into a light-skinned, brilliant, Harvard-trained, doubly-conscious, androgynous, Du Bois-ean African-American. Tashi-Evelyn fights a losing battle, welcoming Pierre to her home with an Irish confetti, for Pierre/Peter epitomizes her failure sexually.

Furthermore, Adam's rejection of Tashi[11] marked by his preference for the uninfibulated Lisette, with its racial, sexual, political, and intellectual implications, aggravates Tashi-Evelyn's maladjustment. Conflated into the concept of Tashi/Tashi-Evelyn is a reading of the black female condition in Africa, the United States, and Europe. Such a character, deliberately made helpless for political reasons, had to originate from Africa, then metamorphose into a mythical figure to experience all the odds stacked against black women everywhere. Achebe's words in a different context describe Tashi in her aloneness: "The fly that has no one to advise it follows the corpse into the grave" (Achebe 1964: 32); she kills M'Lissa and follows her to the grave.

Because of Evelyn's seemingly limited choices, her rival's uncle, in an incredible twist in the plot, becomes her analyst. She draws a huge cock on his wall. The cock highlights the atrophying of marital emotions, underscoring the gender discord between African-Americans with a sexual stereotype. Adam, embarrassed, reads the drawing on the wall: black male sexuality is as problematic in the Western world as it is in Africa. The import of this cock, a huge contrast to her clitoral erasure, is deeply etched between the marks on Adam's face. Evelyn as conjuring woman strips him naked, playing the dozens,[12] cutting him down to size, monstrously exposing his treasure.

However, Tashi (Evelyn) comes from a heritage of pain. Like her mother Catherine, named after the 4th-century Christian martyr St. Catherine of Alexandria, she continues to suffer in the hostile Western environment. In contrast, Lisette, whose name is a reminder of that vulva-shaped fleur-de-lis, that "fortified place enclosed by a circular mound" (Webster's *New International*

Dictionary) of Irish antiquity, produces her beloved Petit Pierre, thereby endangering women's international solidarity. In serving as Adam's "fairy fort," protecting him from an enervating marital war zone, Lisette, here the white woman, contributes to the African-American woman's psychological predicament. When Tashi belatedly acknowledges the late Lisette, a symbiotic relationship develops between the two—in death.

Walker's examination of polygamy in all her novels reaches a climax in *Possessing* with this depiction of the trauma it causes woman. Evelyn resists it with abortion, refusing to uphold patriarchy by birthing more patriarchs-to-be or women to breed and keep the system going. She returns to Africa, the origin, to right wrongs like the vengeful panther in the fable that frames her story. Like Lara, the spurned leopard in another tale, her suicidal attempt at rectification, though narcissistic, precipitates a change when a throng of women assemble outside the prison walls to support her. Tashi's unrelenting struggles dramatize the eternal pain endured by the black woman under patriarchy, imperialism, and racism.

VIII   TOWARD A RECUPERATIVE PROCESS

Anti-mother feelings, manifest hostility toward older women, the killing or cannibalizing of the mother, are prevalent in Africana stories from the new world. Torn from an enervated Africa and languishing under an evil stepmother (Britain/Europe/America), many women writers in the African diaspora understandably search for a desirable mother to fill the emotional vacuum created by the phantom of the rejecting and crushed mother. The alienation concomitant with exile and stepchildhood is part of the complex dynamics of "rebarbarizing civilization," as Brian Shaffer (1993) titles the concept. This countermove engenders a spell at the center of which Africa occasionally serves as a punching bag. *Possessing* partially exemplifies this process, which we can regard as part of a deferred dialogue, inevitably mired in hostility because of centuries of repression and denial.[13]

For many of the African writers, although mother Africa is powerless in the face of colonialisms, she still nurtures them, however poorly. Not surprisingly, *Efuru, Woman at Point Zero,* and "The Collector of Treasures" have an inspirational turn. As on the occasions for liberation in different parts of Africa, ectomies, physical and psychological, will end in Africa when a determined group of Africans (perhaps supported by outsiders) make inroads against them. Since legislation has failed to eradicate them, some of the women's writings can be read as the beginnings of guerrilla warfare to counter them. Reexamining, in the local languages, the religious, health, biological, and cultural aspects impacting ectomies has been guardedly successful in getting a few women to modify conservative attitudes (Zainaba 1987). Gradually, some are beginning to see female circumcision as an inconvenience, like Chinese foot binding; it is beginning to go out of vogue, like facial tattooing in many parts of Nigeria. Since modern education limits the production of traditional midwives, the end might be in sight. More and more girls and their mothers will come to realize that some ectomies are needless. In this difficult phase, what is needed is international support of those Africans in Africa fighting against the procedures, not open anger, contempt, fetishization, voyeurism, or the desire to control Africans for their own good. However well-intentioned an international outcry might be, in being theoretically idealistic, it must guard against the "three traps that were already well marked by feminist theorists and researchers–essentialism, ahistoricism, and false generalization..." (Martin 1996:585).

This essay on ectomies inevitably involves *exclusions*. As a form of textual infibulation, it erases original texts, retaining mere vestiges to produce a reading that will, in its turn, be dissected. Cutting and pasting, or rather stitching, to retain the image of the seamstress/surgeon, or, in this computer age, deleting and inserting, form part of the process of engendering literary discourses. The creative project with its "lying," exaggeration, or gaps also involves surgery to generate a wholesome text. As each writer parries or plays with or preys on a predecessor's text, s/he operates on the reader, who, in turn, responds. So, on and on the discourse goes. *Verbum mirabile*, ectomy!

NOTES:

1. A hortatory opening ritualistically enables the griotte, the professional storyteller, to proceed in unraveling verbal mysteries to ensure efficacious (trans)formations. Similarly reinforced, I grope for interpretive insights and empowering possibilities in negotiating a hazardous yet healing terrain.

2. I do acknowledge the works of such groups as Jubilee 2000, who are fighting to have the debts of the poorest countries cancelled so that they can join in millennial celebrations. Their argument is that bad debts are usually forgiven by banks; further, although the poor in the debtor countries were not signatories to the loans–often diverted to personal use by their leaders as in the case of "Zaire" or Kenya or Nigeria–they have suffered the consequences of budget arrangements that always factor in debt payments first, thereby crippling education, health, etc. For anyone willing to fight the issue of graft and the Northern connection (for example, Swiss banking practices), please write a letter of protest asking for the restoration of illicit moneys to the African countries concerned to:

   > Mr. Cotti
   > Minister of Foreign Affairs
   > Bundeshaus West
   > Bern 3003
   > Switzerland

3. This charged phrase as well as the abbreviation FGM (female genital mutilation)

have gained currency and are used instead of the less controversial female circumcision. It contributes to criminalizing the procedure, generating intense emotions on all sides.

4. It is a commentary on the sexist nature of this marriage arrangement that there is no reciprocal ritual to prepare a man to be a good husband and father. Too many men appropriate and colonize their women's bodies.

5. In her last novel, *The Lake Goddess*, which will be published posthumously, Nwapa debunks the common belief that circumcision guarantees pregnancy and virtue. Contrary to expectation, not only does her uncircumcised character produce children, she later abandons them and her husband to lead a celibate life, worshipping the lake goddess and serving the community as a priestess.

6. Needless to say, her Arabic is comatose to me, as the text is brought to life for me through an English translation.

7. I use this word advisedly. The image of infibulated women in *Possessing* and Gloria Naylor's *Bailey's Cafe* as mad, naive, or mentally retarded continue the stereotype of Africa as child, unable to speak or fend for herself. Instead of concentrating only on aspects of African life that retard progress, it will be more profound to address the intricately connected internal and external factors keeping Africa back, especially as Africa has the potential wealth to develop. International interference, an inability to resist it, and poorly defined goals partly account for her underdevelopment. Of course, Walker's and Naylor's goals are politically and aesthetically different. Their works belong to an American genre defined by critiques, sometimes sensationalized, of third world countries by children of immigrants to the U.S. Recent examples are the works of Paule Marshall and Maxine Hong Kingston and such movies as *Like Water, for Chocolate* and *The Joy Luck Club*. Not only do these critiques represent the cutting of the umbilical links with the place of origin, but also mark out the producers as belonging, as authentic Americans.

8. The pronounced limp of women characters in novels by African-American women is, however, not the result of infibulation, but an infabulation. Toni Morrison's *Sula*, where a leg is amputated; the arched foot and child rape in *The Bluest Eye*; edematous feet and infanticide in *Beloved*; hysterectomy in Gayl Jones' *Corregidora* and penidectomy in *Eva's Man*; abortion and salpingectomy in Walker's *Meridian* and the threat of penidectomy in *The Third Life of Grange Copeland*; sadomasochisms in Gloria Naylor's *Bailey's Cafe* and gang rape in *The Women of Brewster Place*, to mention a few instances, compare in violence with their African counterpart. Marginalization occasionally generates a Morrisonian, viole(n)t, necrophilic response from women fighting back.

9. These blank pages can also be viewed as virginal, a wish for the past, pauses in the narration, blanks in the analysand's text, silences in her telling, the mark for a new beginning.

10. The earth deity is usually female; the abuse the earth receives from many men replicates the ill-treatment of women.

11. In many ways, in his treatment of Tashi as a woman, Adam is his biological father's true son, if I may take the liberty of returning to *The Color Purple*. Tashi's blundering is worse than Celie's, since it leads this African to execution.

12. This scene signifies upon Hurston's *Their Eyes Were Watching God*, when Janie castrates Jody, feminizing him before a large audience by referring to him as the change of life. Words and painting clearly effect penidectomies.

13. For example, the hostile African reception of Maryse Conde's novels based in Africa

and her anguish at its virulence is part of this ongoing though sometimes enervating dialogue.

WORKS CITED:

Achebe,Chinua. *Arrow of God*. London: Heinemann, 1964.

Alcoff, Linda and Laura Gray. "Survivor Discourse: Transgression or Recuperation?" *Signs: Journal of Women in Culture and Society* 18 no. 2 (1993): 260-290.

Balsamo, Anne. "On the Cutting Edge: Cosmetic Surgery and the Technological Production of the Gendered Body." *Camera Obscura* 28 (1992): 206-237.

Beier, Ulli. *Yoruba Myths*. Cambridge: Cambridge University Press, 1980.

Bennett, Paula. 1993. "Critical Clitoridectomy: Female Sexual Imagery and Feminist Psychoanalytic Theory." *Signs: Journal of Women in Culture and Society* 18 no. 2 (1980): 235-259.

Busia, Abena P. A. "Rebellious Women: Fictional Biographies—Nawal el Sa'adawi's *Woman at Point Zero* and Mariama Ba's *So Long a Letter.*" *Motherlands: Black Women's Writing from Africa, the Caribbean and South Asia*. Ed. Susheila Nasta. New Brunswick, NJ: Rutgers University Press, 1992. 88-98.

Chinweizu. "Introduction: Redrawing the Map of African Literature." *Voices from Twentieth-Century Africa: Griots and Towncriers, xvii-xxxix*. London: Faber and Faber, 1988.

Foucault, Michel. *The History of Sexuality: Volume 1: An Introduction*. Trans. Robert Hurley. New York: Pantheon Books, 1978.

Giddings, Paula. "Alice Walker's Appeal." *Essence* 23 no.3 (1992): 58-60, 62, 102.

Head, Bessie. "The Collector of Treasures." *The Collector of Treasures and Other Botswana Village Tales*. London: Heinemann, 1977. 87-103.

Herskovits, Melville J. *Dahomey: An Ancient West African Kingdom, Vol. II*. Evanston: Northwestern University Press, 1967.

Hirsch, Marianne. *The Mother/Daughter Plot: Narrative, Psychoanalysis, Feminism*. Bloomington and Indianapolis: Indiana University Press, 1989.

Johnson-Odim, Cheryl. "Common Themes, Different Contexts: Third World Women and Feminism." *Third World Women and the Politics of Feminism*. Ed., Chandra Talpade Mohanty, Ann Russo, Lourdes Torres. Bloomington and Indianapolis: Indiana University Press, 1991. 314-327.

Kronik, John W. "Editor's Column." PMLA 107.1 (1992): 9-12.

Lightfoot-Klein, Hanny. *Prisoners of Ritual: An Odyssey into Female Genital Circumcision in Africa*. New York: Harrington Park Press, 1989.

McHenry, Susan. "A Dialogue with Alice Walker." *Emerge* (September, 1992): 9-10.

Martin, Jane Roland. "Aerial Distance, Esotericism, and Other Closely Related Traps." *Signs: Journal of Women in Culture and Society* 21 no. 3 (1996): 584-614.

Mernissi, Fatima. *Beyond the Veil: Male-Female Dynamics in Modern Muslim Society*. Rev. ed. Bloomington: Indiana University Press, 1987.

______. *Women's Rebellion and Islamic Memory*. London: Zed Books, 1996.

Minh-ha, Trinh T. *Woman, Native, Other: Writing Postcoloniality and Feminism*. Bloomington and Indianapolis: Indiana University Press, 1989.

Ngugi, wa Thiong'o. *Decolonising the Mind: The Politics of Language in African Literature.* London: James Currey; Nairobi: Heinemann Kenya; Portsmouth, NH: Heinemann, Harare: Zimbabwe Publishing House, 1986.

Nwapa, Flora. *Efuru.* London: Heinemann, 1966.

Okpewho, Isidore. *African Oral Literature: Backgrounds, Character, and Continuity.* Bloomington and Indianapolis: Indiana University Press, 1992.

Overall, Christine. "What's Wrong with Prostitution? Evaluating Sex Work." *Signs:Journal of Women in Culture and Society* 17 no. 4 (1992): 705-724.

Patterson, Tiffany R. and Angela M. Gilliam. "Out of Egypt: A Talk with Nawal El Saadawi." *Freedomways* (Third Quarter 1983): 186-194.

Richburg, Keith B. *Out of America: A Black Man Confronts Africa.* New York: Basicbooks, 1997.

Saadawi, Nawal El. *The Hidden Face of Eve: Women in the Arab World.* Trans. and ed. Sherif Hetata; foreword Irene L. Gendzier. Boston: Beacon Press, 1982.

______. *Woman at Point Zero.* Trans. Sherif Hetata. London: Zed Books, 1975.

Schor, Naomi. "Female Paranoia: The Case for Psychoanalytic Feminist Criticism." *Yale French Studies* 62 (1981): 204-219.

Shaffer, Brian W. "'Rebarbarizing Civilization': Conrad's African Fiction and Spencerian Sociology." *PMLA* 108 no. 1 (1993): 45-58.

Soyinka, Wole. *The Man Died.* New York: Penguin Books, 1972.

Spivak, Gayatri Chakravorty. "French Feminism in an International Frame." *Yale French Studies* 62 (1981): 154-184.

______. "Can the Subaltern Speak?" *Marxism and the Interpretation of Culture.* Ed., Cary Elson and Lawrence Grossberg. Urbana and Chicago: University of Illinois, 1988. 271-313.

______. *The Post-colonial Critic: Interviews, Strategies, Dialogues.* Ed. Sarah Harasym. New York: Routledge, 1988.

Tatlock, Lynne. "Speculum Feminarum: Gendered Perspectives on Obstetrics and Gynecology in Early Modern Germany." *Signs: Journal of Women in Culture and Society* 17 no. 4 (1992): 725-760.

Walker, Alice. *Possessing the Secret of Joy.* New York: Harcourt Brace Jovanovich, 1992.

Zainaba. 1990. "Lecture on Clitoridectomy to the Midwives of Touil." Introduced, ed. and trans. Elizabeth Oram. *Opening the Gates: A Century of Arab Feminist Writing.* Ed. Margot Badran and Miriam Cooke. Bloomington and Indianapolis: Indiana University Press, 1987: 63-71.

10.
IN SEARCH OF CHAINS WITHOUT IRON:
On Sisterhood, History, and the Politics of Location[1]

Abena Busia

I am most honored to be here. For any of us who are asked to be here, this particular venue is a special one. Since its inception, the Women's Caucus Breakfast has been for many of us a high point of the African Studies Association meeting. The moment which we all look forward to hear one of our own, whom we respect, speak to us about those matters that concern us as women, as Africans, as Africanists. I never thought I would be in the position to be speaking, rather than listening on this day, but here I am.

Since I knew I was to do this, I have been wondering what it was really I was going to say. That is not exactly true. I knew really what I wanted to say, what I have been struggling with however, is the language with which to say it. I want to talk today about alliances. What makes them possible, what makes them fraught.

Why are we here? Why are we a community? What makes a women's caucus. What sense of sisterhood is it that binds us together? that binds us against? For as many movements have found out, alliances are strongest in negative definition. We know what binds us when we can agree on what we are against, not simply oppression generally, but this specific white fist, this particular black face; the experiential history of exclusion practiced by this named body to which we belong.

As a generation, it is we who are in the throes of being beneficiaries of centuries long struggle of women around the world to reclaim our place in the institutional histories of the ages. We are dealing with a world resisting the idea of having to change to reconsider itself wherever and whenever we enter.

The reference is of course clear. Paula Giddings in her landmark study reminded us of the place that black fore-mothers cleared for us to empower us to continue their work (Giddings 1984). Speaking here as an African feminist, I acknowledge first those women whose life, whose work, and whose life work have made my words possible: Ama Ata Aidoo, Flora Nwapa, Filomena Steady and Molara Ogundipe. Their work centrally continues to be alliance and coalition building.

That is always a painful task, especially as we frequently get not our objectives, but the road there confused. Much of the difficulty, much of the pain we as women in a political landscape bear, is because, as Bernice Johnson Reagon reminds us, we confuse "home" with coalition politics (Reagon 1983). This is an important point. Despite the fact that we *all* have sisters, we behave as if building sisterly relations is easy and automatic work, rather than the life time process of commitment that it is. We want always to have a sense of alliance that is also always filled with a sense of ease and well-being. And if anything happens to disrupt the faith in that equanimity, we are undone, and the "revolution" stops. It is one of the hardest things to accept that to work towards a common goal, we are not obliged to choose each other as dance partners, bedfellows or any other kind of mate. We are not obliged to break bread together, though that is always comforting. But to work together, what it takes is a deep, enduring respect based on an acceptance of our mutual humanities. But that compassion can only come if we but show charity to each other, and doing that requires a facing of history.

But to face history is often to be forced to recognize a history of horrors, a history of evident betrayals. What is even harder sometimes than facing history is to face not only the extent to which we have been betrayed, but the extent to which we have betrayed others, or been complicit in their continuing violations.

What I am struggling with now is a direct result of having heard Obioma Nnaemeka speak here at this forum in 1993, where she spoke of the disruption at the conference in Nigeria eighteen months before caused by African-American women. It seemed to me there were three central points in Nnaemeka's account of the incident; that the African-American women objected with some force to the prominent role Europeans and Euro-American women felt *entitled* to play; that the voicing of these objections in the manner done caused distress to their Nigerian hosts; and that the conference organizer in her recounting of the story voiced her impatience with the stand of the African-American women.

I will comment on all this by telling another story. But first I want to make it clear that I am treating the story of what happened in Nigeria as told by Nnaemeka as emblematic. It could be replaced with a whole myriad of other similar stories. This story is a good touchstone because it happened to *us*. Some of us where there; some of us were officially told about it even if we were not there. I was not there, and that is indeed part of my point. Furthermore, I was made a participant in the story, as were all of us who heard it last year, by the fact that it was told publicly, in this very forum, at the African Studies Association's Women's Caucus Breakfast, by Obioma Nnaemeka herself.

All stories bear the mark of the teller, all stories are subject to interpretation, and we have all heard by now as many versions of the story of what happened in Nigeria as there have been people to tell it. We have also heard as many versions of the story as it was re-told to us as there were people in the room last year. My concern is not to verify, explain, excuse that story, or to pass judgement on anyone. My aim is to use it to raise questions about what it contributes to our understanding of the intersections of history and locations, power and displacements, that make the search for sisterhood so over-wrought.

Obioma Nnameka's story is a story of a moment—a dramatic moment frozen in time, where a gesture was made, words were spoken which first had to be immediately dealt with. And the word then was broadcast or recorded in multiple ways by many people. My concern is what can these double gestures, of the event and of its historicizing, teach us. To reach for that I want to tell a story.

Sometime ago I heard Carole Boyce Davies speaking on "Migrations of the Subject", the introductory chapter of her book (Davies 1994). In that paper she gave a series of "migration horror stories" which have been haunting me ever since. They were horrors precisely because of the invisible nature of the contradictions of existence that creep up on us and reveal, expose, and betray long patterns of power and displacement. That lecture has ever since left me collecting my own sets of stories, the ones I give you here not on migrations, but on what I call "misalliance".

When I first arrived in the United States in 1980, just prior to Labor Day weekend to come and teach at Yale, my first home was a rented room in the large apartment sublet by the son of long-standing acquaintances of my parents, an American couple who had known my parents since the early 1950s when they were all young together on the campus of the University of Ghana at Legon.

That year at Yale was a painful time, and this story is one of the reasons why. On my arrival at the university I had been made a Fellow of one of the colleges, and was therefore invited to the social events there, which I happily attended. But though I went around being, as I thought, my usual friendly and gregarious self, for the first time in my life in a new place, I made few friends. The graduate students avoided me, and the junior faculty had little time for me. One day when obsessed about this sense of alienation, my roommate offered an explanation.

In order to fully comprehend what was going on you need to know, if you haven't already assumed it, that he was white. He and I were not lovers. He has a relationship with an African American woman also in the graduate program, who was one of the few people who had gone out of her way to be social towards me. She had the answer to the mystery, for she had told him, or so he relayed to me, that they, meaning the black graduate students "just couldn't understand how I could go to those parties and just talk to those whitefolks the way I do".

I was dumbfounded. Here was a white man, sleeping with a Black woman, who sends him to tell me, another Black woman, that she and her friends didn't see how I could be so social to whitefolk??

When I climbed down off the walls, I moved out of that apartment. Then I looked around me, and looked hard. I realized that indeed at those parties the social communication tended, at least at the graduate and very junior faculty level, to be strictly along racial lines. The exception seemed to be amongst the senior or distinguished faculty. So here I was this person of no status, blundering in and behaving like John Blassingame and Robert Farris Thompson. There was a very subtle line of social convention, and I had transgressed it.

The real lesson in this for me, was having to come to terms with my own blind sense of entitlement in transgressing this boundary. I am not saying that the boundary should have been there. In fact, I believe quite resolutely that it should not have been. I am simply saying that being there, I should have noticed it. And the extent to which I failed to see it was a measure of naivete born of absolute entitlement. Coming to terms with my own sense of privilege, my own Independent Ghanaian sense that I could indeed say what I wanted, to whom I wanted, whenever I wanted, regardless of race or status, regardless of danger, struck at the heart of the matter. It was an attitude of safety born of an inattention to differential histories.

Thus, ten years later, hearing a story about the potentially disruptive power of African Americans, though still a sufficiently old-fashioned enough Ghanaian, bound by set notions of hospitality to strangers, to be embarrassed by the episode and the transgressive nature of their behavior in its retelling, I was definitely on the side of the African Americans. Ten years earlier I would not have been. I would not, did not, concede that they could have had a point at all. What had wrought the change in me?

Many of you in this room have heard me say this often, but I did not used to think of myself as "Black" at all. I have known I am an African all my life, I did not know I was Black until I started living in the United States a decade and a half ago, and the difference can mean all the difference in the world.

There is a part of me that misses the young woman who could wander into parties at Yale totally un-self-conscious of the fact that even in that environment she was Black, young, and female, in that order. It is not a lesson any of us should be obliged to learn. But being born Black in the United States, you have no choice. It comes to you, in your mother's milk, so to speak.

Life experiences have led me to have to face the difference between being African, Black-British or Afro-American, and thus the difference between the ways the British, at home, and abroad, and Americans, at home and abroad, interact with us—at home or abroad, and all of those dynamics change, whatever we mean by home, and wherever abroad is. Two more stories:

The first I call my "Shopping with CC" story. This story also takes place during that transformative year at Yale. Later on that year, when I had indeed made connections and lasting friends, I went shopping in one of the two large department stores in the center of New Haven with a group of sisters. We were relaxed and having fun trying to find an outfit for one of us; all the others were African American or Afro-Caribbean. I was the only African, the only newcomer. I was doing little talking, and hadn't addressed myself to any of the staff. Then at one point we saw something that we liked. I wanted to try it myself, but my size was not out, and I wanted one of my friends to try it in a different color. I went to ask for what we wanted.

Up until then we had largely been treated with the attentive indifference that large numbers of black women become accustomed to when shopping together in this country. Attentive because you can feel them just waiting for you to shop-lift or spoil something, indifference because when we asked for service what we received could scarcely be called that; until I spoke. The reaction to what actors politely call my South of England "received pronunciation" voice, was instantaneous. For reasons which still bewilder me, the service became solicitous, swift, efficient, and friendly—clearly to be an exotic Negro is more acceptable than being a domestic Negro.

The counter clerk's response was an informal institutionalization of a mythological history that separated myself from my sister. We all know that Africa is the darkest of continents, and her people the most backwards of natives—except, it seems, when they arrive on these shores, then in many subtle ways a space is cleared to privilege us over "them." As Gayatri Spivak reminds us, we must always be aware of the moments we are in danger of becoming co-opted, whether as Caliban, or as Ariel.

My next story is my "Shopping with Sarah" story. (As you see, shopping features largely in the social fabric of my life). I have a very close friend, born and raised in Westchester county, who I met when we started graduate school together the same year at Oxford. Many years ago, shortly after the birth of her second child, she needed to attend a social function connected to her husband's work. She didn't much feel like going, she had had her fill of Wall Street bankers, and was anyway suffering from post-partum blues. We decided to go shopping for a new evening dress for the occasion—and we took the children with us.

We were buying a number of other things that day, and she was doing most of the searching, while I was watching the children. Every time she purchased something, the counter clerks would, without thinking twice, charge the item, hand her card back to her and give me the package! This woman is one of my closest friends whose home is my safe haven, whose children are my first born. We are very intimate friends, yet strangers in that setting did not seem to be able to look at us and realize that possibility. Shopping with her as girls together in Westchester county, there was no way in the informal institutionalizing of historical racism to make a social space for the nature of our friendship. In the history of relations between black women and white women in creating alliances, the starting ground has always been unequal.

This is hard to talk about. I would rather in one sense keep silent. I am resisting the need to apologize, to say things to the Euro-American women present, like you know some of you are my closest friends; or my longest standing friends and confidants are all white women; or the first man I nearly married was white. And can't you just hear yourselves in similar situations, "some of my best friends are blacks, or jews", or whatever else. Can't we just hear our own fears, our own pains.

I am trying to talk about the burdens of collective histories, and I am terrified that the white women who have been my close personal friends for decades will feel betrayed. And anyway, will articulating these fears, naming them, help to heal the sources of our discomfort, or exacerbate the wounds and harm us further? Living in the United States has turned me, of all people, painfully race conscious. Yet I am speaking because we need so desperately to find a place to see clear-sightedly, all those simple gestures, and read them through the legacy of our histories so that the meaning of simple acts and desperate performances does not get lost in the enactment, or in the re-telling.

Adrienne Rich, in what is for me one of her most poignant and powerful pieces, "Notes Towards a Politics of Location," in speaking about how she constructs her own self-identity, articulates the awful truth that by virtue of being born a US citizen, at a time of defacto segregation, she was in fact classified as white before she was born a female (Rich 1984). What she was coming to terms with was that all of her subsequent alliance building was therefore built on that assumption of privilege which it was a long slow process for her to learn to interrogate.

But to build the alliances she did, she had to interrogate. "Knowing ignorance is Strength. Ignoring knowledge is Sickness" I know Lao Tzu through Trin-h T. Min-ha. Can we bear to hear our pain?

I called this talk "In Search of Chains Without Iron" in recognition of a hope; that sisterhood is the kente tie that binds us. But can we celebrate those when the marks of iron are still sore on our wrists and ankles? We have not yet come out from under the shadow, the very long shadow cast by imperial masters and plantation overlords, on a geographic landscape scarred by time.

We need to negotiate our way, not around, but through the long shadows of our histories. Those histories have been histories of separation, of fragmentation, and they have necessarily been constructed as such. And speaking as an African woman, it is a painful thing to acknowledge the "success" of the strategies. As African descent sisters, we are always, in those power constructs, articulated as fragmented—or monolithic only in ways that disempower. And sometimes we truly are so fragmented.

In the field of identity politics, imperial and colonial histories can still take hold. There was a time when it was as unthinkable for a West Indian woman to contemplate marrying a West African, for one thing she would never be heard of again; or she would have to go home and deal with all those other backward wives, and so on and so on. Or, for some of us dark-skinned and nappy haired, there have been one too many "Miss Black" something or other who looked more like Cinderella than.. than who? what beautiful culture heroes do our children have? I am not saying that we all desire to be Cinderella, simply pointing out the absence of a popular social currency, a name even, to replace what she stands for.

But in the nature of political alliances, that also has its reverse side. We must recognize that also as part of the same legacy which might tie a Jamaican more firmly to a Ghanaian, than to someone from the United States, despite the greater proximity of the latter. And the tie would be based on the profound and continuing impact, for example, that a British education, or more importantly, mercantile system can have. A triumph of history over geography.

One more story. A few years ago one of my colleagues at Rutgers held a dinner party in honor of a visiting British scholar. She herself was born and raised in Hong Kong, and came to this country for graduate school. The other guests were; an Indian man whose family had been displaced to Pakistan at the time of the partition; a married couple, the wife a Euro-American colleague of ours whose husband is British, two other Euro-American colleagues, and myself, born in Ghana, raised in England, and like everyone else around that table, working in the United States. The age spread amongst us was almost twenty years.

During the course of the evening the conversation turned to the BBC world service, and from there to Alistair Cook and other British exports. A most extraordinary thing happened. Those of us from the "far flung ports" of the former British Empire discovered we had one noticeable thing in common. Despite the age range and geographic spread, England, Pakistan, Ghana, Hong Kong, we had all grown up not only eating Marmite, but swallowing Seven Seas cod liver oil, eating Huntley and Palmer's biscuits and Rountree's Fruit Gums, being rubbed with Sloan's lineament, and could sing the same advertising jingles for Blue Star Omo and Palmolive soap. And the brand names were important; we dredged the names and the tunes up from our individual and collective memories as the Americans listened to us, stunned. And we could none of us cry for laughing.

Yet at the same time, a Trinidadian is not simply part of a past tied to Britain, she is also part of a present tied to the United States in ways that could separate not only from Ghana, but from her own sister in Britain busy making alliances with Ghanaians, and Pakistanis, and so on. To return to a point I made right at the start, in Britain it was always easier to form coalitions across non-white racial and ethnic groups. "We was all wogs together" so to speak—all of us, as Meiling Jin would remind us, Strangers in a Hostile Landscape, with "no place to be somebody".

It is that "place to be somebody" that tears at the heart of that encounter Obioma Nnameka recounted. We must acknowledge that the aggression of the African-Americans, whatever the source, was felt to be a violation. And in that standoff between African American and Euro-American women locked in their continuing incestuous embrace, how can African women feel at home, even in their own home?

Yet at a conference on the African continent discussing black women in the diaspora, who was it who needed to be made to feel safe enough to speak her experiences? Whose homecoming was it supposed to be? And if the African-American women couldn't claim their voices there, is there anyplace on earth they could claim it?

Once again, it was the most dispossessed, thinking they had finally come to a resting place for a conversation, who were being asked to lay their burden down before anyone had acknowledged what a heavy load they had been carrying for so long. Perhaps it is only those truly with a sense of entitlement, however acquired, who can treat all comers at the gate with equal magnanimity, wherever they come from. And it is always those who have never been afforded that entitlement who must fight for ways to establish it, whatever it costs.

One last story. Nearly twenty years ago I traveled from Oxford to go to London to see a show. It was the Amnesty International Benefit concert for Evita. I was with several friends, all white, though one of them had been raised in Ghana and other parts of West Africa, and the other, whose mother was half Japanese, had been raised in Jamaica and Pakistan. This did not show on their faces. Whilst sitting in a pub across the street from the theatre waiting for the doors to open, a drunken (ironically in the context, Irish) man came up to me and started berating me for my very presence there, not only in the pub, but in the country at all— invoking at the top of his voice the name of Enoch Powell, and making declarations about the number of blacks on the dole and how South Africa had it right. All my friends remained silent.

Ten years later, the one to whom I am closest apologized to me. She had been forever haunted by that vision of herself being silent. And this had forced her to do what Adrienne Rich had done, and what we all must do; to ask at what point she as a white woman was going to divest herself of that safety and simply interrupt, to interrogate our own positionalities and the power of our own privileges.

What I ask is to create a world in which that is possible. To make spaces to interrogate those moments in safety. If we are Unequal Sisters, we must first begin with an address to that inequality before we can presume that a sisterhood will survive. Unless each of us takes on the responsibility for those small moments or dramatic gestures, to understand them, truly understand them in the depth of their historical resonance, we will be building alliances on quicksand rather than rock. It takes a lot of hard work to change. And we need above all, respect.

Respect indeed for those of us who have faced history, and from whose struggles we can learn. For me, as an African, as a Ghanaian, to acknowledge the wisdom of the work done by our elders; of Ama Ata Aidoo whose *Dilemma of a Ghost*, published approximately twenty-five years ago now remains one of the most emotionally telling and politically astute investigations in our literature of the manifold aspects of what Carol Boyce Davies calls our "cross-cultural misknowledges"; of Molara Ogundipe Leslie, a warrior in the trenches for so long, she is only now finding a place to come up for air; and of the ancestors, Flora Nwapa, who was here with us the year before and whose death cheated us of her sterling and quiet example, not so much even in her works, but with her life. Our list is long and history is nobody's fault, but everybody's responsibility:

> We are all mothers,
> and we have that fire within us,

of powerful women
whose spirits are so angry
we can laugh beauty into life
and still make you taste
the salt tears of our knowledge.
For we are not tortured
anymore;
we have seen beyond your lies and disguises,
and *we* have mastered the language of words,
we have mastered speech.
And yes,
we have also seen ourselves.
We have stripped ourselves raw
and naked piece by piece, until our flesh lies flayed
with blood on our *own* hands.
What terrible thing can you do us
which we have not done to ourselves?
What can you tell us
which we didn't deceive ourselves with
a long time ago?
You cannot know how long we cried
until we laughed
over the broken pieces of our dreams.
Ignorance
shattered us into such fragments
we had to unearth ourselves piece by piece,
to uncover with our own hands such unexpected relics
even we wondered
how we could hold such treasure.
And yes, we have conceived
to force our mutilated hopes
into the substance of visions
beyond your imaginings
to declare through pain our deliverance:
So do not even ask,
do not ask what it is we are laboring with *this* time;
Dreamers remember their dreams
when they are disturbed -
And you shall not escape
what we *will* make
of the broken pieces of our lives.
(Busia 1990)

NOTES:

1 This paper is the transcript of a talk delivered at the African Studies Association's Women's Caucus Breakfast at the annual conference in November 1993.

WORKS CITED:

Giddings, Paula. *When and Where I Enter... The Impact of Black Women on Race and Sex in America.* New York: William & Morrow & Co. Inc, 1984.

Reagon, Bernice Johnson. "Coaltion Politics: Turning the Century," in *Home Girls: A Black Feminist Anthology*, ed. Barbara Smith. New York: Kitchen Table:Women of Color Press, 1983.

Davies, Carole Boyce. *Migrations of the Subject: Black Women Writing and Identity.* New York: Routledge, 1994.

Rich, Adrienne. "Notes Toward a Politics of Location" in *Blood, Bread and Poetry: Selected Prose 1979-1985.* New York: Norton, 1994. pp210-231.

Busia, Abena P.A. "Liberation", in *Testimonies of Exile.* Trenton NJ: Africa World Press, 1990. pp. 35-36.

Contributors:

Abena Busia is an Associate Professor in the Department of Literatures in English at Rutgers, The State University of New Jersey. She is co-editor, with Stanlie James, of *Theorizing Black Feminisms: The Visionary Pragmatism of Black Women*, and *Beyond Survival: African Literature & the Search for New Life: Proceedings of the African Literature Association Conference*, with Kofi Anyidoho and Anne Adams. She is also coordinating, with Tuzyline Jita Allen, and Florence Howe of the Feminist Press, *Women Writing Africa*, a multi-volume continent-wide publishing project of cultural reconstruction.

Nontsasa Nako is a graduate student in the Department of Literature at the University of Cape Town in South Africa.

Nkiru Nzegwu is Associate Professor in the Department of Africana Studies and the Graduate Program of Philosophy, Interpretation, and Culture Program at Binghamton University, New York. She has published extensively in art history, feminism, and culture studies.

Leslye Amede Obiora is Associate Professor at the College of Law, University of Arizona at Tucson. She has written extensively on human rights, gender equity, development and jurisprudence. Recently, she was a residential fellow at the Institute for Advanced Studies at Princeton and at the Rockefeller Study Center in Bellagio, Italy.

Chikwenye Okonjo Ogunyemi is Professor of African, African-American, and Caribbean literature at Sarah Lawrence College, Bronxville, New York. She is particularly interested in the writings of black women throughout the Diaspora. Her latest book is, *Africa Wo/man Palava: The Nigerian Novel by Women* (University of Chicago Press, 1996).

Mojúbàolú Olúfunké Okome is an Associate Professor in the Department of Political Science at Brooklyn College. She was a postdoctoral research fellow and a visiting professor in the Department of African and African American Studies at Fordham University in 1996-97. Her research interests include African Politics, African women, globalization, democracy and development, and African immigration to the United States. Okome is the author of *A Sapped Democracy: The Political Economy of the Structural Adjustment Program* *and Political Transition in Nigeria, 1983-1993* (University Press of America, 1998). She is also coeditor of an online journal, *Jenda: Journal of African Culture and Women's Studies*, www.jendajournal.com.

Oyèrónké Oyewùmí is Associate Professor in the Department of Sociology at the State University of New York at Stony Brook. Her areas of interest include African Epistemologies, Critical Social Theory, Globalization, Social Inequalities and Western Culture. She is the author of the award-winning book, *The Invention of Women: Making an African Sense of Western Gender Discourses* (University of Minnesota Press, 1997).

Olufemi Taiwo is an Associate Professor of Philosophy and African and African-American Studies at Seattle University, Seattle, Washington. In the 2000/2001 academic year, he was a Ford Foundation Visiting Postdoctoral Research and Teaching Fellow at the Carter G. Woodson Institute for Afro-American and African Studies, University of Virginia, Charlottesville, Virginia, U.S.A. Taiwo was also a Visiting Distinguished Minority Scholar at the University of Wisconsin at Eau Claire, Eau Claire, Wisconsin, U.S.A. He has served as a Visiting Professor at the Institut für Afrikastudien, Universität Bayreuth, Beyreuth, Germany. His book *Legal Naturalism: A Marxist Theory of Law* was published in 1996 by Cornell University Press. He is currently completing a collection of essays tentatively titled *Colonialism and Modernity*. Taiwo's interests include philosophy of law, political philosophy, African philosophy, women and politics, and philosophy of history.

INDEX